Developers from around the world are using the Ruby language. Here's what they're saying about *Programming Ruby*...

"In their first landmark book, *The Pragmatic Programmer*, Dave and Andy urged us to learn at least one new programming language every year. It may follow the principle of least surprise that the authors would bring us this year's candidate, accompanied with a pragmatic philosophy of how to learn your new OO scripting language of choice."

► **Frank Westphal** , independent consultant

"Ruby is an exciting new language, worth knowing about and well worth considering for an upcoming project. It's rare to see such a useful book this early in the life of a new language. But of course I would expect no less from the authors of *The Pragmatic Programmer*. Andy and Dave: Thanks!"

► **Ron Jeffries** , author of Extreme Programming Installed

"I have used Perl and Python for my work ... but Ruby just turns my work into fun!"

► **Clemens Hintze** , programmer

"Ruby is a remarkably clean, simple, powerful, and practical dynamic OO programming language. Ruby fully deserves this correspondingly best-of-breed book. This book is a "must have" wizard's workshop for using Ruby to boost your programming power and productivity. This book will greatly amplify the worldwide use of Ruby, stimulate powerful Ruby extensions, and generate demand for second and third editions. I look forward to telling later legions of Ruby users that I was farsighted enough to master Ruby using the classic first edition of *Programming Ruby*."

► **Conrad Schneiker**

"A good book by a great pair of programmers about a language with a great future. This should be the first Ruby book anyone buys."

► **Hal Fulton**

"Dave and Andy are among the western pioneers who understand the value of this precious gem of a language. They cleaned and polished it well, dazzling us all with its depth and transparency. It's almost magical."

► **Aleksi Niemelä**

Programming Ruby

Programming Ruby
The Pragmatic Programmer's Guide

David Thomas
Andrew Hunt

ADDISON–WESLEY

Boston • San Francisco • New York • Toronto • Montreal
London • Munich • Paris • Madrid
Capetown • Sydney • Tokyo • Singapore • Mexico City

Many of the designations used by manufacturers and sellers to distinguish their products are claimed as trademarks. Where those designations appear in this book, and Addison-Wesley was aware of a trademark claim, the designations have been printed with initial capital letters or in all capitals.

The authors and publisher have taken care in the preparation of this book, but make no express or implied warranty of any kind and assume no responsibility for errors or omissions. No liability is assumed for incidental or consequential damages in connection with or arising out of the use of the information or programs contained herein.

The publisher offers discounts on this book when ordered in quantity for special sales. For more information, please contact:

Pearson Education Corporate Sales Division
One Lake Street
Upper Saddle River, NJ   07458
(800) 382-3419
corpsales@pearsontechgroup.com

Visit AW on the Web: www.awl.com/cseng

Library of Congress Cataloging-in-Publication Data

Thomas, David,
   Programming Ruby : the pragmatic programmer's guide / David Thomas,   Andrew Hunt.
         p.   cm.
   Includes bibliographical references and index.
   ISBN 0-201-71089-7
   1. Object-oriented programming (Computer science) 2. Ruby (Computer program language)
I. Hunt, Andrew

QA76.64.T494.2000
005.13'3--dc21   00–045390
                                                                              CIP

Copyright © 2001 by Addison-Wesley

ISBN 0-201-71089-7
Text printed on recycled paper.
1 2 3 4 5 6 7 8 9 10—CRS—0403020100
First printing, October 2000

For Juliet and Ellie,
Zachary and Elizabeth,
Henry and Stuart

Contents

PART I—FACETS OF RUBY

PART II—RUBY IN ITS SETTING

PART III—RUBY CRYSTALLIZED

PART IV—RUBY LIBRARY REFERENCE

PART V—APPENDICES

List of Tables

List of Figures

Foreword

Man is driven to create; I know I really love to create things. And while I'm not good at painting, drawing, or music, I can write software.

Shortly after I was introduced to computers, I became interested in programming languages. I believed that an ideal programming language must be attainable, and I wanted to be the designer of it. Later, after gaining some experience, I realized that this kind of ideal, all-purpose language might be more difficult than I had thought. But I was still hoping to design a language that would work for most of the jobs I did everyday. That was my dream as a student.

Years later I talked with colleagues about scripting languages, about their power and possibility. As an object-oriented fan for more than fifteen years, it seemed to me that OO programming was very suitable for scripting too. I did some research on the 'net for a while, but the candidates I found, Perl and Python, were not exactly what I was looking for. I wanted a language more powerful than Perl, and more object-oriented than Python.

Then, I remembered my old dream, and decided to design my own language. At first I was just was toying around with it at work. But gradually it grew to be a tool good enough to replace Perl. I named it *Ruby*—after the precious red stone—and released it to the public in 1995.

Since then a lot of people have become interested in Ruby. Believe it or not, Ruby is actually more popular than Python in Japan right now. I hope that eventually it will be just as well received all over the world.

I believe that the purpose of life is, at least in part, to be happy. Based on this belief, Ruby is designed to make programming not only easy, but also fun. It allows you to concentrate on the creative side of programming, with less stress. If you don't believe me, read this book and try Ruby. I'm sure you'll find out for yourself.

I'm very thankful to the people who have joined the Ruby community; they have helped me a lot. I almost feel like Ruby is one of my children, but in fact, it is the result of the combined efforts of many people. Without their help, Ruby could never have become what it is.

I am especially thankful to the authors of this book, Dave Thomas and Andy Hunt. Ruby has never been a well-documented language. Because I have always preferred writing programs over writing documents, the Ruby manuals tend to be less thorough than they should be. You had to read the source to know the exact behavior of the language. But now Dave and Andy have done the work for you.

They became interested in a lesser-known language from the Far East. They researched it, read thousands of lines of source code, wrote uncountable test scripts and e-mails, clarified the ambiguous behavior of the language, found bugs (and even fixed some of them), and finally compiled this great book. Ruby is certainly well documented now!

Their work on this book has not been trivial. While they were writing it, I was modifying the language itself. But we worked together on the updates, and this book is as accurate as possible.

It is my hope that both Ruby and this book will serve to make your programming easy and enjoyable. Have fun!

Yukihiro Matsumoto, a.k.a. *"Matz"*
まつもと ゆきひろ
Japan, October 2000

Preface

This book is a tutorial and reference for the Ruby programming language. Use Ruby, and you'll write better code, be more productive, and enjoy programming more.

These are bold claims, but we think that after reading this book you'll agree with them. And we have the experience to back up this belief.

As Pragmatic Programmers we've tried many, many languages in our search for tools to make our lives easier, for tools to help us do our jobs better. Until now, though, we'd always been frustrated by the languages we were using.

Our job is to solve problems, not spoonfeed compilers, so we like dynamic languages that adapt to us, without arbitrary, rigid rules. We need clarity so we can communicate using our code. We value conciseness and the ability to express a requirement in code accurately and efficiently. The less code we write, the less that can go wrong. (And our wrists and fingers are thankful, too.)

We want to be as productive as possible, so we want our code to run the first time; time spent in the debugger is time stolen from the development clock. It also helps if we can try out code as we edit it; if you have to wait for a 2-hour make cycle, you may as well be using punch cards and submitting your work for batch compilation.

We want a language that works at a high level of abstraction. The higher level the language, the less time we spend translating our requirements into code.

When we discovered Ruby, we realized that we'd found what we'd been looking for. More than any other language with which we have worked, Ruby *stays out of your way*. You can concentrate on solving the problem at hand, instead of struggling with compiler and language issues. That's how it can help you become a better programmer: by giving you the chance to spend your time creating solutions for your users, not for the compiler.

Ruby Sparkles

Take a true object-oriented language, such as Smalltalk. Drop the unfamiliar syntax and move to more conventional, file-based source code. Now add in a good measure of the flexibility and convenience of languages such as Python and Perl.

You end up with Ruby.

OO aficionados will find much to like in Ruby: things such as pure object orientation (everything's an object), metaclasses, closures, iterators, and ubiquitous heterogeneous collections. Smalltalk users will feel right at home (and C++ and Java users will feel jealous).

At the same time, Perl and Python wizards will find many of their favorite features: full regular expression support, tight integration with the underlying operating system, convenient shortcuts, and dynamic evaluation.

Ruby is easy to learn. Everyday tasks are simple to code, and once you've done them, they are easy to maintain and grow. Apparently difficult things often turn out not to have been difficult after all. Ruby follows the *Principle of Least Surprise*—things work the way you would expect them to, with very few special cases or exceptions. And that really *does* make a difference when you're programming.

We call Ruby a *transparent* language. By that we mean that Ruby doesn't obscure the solutions you write behind lots of syntax and the need to churn out reams of support code just to get simple things done. With Ruby you write programs close to the problem domain. Rather than constantly mapping your ideas and designs down to the pedestrian level of most languages, with Ruby you'll find you can express them directly and express them elegantly. This means you code faster. It also means your programs stay readable and maintainable.

Using Ruby, we are constantly amazed at how much code we can write in one sitting, code that works the first time. There are very few syntax errors, no type violations, and far fewer bugs than usual. This makes sense: there's less to get wrong. No bothersome semicolons to type mechanically at the end of each line. No troublesome type declarations to keep in sync (especially in separate files). No unnecessary words just to keep the compiler happy. No error-prone framework code.

So why learn Ruby? Because we think it will help you program *better*. It will help you to focus on the problem at hand, with fewer distractions. It will make your life easier.

What Kind of Language Is Ruby?

In the old days, the distinction between languages was simple: they were either compiled, like C or Fortran, or interpreted, like BASIC. Compiled languages gave you speed and low-level access; interpreted languages were higher-level but slower.

Times change, and things aren't that simple anymore. Some language designers have taken to calling their creations "scripting languages." By this, we guess they mean that their languages are interpreted and can be used to replace batch files and shell scripts, orchestrating the behavior of other programs and the underlying operating system. Perl, TCL, and Python have all been called scripting languages.

What exactly *is* a scripting language? Frankly we don't know if it's a distinction worth making. In Ruby, you can access all the underlying operating system features. You can do the same stuff in Ruby that you can in Perl or Python, and you can do it more cleanly. But Ruby is fundamentally different. It is a true programming language, too, with strong theoretical roots and an elegant, lightweight syntax. You *could* hack together a mess of "scripts" with Ruby, but you probably won't. Instead, you'll be more inclined to *engineer* a solution, to produce a program than is easy to understand, simple to maintain, and a piece of cake to extend and reuse in the future.

Although we have used Ruby for scripting jobs, most of the time we use it as a general-purpose programming language. We've used it to write GUI applications and middle-tier server processes, and we're using it to format large parts of this book. Others have used it for managing server machines and databases. Ruby is serving Web pages, interfacing to databases and generating dynamic content. People are writing artificial intelligence and machine learning programs in Ruby, and at least one person is using it to investigate natural evolution. Ruby's finding a home as a vehicle for exploratory mathematics. And people all over the world are using it as a way of gluing together all their different applications. It truly is a great language for producing solutions in a wide variety of problem domains.

Is Ruby for Me?

Ruby is not the universal panacea for programmers' problems. There will always be times when you'll need a particular language: the environment may dictate it, you may have special libraries you need, performance concerns, or simply an issue with training. We haven't given up languages such as Java and C++ entirely (although there are times when we wish we could).

However, Ruby is probably more applicable than you might think. It is easy to extend, both from within the language and by linking in third-party libraries. It is portable across a number of platforms. It's relatively lightweight and consumes only modest system resources. And it's easy to learn; we've known people who've put Ruby code into production systems within a day of picking up drafts of this book. We've used Ruby to implement parts of an X11 window manager, a task that's normally considered severe C coding. Ruby excelled, and helped us write code in hours that would otherwise have taken days.

Once you get comfortable with Ruby, we think you'll keep coming back to it as your language of choice.

Why Did We Write This Book?

So we'd just finished writing *The Pragmatic Programmer,* our families had just started talking to us again, and suddenly we felt the need to write another book. Why? We guess it comes down to a kind of missionary zeal.

Ruby was created by Yukihiro Matsumoto (Matz) in Japan. Since 1995, its popularity in Japan has grown at an astounding rate; there are rumors that Ruby is more popular than Python in Japan. But to date, much of the detailed Ruby documentation is in Japanese. It probably isn't a programming language you'd just stumble across.

We wanted to spread the word, to have more people outside Japan using Ruby and enjoying the benefits, so we decided to document Ruby in English. And what started out as a small project just sort of grew....

Ruby Versions

This book documents Version 1.6 of Ruby, which was released in September 2000.

Ruby version numbering follows the same scheme used for many other open source projects. Releases with even subversion numbers (1.0, 1.2, 1.4, and so on) are stable, public releases. These are the releases that are prepackaged and made available on the various Ruby Web sites.

Development versions of the software have odd subversion numbers, such as 1.1 and 1.3. These you'll have to download and build for yourself, as described in the box on page xxvii.

Installing Ruby

You can get Ruby from `ftp://ftp.netlab.co.jp/pub/lang/ruby`, or from the mirror sites listed on page 532 in Appendix C. There you will find the latest stable release, as well as various development releases.

You'll always find source code releases of Ruby; you may also find prebuilt binaries for Windows or other operating systems.

Building Ruby

In the Ruby distribution you'll find a file named README, which explains the installation procedure in detail. To summarize, you build Ruby on POSIX-based systems using the same four commands you use for most other open source applications: `./configure`, `make`, `make test`, and `make install`. You can build Ruby under other environments

---

The Very Latest Ruby

For those who just have to be on the very latest, hot-off-the-press and *untested* cutting edge (as we were while writing this book), you can get development versions straight from the developers' working repository.

The Ruby developers use CVS (Concurrent Version System, freely available from `www.cvshome.com`) as their revision control system. You can check files out as an anonymous user from their archive by executing the following CVS commands:

```
% cvs -d :pserver:anonymous@cvs.netlab.co.jp:/home/cvs ↵
    login
(Logging in to anonymous@cvs.netlab.co.jp)
CVS password: guest
% cvs -d :pserver:anonymous@cvs.netlab.co.jp:/home/cvs ↵
    checkout ruby
```

The complete source code tree, just as the developers last left it, will now be copied to a "ruby" subdirectory on your machine, updating your local source tree from a repository on the other side of the world. Isn't it a great time to be alive?

(including Windows) by using a POSIX emulation environment such as `cygwin`[1] or by using native compilers—see "`ntsetup.bat`" in the distribution's `win32` subdirectory as a starting point.

Running Ruby

Now that Ruby is installed, you'd probably like to run some programs. Unlike compiled environments, there are two ways to run Ruby—interactively and as a program.

Interactive Ruby

The easiest way to run Ruby interactively is simply to type "ruby" at the shell prompt.

```
% ruby
puts "Hello, world!"
^D
Hello, world!
```

---

1.   See `sourceware.cygnus.com/cygwin` for details.

Here we typed in the single `puts` expression and an end of file character (which is control-D on our system). This process works, but it's sort of painful if you make a typo, and you can't really see what's going on as you type.

In the `sample` directory in the Ruby distribution you'll find a script named "`eval.rb`". It goes one step better by showing us the value of each expression as it is entered:

```
% cd sample
% ruby eval.rb
ruby> a = "Hello, world!"
"Hello, world!"
ruby> puts a
Hello, world!
nil
ruby> ^D
%
```

Here we can see the output from `puts`, and then the return value from `puts` (which is `nil`).

That's all fine and well, except that multiline expressions do not work, and you can't edit the line you're on, or go back and use previous lines (as you might with command history in a shell).

For the next step up from `eval.rb`, we have `irb`—Interactive Ruby. `irb` is a Ruby Shell, complete with command-line history, line editing capabilities, and job control. It is quite configurable and has many options, so much so that it has its own appendix beginning on page 523. We recommend that you get familiar with `irb` so you can try some of our examples interactively.

Ruby Programs

Finally, you can run a Ruby program from a file as you would any other shell script, Perl program, or Python program. You can simply run Ruby giving the script name as an argument:

```
% ruby myprog.rb
```

Or you can use the Unix "shebang" notation as the first line of the program file.[2]

```
#!/usr/local/bin/ruby -w

puts "Hello, World!"
```

---

2.   If your system supports it, you can avoid hard-coding the path to Ruby in the *shebang* line by using `#!/usr/bin/env ruby`, which will search your path for `ruby` and then execute it.

If you make this source file executable (using, for instance, `chmod +x myprog.rb`), Unix lets you run the file as a program:

```
% ./myprog.rb
Hello, World!
```

You can do something similar under Microsoft Windows using file associations.

Get Involved

Visit the Ruby Web sites, `www.rubycentral.com` and `www.ruby-lang.org`, to see what's new, and chat with other Ruby users on the newsgroup or mailing lists (see Appendix C).

And we'd certainly appreciate hearing from you. Comments, suggestions, errors in the text, and problems in the examples are all welcome. E-mail us at:

```
rubybook@pragmaticprogrammer.com
```

Acknowledgments

A book is a massive undertaking, one that we would never be able to complete without help from our all our friends, old and new. We're proud to count among our old friends the team at Addison-Wesley: Mike Hendrickson, John Fuller, the ever-helpful Julie Steele, and the wonderful Julie DiNicola. Thank you all.

Our reviewers were fantastic. We put them up against some incredibly tight deadlines and they came through for us. Reviewing a book full of technical detail isn't easy, so we're especially grateful to George Coe, Bob Davison, Jeff Deifik, Hal Fulton, Tadayoshi Funaba, Clemens Hintze, Kazuhiro Hiwada, Kikutani Makoto, Mike Linksvayer, Aleksi Niemelä, Lew Perin, Jared Richardson, Armin Roehrl, Conrad Schneiker, Patrick Schoenbach, and Eric Vought. Thanks also go to the two Julies at Addison-Wesley for coordinating this truly international effort.

Several people helped us with specific areas of this book. Tadayoshi Funaba exchanged countless e-mails with us until we finally understood the `Date` module. Guy Decoux and Clemens Hintze patiently answered our questions about writing Ruby extensions, and Masaki Suketa helped us understand the `WinOLE` module.

Although much of the original Ruby documentation is in Japanese, there is a growing body of English translations, mostly undertaken by Japanese developers whose skills with English never cease to amaze us. Although there are too many individual contributions to this effort to name each author, we would like to single out Goto Kentaro, who has produced a large volume of high-quality documentation and placed it online.

Finally, we have to thank Yukihiro "Matz" Matsumoto, the creator of Ruby. We've lost count of the number of questions we've asked of him, and the number of patient and detailed answers he's sent back. As well as creating a truly wonderful language, Matz has fostered a wonderfully supportive and open culture in which that language can prosper.

Thank you all. Domo arigato gozaimasu.

Dave Thomas and *Andy Hunt*
THE PRAGMATIC PROGRAMMERS
`www.pragmaticprogrammer.com`

Notation Conventions

Throughout this book, we use the following typographic notations.

Literal code examples are shown using a typewriter-like font:

```
class SampleCode
  def run
    #...
  end
end
```

Within the text, `Fred#doIt` is a reference to an instance method (`doIt`) of class `Fred`, while `Fred.new`[3] is a class method, and `Fred::EOF` is a class constant.

The book contains many snippets of Ruby code. Where possible, we've tried to show what happens when they run. In simple cases, we show the value of expressions on the same line as the expression. For example:

```
a = 1
b = 2
a + b   →   3
```

At times, we're also interested in the values of assignment statements, in which case we'll show them.

```
a = 1   →   1
b = 2   →   2
a + b   →   3
```

If the program produces more complex output, we show it below the program code:

```
3.times { puts "Hello!" }
```

produces:

```
Hello!
Hello!
Hello!
```

In some of the library documentation, we wanted to show where spaces appear in the output. You'll see these spaces as "␣" characters.

Command-line invocations are shown with literal text in a Roman font, and parameters you supply in an *italic* font. Optional elements are shown in large square brackets.

ruby [*flags,* ...] [*progname*] *arguments* [, *arguments*]...

---

3. In some other Ruby documentation, you may see class methods written as `Fred::new`. This is perfectly valid Ruby syntax; we just happen to feel that `Fred.new` is less distracting to read.

## Chapter 1

Roadmap

The main text of this book has four separate parts, each with its own personality, and each addressing different aspects of the Ruby language.

In Part I, *Facets of Ruby*, you'll find a Ruby tutorial. It starts off with a short chapter on some of the terminology and concepts that are unique to Ruby. This chapter also includes enough basic syntax so that the other chapters will make sense. The rest of the tutorial is a top-down look at the language. There we talk about classes and objects, types, expressions, and all the other things that make up the language. We even end with a short chapter on digging yourself out when trouble strikes.

One of the great things about Ruby is how well it integrates with its environment. Part II, *Ruby in Its Setting*, investigates this. Here you'll find practical information on running Ruby, and using Ruby with the Web. You'll learn how to create GUI applications using Tk, and how to use Ruby in a Microsoft Windows environment, including wonderful things such as making native API calls, COM integration, and Windows Automation. And you'll discover just how easy it is to extend Ruby and to embed Ruby within your own code.

Part III, *Ruby Crystallized*, contains more advanced material. Here you'll find all the gory details about the language, the metaclass model, tainting, reflection, and marshaling. You could probably speed-read this the first time through, but we found ourselves using the tables in this section even as we were writing the rest of the book.

The *Ruby Library Reference* is Part IV. It's big. We document over 800 methods in more than 40 built-in classes and modules. On top of that, we have another 70 pages describing some of the more useful library modules that come with Ruby.

So, how should you read this book? Well, it depends on you.

Depending on your level of expertise with programming in general, and OO in particular, you may want to read just a few portions of the book to start with. Here are our recommendations.

If you're a beginner, you may want to start with the tutorial material in Part I. Keep the library reference close at hand as you start to write programs. Get familiar with the basic classes such as **Array**, **Hash**, and **String**. As you become more comfortable in the environment, you may want to investigate some of the more advanced topics in Part III.

If you're already comfortable with Perl, Python, Java, or Smalltalk, then we'd suggest reading the introduction in Chapter 2 first. From there, you may want to take the slower approach and keep going with the tutorial that follows, or skip ahead to the gritty details starting in Part III, followed by the library reference in Part IV.

Experts, gurus, and "I-don't-need-no-stinking-tutorial" types can dive straight into the language reference in Chapter 18, which begins on page 201, skim the library reference, then use the book as a (rather attractive) coffee coaster.

Of course, there's nothing wrong with just starting at the beginning and working your way through.

And don't forget, if you run into a problem that you can't figure out, help is available. See Appendix C beginning on page 531 for more information.

Part I

Facets of Ruby

## Chapter 2

Ruby.new

When we originally wrote this book, we had a grand plan (we were younger then). We wanted to document the language from the top down, starting with classes and objects, and ending with the nitty-gritty syntax details. It seemed like a good idea at the time. After all, most everything in Ruby is an object, so it made sense to talk about objects first.

Or so we thought.

Unfortunately, it turns out to be difficult to describe a language that way. If you haven't covered strings, `if` statements, assignments, and other details, it's difficult to write examples of classes. Throughout our top-down description, we kept coming across low-level details we needed to cover so that the example code would make sense.

So, we came up with another grand plan (they don't call us pragmatic for nothing). We'd still describe Ruby starting at the top. But before we did that, we'd add a short chapter that described all the common language features used in the examples along with the special vocabulary used in Ruby, a kind of minitutorial to bootstrap us into the rest of the book.

Ruby Is an Object-Oriented Language

Let's say it again. Ruby is a genuine object-oriented language. Everything you manipulate is an object, and the results of those manipulations are themselves objects. However, many languages make the same claim, and they often have a different interpretation of what object-oriented means and a different terminology for the concepts they employ.

So, before we get too far into the details, let's briefly look at the terms and notation that *we'll* be using.

When you write object-oriented code, you're normally looking to model concepts from the real world in your code. Typically during this modeling process you'll discover categories of things that need to be represented in code. In a jukebox, the concept of a "song" might be such a category. In Ruby, you'd define a *class* to represent each of these entities. A class is a combination of state (for example, the name of the song) and methods that use that state (perhaps a method to play the song).

Once you have these classes, you'll typically want to create a number of *instances* of each. For the jukebox system containing a class called `Song`, you'd have separate instances for popular hits such as "Ruby Tuesday," "Enveloped in Python," "String of Pearls," "Small talk," and so on. The word *object* is used interchangeably with class instance (and being lazy typists, we'll probably be using the word "object" more frequently).

In Ruby, these objects are created by calling a constructor, a special method associated with a class. The standard constructor is called `new`.

```
song1 = Song.new("Ruby Tuesday")
song2 = Song.new("Enveloped in Python")
# and so on
```

These instances are both derived from the same class, but they have unique characteristics. First, every object has a unique *object identifier* (abbreviated as *object id*). Second, you can define *instance variables*, variables with values that are unique to each instance. These instance variables hold an object's state. Each of our songs, for example, will probably have an instance variable that holds the song title.

Within each class, you can define *instance methods*. Each method is a chunk of functionality which may be called from within the class and (depending on accessibility constraints) from outside. These instance methods in turn have access to the object's instance variables, and hence to the object's state.

Methods are invoked by sending a message to an object. The message contains the method's name, along with any parameters the method may need.[1] When an object receives a message, it looks into its own class for a corresponding method. If found, that method is executed. If the method *isn't* found, ... well, we'll get to that later.

This business of methods and messages may sound complicated, but in practice it is very natural. Let's look at some method calls. (Remember that the arrows in the code examples show the values returned by the corresponding expressions.)

```
"gin joint".length   →   9
"Rick".index("c")    →   2
-1942.abs            →   1942
sam.play(aSong)      →   "duh dum, da dum de dum ..."
```

---

1.   This idea of expressing method calls in the form of messages comes from Smalltalk.

Here, the thing before the period is called the *receiver*, and the name after the period is the method to be invoked. The first example asks a string for its length, and the second asks a different string to find the index of the letter "c." The third line has a number calculate its absolute value. Finally, we ask Sam to play us a song.

It's worth noting here a major difference between Ruby and most other languages. In (say) Java, you'd find the absolute value of some number by calling a separate function and passing in that number. You might write

```
number = Math.abs(number)     // Java code
```

In Ruby, the ability to determine an absolute value is built into numbers—they take care of the details internally. You simply send the message **abs** to a number object and let it do the work.

```
number = number.abs
```

The same applies to all Ruby objects: in C you'd write **strlen(name)**, while in Ruby it's **name.length**, and so on. This is part of what we mean when we say that Ruby is a genuine OO language.

Some Basic Ruby

Not many people like to read heaps of boring syntax rules when they're picking up a new language. So we're going to cheat. In this section we'll hit some of the highlights, the stuff you'll just *have* to know if you're going to write Ruby programs. Later, in Chapter 18, which begins on page 201, we'll go into all the gory details.

Let's start off with a simple Ruby program. We'll write a method that returns a string, adding to that string a person's name. We'll then invoke that method a couple of times.

```
def sayGoodnight(name)
  result = "Goodnight, " + name
  return result
end

# Time for bed...
puts sayGoodnight("John-Boy")
puts sayGoodnight("Mary-Ellen")
```

First, some general observations. Ruby syntax is clean. You don't need semicolons at the ends of statements as long as you put each statement on a separate line. Ruby comments start with a # character and run to the end of the line. Code layout is pretty much up to you; indentation is not significant.

Methods are defined with the keyword **def**, followed by the method name (in this case, "**sayGoodnight**") and the method's parameters between parentheses. Ruby doesn't use braces to delimit the bodies of compound statements and definitions. Instead, you simply finish the body with the keyword **end**. Our method's body is pretty simple. The first line concatenates the literal string "Goodnight,␣" to the parameter **name** and assigns the result to the local variable result. The next line returns that result to the caller. Note that we didn't have to declare the variable **result**; it sprang into existence when we assigned to it.

Having defined the method, we call it twice. In both cases we pass the result to the method **puts**, which simply outputs its argument followed by a newline.

```
Goodnight, John-Boy
Goodnight, Mary-Ellen
```

The line "**puts sayGoodnight("John-Boy")**" contains two method calls, one to **sayGoodnight** and the other to **puts**. Why does one call have its arguments in parentheses while the other doesn't? In this case it's purely a matter of taste. The following lines are all equivalent.

```
puts sayGoodnight "John-Boy"
puts sayGoodnight("John-Boy")
puts(sayGoodnight "John-Boy")
puts(sayGoodnight("John-Boy"))
```

However, life isn't always that simple, and precedence rules can make it difficult to know which argument goes with which method invocation, so we recommend using parentheses in all but the simplest cases.

This example also shows some Ruby string objects. There are many ways to create a string object, but probably the most common is to use string literals: sequences of characters between single or double quotation marks. The difference between the two forms is the amount of processing Ruby does on the string while constructing the literal. In the single-quoted case, Ruby does very little. With a few exceptions, what you type into the string literal becomes the string's value.

In the double-quoted case, Ruby does more work. First, it looks for substitutions—sequences that start with a backslash character—and replaces them with some binary value. The most common of these is "\n", which is replaced with a newline character. When a string containing a newline is output, the "\n" forces a line break.

```
puts "And Goodnight,\nGrandma"
```

produces:

```
And Goodnight,
Grandma
```

The second thing that Ruby does with double-quoted strings is expression interpolation. Within the string, the sequence #{*expression*} is replaced by the value of *expression*. We could use this to rewrite our previous method.

```
def sayGoodnight(name)
  result = "Goodnight, #{name}"
  return result
end
```

When Ruby constructs this string object, it looks at the current value of **name** and substitutes it into the string. Arbitrarily complex expressions are allowed in the #{...} construct. As a shortcut, you don't need to supply the braces when the expression is simply a global, instance, or class variable. For more information on strings, as well as on the other Ruby standard types, see Chapter 5, which begins on page 49.

Finally, we could simplify this method some more. The value returned by a Ruby method is the value of the last expression evaluated, so we can get rid of the **return** statement altogether.

```
def sayGoodnight(name)
  "Goodnight, #{name}"
end
```

We promised that this section would be brief. We've got just one more topic to cover: Ruby names. For brevity, we'll be using some terms (such as class variable) that we aren't going to define here. However, by talking about the rules now, you'll be ahead of the game when we actually come to discuss instance variables and the like later.

Ruby uses a convention to help it distinguish the usage of a name: the first characters of a name indicate how the name is used. Local variables, method parameters, and method names should all start with a lowercase letter or with an underscore. Global variables are prefixed with a dollar sign ($), while instance variables begin with an "at" sign (@). Class variables start with two "at" signs (@@). Finally, class names, module names, and constants should start with an uppercase letter. Samples of different names are given in Table 2.1 on the next page.

Following this initial character, a name can be any combination of letters, digits, and underscores (with the proviso that the character following an @ sign may not be a digit).

Arrays and Hashes

Ruby's arrays and hashes are indexed collections. Both store collections of objects, accessible using a key. With arrays, the key is an integer, whereas hashes support any object as a key. Both arrays and hashes grow as needed to hold new elements. It's more efficient to access array elements, but hashes provide more flexibility. Any particular array or hash can hold objects of differing types; you can have an array containing an integer, a string, and a floating point number, as we'll see in a minute.

Table 2.1. Example variable and class names

——————— Variables ———————				Constants and
Local	**Global**	**Instance**	**Class**	**Class Names**
name	$debug	@name	@@total	PI
fishAndChips	$CUSTOMER	@point_1	@@symtab	FeetPerMile
x_axis	$_	@X	@@N	String
thx1138	$plan9	@_	@@x_pos	MyClass
_26	$Global	@plan9	@@SINGLE	Jazz_Song

You can create and initialize a new array using an array literal—a set of elements between square brackets. Given an array object, you can access individual elements by supplying an index between square brackets, as the next example shows.

```
a = [ 1, 'cat', 3.14 ]   # array with three elements
# access the first element
a[0]   →   1
# set the third element
a[2] = nil
# dump out the array
a      →   [1, "cat", nil]
```

You can create empty arrays either by using an array literal with no elements or by using the array object's constructor, `Array.new`.

```
empty1 = []
empty2 = Array.new
```

Sometimes creating arrays of words can be a pain, what with all the quotes and commas. Fortunately, there's a shortcut: `%w` does just what we want.

```
a = %w{ ant bee cat dog elk }
a[0]   →   "ant"
a[3]   →   "dog"
```

Ruby hashes are similar to arrays. A hash literal uses braces rather than square brackets. The literal must supply two objects for every entry: one for the key, the other for the value.

For example, you might want to map musical instruments to their orchestral sections. You could do this with a hash.

```
instSection = {
  'cello'    => 'string',
  'clarinet' => 'woodwind',
  'drum'     => 'percussion',
  'oboe'     => 'woodwind',
```

```
     'trumpet'    => 'brass',
     'violin'     => 'string'
}
```

Hashes are indexed using the same square bracket notation as arrays.

```
instSection['oboe']      →   "woodwind"
instSection['cello']     →   "string"
instSection['bassoon']   →   nil
```

As the last example shows, a hash by default returns **nil** when indexed by a key it doesn't contain. Normally this is convenient, as **nil** means **false** when used in conditional expressions. Sometimes you'll want to change this default. For example, if you're using a hash to count the number of times each key occurs, it's convenient to have the default value be zero. This is easily done by specifying a default value when you create a new, empty hash.

```
histogram = Hash.new(0)
histogram['key1']  →   0
histogram['key1'] = histogram['key1'] + 1
histogram['key1']  →   1
```

Array and hash objects have lots of useful methods: see the discussion starting on page 35, and the reference sections starting on pages 282 and 321, for details.

Control Structures

Ruby has all the usual control structures, such as **if** statements and **while** loops. Java, C, and Perl programmers may well get caught by the lack of braces around the bodies of these statements. Instead, Ruby uses the keyword **end** to signify the end of a body.

```
if count > 10
  puts "Try again"
elsif tries == 3
  puts "You lose"
else
  puts "Enter a number"
end
```

Similarly, **while** statements are terminated with **end**.

```
while weight < 100 and numPallets <= 30
  pallet = nextPallet()
  weight += pallet.weight
  numPallets += 1
end
```

Ruby *statement modifiers* are a useful shortcut if the body of an `if` or `while` statement is just a single expression. Simply write the expression, followed by `if` or `while` and the condition. For example, here's a simple `if` statement.

```
if radiation > 3000
  puts "Danger, Will Robinson"
end
```

Here it is again, rewritten using a statement modifier.

```
puts "Danger, Will Robinson" if radiation > 3000
```

Similarly, a `while` loop such as

```
while square < 1000
   square = square*square
end
```

becomes the more concise

```
square = square*square  while square < 1000
```

These statement modifiers should seem familiar to Perl programmers.

Regular Expressions

Most of Ruby's built-in types will be familiar to all programmers. A majority of languages have strings, integers, floats, arrays, and so on. However, until Ruby came along, regular expression support was generally built into only the so-called scripting languages, such as Perl, Python, and awk. This is a shame: regular expressions, although cryptic, are a powerful tool for working with text.

Entire books have been written about regular expressions (for example, *Mastering Regular Expressions* [Fri97]), so we won't try to cover everything in just a short section. Instead, we'll look at just a few examples of regular expressions in action. You'll find full coverage of regular expressions starting on page 58.

A regular expression is simply a way of specifying a *pattern* of characters to be matched in a string. In Ruby, you typically create a regular expression by writing a pattern between slash characters (*/pattern/*). And, Ruby being Ruby, regular expressions are of course objects and can be manipulated as such.

For example, you could write a pattern that matches a string containing the text "Perl" or the text "Python" using the following regular expression.

```
/Perl|Python/
```

The forward slashes delimit the pattern, which consists of the two things we're matching, separated by a pipe character ("|"). You can use parentheses within patterns, just as you can in arithmetic expressions, so you could also have written this pattern as

```
/P(erl|ython)/
```

You can also specify repetition within patterns. /ab+c/ matches a string containing an "a" followed by one or more "b"s, followed by a "c". Change the plus to an asterisk, and /ab*c/ creates a regular expression that matches an "a", zero or more "b"s, and a "c".

You can also match one of a group of characters within a pattern. Some common examples are character classes such as "\s", which matches a whitespace character (space, tab, newline, and so on), "\d", which matches any digit, and "\w", which matches any character that may appear in a typical word. The single character "." (a period) matches any character.

We can put all this together to produce some useful regular expressions.

```
/\d\d:\d\d:\d\d/       # a time such as 12:34:56
/Perl.*Python/         # Perl, zero or more other chars, then Python
/Perl\s+Python/        # Perl, one or more spaces, then Python
/Ruby (Perl|Python)/   # Ruby, a space, and either Perl or Python
```

Once you have created a pattern, it seems a shame not to use it. The match operator "=~" can be used to match a string against a regular expression. If the pattern is found in the string, =~ returns its starting position, otherwise it returns nil. This means you can use regular expressions as the condition in if and while statements. For example, the following code fragment writes a message if a string contains the text 'Perl' or 'Python'.

```
if line =~ /Perl|Python/
  puts "Scripting language mentioned: #{line}"
end
```

The part of a string matched by a regular expression can also be replaced with different text using one of Ruby's substitution methods.

```
line.sub(/Perl/, 'Ruby')    # replace first 'Perl' with 'Ruby'
line.gsub(/Python/, 'Ruby') # replace every 'Python' with 'Ruby'
```

We'll have a lot more to say about regular expressions as we go through the book.

Blocks and Iterators

This section briefly describes one of Ruby's particular strengths. We're about to look at code blocks: chunks of code that you can associate with method invocations, almost as if they were parameters. This is an incredibly powerful feature. You can use code blocks to implement callbacks (but they're simpler than Java's anonymous inner classes), to pass around chunks of code (but they're more flexible than C's function pointers), and to implement iterators.

Code blocks are just chunks of code between braces or do...end.

```
{ puts "Hello" }         # this is a block
do                       #
  club.enroll(person)    # and so is this
  person.socialize       #
end                      #
```

Once you've created a block, you can associate it with a call to a method. That method can then invoke the block one or more times using the Ruby `yield` statement. The following example shows this in action. We define a method that calls `yield` twice. We then call it, putting a block on the same line, after the call (and after any arguments to the method).[2]

```
def callBlock
  yield
  yield
end

callBlock { puts "In the block" }
```

produces:

```
In the block
In the block
```

See how the code in the block (`puts "In the block"`) is executed twice, once for each call to `yield`.

You can provide parameters to the call to `yield`: these will be passed to the block. Within the block, you list the names of the arguments to receive these parameters between vertical bars ("|").

```
def callBlock
  yield "hello", 99
end              \     \

callBlock { |str, num| ... }
```

Code blocks are used throughout the Ruby library to implement iterators: methods that return successive elements from some kind of collection, such as an array.

---

2.   Some people like to think of the association of a block with a method as a kind of parameter passing. This works on one level, but it isn't really the whole story. You might be better off thinking of the block and the method as coroutines, which transfer control back and forth between themselves.

```
a = %w( ant bee cat dog elk )    # create an array
a.each { |animal| puts animal }  # iterate over the contents
```

produces:

```
ant
bee
cat
dog
elk
```

Let's look at how we might implement the **Array** class's **each** iterator that we used in the previous example. The **each** iterator loops through every element in the array, calling **yield** for each one. In pseudo code, this might look like:

```
# within class Array...
def each
  for each element
    yield(element)
  end
end
```

You could then iterate over an array's elements by calling its **each** method and supplying a block. This block would be called for each element in turn.

```
[ 'cat', 'dog', 'horse' ].each do |animal|
  print animal, " -- "
end
```

produces:

```
cat -- dog -- horse --
```

Similarly, many looping constructs that are built into languages such as C and Java are simply method calls in Ruby, with the methods invoking the associated block zero or more times.

```
5.times {  print "*" }
3.upto(6) {|i|  print i }
('a'..'e').each {|char| print char }
```

produces:

```
*****3456abcde
```

Here we ask the number 5 to call a block five times, then ask the number 3 to call a block, passing in successive values until it reaches 6. Finally, the range of characters from "a" to "e" invokes a block using the method **each**.

Reading and 'Riting

Ruby comes with a comprehensive I/O library. However, in most of the examples in this book we'll stick to a few simple methods. We've already come across two methods that do output. `puts` writes each of its arguments, adding a newline after each. `print` also writes its arguments, but with no newline. Both can be used to write to any I/O object, but by default they write to the console.

Another output method we use a lot is `printf`, which prints its arguments under the control of a format string (just like `printf` in C or Perl).

```
printf "Number: %5.2f, String: %s", 1.23, "hello"
```

produces:

```
Number:  1.23, String: hello
```

In this example, the format string `"Number: %5.2f, String: %s"` tells `printf` to substitute in a floating point number (allowing five characters in total, with two after the decimal point) and a string.

There are many ways to read input into your program. Probably the most traditional is to use the routine `gets`, which returns the next line from your program's standard input stream.

```
line = gets
print line
```

The `gets` routine has a side effect: as well as returning the line just read, it also stores it into the global variable `$_`. This variable is special, in that it is used as the default argument in many circumstances. If you call `print` with no argument, it prints the contents of `$_`. If you write an `if` or `while` statement with just a regular expression as the condition, that expression is matched against `$_`. While viewed by some purists as a rebarbative barbarism, these abbreviations can help you write some concise programs. For example, the following program prints all lines in the input stream that contain the word "Ruby."

```
while gets           # assigns line to $_
  if /Ruby/          # matches against $_
    print            # prints $_
  end
end
```

The "Ruby way" to write this would be to use an iterator.

```
ARGF.each { |line|  print line  if line =~ /Ruby/ }
```

This uses the predefined object `ARGF`, which represents the input stream that can be read by a program.

Onward and Upward

That's it. We've finished our lightning-fast tour of some of the basic features of Ruby. We've had a brief look at objects, methods, strings, containers, and regular expressions, seen some simple control structures, and looked at some rather nifty iterators. Hopefully, this chapter has given you enough ammunition to be able to attack the rest of this book.

Time to move on, and up—up to a higher level. Next, we'll be looking at classes and objects, things that are at the same time both the highest-level constructs in Ruby and the essential underpinnings of the entire language.

## Chapter 3

Classes, Objects, and Variables

From the examples we've shown so far, you might be wondering about our earlier assertion that Ruby is an object-oriented language. Well, this chapter is where we justify that claim. We're going to be looking at how you create classes and objects in Ruby, and at some of the ways in which Ruby is more powerful than most object-oriented languages. Along the way, we'll be implementing part of our next billion-dollar product, the Internet Enabled Jazz and Blue Grass jukebox.

After months of work, our highly paid Research and Development folks have determined that our jukebox needs *songs*. So it seems like a good idea to start off by setting up a Ruby class that represents things that are songs. We know that a real song has a name, an artist, and a duration, so we'll want to make sure that the song objects in our program do, too.

We'll start off by creating a basic class **Song**,[1] which contains just a single method, `initialize`.

```
class Song
  def initialize(name, artist, duration)
    @name     = name
    @artist   = artist
    @duration = duration
  end
end
```

`initialize` is a special method in Ruby programs. When you call **Song.new** to create a new **Song** object, Ruby creates an uninitialized object and then calls that object's

---

1.   As we mentioned on page 9, class names start with an uppercase letter, while method names start with a lowercase letter.

`initialize` method, passing in any parameters that were passed to `new`. This gives you a chance to write code that sets up your object's state.

For class `Song`, the `initialize` method takes three parameters. These parameters act just like local variables within the method, so they follow the local variable naming convention of starting with a lowercase letter.

Each object represents its own song, so we need each of our `Song` objects to carry around its own song name, artist, and duration. This means we need to store these values as *instance variables* within the object. In Ruby, an instance variable is simply a name preceded by an "at" sign ("@"). In our example, the parameter `name` is assigned to the instance variable `@name`, `artist` is assigned to `@artist`, and `duration` (the length of the song in seconds) is assigned to `@duration`.

Let's test our spiffy new class.

```
aSong = Song.new("Bicylops", "Fleck", 260)
aSong.inspect   →   "#<Song:0x40189104 @duration=260,
                    @artist=\"Fleck\", @name=\"Bicylops\">"
```

Well, it seems to work. By default, the `inspect` message, which can be sent to any object, dumps out the object's id and instance variables. It looks as though we have them set up correctly.

Our experience tells us that during development we'll be printing out the contents of a `Song` object many times, and `inspect`'s default formatting leaves something to be desired. Fortunately, Ruby has a standard message, `to_s`, which it sends to any object it wants to render as a string. Let's try it on our song.

```
aSong = Song.new("Bicylops", "Fleck", 260)
aSong.to_s   →   "#<Song:0x401892f8>"
```

That wasn't too useful—it just reported the object id. So, let's override `to_s` in our class. As we do this, we should also take a moment to talk about how we're showing the class definitions in this book.

In Ruby, classes are never closed: you can always add methods to an existing class. This applies to the classes you write as well as the standard, built-in classes. All you have to do is open up a class definition for an existing class, and the new contents you specify will be added to whatever's there.

This is great for our purposes. As we go through this chapter, adding features to our classes, we'll show just the class definitions for the new methods; the old ones will still be there. It saves us having to repeat redundant stuff in each example. Obviously, though, if you were creating this code from scratch, you'd probably just throw all the methods into a single class definition.

Enough detail! Let's get back to adding a `to_s` method to our `Song` class.

```
class Song
  def to_s
    "Song: #{@name}-#{@artist} (#{@duration})"
  end
end
aSong = Song.new("Bicylops", "Fleck", 260)
aSong.to_s  →  "Song: Bicylops-Fleck (260)"
```

Excellent, we're making progress. However, we've slipped in something subtle. We said that Ruby supports to_s for all objects, but we didn't say how. The answer has to do with inheritance, subclassing, and how Ruby determines what method to run when you send a message to an object. This is a subject for a new section, so....

Inheritance and Messages

Inheritance allows you to create a class that is a refinement or specialization of another class. For example, our jukebox has the concept of songs, which we encapsulate in class Song. Then marketing comes along and tells us that we need to provide karaoke support. A karaoke song is just like any other (there's no vocal on it, but that doesn't concern us). However, it also has an associated set of lyrics, along with timing information. When our jukebox plays a karaoke song, the lyrics should flow across the screen on the front of the jukebox in time with the music.

An approach to this problem is to define a new class, KaraokeSong, which is just like Song, but with a lyric track.

```
class KaraokeSong < Song
  def initialize(name, artist, duration, lyrics)
    super(name, artist, duration)
    @lyrics = lyrics
  end
end
```

The "< Song" on the class definition line tells Ruby that a KaraokeSong is a *subclass* of Song. (Not surprisingly, this means that Song a *superclass* of KaraokeSong. People also talk about parent-child relationships, so KaraokeSong's parent would be Song.) For now, don't worry too much about the initialize method; we'll talk about that super call later.

Let's create a KaraokeSong and check that our code worked. (In the final system, the lyrics will be held in an object that includes the text and timing information. To test out our class, though, we'll just use a string. This is another benefit of untyped languages—we don't have to define everything before we start running code.

```
aSong = KaraokeSong.new("My Way", "Sinatra", 225, "And now, the...")
aSong.to_s  →  "Song: My Way-Sinatra (225)"
```

Well, it ran, but why doesn't the to_s method show the lyric?

The answer has to do with the way Ruby determines which method should be called when you send a message to an object. When Ruby compiles the method invocation aSong.to_s, it doesn't actually know where to find the method to_s. Instead, it defers the decision until the program is run. At that time, it looks at the class of aSong. If that class implements a method with the same name as the message, that method is run. Otherwise, Ruby looks for a method in the parent class, and then in the grandparent, and so on up the ancestor chain. If it runs out of ancestors without finding the appropriate method, it takes a special action that normally results in an error being raised.[2]

So, back to our example. We sent the message to_s to aSong, an object of class KaraokeSong. Ruby looks in KaraokeSong for a method called to_s, but doesn't find it. The interpreter then looks in KaraokeSong's parent, class Song, and there it finds the to_s method that we defined on page 20. That's why it prints out the song details but not the lyrics—class Song doesn't know anything about lyrics.

Let's fix this by implementing KaraokeSong#to_s. There are a number of ways to do this. Let's start with a bad way. We'll copy the to_s method from Song and add on the lyric.

```ruby
class KaraokeSong
  # ...
  def to_s
    "KS: #{@name}-#{@artist} (#{duration}) [#{@lyrics}]"
  end
end
aSong = KaraokeSong.new("My Way", "Sinatra", 225, "And now, the...")
aSong.to_s   →   "KS: My Way-Sinatra (225) [And now, the...]"
```

We're correctly displaying the value of the @lyrics instance variable. To do this, the subclass directly accesses the instance variables of its ancestors. So why is this a bad way to implement to_s?

The answer has to do with good programming style (and something called *decoupling*). By poking around in our parent's internal state, we're tying ourselves tightly to its implementation. Say we decided to change Song to store the duration in milliseconds. Suddenly, KaraokeSong would start reporting ridiculous values. The idea of a karaoke version of "My Way" that lasts for 3750 minutes is just too frightening to consider.

We get around this problem by having each class handle its own internal state. When KaraokeSong#to_s is called, we'll have it call its parent's to_s method to get the song details. It will then append to this the lyric information and return the result. The

---

2. In fact, you can intercept this error, which allows you to fake out methods at runtime. This is described under Object#method_missing on page 360.

trick here is the Ruby keyword "super". When you invoke **super** with no arguments, Ruby sends a message to the current object's parent, asking it to invoke a method of the same name as the current method, and passing it the parameters that were passed to the current method. Now we can implement our new and improved **to_s**.

```
class KaraokeSong < Song
  # Format ourselves as a string by appending
  # our lyrics to our parent's #to_s value.
  def to_s
    super + " [#{@lyrics}]"
  end
end
aSong = KaraokeSong.new("My Way", "Sinatra", 225, "And now, the...")
aSong.to_s   →   "Song: My Way-Sinatra (225) [And now, the...]"
```

We explicitly told Ruby that **KaraokeSong** was a subclass of **Song**, but we didn't specify a parent class for **Song** itself. If you don't specify a parent when defining a class, Ruby supplies class **Object** as a default. This means that all objects have **Object** as an ancestor, and that **Object**'s instance methods are available to every object in Ruby. Back on page 20 we said that **to_s** is available to all objects. Now we know why; **to_s** is one of more than 35 instance methods in class **Object**. The complete list begins on page 356.

Inheritance and Mixins

Some object-oriented languages (notably C++) support multiple inheritance, where a class can have more than one immediate parent, inheriting functionality from each. Although powerful, this technique can be dangerous, as the inheritance hierarchy can become ambiguous.

Other languages, such as Java, support single inheritance. Here, a class can have only one immediate parent. Although cleaner (and easier to implement), single inheritance also has drawbacks—in the real world things often inherit attributes from multiple sources (a ball is both a *bouncing thing* and a *spherical thing*, for example).

Ruby offers an interesting and powerful compromise, giving you the simplicity of single inheritance and the power of multiple inheritance. A Ruby class can have only one direct parent, and so Ruby is a single-inheritance language. However, Ruby classes can include the functionality of any number of mixins (a mixin is like a partial class definition). This provides a controlled multiple-inheritance-like capability with none of the drawbacks. We'll explore mixins more beginning on page 100.

So far in this chapter we've been looking at classes and their methods. Now it's time to move on to the objects, such as the instances of class **Song**.

Objects and Attributes

The **Song** objects we've created so far have an internal state (such as the song title and artist). That state is private to those objects—no other object can access an object's instance variables. In general, this is a Good Thing. It means that the object is solely responsible for maintaining its own consistency.

However, an object that is totally secretive is pretty useless—you can create it, but then you can't do anything with it. You'll normally define methods that let you access and manipulate the state of an object, allowing the outside world to interact with the object. These externally visible facets of an object are called its *attributes*.

For our **Song** objects, the first thing we may need is the ability to find out the title and artist (so we can display them while the song is playing) and the duration (so we can display some kind of progress bar).

```
class Song
  def name
    @name
  end
  def artist
    @artist
  end
  def duration
    @duration
  end
end
aSong = Song.new("Bicylops", "Fleck", 260)
aSong.artist    →    "Fleck"
aSong.name      →    "Bicylops"
aSong.duration  →    260
```

Here we've defined three accessor methods to return the values of the three instance attributes. Because this is such a common idiom, Ruby provides a convenient shortcut: **attr_reader** creates these accessor methods for you.

```
class Song
  attr_reader :name, :artist, :duration
end
aSong = Song.new("Bicylops", "Fleck", 260)
aSong.artist    →    "Fleck"
aSong.name      →    "Bicylops"
aSong.duration  →    260
```

This example has introduced something new. The construct **:artist** is an expression that returns a **Symbol** object corresponding to **artist**. You can think of **:artist** as meaning the *name* of the variable **artist**, while plain **artist** is the *value* of the variable. In this example, we named the accessor methods **name**, **artist**, and **duration**. The corresponding instance variables, **@name**, **@artist**, and **@duration**, will be created automatically. These accessor methods are identical to the ones we wrote by hand earlier.

Writable Attributes

Sometimes you need to be able to set an attribute from outside the object. For example, let's assume that the duration that is initially associated with a song is an estimate (perhaps gathered from information on a CD or in the MP3 data). The first time we play the song, we get to find out how long it actually is, and we store this new value back in the Song object.

In languages such as C++ and Java, you'd do this with *setter functions.*

```
class JavaSong {                      // Java code
  private Duration myDuration;
  public void setDuration(Duration newDuration) {
    myDuration = newDuration;
  }
}
s = new Song(....)
s.setDuration(length)
```

In Ruby, the attributes of an object can be accessed as if they were any other variable. We've seen this above with phrases such as aSong.name. So, it seems natural to be able to assign to these variables when you want to set the value of an attribute. In keeping with the Principle of Least Surprise, that's just what you do in Ruby.

```
class Song
  def duration=(newDuration)
    @duration = newDuration
  end
end
aSong = Song.new("Bicylops", "Fleck", 260)
aSong.duration   →   260
aSong.duration = 257   # set attribute with updated value
aSong.duration   →   257
```

The assignment "aSong.duration = 257" invokes the method duration= in the aSong object, passing it 257 as an argument. In fact, defining a method name ending in an equals sign makes that name eligible to appear on the left-hand side of an assignment.

Again, Ruby provides a shortcut for creating these simple attribute setting methods.

```
class Song
  attr_writer :duration
end
aSong = Song.new("Bicylops", "Fleck", 260)
aSong.duration = 257
```

Virtual Attributes

These attribute accessing methods do not have to be just simple wrappers around an object's instance variables. For example, you might want to access the duration in minutes and fractions of a minute, rather than in seconds as we've been doing.

```
class Song
  def durationInMinutes
    @duration/60.0   # force floating point
  end
  def durationInMinutes=(value)
    @duration = (value*60).to_i
  end
end
aSong = Song.new("Bicylops", "Fleck", 260)
aSong.durationInMinutes    →   4.333333333
aSong.durationInMinutes = 4.2
aSong.duration             →   252
```

Here we've used attribute methods to create a virtual instance variable. To the outside world, `durationInMinutes` seems to be an attribute like any other. Internally, though, there is no corresponding instance variable.

This is more than a curiosity. In his landmark book *Object-Oriented Software Construction* [Mey97], Bertrand Meyer calls this the *Uniform Access Principle*. By hiding the difference between instance variables and calculated values, you are shielding the rest of the world from the implementation of your class. You're free to change how things work in the future without impacting the millions of lines of code that use your class. This is a big win.

Class Variables and Class Methods

So far, all the classes we've created have contained instance variables and instance methods: variables that are associated with a particular instance of the class, and methods that work on those variables. Sometimes classes themselves need to have their own states. This is where class variables come in.

Class Variables

A class variable is shared among all objects of a class, and it is also accessible to the class methods that we'll describe later. There is only one copy of a particular class variable for a given class. Class variable names start with two "at" signs, such as "`@@count`". Unlike global and instance variables, class variables must be initialized before they are used. Often this initialization is just a simple assignment in the body of the class definition.

For example, our jukebox may want to record how many times each particular song has been played. This count would probably be an instance variable of the **Song** object. When a song is played, the value in the instance is incremented. But say we also want to know how many songs have been played in total. We could do this by searching for all the **Song** objects and adding up their counts, or we could risk excommunication from the Church of Good Design and use a global variable. Instead, we'll use a class variable.

```
class Song
  @@plays = 0
  def initialize(name, artist, duration)
    @name     = name
    @artist   = artist
    @duration = duration
    @plays    = 0
  end
  def play
    @plays += 1
    @@plays += 1
    "This  song: #@plays plays. Total #@@plays plays."
  end
end
```

For debugging purposes, we've arranged for **Song#play** to return a string containing the number of times this song has been played, along with the total number of plays for all songs. We can test this easily.

```
s1 = Song.new("Song1", "Artist1", 234)  # test songs..
s2 = Song.new("Song2", "Artist2", 345)
s1.play   →   "This  song: 1 plays. Total 1 plays."
s2.play   →   "This  song: 1 plays. Total 2 plays."
s1.play   →   "This  song: 2 plays. Total 3 plays."
s1.play   →   "This  song: 3 plays. Total 4 plays."
```

Class variables are private to a class and its instances. If you want to make them accessible to the outside world, you'll need to write an accessor method. This method could be either an instance method or, leading us neatly to the next section, a class method.

Class Methods

Sometimes a class needs to provide methods that work without being tied to any particular object. We've already come across one such method. The **new** method creates a new **Song** object but is not itself associated with a particular song.

```
aSong = Song.new(....)
```

You'll find class methods sprinkled throughout the Ruby libraries. For example, objects of class **File** represent open files in the underlying file system. However, class **File** also provides several class methods for manipulating files that aren't open and therefore don't have a `File` object. If you want to delete a file, you call the class method `File.delete`, passing in the name.

```
File.delete("doomedFile")
```

Class methods are distinguished from instance methods by their definition. Class methods are defined by placing the class name and a period in front of the method name.

```
class Example

  def instMeth                # instance method
  end

  def Example.classMeth       # class method
  end

end
```

Jukeboxes charge money for each song played, not by the minute. That makes short songs more profitable than long ones. We may want to prevent songs that take too long from being available on the SongList. We could define a class method in `SongList` that checked to see if a particular song exceeded the limit. We'll set this limit using a class constant, which is simply a constant (remember constants? they start with an uppercase letter) that is initialized in the class body.

```
class SongList
  MaxTime = 5*60             #  5 minutes

  def SongList.isTooLong(aSong)
    return aSong.duration > MaxTime
  end
end
song1 = Song.new("Bicylops", "Fleck", 260)
SongList.isTooLong(song1)   →    false
song2 = Song.new("The Calling", "Santana", 468)
SongList.isTooLong(song2)   →    true
```

Singletons and Other Constructors

Sometimes you want to override the default way in which Ruby creates objects. As an example, let's look at our jukebox. Because we'll have many jukeboxes, spread all over the country, we want to make maintenance as easy as possible. Part of the requirement is to log everything that happens to a jukebox: the songs that are played, the money received, the strange fluids poured into it, and so on. Because we want to reserve the network bandwidth for music, we'll store these logfiles locally. This means we'll need a class that handles logging. However, we want only one logging object per jukebox, and we want that object to be shared among all the other objects that use it.

Enter the Singleton pattern, documented in *Design Patterns* [GHJV95]. We'll arrange things so that the only way to create a logging object is to call **Logger.create**, and we'll ensure that only one logging object is ever created.

```
class Logger
  private_class_method :new
  @@logger = nil
  def Logger.create
    @@logger = new unless @@logger
    @@logger
  end
end
```

By making **Logger**'s method **new** private, we prevent anyone from creating a logging object using the conventional constructor. Instead, we provide a class method, **Logger.create**. This uses the class variable **@@logger** to keep a reference to a single instance of the logger, returning that instance every time it is called.[3] We can check this by looking at the object identifiers the method returns.

```
Logger.create.id   →   537678716
Logger.create.id   →   537678716
```

Using class methods as pseudo-constructors can also make life easier for users of your class. As a trivial example, let's look at a class **Shape** that represents a regular polygon. Instances of **Shape** are created by giving the constructor the required number of sides and the total perimeter.

```
class Shape
  def initialize(numSides, perimeter)
    # ...
  end
end
```

However, a couple of years later, this class is used in a different application, where the programmers are used to creating shapes by name, and by specifying the length of the side, not the perimeter. Simply add some class methods to **Shape**.

```
class Shape
  def Shape.triangle(sideLength)
    Shape.new(3, sideLength*3)
  end
  def Shape.square(sideLength)
    Shape.new(4, sideLength*4)
  end
end
```

---

3.   The implementation of singletons that we present here is not thread-safe; if multiple threads were running, it would be possible to create multiple logger objects. Rather than add thread safety ourselves, however, we'd probably use the **Singleton** mixin supplied with Ruby, which is documented on page 472.

There are many interesting and powerful uses of class methods, but exploring them won't get our jukebox finished any sooner, so let's move on.

Access Control

When designing a class interface, it's important to consider just how much access to your class you'll be exposing to the outside world. Allow too much access into your class, and you risk increasing the coupling in your application—users of your class will be tempted to rely on details of your class's implementation, rather than on its logical interface. The good news is that the only way to change an object's state in Ruby is by calling one of its methods. Control access to the methods and you've controlled access to the object. A good rule of thumb is never to expose methods that could leave an object in an invalid state. Ruby gives us three levels of protection.

- **Public methods** can be called by anyone—there is no access control. Methods are public by default (except for `initialize`, which is always private).

- **Protected methods** can be invoked only by objects of the defining class and its subclasses. Access is kept within the family.

- **Private methods** cannot be called with an explicit receiver. Because you cannot specify an object when using them, private methods can be called only in the defining class and by direct descendents within that same object.

The difference between "protected" and "private" is fairly subtle, and is different in Ruby than in most common OO languages. If a method is protected, it may be called by *any* instance of the defining class or its subclasses. If a method is private, it may be called only within the context of the calling object—it is never possible to access another object's private methods directly, even if the object is of the same class as the caller.

Ruby differs from other OO languages in another important way. Access control is determined dynamically, as the program runs, not statically. You will get an access violation only when the code attempts to execute the restricted method.

Specifying Access Control

You specify access levels to methods within class or module definitions using one or more of the three functions `public`, `protected`, and `private`. Each function can be used in two different ways.

If used with no arguments, the three functions set the default access control of subsequently defined methods. This is probably familiar behavior if you're a C++ or Java programmer, where you'd use keywords such as `public` to achieve the same effect.

```
class MyClass
    def method1      # default is 'public'
      #...
    end

  protected          # subsequent methods will be 'protected'

    def method2      # will be 'protected'
      #...
    end

  private            # subsequent methods will be 'private'

    def method3      # will be 'private'
      #...
    end

  public             # subsequent methods will be 'public'

    def method4      # and this will be 'public'
      #...
    end
end
```

Alternatively, you can set access levels of named methods by listing them as arguments to the access control functions.

```
class MyClass
  def method1
  end

  # ... and so on

  public    :method1, :method4
  protected :method2
  private   :method3
end
```

A class's `initialize` method is automatically declared to be private.

It's time for some examples. Perhaps we're modeling an accounting system where every debit has a corresponding credit. Because we want to ensure that no one can break this rule, we'll make the methods that do the debits and credits private, and we'll define our external interface in terms of transactions.

```
class Accounts

  private

    def debit(account, amount)
      account.balance -= amount
    end
    def credit(account, amount)
      account.balance += amount
    end
```

```
public

  #...
  def transferToSavings(amount)
    debit(checking, amount)
    credit(savings, amount)
  end
  #...
end
```

Protected access is used when objects need to access the internal state of other objects of the same class. For example, we may want to allow the individual `Account` objects to compare their raw balances, but may want to hide those balances from the rest of the world (perhaps because we present them in a different form).

```
class Account
  attr_reader :balance      # accessor method 'balance'

  protected :balance        # and make it protected

  def greaterBalanceThan(other)
    return @balance > other.balance
  end
end
```

Because the attribute `balance` is protected, it's available only within `Account` objects.

Variables

Now that we've gone to the trouble to create all these objects, let's make sure we don't lose them. Variables are used to keep track of objects; each variable holds a reference to an object.

Let's confirm this with some code.

```
person = "Tim"
person.id    →   537678996
person.type  →   String
person       →   "Tim"
```

On the first line, Ruby creates a new `String` object with the value "Tim." A reference to this object is placed in the local variable `person`. A quick check shows that the variable has indeed taken on the personality of a string, with an object id, a type, and a value.

So, is a variable an object?

In Ruby, the answer is "no." A variable is simply a reference to an object. Objects float around in a big pool somewhere (the heap, most of the time) and are pointed to by variables.

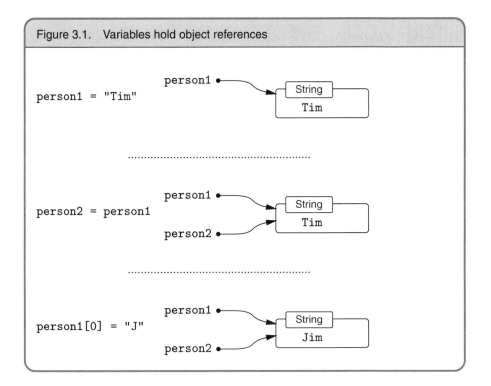

Figure 3.1.   Variables hold object references

Let's make the example slightly more complicated.

```
person1 = "Tim"
person2 = person1

person1[0] = 'J'

person1    →    "Jim"
person2    →    "Jim"
```

What happened here? We changed the first character of **person1**, but both **person1** and **person2** changed from "Tim" to "Jim."

It all comes back to the fact that variables hold references to objects, not the objects themselves. The assignment of **person1** to **person2** doesn't create any new objects; it simply copies **person1**'s object reference to **person2**, so that both **person1** and **person2** refer to the same object. We show this in Figure 3.1.

Assignment *aliases* objects, potentially giving you multiple variables that reference the same object. But can't this cause problems in your code? It can, but not as often as you'd think (objects in Java, for example, work exactly the same way). For instance, in the example in Figure 3.1, you could avoid aliasing by using the **dup** method of **String**, which creates a new **String** object with identical contents.

```
person1 = "Tim"
person2 = person1.dup
person1[0] = "J"
person1   →   "Jim"
person2   →   "Tim"
```

You can also prevent anyone from changing a particular object by freezing it (we talk more about freezing objects on page 255). Attempt to alter a frozen object, and Ruby will raise a **TypeError** exception.

```
person1 = "Tim"
person2 = person1
person1.freeze        # prevent modifications to the object
person2[0] = "J"
```

produces:

```
prog.rb:4:in `[]=': can't modify frozen string (TypeError)
from prog.rb:4
```

## Chapter 4

Containers, Blocks, and Iterators

A jukebox with one song is unlikely to be popular (except perhaps in some very, very scary bars), so pretty soon we'll have to start thinking about producing a catalog of available songs and a playlist of songs waiting to be played. Both of these are containers: objects that hold references to one or more other objects.

Both the catalog and the playlist need a similar set of methods: add a song, remove a song, return a list of songs, and so on. The playlist may perform additional tasks, such as inserting advertising every so often or keeping track of cumulative play time, but we'll worry about these things later. In the meantime, it seems like a good idea to develop some kind of generic `SongList` class, which we can specialize into catalogs and playlists.

Containers

Before we start implementing, we'll need to work out how to store the list of songs inside a `SongList` object. We have three obvious choices. We could use the Ruby `Array` type, use the Ruby `Hash` type, or create our own list structure. Being lazy, for now we'll look at arrays and hashes, and choose one of these for our class.

Arrays

The class `Array` holds a collection of object references. Each object reference occupies a position in the array, identified by a non-negative integer index.

You can create arrays using literals or by explicitly creating an `Array` object. A literal array is simply a list of objects between square brackets.

```
a = [ 3.14159, "pie", 99 ]
a.type      →   Array
a.length    →   3
a[0]        →   3.14159
a[1]        →   "pie"
a[2]        →   99
a[3]        →   nil

b = Array.new
b.type      →   Array
b.length    →   0
b[0] = "second"
b[1] = "array"
b           →   ["second", "array"]
```

Arrays are indexed using the [ ] operator. As with most Ruby operators, this is actually
a method (in class **Array**) and hence can be overridden in subclasses. As the example
shows, array indices start at zero. Index an array with a single integer, and it returns the
object at that position or returns **nil** if nothing's there. Index an array with a negative
integer, and it counts from the end. This is shown in Figure 4.1 on the next page.

```
a = [ 1, 3, 5, 7, 9 ]
a[-1]    →   9
a[-2]    →   7
a[-99]   →   nil
```

You can also index arrays with a pair of numbers, [start, count]. This returns a
new array consisting of references to **count** objects starting at position **start**.

```
a = [ 1, 3, 5, 7, 9 ]
a[1, 3]    →   [3, 5, 7]
a[3, 1]    →   [7]
a[-3, 2]   →   [5, 7]
```

Finally, you can index arrays using ranges, in which start and end positions are separated by two or three periods. The two-period form includes the end position, while the
three-period form does not.

```
a = [ 1, 3, 5, 7, 9 ]
a[1..3]     →   [3, 5, 7]
a[1...3]    →   [3, 5]
a[3..3]     →   [7]
a[-3..-1]   →   [5, 7, 9]
```

The [ ] operator has a corresponding [ ]= operator, which lets you set elements in the
array. If used with a single integer index, the element at that position is replaced by
whatever is on the right-hand side of the assignment. Any gaps that result will be filled
with **nil**.

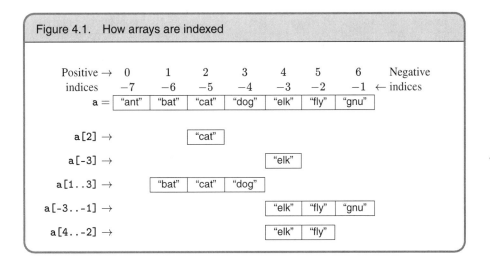

Figure 4.1. How arrays are indexed

```
a = [ 1, 3, 5, 7, 9 ]       →    [1, 3, 5, 7, 9]
a[1] = 'bat'                →    [1, "bat", 5, 7, 9]
a[-3] = 'cat'               →    [1, "bat", "cat", 7, 9]
a[3] = [ 9, 8 ]             →    [1, "bat", "cat", [9, 8], 9]
a[6] = 99                   →    [1, "bat", "cat", [9, 8], 9, nil, 99]
```

If the index to [ ]= is two numbers (a start and a length) or a range, then those elements in the original array are replaced by whatever is on the right-hand side of the assignment. If the length is zero, the right-hand side is inserted into the array before the start position; no elements are removed. If the right-hand side is itself an array, its elements are used in the replacement. The array size is automatically adjusted if the index selects a different number of elements than are available on the right-hand side of the assignment.

```
a = [ 1, 3, 5, 7, 9 ]       →    [1, 3, 5, 7, 9]
a[2, 2] = 'cat'             →    [1, 3, "cat", 9]
a[2, 0] = 'dog'             →    [1, 3, "dog", "cat", 9]
a[1, 1] = [ 9, 8, 7 ]       →    [1, 9, 8, 7, "dog", "cat", 9]
a[0..3] = []                →    ["dog", "cat", 9]
a[5] = 99                   →    ["dog", "cat", 9, nil, nil, 99]
```

Arrays have a large number of other useful methods. Using these, you can treat arrays as stacks, sets, queues, dequeues, and fifos. A complete list of array methods starts on page 282.

Hashes

Hashes (sometimes known as associative arrays or dictionaries) are similar to arrays, in that they are indexed collectives of object references. However, while you index arrays with integers, you can index a hash with objects of any type: strings, regular expressions, and so on. When you store a value in a hash, you actually supply two objects—the key and the value. You can subsequently retrieve the value by indexing the hash with the same key. The values in a hash can be any objects of any type. The example that follows uses hash literals: a list of *key => value* pairs between braces.

```
h = { 'dog' => 'canine', 'cat' => 'feline', 'donkey' => 'asinine' }

h.length    →    3
h['dog']    →    "canine"
h['cow']    = 'bovine'
h[12]       = 'dodecine'
h['cat']    = 99
h           →    {"cow"=>"bovine", 12=>"dodecine", "dog"=>"canine",
                  "donkey"=>"asinine", "cat"=>99}
```

Compared with arrays, hashes have one significant advantage: they can use any object as an index. However, they also have a significant disadvantage: their elements are not ordered, so you cannot easily use a hash as a stack or a queue.

You'll find that hashes are one of the most commonly used data structures in Ruby. A full list of the methods implemented by class `Hash` starts on page 321.

Implementing a SongList Container

After that little diversion into arrays and hashes, we're now ready to implement the jukebox's `SongList`. Let's invent a basic list of methods we need in our `SongList`. We'll want to add to it as we go along, but it will do for now.

append(aSong) → list
>   Append the given song to the list.

deleteFirst() → aSong
>   Remove the first song from the list, returning that song.

deleteLast() → aSong
>   Remove the last song from the list, returning that song.

[anIndex] → aSong
>   Return the song identified by *anIndex*, which may be an integer index or a song title.

This list gives us a clue to the implementation. The ability to append songs at the end, and remove them from both the front and end, suggests a dequeue—a double-ended queue—which we know we can implement using an `Array`. Similarly, the ability to return a song at an integer position in the list is supported by arrays.

However, there's also the need to be able to retrieve songs by title, which might suggest using a hash, with the title as a key and the song as a value. Could we use a hash? Well, possibly, but there are problems. First a hash is unordered, so we'd probably need to use an ancillary array to keep track of the list. A bigger problem is that a hash does not support multiple keys with the same value. That would be a problem for our playlist, where the same song might be queued up for playing multiple times. So, for now we'll stick with an array of songs, searching it for titles when needed. If this becomes a performance bottleneck, we can always add some kind of hash-based lookup later.

We'll start our class with a basic `initialize` method, which creates the `Array` we'll use to hold the songs and stores a reference to it in the instance variable `@songs`.

```
class SongList
  def initialize
    @songs = Array.new
  end
end
```

The `SongList#append` method adds the given song to the end of the `@songs` array. It also returns *self*, a reference to the current `SongList` object. This is a useful convention, as it lets us chain together multiple calls to `append`. We'll see an example of this later.

```
class SongList
  def append(aSong)
    @songs.push(aSong)
    self
  end
end
```

Then we'll add the `deleteFirst` and `deleteLast` methods, trivially implemented using `Array#shift` and `Array#pop`, respectively.

```
class SongList
  def deleteFirst
    @songs.shift
  end
  def deleteLast
    @songs.pop
  end
end
```

At this point, a quick test might be in order. First, we'll append four songs to the list. Just to show off, we'll use the fact that `append` returns the `SongList` object to chain together these method calls.

```
list = SongList.new
list.
  append(Song.new('title1', 'artist1', 1)).
  append(Song.new('title2', 'artist2', 2)).
  append(Song.new('title3', 'artist3', 3)).
  append(Song.new('title4', 'artist4', 4))
```

Then we'll check that songs are taken from the start and end of the list correctly, and that `nil` is returned when the list becomes empty.

```
list.deleteFirst   →   Song: title1-artist1 (1)
list.deleteFirst   →   Song: title2-artist2 (2)
list.deleteLast    →   Song: title4-artist4 (4)
list.deleteLast    →   Song: title3-artist3 (3)
list.deleteLast    →   nil
```

So far so good. Our next method is [ ], which accesses elements by index. If the index is a number (which we check using `Object#kind_of?`), we just return the element at that position.

```
class SongList
  def [](key)
    if key.kind_of?(Integer)
      @songs[key]
    else
      # ...
    end
  end
end
```

Again, testing this is pretty trivial.

```
list[0]   →   Song: title1-artist1 (1)
list[2]   →   Song: title3-artist3 (3)
list[9]   →   nil
```

Now we need to add the facility that lets us look up a song by title. This is going to involve scanning through the songs in the list, checking the title of each. To do this, we first need to spend a couple of pages looking at one of Ruby's neatest features: iterators.

Blocks and Iterators

So, our next problem with `SongList` is to implement the code in method [ ] that takes a string and searches for a song with that title. This seems straightforward: we have an array of songs, so we just go through it one element at a time, looking for a match.

```
class SongList
  def [](key)
    if key.kind_of?(Integer)
      return @songs[key]
    else
      for i in 0...@songs.length
        return @songs[i] if key == @songs[i].name
      end
    end
    return nil
  end
end
```

This works, and it looks comfortingly familiar: a `for` loop iterating over an array. What could be more natural?

It turns out there *is* something more natural. In a way, our `for` loop is somewhat too intimate with the array; it asks for a length, then retrieves values in turn until it finds a match. Why not just ask the array to apply a test to each of its members? That's just what the `find` method in `Array` does.

```
class SongList
  def [](key)
    if key.kind_of?(Integer)
      result = @songs[key]
    else
      result = @songs.find { |aSong| key == aSong.name }
    end
    return result
  end
end
```

We could use `if` as a statement modifier to shorten the code even more.

```
class SongList
  def [](key)
    return @songs[key] if key.kind_of?(Integer)
    return @songs.find { |aSong| aSong.name == key }
  end
end
```

The method `find` is an iterator—a method that invokes a block of code repeatedly. Iterators and code blocks are among the more interesting features of Ruby, so let's spend a while looking into them (and in the process we'll find out exactly what that line of code in our `[]` method actually does).

Implementing Iterators

A Ruby iterator is simply a method that can invoke a block of code. At first sight, a block in Ruby looks just like a block in C, Java, or Perl. Unfortunately, in this case looks are deceiving—a Ruby block *is* a way of grouping statements, but not in the conventional way.

First, a block may appear only in the source adjacent to a method call; the block is written starting on the same line as the method's last parameter. Second, the code in the block is not executed at the time it is encountered. Instead, Ruby remembers the context in which the block appears (the local variables, the current object, and so on), and then enters the method. This is where the magic starts.

Within the method, the block may be invoked, almost as if it were a method itself, using the `yield` statement. Whenever a `yield` is executed, it invokes the code in the block.

When the block exits, control picks back up immediately after the `yield`.[1] Let's start with a trivial example.

```
def threeTimes
  yield
  yield
  yield
end
threeTimes { puts "Hello" }
```

produces:

```
Hello
Hello
Hello
```

The block (the code between the braces) is associated with the call to the method **threeTimes**. Within this method, `yield` is called three times in a row. Each time, it invokes the code in the block, and a cheery greeting is printed. What makes blocks interesting, however, is that you can pass parameters to them and receive values back from them. For example, we could write a simple function that returns members of the Fibonacci series up to a certain value.[2]

```
def fibUpTo(max)
  i1, i2 = 1, 1          # parallel assignment
  while i1 <= max
    yield i1
    i1, i2 = i2, i1+i2
  end
end
fibUpTo(1000) { |f| print f, " " }
```

produces:

```
1 1 2 3 5 8 13 21 34 55 89 144 233 377 610 987
```

In this example, the `yield` statement has a parameter. This value is passed to the associated block. In the definition of the block, the argument list appears between vertical bars. In this instance, the variable **f** receives the value passed to the `yield`, so the block prints successive members of the series. (This example also shows parallel assignment in action. We'll come back to this on page 77.) Although it is common to pass just one value to a block, this is not a requirement; a block may have any number of parame-

---

1.   Programming-language buffs will be pleased to know that the keyword `yield` was chosen to echo the `yield` function in Liskov's language CLU, a language that is over 20 years old and yet contains features that still haven't been widely exploited by the CLU-less.

2.   The basic Fibonacci series is a sequence of integers, starting with two 1's, in which each subsequent term is the sum of the two preceding terms. The series is sometimes used in sorting algorithms and in analyzing natural phenomena.

ters. If a `yield` statement passes more parameters than a block is expecting, the excess parameters are silently, but brutally, ignored.

Parameters to a block may be existing local variables; if so, the new value of the variable will be retained after the block completes. This may lead to unexpected behavior, but there is also a performance gain to be had by using variables that already exist.[3]

A block may also return a value to the method. The value of the last expression evaluated in the block is passed back to the method as the value of the `yield`. This is how the `find` method used by class `Array` works.[4] Its implementation would look something like the following.

```
class Array
  def find
    for i in 0...size
      value = self[i]
      return value if yield(value)
    end
    return nil
  end
end

[1, 3, 5, 7, 9].find {|v| v*v > 30 }   →   7
```

This passes successive elements of the array to the associated block. If the block returns `true`, the method returns the corresponding element. If no element matches, the method returns `nil`. The example shows the benefit of this approach to iterators. The **Array** class does what it does best, accessing array elements, leaving the application code to concentrate on its particular requirement (in this case, finding an entry that meets some mathematical criteria).

Some iterators are common to many types of Ruby collections. We've looked at `find` already. Two others are `each` and `collect`.

`each` is probably the simplest iterator—all it does is yield successive elements of its collection.

```
[ 1, 3, 5 ].each { |i| puts i }
```

produces:

```
1
3
5
```

---

3. For more information on this and other "gotchas," see the list beginning on page 129; more performance information begins on page 130.

4. The `find` method is actually defined in module **Enumerable**, which is mixed into class **Array**.

The `each` iterator has a special place in Ruby; on page 87 we'll describe how it's used as the basis of the language's `for` loop, and starting on page 104 we'll see how defining an `each` method can add a whole lot more functionality to your class for free.

Another common iterator is `collect`, which takes each element from the collection and passes it to the block. The results returned by the block are used to construct a new array. For instance:

```
["H", "A", "L"].collect { |x| x.succ }   →   ["I", "B", "M"]
```

Ruby Compared with C++ and Java

It's worth spending a paragraph comparing Ruby's approach to iterators to that of C++ and Java. In the Ruby approach, the iterator is simply a method, identical to any other, that happens to call `yield` whenever it generates a new value. The thing that uses the iterator is simply a block of code associated with this method. There is no need to generate helper classes to carry the iterator state, as in Java and C++. In this, as in many other ways, Ruby is a transparent language. When you write a Ruby program, you concentrate on getting the job done, not on building scaffolding to support the language itself.

Iterators are not limited to accessing existing data in arrays and hashes. As we saw in the Fibonacci example, an iterator can return derived values. This capability is used by the Ruby input/output classes, which implement an iterator interface returning successive lines (or bytes) in an I/O stream.

```
f = File.open("testfile")
f.each do |line|
  print line
end
f.close
```

produces:

```
This is line one
This is line two
This is line three
And so on...
```

Let's look at just one more iterator implementation. The Smalltalk language also supports iterators over collections. If you ask Smalltalk programmers to sum the elements in an array, it's likely that they'd use the `inject` function.

```
sumOfValues                    "Smalltalk method"
    ^self values
        inject: 0
        into: [ :sum :element | sum + element value]
```

`inject` works like this. The first time the associated block is called, `sum` is set to `inject`'s parameter (zero in this case), and `element` is set to the first element in the array. The second and subsequent times the block is called, `sum` is set to the value returned by the block on the previous call. This way, `sum` can be used to keep a running total. The final value of `inject` is the value returned by the block the last time it was called.

Ruby does not have an `inject` method, but it's easy to write one. In this case we'll add it to the `Array` class, while on page 102 we'll see how to make it more generally available.

```
class Array
  def inject(n)
      each { |value| n = yield(n, value) }
      n
  end
  def sum
    inject(0) { |n, value| n + value }
  end
  def product
    inject(1) { |n, value| n * value }
  end
end
[ 1, 2, 3, 4, 5 ].sum        →    15
[ 1, 2, 3, 4, 5 ].product    →    120
```

Although blocks are often the target of an iterator, they also have other uses. Let's look at a few.

Blocks for Transactions

Blocks can be used to define a chunk of code that must be run under some kind of transactional control. For example, you'll often open a file, do something with its contents, and then want to ensure that the file is closed when you finish. Although you can do this using conventional code, there's an argument for making the file responsible for closing itself. We can do this with blocks. A naive implementation (ignoring error handling) might look something like the following.

```
class File
  def File.openAndProcess(*args)
    f = File.open(*args)
    yield f
    f.close()
  end
end

File.openAndProcess("testfile", "r") do |aFile|
  print while aFile.gets
end
```

produces:

```
This is line one
This is line two
This is line three
And so on...
```

This small example illustrates a number of techniques. The `openAndProcess` method is a *class method*—it may be called independent of any particular `File` object. We want it to take the same arguments as the conventional `File.open` method, but we don't really care what those arguments are. Instead, we specified the arguments as `*args`, meaning "collect the actual parameters passed to the method into an array." We then call `File.open`, passing it `*args` as a parameter. This expands the array back into individual parameters. The net result is that `openAndProcess` transparently passes whatever parameters it received to `File.open`.

Once the file has been opened, `openAndProcess` calls `yield`, passing the open file object to the block. When the block returns, the file is closed. In this way, the responsibility for closing an open file has been passed from the user of file objects back to the files themselves.

Finally, this example uses **do. . . end** to define a block. The only difference between this notation and using braces to define blocks is precedence: **do. . . end** binds lower than "{ . . . }". We discuss the impact of this on page 236.

The technique of having files manage their own lifecycle is so useful that the class `File` supplied with Ruby supports it directly. If `File.open` has an associated block, then that block will be invoked with a file object, and the file will be closed when the block terminates. This is interesting, as it means that `File.open` has two different behaviors: when called with a block, it executes the block and closes the file. When called without a block, it returns the file object. This is made possible by the method `Kernel.block_given?`, which returns `true` if a block is associated with the current method. Using it, you could implement `File.open` (again, ignoring error handling) using something like the following.

```
class File
  def File.myOpen(*args)
    aFile = File.new(*args)
    # If there's a block, pass in the file and close
    # the file when it returns
    if block_given?
      yield aFile
      aFile.close
      aFile = nil
    end
    return aFile
  end
end
```

Blocks Can Be Closures

Let's get back to our jukebox for a moment (remember the jukebox?). At some point we'll be working on the code that handles the user interface—the buttons that people press to select songs and control the jukebox. We'll need to associate actions with those buttons: press STOP and the music stops. It turns out that Ruby's blocks are a convenient way to do this. Let's start out by assuming that the people who made the hardware implemented a Ruby extension that gives us a basic button class. (We talk about extending Ruby beginning on page 171.)

```
bStart = Button.new("Start")
bPause = Button.new("Pause")
# ...
```

What happens when the user presses one of our buttons? In the `Button` class, the hardware folks rigged things so that a callback method, `buttonPressed`, will be invoked. The obvious way of adding functionality to these buttons is to create subclasses of `Button` and have each subclass implement its own `buttonPressed` method.

```
class StartButton < Button
  def initialize
    super("Start")        # invoke Button's initialize
  end
  def buttonPressed
    # do start actions...
  end
end

bStart = StartButton.new
```

There are two problems here. First, this will lead to a large number of subclasses. If the interface to `Button` changes, this could involve us in a lot of maintenance. Second, the actions performed when a button is pressed are expressed at the wrong level; they are not a feature of the button, but are a feature of the jukebox that uses the buttons. We can fix both of these problems using blocks.

```
class JukeboxButton < Button
  def initialize(label, &action)
    super(label)
    @action = action
  end
  def buttonPressed
    @action.call(self)
  end
end

bStart = JukeboxButton.new("Start") { songList.start }
bPause = JukeboxButton.new("Pause") { songList.pause }
```

The key to all this is the second parameter to `JukeboxButton#initialize`. If the last parameter in a method definition is prefixed with an ampersand (such as `&action`),

Ruby looks for a code block whenever that method is called. That code block is converted to an object of class **Proc** and assigned to the parameter. You can then treat the parameter as any other variable. In our example, we assigned it to the instance variable **@action**. When the callback method **buttonPressed** is invoked, we use the **Proc#call** method on that object to invoke the block.

So what exactly do we have when we create a **Proc** object? The interesting thing is that it's more than just a chunk of code. Associated with a block (and hence a **Proc** object) is all the context in which the block was *defined*: the value of **self**, and the methods, variables, and constants in scope. Part of the magic of Ruby is that the block can still use all this original scope information even if the environment in which it was defined would otherwise have disappeared. In other languages, this facility is called a *closure*.

Let's look at a contrived example. This example uses the method **proc**, which converts a block to a **Proc** object.

```
def nTimes(aThing)
  return proc { |n| aThing * n }
end

p1 = nTimes(23)
p1.call(3)    →    69
p1.call(4)    →    92
p2 = nTimes("Hello ")
p2.call(3)    →    "Hello Hello Hello "
```

The method **nTimes** returns a **Proc** object that references the method's parameter, **aThing**. Even though that parameter is out of scope by the time the block is called, the parameter remains accessible to the block.

## Chapter 5

Standard Types

So far we've been having fun implementing pieces of our jukebox code, but we've been negligent. We've looked at arrays, hashes, and procs, but we haven't really covered the other basic types in Ruby: numbers, strings, ranges, and regular expressions. Let's spend a few pages on these basic building blocks now.

Numbers

Ruby supports integers and floating point numbers. Integers can be any length (up to a maximum determined by the amount of free memory on your system). Integers within a certain range (normally -2^{31} to 2^{31} or -2^{63} to 2^{63}) are held internally in binary form, and are objects of class `Fixnum`. Integers outside this range are stored in objects of class `Bignum` (currently implemented as a variable-length set of short integers). This process is transparent, and Ruby automatically manages the conversion back and forth.

```
num = 8
7.times do
  print num.type, " ", num, "\n"
  num *= num
end
```

produces:

```
Fixnum 8
Fixnum 64
Fixnum 4096
Fixnum 16777216
Bignum 281474976710656
Bignum 79228162514264337593543950336
Bignum 6277101735386680763835789423207666416102355444464034512896
```

You write integers using an optional leading sign, an optional base indicator (0 for octal, 0x for hex, or 0b for binary), followed by a string of digits in the appropriate base. Underscore characters are ignored in the digit string.

```
123456                      # Fixnum
123_456                     # Fixnum (underscore ignored)
-543                        # Negative Fixnum
123_456_789_123_345_789     # Bignum
0xaabb                      # Hexadecimal
0377                        # Octal
-0b101_010                  # Binary (negated)
```

You can also get the integer value corresponding to an ASCII character or escape sequence by preceding it with a question mark. Control and meta combinations can also be generated using ?\C-*x*, ?\M-*x*, and ?\M-\C-*x*. The control version of a value is the same as "value & 0x9f". The meta version of a value is "value | 0x80". Finally, the sequence ?\C-? generates an ASCII delete, 0177.

```
?a                      # character code
?\n                     # code for a newline (0x0a)
?\C-a                   # control a = ?A & 0x9f = 0x01
?\M-a                   # meta sets bit 7
?\M-\C-a                # meta and control a
?\C-?                   # delete character
```

A numeric literal with a decimal point and/or an exponent is turned into a Float object, corresponding to the native architecture's double data type. You must follow the decimal point with a digit, as 1.e3 tries to invoke the method e3 in class Fixnum.

All numbers are objects, and respond to a variety of messages (listed in full starting on pages 294, 318, 319, 328, and 354). So, unlike (say) C++, you find the absolute value of a number by writing aNumber.abs, not abs(aNumber).

Integers also support several useful iterators. We've seen one already—7.times in the code example on the preceding page. Others include upto and downto, for iterating up and down between two integers, and step, which is more like a traditional for loop.

```
3.times        { print "X " }
1.upto(5)      { |i| print i, " " }
99.downto(95)  { |i| print i, " " }
50.step(80, 5) { |i| print i, " " }
```

produces:

```
X X X 1 2 3 4 5 99 98 97 96 95 50 55 60 65 70 75 80
```

Finally, a warning for Perl users. Strings that contain numbers are not automatically converted into numbers when used in expressions. This tends to bite most often when reading numbers from a file. The following code (probably) doesn't do what was intended.

```
DATA.each do |line|
  vals = line.split    # split line, storing tokens in val
  print vals[0] + vals[1], " "
end
```

Feed it a file containing

```
3 4
5 6
7 8
```

and you'll get the output "34 56 78." What happened?

The problem is that the input was read as strings, not numbers. The plus operator concatenates strings, so that's what we see in the output. To fix this, use the `String#to_i` method to convert the string to an integer.

```
DATA.each do |line|
  vals = line.split
  print vals[0].to_i + vals[1].to_i, " "
end
```

produces:

```
7 11 15
```

Strings

Ruby strings are simply sequences of 8-bit bytes. They normally hold printable characters, but that is not a requirement; a string can also hold binary data. Strings are objects of class `String`.

Strings are often created using string literals—sequences of characters between delimiters. Because binary data is otherwise difficult to represent within program source, you can place various escape sequences in a string literal. Each is replaced with the corresponding binary value as the program is compiled. The type of string delimiter determines the degree of substitution performed. Within single-quoted strings, two consecutive backslashes are replaced by a single backslash, and a backslash followed by a single quote becomes a single quote.

```
'escape using "\\"'    →   escape using "\"
'That\'s right'        →   That's right
```

Double-quoted strings support a boatload more escape sequences. The most common is probably "\n", the newline character. Table 18.2 on page 205 gives the complete list. In addition, you can substitute the value of any Ruby expression into a string using the sequence #{ *expr* }. If the expression is just a global variable, a class variable, or an instance variable, you can omit the braces.

```
"Seconds/day: #{24*60*60}"    →   Seconds/day: 86400
"#{'Ho! '*3}Merry Christmas"  →   Ho! Ho! Ho! Merry Christmas
"This is line #$."            →   This is line 3
```

There are three more ways to construct string literals: %q, %Q, and "here documents."

%q and %Q start delimited single- and double-quoted strings.

```
%q/general single-quoted string/    →    general single-quoted string
%Q!general double-quoted string!    →    general double-quoted string
%Q{Seconds/day: #{24*60*60}}        →    Seconds/day: 86400
```

The character following the "q" or "Q" is the delimiter. If it is an opening bracket, brace, parenthesis, or less-than sign, the string is read until the matching close symbol is found. Otherwise the string is read until the next occurrence of the same delimiter.

Finally, you can construct a string using a *here document*.

```
aString = <<END_OF_STRING
    The body of the string
    is the input lines up to
    one ending with the same
    text that followed the '<<'
END_OF_STRING
```

A here document consists of lines in the source up to, but not including, the terminating string that you specify after the < < characters. Normally, this terminator must start in the first column. However, if you put a minus sign after the < < characters, you can indent the terminator.

```
print <<-STRING1, <<-STRING2
    Concat
    STRING1
        enate
        STRING2
```

produces:

```
        Concat
            enate
```

Working with Strings

String is probably the largest built-in Ruby class, with over 75 standard methods. We won't go through them all here; the library reference has a complete list. Instead, we'll look at some common string idioms—things that are likely to pop up during day-to-day programming.

Let's get back to our jukebox. Although it's designed to be connected to the Internet, it also holds copies of some popular songs on a local hard drive. That way, if a squirrel chews through our 'net connection we'll still be able to entertain the customers.

For historical reasons (are there any other kind?), the list of songs is stored as rows in a flat file. Each row holds the name of the file containing the song, the song's duration, the artist, and the title, all in vertical-bar-separated fields. A typical file might start:

```
/jazz/j00132.mp3  | 3:45 | Fats      Waller     | Ain't Misbehavin'
/jazz/j00319.mp3  | 2:58 | Louis     Armstrong  | Wonderful World
/bgrass/bg0732.mp3| 4:09 | Strength in Numbers | Texas Red
          :                    :          :                :
```

Looking at the data, it's clear that we'll be using some of class **String**'s many methods to extract and clean up the fields before we create **Song** objects based on them. At a minimum, we'll need to:

- break the line into fields,

- convert the running time from mm:ss to seconds, and

- remove those extra spaces from the artist's name.

Our first task is to split each line into fields, and **String#split** will do the job nicely. In this case, we'll pass **split** a regular expression, /*|*/, which splits the line into tokens wherever **split** finds a vertical bar, optionally surrounded by spaces. And, because the line read from the file has a trailing newline, we'll use **String#chomp** to strip it off just before we apply the split.

```
songs = SongList.new
songFile.each do |line|
  file, length, name, title = line.chomp.split(/\s*\|\s*/)
  songs.append Song.new(title, name, length)
end
puts songs[1]
```

produces:

```
Song: Wonderful World--Louis     Armstrong (2:58)
```

Unfortunately, whoever created the original file entered the artists' names in columns, so some of them contain extra spaces. These will look ugly on our high-tech, super-twist, flat-panel Day-Glo display, so we'd better remove these extra spaces before we go much further. There are many ways of doing this, but probably the simplest is **String#squeeze**, which trims runs of repeated characters. We'll use the **squeeze!** form of the method, which alters the string in place.

```
songs = SongList.new
songFile.each do |line|
  file, length, name, title = line.chomp.split(/\s*\|\s*/)
  name.squeeze!(" ")
  songs.append Song.new(title, name, length)
end
puts songs[1]
```

produces:

```
Song: Wonderful World--Louis Armstrong (2:58)
```

Finally, there's the minor matter of the time format: the file says 2:58, and we want the number of seconds, 178. We could use `split` again, this time splitting the time field around the colon character.

```
mins, secs = length.split(/:/)
```

Instead, we'll use a related method. `String#scan` is similar to `split` in that it breaks a string into chunks based on a pattern. However, unlike `split`, with `scan` you specify the pattern that you want the chunks to match. In this case, we want to match one or more digits for both the minutes and seconds component. The pattern for one or more digits is /\d+/.

```
songs = SongList.new
songFile.each do |line|
  file, length, name, title = line.chomp.split(/\s*\|\s*/)
  name.squeeze!(" ")
  mins, secs = length.scan(/\d+/)
  songs.append Song.new(title, name, mins.to_i*60+secs.to_i)
end
puts songs[1]
```

produces:

```
Song: Wonderful World--Louis Armstrong (178)
```

Our jukebox has a keyword search capability. Given a word from a song title or an artist's name, it will list all matching tracks. Type in "fats," and it might come back with songs by Fats Domino, Fats Navarro, and Fats Waller, for example. We'll implement this by creating an indexing class. Feed it an object and some strings, and it will index that object under every word (of two or more characters) that occurs in those strings. This will illustrate a few more of class `String`'s many methods.

```
class WordIndex
  def initialize
    @index = Hash.new(nil)
  end
  def index(anObject, *phrases)
    phrases.each do |aPhrase|
      aPhrase.scan /\w[-\w']+/ do |aWord|    # extract each word
        aWord.downcase!
        @index[aWord] = [] if @index[aWord].nil?
        @index[aWord].push(anObject)
      end
    end
  end
  def lookup(aWord)
    @index[aWord.downcase]
  end
end
```

The `String#scan` method extracts elements from a string that match a regular expression. In this case, the pattern "`\w[-\w']+`" matches any character that can appear in a word, followed by one or more of the things specified in the brackets (a hyphen, another word character, or a single quote). We'll talk more about regular expressions beginning on page 58. To make our searches case insensitive, we map both the words we extract and the words used as keys during the lookup to lowercase. Note the exclamation mark at the end of the first `downcase!` method name. As with the `squeeze!` method we used previously, this is an indication that the method will modify the receiver in place, in this case converting the string to lowercase.[1]

We'll extend our `SongList` class to index songs as they're added, and add a method to look up a song given a word.

```
class SongList
  def initialize
    @songs = Array.new
    @index = WordIndex.new
  end
  def append(aSong)
    @songs.push(aSong)
    @index.index(aSong, aSong.name, aSong.artist)
    self
  end
  def lookup(aWord)
    @index.lookup(aWord)
  end
end
```

Finally, we'll test it all.

```
songs = SongList.new
songFile.each do |line|
  file, length, name, title = line.chomp.split(/\s*\|\s*/)
  name.squeeze!(" ")
  mins, secs = length.scan(/\d+/)
  songs.append Song.new(title, name, mins.to_i*60+secs.to_i)
end
puts songs.lookup("Fats")
puts songs.lookup("ain't")
puts songs.lookup("RED")
puts songs.lookup("WoRlD")
```

produces:

```
Song: Ain't Misbehavin'--Fats Waller (225)
Song: Ain't Misbehavin'--Fats Waller (225)
Song: Texas Red--Strength in Numbers (249)
Song: Wonderful World--Louis Armstrong (178)
```

---

1.   There's a minor bug in this code example: the song "Gone, Gone, Gone" would get indexed three times. Can you come up with a fix?

We could spend the next 50 pages looking at all the methods in class `String`. However, let's move on instead to look at a simpler datatype: ranges.

Ranges

Ranges occur everywhere: January to December, 0 to 9, rare to well-done, lines 50 through 67, and so on. If Ruby is to help us model reality, it seems natural for it to support these ranges. In fact, Ruby goes one better: it actually uses ranges to implement three separate features: sequences, conditions, and intervals.

Ranges as Sequences

The first and perhaps most natural use of ranges is to express a sequence. Sequences have a start point, an end point, and a way to produce successive values in the sequence. In Ruby, these sequences are created using the "``.``" and "``...``" range operators. The two-dot form creates an inclusive range, while the three-dot form creates a range that excludes the specified high value.

```
1..10
'a'..'z'
0...anArray.length
```

In Ruby, unlike in some earlier versions of Perl, ranges are not represented internally as lists: the sequence 1..100000 is held as a `Range` object containing references to two `Fixnum` objects. If you need to, you can convert a range to a list using the `to_a` method.

```
(1..10).to_a          →    [1, 2, 3, 4, 5, 6, 7, 8, 9, 10]
('bar'..'bat').to_a   →    ["bar", "bas", "bat"]
```

Ranges implement methods that let you iterate over them and test their contents in a variety of ways.

```
digits = 0..9
digits.include?(5)          →    true
digits.min                  →    0
digits.max                  →    9
digits.reject {|i| i < 5 }  →    [5, 6, 7, 8, 9]
digits.each do |digit|
  dial(digit)
end
```

So far we've shown ranges of numbers and strings. However, as you'd expect from an object-oriented language, Ruby can create ranges based on objects that you define. The only constraints are that the objects must respond to `succ` by returning the next object in sequence and the objects must be comparable using `<=>`, the general comparison operator. Sometimes called the spaceship operator, `<=>` compares two values, returning

−1, 0, or +1 depending on whether the first is less than, equal to, or greater than the second.

Here's a simple class that represents rows of "#" signs. We might use it as a text-based stub when testing the jukebox volume control.

```
class VU

  include Comparable

  attr :volume

  def initialize(volume)  # 0..9
    @volume = volume
  end

  def inspect
    '#' * @volume
  end

  # Support for ranges

  def <=>(other)
    self.volume <=> other.volume
  end

  def succ
    raise(IndexError, "Volume too big") if @volume >= 9
    VU.new(@volume.succ)
  end
end
```

We can test it by creating a range of VU objects.

```
medium = VU.new(4)..VU.new(7)
medium.to_a                      →   [####, #####, ######, #######]
medium.include?(VU.new(3))       →   false
```

Ranges as Conditions

As well as representing sequences, ranges may also be used as conditional expressions. For example, the following code fragment prints sets of lines from standard input, where the first line in each set contains the word "start" and the last line the word "end."

```
while gets
  print if /start/../end/
end
```

Behind the scenes, the range keeps track of the state of each of the tests. We'll show some examples of this in the description of loops that starts on page 84.

Ranges as Intervals

A final use of the versatile range is as an interval test: seeing if some value falls within the interval represented by the range. This is done using ===, the case equality operator.

```
(1..10)     === 5        →    true
(1..10)     === 15       →    false
(1..10)     === 3.14159  →    true
('a'..'j') === 'c'       →    true
('a'..'j') === 'z'       →    false
```

The example of a case expression on page 83 shows this test in action, determining a jazz style given a year.

Regular Expressions

Back on page 53 when we were creating a song list from a file, we used a regular expression to match the field delimiter in the input file. We claimed that the expression line.split(/\s*\|\s*/) matched a vertical bar surrounded by optional whitespace. Let's explore regular expressions in more detail to see why this claim is true.

Regular expressions are used to match patterns against strings. Ruby provides built-in support that makes pattern matching and substitution convenient and concise. In this section we'll work through all the main features of regular expressions. There are some details we won't cover: have a look at page 207 for more information.

Regular expressions are objects of type **Regexp**. They can be created by calling the constructor explicitly or by using the literal forms /pattern/ and %r{pattern}.

```
a = Regexp.new('^\s*[a-z]')   →    /^\s*[a-z]/
b = /^\s*[a-z]/               →    /^\s*[a-z]/
c = %r{^\s*[a-z]}             →    /^\s*[a-z]/
```

Once you have a regular expression object, you can match it against a string using **Regexp.match(aString)** or the match operators =~ (positive match) and !~ (negative match). The match operators are defined for both **String** and **Regexp** objects. If both operands of the match operator are **Strings**, the one on the right will be converted to a regular expression.

```
a = "Fats Waller"
a =~ /a/    →    1
a =~ /z/    →    nil
a =~ "ll"   →    7
```

The match operators return the character position at which the match occurred. They also have the side effect of setting a whole load of Ruby variables. $& receives the part of the string that was matched by the pattern, $' receives the part of the string that preceded the match, and **$'** receives the string after the match. We can use this to write a method, showRE, which illustrates where a particular pattern matches.

```
def showRE(a,re)
  if a =~ re
    "#{$`}<<#{$&}>>#{$'}"
  else
    "no match"
  end
end

showRE('very interesting', /t/)  →  very in<<t>>eresting
showRE('Fats Waller', /ll/)      →  Fats Wa<<ll>>er
```

The match also sets the thread-global variables **$~** and **$1** through **$9**. The variable **$~** is a MatchData object (described beginning on page 340) that holds everything you might want to know about the match. **$1** and so on hold the values of parts of the match. We'll talk about these later. And for people who cringe when they see these Perl-like variable names, stay tuned. There's good news at the end of the chapter.

Patterns

Every regular expression contains a pattern, which is used to match the regular expression against a string.

Within a pattern, all characters except ., |, (,), [, {, +, \, ^, $, *, and ? match themselves.

```
showRE('kangaroo', /angar/)    →  k<<angar>>oo
showRE('!@%&-_=+', /%&/)        →  !@<<%&>>-_=+
```

If you want to match one of these special characters literally, precede it with a backslash. This explains part of the pattern we used to split the song line, /\s*\|\s*/. The \| means "match a vertical bar." Without the backslash, the "|" would have meant *alternation* (which we'll describe later).

```
showRE('yes | no', /\|/)       →  yes <<|>> no
showRE('yes (no)', /\(no\)/)   →  yes <<(no)>>
showRE('are you sure?', /e\?/)  →  are you sur<<e?>>
```

A backslash followed by an alphanumeric character is used to introduce a special match construct, which we'll cover later. In addition, a regular expression may contain #{...} expression substitutions.

Anchors

By default, a regular expression will try to find the first match for the pattern in a string. Match /iss/ against the string "Mississippi," and it will find the substring "iss" starting at position one. But what if you want to force a pattern to match only at the start or end of a string?

The patterns ^ and $ match the beginning and end of a line, respectively. These are often used to *anchor* a pattern match: for example, /^option/ matches the word "option" only if it appears at the start of a line. The sequence \A matches the beginning of a string, and \z and \Z match the end of a string. (Actually, \Z matches the end of a string *unless* the string ends with a "\n", it which case it matches just before the "\n".)

```
showRE("this is\nthe time", /^the/)     →   this is\n<<the>> time
showRE("this is\nthe time", /is$/)      →   this <<is>>\nthe time
showRE("this is\nthe time", /\Athis/)   →   <<this>> is\nthe time
showRE("this is\nthe time", /\Athe/)    →   no match
```

Similarly, the patterns \b and \B match word boundaries and nonword boundaries, respectively. Word characters are letters, numbers, and underscore.

```
showRE("this is\nthe time", /\bis/)     →   this <<is>>\nthe time
showRE("this is\nthe time", /\Bis/)     →   th<<is>> is\nthe time
```

Character Classes

A character class is a set of characters between brackets: [*characters*] matches any single character between the brackets. [aeiou] will match a vowel, [,.:;!?] matches punctuation, and so on. The significance of the special regular expression characters— . | () [{+^$*?—is turned off inside the brackets. However, normal string substitution still occurs, so (for example) \b represents a backspace character and \n a newline (see Table 18.2 on page 205). In addition, you can use the abbreviations shown in Table 5.1 on page 62, so that (for example) \s matches any whitespace character, not just a literal space.

```
showRE('It costs $12.', /[aeiou]/)   →   It c<<o>>sts $12.
showRE('It costs $12.', /[\s]/)      →   It<< >>costs $12.
```

Within the brackets, the sequence c_1-c_2 represents all the characters between c_1 and c_2, inclusive.

If you want to include the literal characters] and - within a character class, they must appear at the start.

```
a = 'Gamma [Design Patterns-page 123]'
showRE(a, /[]]/)    →   Gamma [Design Patterns-page 123<<]>>
showRE(a, /[B-F]/)  →   Gamma [<<D>>esign Patterns-page 123]
showRE(a, /[-]/)    →   Gamma [Design Patterns<<->>page 123]
showRE(a, /[0-9]/)  →   Gamma [Design Patterns-page <<1>>23]
```

Put a ^ immediately after the opening bracket to negate a character class: [^a-z] matches any character that isn't a lowercase alphabetic.

Some character classes are used so frequently that Ruby provides abbreviations for them. These abbreviations are listed in Table 5.1 on page 62—they may be used both within brackets and in the body of a pattern.

```
showRE('It costs $12.', /\s/)   →   It<< >>costs $12.
showRE('It costs $12.', /\d/)   →   It costs $<<1>>2.
```

Finally, a period (".") appearing outside brackets represents any character except a new-line (and in multiline mode it matches a newline, too).

```
a = 'It costs $12.'
showRE(a, /c.s/)   →   It <<cos>>ts $12.
showRE(a, /./)     →   <<I>>t costs $12.
showRE(a, /\./)    →   It costs $12<<.>>
```

Repetition

When we specified the pattern that split the song list line, /\s*\|\s*/, we said we wanted to match a vertical bar surrounded by an arbitrary amount of whitespace. We now know that the \s sequences match a single whitespace character, so it seems likely that the asterisks somehow mean "an arbitrary amount." In fact, the asterisk is one of a number of modifiers that allow you to match multiple occurrences of a pattern.

If *r* stands for the immediately preceding regular expression within a pattern, then:

*r**   matches zero or more occurrences of *r*.
r+   matches one or more occurrences of *r*.
r?   matches zero or one occurrence of *r*.
r{m,n}   matches at least "m" and at most "n" occurrences of *r*.
r{m,}   matches at least "m" occurrences of *r*.

These repetition constructs have a high precedence—they bind only to the immediately preceding regular expression in the pattern. /ab+/ matches an "a" followed by one or more "b"s, not a sequence of "ab"s. You have to be careful with the * construct too—the pattern /a*/ will match any string; every string has zero or more "a"s.

These patterns are called *greedy*, because by default they will match as much of the string as they can. You can alter this behavior, and have them match the minimum, by adding a question mark suffix.

```
a = "The moon is made of cheese"
showRE(a, /\w+/)             →   <<The>> moon is made of cheese
showRE(a, /\s.*\s/)          →   The<< moon is made of >>cheese
showRE(a, /\s.*?\s/)         →   The<< moon >>is made of cheese
showRE(a, /[aeiou]{2,99}/)   →   The m<<oo>>n is made of cheese
showRE(a, /mo?o/)            →   The <<moo>>n is made of cheese
```

Alternation

We know that the vertical bar is special, because our line splitting pattern had to escape it with a backslash. That's because an unescaped vertical bar "|" matches either the regular expression that precedes it or the regular expression that follows it.

Table 5.1. Character class abbreviations

Sequence	As [...]	Meaning
\d	[0-9]	Digit character
\D	[^0-9]	Nondigit
\s	[\s\t\r\n\f]	Whitespace character
\S	[^\s\t\r\n\f]	Nonwhitespace character
\w	[A-Za-z0-9_]	Word character
\W	[^A-Za-z0-9_]	Nonword character

```
a = "red ball blue sky"
showRE(a, /d|e/)                    →   r<<e>>d ball blue sky
showRE(a, /al|lu/)                  →   red b<<al>>l blue sky
showRE(a, /red ball|angry sky/)   →   <<red ball>> blue sky
```

There's a trap for the unwary here, as "|" has a very low precedence. The last example above matches "red ball" or "angry sky", not "red ball sky" or "red angry sky". To match "red ball sky" or "red angry sky", you'd need to override the default precedence using grouping.

Grouping

You can use parentheses to group terms within a regular expression. Everything within the group is treated as a single regular expression.

```
showRE('banana', /an*/)     →   b<<an>>ana
showRE('banana', /(an)*/)   →   <<>>banana
showRE('banana', /(an)+/)   →   b<<anan>>a

a = 'red ball blue sky'
showRE(a, /blue|red/)          →   <<red>> ball blue sky
showRE(a, /(blue|red) \w+/)    →   <<red ball>> blue sky
showRE(a, /(red|blue) \w+/)    →   <<red ball>> blue sky
showRE(a, /red|blue \w+/)      →   <<red>> ball blue sky

showRE(a, /red (ball|angry) sky/)   →   no match
a = 'the red angry sky'
showRE(a, /red (ball|angry) sky/)   →   the <<red angry sky>>
```

Parentheses are also used to collect the results of pattern matching. Ruby counts opening parentheses, and for each stores the result of the partial match between it and the corresponding closing parenthesis. You can use this partial match both within the remainder of the pattern and in your Ruby program. Within the pattern, the sequence \1 refers to the match of the first group, \2 the second group, and so on. Outside the pattern, the special variables $1, $2, and so on, serve the same purpose.

```
"12:50am" =~ /(\d\d):(\d\d)(..)/     →    0
"Hour is #$1, minute #$2"            →    "Hour is 12, minute 50"
"12:50am" =~ /((\d\d):(\d\d))(..)/   →    0
"Time is #$1"                        →    "Time is 12:50"
"Hour is #$2, minute #$3"            →    "Hour is 12, minute 50"
"AM/PM is #$4"                       →    "AM/PM is am"
```

The ability to use part of the current match later in that match allows you to look for various forms of repetition.

```
# match duplicated letter
showRE('He said "Hello"', /(\w)\1/)    →    He said "He<<ll>>o"
# match duplicated substrings
showRE('Mississippi', /(\w+)\1/)       →    M<<ississ>>ippi
```

You can also use back references to match delimiters.

```
showRE('He said "Hello"', /(["']).*?\1/)    →    He said <<"Hello">>
showRE("He said 'Hello'", /(["']).*?\1/)    →    He said <<'Hello'>>
```

Pattern-Based Substitution

Sometimes finding a pattern in a string is good enough. If a friend challenges you to find a word that contains the letters a, b, c, d, and e in order, you could search a word list with the pattern /a.*b.*c.*d.*e/ and find "absconded" and "ambuscade." That has to be worth something.

However, there are times when you need to change things based on a pattern match. Let's go back to our song list file. Whoever created it entered all the artists' names in lowercase. When we display them on our jukebox's screen, they'd look better in mixed case. How can we change the first character of each word to uppercase?

The methods String#sub and String#gsub look for a portion of a string matching their first argument and replace it with their second argument. String#sub performs one replacement, while String#gsub replaces every occurrence of the match. Both routines return a new copy of the String containing the substitutions. Mutator versions String#sub! and String#gsub! modify the original string.

```
a = "the quick brown fox"
a.sub(/[aeiou]/, '*')    →    "th* quick brown fox"
a.gsub(/[aeiou]/, '*')   →    "th* q**ck br*wn f*x"
a.sub(/\s\S+/, '')       →    "the brown fox"
a.gsub(/\s\S+/, '')      →    "the"
```

The second argument to both functions can be either a String or a block. If a block is used, the block's value is substituted into the String.

```
a = "the quick brown fox"
a.sub(/^./) { $&.upcase }        →    "The quick brown fox"
a.gsub(/[aeiou]/) { $&.upcase }  →    "thE qUIck brOwn fOx"
```

So, this looks like the answer to converting our artists' names. The pattern that matches the first character of a word is \b\w—look for a word boundary followed by a word character. Combine this with **gsub** and we can hack the artists' names.

```
def mixedCase(aName)
  aName.gsub(/\b\w/) { $&.upcase }
end
```

```
mixedCase("fats waller")          →   "Fats Waller"
mixedCase("louis armstrong")      →   "Louis Armstrong"
mixedCase("strength in numbers")  →   "Strength In Numbers"
```

Backslash Sequences in the Substitution

Earlier we noted that the sequences \1, \2, and so on are available in the pattern, standing for the *n*th group matched so far. The same sequences are available in the second argument of **sub** and **gsub**.

```
"fred:smith".sub(/(\w+):(\w+)/, '\2, \1')   →   "smith, fred"
"nercpyitno".gsub(/(.)(.)/, '\2\1')         →   "encryption"
```

There are additional backslash sequences that work in substitution strings: \& (last match), \+ (last matched group), \' (string prior to match), \' (string after match), and \\ (a literal backslash).

It gets confusing if you want to include a literal backslash in a substitution. The obvious thing is to write

```
str.gsub(/\\/, '\\\\')
```

Clearly, this code is trying to replace each backslash in **str** with two. The programmer doubled up the backslashes in the replacement text, knowing that they'd be converted to "\\" in syntax analysis. However, when the substitution occurs, the regular expression engine performs another pass through the string, converting "\\" to "\", so the net effect is to replace each single backslash with another single backslash. You need to write gsub(/\\/, '\\\\\\\\')!

```
str = 'a\b\c'                       →   "a\b\c"
str.gsub(/\\/, '\\\\\\\\')          →   "a\\b\\c"
```

However, using the fact that \& is replaced by the matched string, you could also write

```
str = 'a\b\c'                       →   "a\b\c"
str.gsub(/\\/, '\&\&')              →   "a\\b\\c"
```

If you use the block form of **gsub**, the string for substitution is analyzed only once (during the syntax pass) and the result is what you intended.

```
str = 'a\b\c'                       →   "a\b\c"
str.gsub(/\\/) { '\\\\' }           →   "a\\b\\c"
```

Finally, as an example of the wonderful expressiveness of combining regular expressions with code blocks, consider the following code fragment from the CGI library module, written by Wakou Aoyama. The code takes a string containing HTML escape sequences and converts it into normal ASCII. Because it was written for a Japanese audience, it uses the "n" modifier on the regular expressions, which turns off wide-character processing. It also illustrates Ruby's `case` expression, which we discuss starting on page 83.

```
def unescapeHTML(string)
  str = string.dup
  str.gsub!(/&(.*?);/n) {
    match = $1.dup
    case match
    when /\Aamp\z/ni         then '&'
    when /\Aquot\z/ni        then '"'
    when /\Agt\z/ni          then '>'
    when /\Alt\z/ni          then '<'
    when /\A#(\d+)\z/n       then Integer($1).chr
    when /\A#x([0-9a-f]+)\z/ni then $1.hex.chr
    end
  }
  str
end
puts unescapeHTML("1&lt;2 &amp;&amp; 4&gt;3")
puts unescapeHTML("&quot;A&quot; = &#65; = &#x41;")
```

produces:

```
1<2 && 4>3
"A" = A = A
```

Object-Oriented Regular Expressions

We have to admit that while all these weird variables are very convenient to use, they aren't very object oriented, and they're certainly cryptic. And didn't we say that everything in Ruby was an object? What's gone wrong here?

Nothing, really. It's just that when Matz designed Ruby, he produced a fully object-oriented regular expression handling system. He then made it look familiar to Perl programmers by wrapping all these $-variables on top of it all. The objects and classes are still there, underneath the surface. So let's spend a while digging them out.

We've already come across one class: regular expression literals create instances of class `Regexp` (documented beginning on page 366).

```
re = /cat/
re.type   →   Regexp
```

The method `Regexp#match` matches a regular expression against a string. If unsuccessful, the method returns `nil`. On success, it returns an instance of class `MatchData`, documented beginning on page 340. And that `MatchData` object gives you access to all available information about the match. All that good stuff that you can get from the $-variables is bundled in a handy little object.

```
re = /(\d+):(\d+)/      # match a time hh:mm
md = re.match("Time: 12:34am")
md.type                      →   MatchData
md[0]          # == $&     →   "12:34"
md[1]          # == $1     →   "12"
md[2]          # == $2     →   "34"
md.pre_match   # == $`     →   "Time: "
md.post_match  # == $'     →   "am"
```

Because the match data is stored in its own object, you can keep the results of two or more pattern matches available at the same time, something you can't do using the $-variables. In the next example, we're matching the same `Regexp` object against two strings. Each match returns a unique `MatchData` object, which we verify by examining the two subpattern fields.

```
re = /(\d+):(\d+)/      # match a time hh:mm
md1 = re.match("Time: 12:34am")
md2 = re.match("Time: 10:30pm")
md1[1, 2]   →   ["12", "34"]
md2[1, 2]   →   ["10", "30"]
```

So how do the $-variables fit in? Well, after every pattern match, Ruby stores a reference to the result (`nil` or a `MatchData` object) in a thread-local variable (accessible using $~). All the other regular expression variables are then derived from this object. Although we can't really think of a use for the following code, it demonstrates that all the other `MatchData`-related $-variables are indeed slaved off the value in $~.

```
re = /(\d+):(\d+)/
md1 = re.match("Time: 12:34am")
md2 = re.match("Time: 10:30pm")
[ $1, $2 ]   # last successful match       →   ["10", "30"]
$~ = md1
[ $1, $2 ]   # previous successful match   →   ["12", "34"]
```

Having said all this, we have to 'fess up. Andy and Dave normally use the $-variables rather than worrying about `MatchData` objects. For everyday use, they just end up being more convenient. Sometimes we just can't help being pragmatic.

## Chapter 6

More About Methods

Other languages have functions, procedures, methods, or routines, but in Ruby there is only the *method*—a chunk of expressions that return a value.

So far in this book, we've been defining and using methods without much thought. Now it's time to get into the details.

Defining a Method

As we've seen throughout this book, a method is defined using the keyword `def`. Method names should begin with a lowercase letter.[1] Methods that act as queries are often named with a trailing "?", such as `instance_of?`. Methods that are "dangerous," or modify the receiver, might be named with a trailing "!". For instance, `String` provides both a `chop` and a `chop!`. The first one returns a modified string; the second modifies the receiver in place. "?" and "!" are the only weird characters allowed as method name suffixes.

Now that we've specified a name for our new method, we may need to declare some parameters. These are simply a list of local variable names in parentheses. Some sample method declarations are

```
def myNewMethod(arg1, arg2, arg3)      # 3 arguments
  # Code for the method would go here
end

def myOtherNewMethod                   # No arguments
  # Code for the method would go here
end
```

---

1.   You won't get an immediate error if you use an uppercase letter, but when Ruby sees you calling the method, it will first guess that it is a constant, not a method invocation, and as a result it may parse the call incorrectly.

Ruby lets you specify default values for a method's arguments—values that will be used if the caller doesn't pass them explicitly. This is done using the assignment operator.

```
def coolDude(arg1="Miles", arg2="Coltrane", arg3="Roach")
  "#{arg1}, #{arg2}, #{arg3}."
end
```

```
coolDude                             →    "Miles, Coltrane, Roach."
coolDude("Bart")                     →    "Bart, Coltrane, Roach."
coolDude("Bart", "Elwood")           →    "Bart, Elwood, Roach."
coolDude("Bart", "Elwood", "Linus")  →    "Bart, Elwood, Linus."
```

The body of a method contains normal Ruby expressions, except that you may not define an instance method, class, or module within a method. The return value of a method is the value of the last expression executed, or the result of an explicit `return` expression.

Variable-Length Argument Lists

But what if you want to pass in a variable number of arguments, or want to capture multiple arguments into a single parameter? Placing an asterisk before the name of the parameter after the "normal" parameters does just that.

```
def varargs(arg1, *rest)
  "Got #{arg1} and #{rest.join(', ')}"
end
```

```
varargs("one")                  →    "Got one and "
varargs("one", "two")           →    "Got one and two"
varargs "one", "two", "three"   →    "Got one and two, three"
```

In this example, the first argument is assigned to the first method parameter as usual. However, the next parameter is prefixed with an asterisk, so all the remaining arguments are bundled into a new `Array`, which is then assigned to that parameter.

Methods and Blocks

As we discussed in the section on blocks and iterators beginning on page 40, when a method is called, it may be associated with a block. Normally, you simply call the block from within the method using `yield`.

```
def takeBlock(p1)
  if block_given?
    yield(p1)
  else
    p1
  end
end
```

```
takeBlock("no block")                              →    "no block"
takeBlock("no block") { |s| s.sub(/no /, '') }    →    "block"
```

However, if the last parameter in a method definition is prefixed with an ampersand, any associated block is converted to a **Proc** object, and that object is assigned to the parameter.

```
class TaxCalculator
  def initialize(name, &block)
    @name, @block = name, block
  end
  def getTax(amount)
    "#@name on #{amount} = #{ @block.call(amount) }"
  end
end

tc = TaxCalculator.new("Sales tax") { |amt| amt * 0.075 }

tc.getTax(100)    →    "Sales tax on 100 = 7.5"
tc.getTax(250)    →    "Sales tax on 250 = 18.75"
```

Calling a Method

You call a method by specifying a receiver, the name of the method, and optionally some parameters and an associated block.

```
connection.downloadMP3("jitterbug") { |p| showProgress(p) }
```

In this example, the object **connection** is the receiver, **downloadMP3** is the name of the method, **"jitterbug"** is the parameter, and the stuff between the braces is the associated block.

For class and module methods, the receiver will be the class or module name.

```
File.size("testfile")
Math.sin(Math::PI/4)
```

If you omit the receiver, it defaults to **self**, the current object.

```
self.id      →    537706116
id           →    537706116
self.type    →    Object
type         →    Object
```

This defaulting mechanism is how Ruby implements private methods. Private methods may *not* be called with a receiver, so they must be methods available in the current object.

The optional parameters follow the method name. If there is no ambiguity you can omit the parentheses around the argument list when calling a method.[2] However, except in the simplest cases we don't recommend this—there are some subtle problems that can trip you up.[3] Our rule is simple: if there's any doubt, use parentheses.

```
a = obj.hash    # Same as
a = obj.hash()  # this.

obj.someMethod "Arg1", arg2, arg3   # Same thing as
obj.someMethod("Arg1", arg2, arg3)  # with parentheses.
```

Expanding Arrays in Method Calls

Earlier we saw that if you put an asterisk in front of a formal parameter in a method definition, multiple arguments in the call to the method will be bundled up into an array. Well, the same thing works in reverse.

When you call a method, you can explode an array, so that each of its members is taken as a separate parameter. Do this by prefixing the array argument (which must follow all the regular arguments) with an asterisk.

```
def five(a, b, c, d, e)
  "I was passed #{a} #{b} #{c} #{d} #{e}"
end

five(1, 2, 3, 4, 5 )       →   "I was passed 1 2 3 4 5"
five(1, 2, 3, *['a', 'b'])  →   "I was passed 1 2 3 a b"
five(*(10..14).to_a)       →   "I was passed 10 11 12 13 14"
```

Making Blocks More Dynamic

We've already seen how you can associate a block with a method call.

```
listBones("aardvark") do |aBone|
  # ...
end
```

Normally, this is perfectly good enough—you associate a fixed block of code with a method, in the same way you'd have a chunk of code after an `if` or `while` statement.

Sometimes, however, you'd like to be more flexible. For example, we may be teaching math skills.[4] The student could ask for an *n*-plus table or an *n*-times table. If the student

---

2.   Other Ruby documentation sometimes calls these method calls without parentheses "commands."

3.   In particular, you *must* use parentheses on a method call that is itself a parameter to another method call (unless it is the last parameter).

4.   Of course, Andy and Dave would have to *learn* math skills first. Conrad Schneiker reminded us that there are three kinds of people: those who can count and those who can't.

asked for a 2-times table, we'd output 2, 4, 6, 8, and so on. (This code does not check its inputs for errors.)

```ruby
print "(t)imes or (p)lus: "
times = gets
print "number: "
number = gets.to_i

if times =~ /^t/
  puts((1..10).collect { |n| n*number }.join(", "))
else
  puts((1..10).collect { |n| n+number }.join(", "))
end
```

produces:

```
(t)imes or (p)lus: t
number: 2
2, 4, 6, 8, 10, 12, 14, 16, 18, 20
```

This works, but it's ugly, with virtually identical code on each branch of the `if` statement. If would be nice if we could factor out the block that does the calculation.

```ruby
print "(t)imes or (p)lus: "
times = gets
print "number: "
number = gets.to_i

if times =~ /^t/
  calc = proc { |n| n*number }
else
  calc = proc { |n| n+number }
end
puts((1..10).collect(&calc).join(", "))
```

produces:

```
(t)imes or (p)lus: t
number: 2
2, 4, 6, 8, 10, 12, 14, 16, 18, 20
```

If the last argument to a method is preceded by an ampersand, Ruby assumes that it is a `Proc` object. It removes it from the parameter list, converts the `Proc` object into a block, and associates it with the method.

This technique can also be used to add some syntactic sugar to block usage. For example, you sometimes want to take an iterator and store each value it yields into an array. We'll reuse our Fibonacci number generator from page 42.

```ruby
a = []
fibUpTo(20) { |val| a << val }   →   nil
a.inspect                        →   "[1, 1, 2, 3, 5, 8, 13]"
```

This works, but our intention isn't quite as transparent as we may like. Instead, we'll define a method called `into`, which returns the block that fills the array. (Notice at the same time that the block returned really is a closure—it references the parameter *anArray* even after method `into` has returned.)

```ruby
def into(anArray)
  return proc { |val| anArray << val }
end

fibUpTo 20, &into(a = [])
a.inspect    →    "[1, 1, 2, 3, 5, 8, 13]"
```

Collecting Hash Arguments

Some languages feature "keyword arguments"—that is, instead of passing arguments in a given order and quantity, you pass the name of the argument with its value, in any order. Ruby 1.6 does not have keyword arguments (although they are scheduled to be implemented in Ruby 1.8).

In the meantime, people are using hashes as a way of achieving the same effect. For example, we might consider adding a more powerful named-search facility to our `SongList`.

```ruby
class SongList
  def createSearch(name, params)
    # ...
  end
end
aList.createSearch("short jazz songs", {
                    'genre'             => "jazz",
                    'durationLessThan' => 270
                    } )
```

The first parameter is the search name, and the second is a hash literal containing search parameters. The use of a hash means that we can simulate keywords: look for songs with a genre of "jazz" and a duration less than $4\frac{1}{2}$ minutes. However, this approach is slightly clunky, and that set of braces could easily be mistaken for a block associated with the method. So, Ruby has a short cut. You can place *key => value* pairs in an argument list, as long as they follow any normal arguments and precede any array and block arguments. All these pairs will be collected into a single hash and passed as one argument to the method. No braces are needed.

```ruby
aList.createSearch("short jazz songs",
                    'genre'             => "jazz",
                    'durationLessThan' => 270
                    )
```

Chapter 7

Expressions

So far we've been fairly cavalier in our use of expressions in Ruby. After all, a = b + c is pretty standard stuff. You could write a whole heap of Ruby code without reading any of this chapter.

But it wouldn't be as much fun ;-).

One of the first differences with Ruby is that anything that can reasonably return a value does: just about everything is an expression. What does this mean in practice?

Some obvious things include the ability to chain statements together.

```
a = b = c = 0                      →    0
[ 3, 1, 7, 0 ].sort.reverse   →    [7, 3, 1, 0]
```

Perhaps less obvious, things that are normally statements in C or Java are expressions in Ruby. For example, the `if` and `case` statements both return the value of the last expression executed.

```
songType = if song.mp3Type == MP3::Jazz
             if song.written < Date.new(1935, 1, 1)
               Song::TradJazz
             else
               Song::Jazz
             end
           else
             Song::Other
           end

rating = case votesCast
         when 0...10      then Rating::SkipThisOne
         when 10...50     then Rating::CouldDoBetter
         else                  Rating::Rave
         end
```

We'll talk more about `if` and `case` starting on page 81.

Operator Expressions

Ruby has the basic set of operators (+, -, *, /, and so one) as well as a few surprises. A complete list of the operators, and their precedences, is given in Table 18.4 on page 221.

In Ruby, many operators are actually method calls. When you write a*b + c you're actually asking the object referenced by a to execute the method "*", passing in the parameter b. You then ask the object that results from that calculation to execute "+", passing c as a parameter. This is exactly equivalent to writing

```
(a.*(b)).+(c)
```

Because everything is an object, and because you can redefine instance methods, you can always redefine basic arithmetic if you don't like the answers you're getting.

```
class Fixnum
  alias oldPlus +
  def +(other)
    oldPlus(other).succ
  end
end

1 + 2    →    4
a = 3
a += 4   →    8
```

More useful is the fact that classes that you write can participate in operator expressions just as if they were built-in objects. For example, we might want to be able to extract a number of seconds of music from the middle of a song. We could using the indexing operator "[]" to specify the music to be extracted.

```
class Song
  def [](fromTime, toTime)
    result = Song.new(self.title + " [extract]",
                      self.artist,
                      toTime - fromTime)
    result.setStartTime(fromTime)
    result
  end
end
```

This code fragment extends class Song with the method "[]", which takes two parameters (a start time and an end time). It returns a new song, with the music clipped to the given interval. We could then play the introduction to a song with code such as:

```
aSong[0, 0.15].play
```

Miscellaneous Expressions

As well as the obvious operator expressions and method calls, and the (perhaps) less obvious statement expressions (such as `if` and `case`), Ruby has a few more things that you can use in expressions.

Command Expansion

If you enclose a string in backquotes, or use the delimited form prefixed by `%x`, it will (by default) be executed as a command by your underlying operating system. The value of the expression is the standard output of that command. Newlines will not be stripped, so it is likely that the value you get back will have a trailing return or linefeed character.

```
`date`                  →    "Wed Sep 20 10:32:12 CDT 2000\n"
`dir`.split[34]         →    "bad.tgz"
%x{echo "Hello there"}  →    "Hello there\n"
```

You can use expression expansion and all the usual escape sequences in the command string.

```
for i in 0..3
  status = `dbmanager status id=#{i}`
  # ...
end
```

The exit status of the command is available in the global variable `$?`.

Backquotes Are Soft

In the description of the command output expression, we said that the string in backquotes would "by default" be executed as a command. In fact, the string is passed to the method called `Kernel.`` ` (a single backquote). If you want, you can override this.

```
alias oldBackquote `
def `(cmd)
  result = oldBackquote(cmd)
  if $? != 0
    raise "Command #{cmd} failed"
  end
  result
end
print `date`
print `data`
```

produces:

```
Wed Sep 20 10:32:12 CDT 2000
prog.rb:3: command not found: data
prog.rb:5:in ``': Command data failed (RuntimeError)
        from prog.rb:10
```

Assignment

Just about every example we've given so far in this book has featured assignment. Perhaps it's about time we said something about it.

An assignment statement sets the variable or attribute on its left side (the *lvalue*) to refer to the value on the right (the *rvalue*). It then returns that value as the result of the assignment expression. This means that you can chain assignments and that you can perform assignments in some unexpected places.

```
a = b = 1 + 2 + 3
a  →  6
b  →  6
a = (b = 1 + 2) + 3
a  →  6
b  →  3
File.open(name = gets.chomp)
```

There are two basic forms of assignment in Ruby. The first assigns an object reference to a variable or constant. This form of assignment is hard-wired into the language.

```
instrument = "piano"
MIDDLE_A   = 440
```

The second form of assignment involves having an object attribute or element reference on the left-hand side.

```
aSong.duration    = 234
instrument["ano"] = "ccolo"
```

These forms are special, because they are implemented by calling methods in the lvalues, which means you can override them.

We've already seen how to define a writable object attribute. Simply define a method name ending in an equals sign. This method receives as its parameter the assignment's rvalue.

```
class Song
  def duration=(newDuration)
    @duration = newDuration
  end
end
```

There is no reason that these attribute setting methods must correspond with internal instance variables, or that there has to be an attribute reader for every attribute writer (or vice versa).

```
class Amplifier
  def volume=(newVolume)
    self.leftChannel = self.rightChannel = newVolume
```

```
    end
    # ...
end
```

Parallel Assignment

During your first week in a programming course (or the second semester if it was a party school), you may have had to write code to swap the values in two variables:

```
int a = 1;
int b = 2;
int temp;

temp = a;
a = b;
b = temp;
```

You can do this much more cleanly in Ruby:

```
a, b = b, a
```

Ruby assignments are effectively performed in parallel, so the values assigned are not affected by the assignment itself. The values on the right-hand side are evaluated in the order in which they appear before any assignment is made to variables or attributes on the left. A somewhat contrived example illustrates this. The second line assigns to the variables a, b, and c the values of the expressions x, x += 1, and x += 1, respectively.

```
x = 0                                    →   0
a, b, c  =  x, (x += 1), (x += 1)   →   [0, 1, 2]
```

When an assignment has more than one lvalue, the assignment expression returns an array of the rvalues.

If an assignment contains more lvalues than rvalues, the excess lvalues are set to nil. If a multiple assignment contains more rvalues than lvalues, the extra rvalues are ignored.

You can collapse and expand arrays using Ruby's parallel assignment operator. If the last lvalue is preceded by an asterisk, all the remaining rvalues will be collected and assigned to that lvalue as an array. Similarly, if the last rvalue is an array, you can prefix it with an asterisk, which effectively expands it into its constituent values in place. (This is not necessary if the rvalue is the only thing on the right-hand side—the array will be expanded automatically.)

```
a = [1, 2, 3, 4 ]
b,  c = a          →   b == 1,    c == 2
b, *c = a          →   b == 1,    c == [2, 3, 4]
b,  c = 99, a      →   b == 99,   c == [1, 2, 3, 4]
b, *c = 99, a      →   b == 99,   c == [[1, 2, 3, 4]]
b,  c = 99, *a     →   b == 99,   c == 1
b, *c = 99, *a     →   b == 99,   c == [1, 2, 3, 4]
```

Using Accessors Within a Class

Why did we write `self.leftChannel` in the example on page 76? Well, there's a hidden gotcha with writable attributes. Normally, methods within a class can invoke other methods in the same class and its superclasses in functional form (that is, with an implicit receiver of `self`). However, this doesn't work with attribute writers. Ruby sees the assignment and decides that the name on the left must be a local variable, not a method call to an attribute writer.

```ruby
class BrokenAmplifier
  attr_accessor :leftChannel, :rightChannel
  def volume=(vol)
    leftChannel = self.rightChannel = vol
  end
end

ba = BrokenAmplifier.new
ba.leftChannel = ba.rightChannel = 99
ba.volume = 5
ba.leftChannel    →    99
ba.rightChannel   →    5
```

We forgot to put "self." in front of the assignment to `leftChannel`, so Ruby stored the new value in a local variable of method `volume`; the object's attribute never got updated. This can be a tricky bug to track down.

Nested Assignments

Parallel assignments have one more feature worth mentioning. The left-hand side of an assignment may contain a parenthesized list of terms. Ruby treats these terms as if they were a nested assignment statement. It extracts out the corresponding rvalue, assigning it to the parenthesized terms, before continuing with the higher-level assignment.

```
b, (c, d), e = 1,2,3,4      →   b == 1, c == 2, d == nil,    e == 3
b, (c, d), e = [1,2,3,4]    →   b == 1, c == 2, d == nil,    e == 3
b, (c, d), e = 1,[2,3],4    →   b == 1, c == 2, d == 3,      e == 4
b, (c, d), e = 1,[2,3,4],5  →   b == 1, c == 2, d == 3,      e == 5
b, (c,*d), e = 1,[2,3,4],5  →   b == 1, c == 2, d == [3, 4], e == 5
```

Other Forms of Assignment

In common with many other languages, Ruby has a syntactic shortcut: a = a + 2 may be written as a += 2.

The second form is converted internally to the first. This means that operators that you have defined as methods in your own classes work as you'd expect.

```
class Bowdlerize
  def initialize(aString)
    @value = aString.gsub(/[aeiou]/, '*')
  end
  def +(other)
    Bowdlerize.new(self.to_s + other.to_s)
  end
  def to_s
    @value
  end
end

a = Bowdlerize.new("damn ")    →    d*mn
a += "shame"                   →    d*mn sh*m*
```

Conditional Execution

Ruby has several different mechanisms for conditional execution of code; most of them should feel familiar, and many have some neat twists. Before we get into them, though, we need to spend a short time looking at boolean expressions.

Boolean Expressions

Ruby has a simple definition of truth. Any value that is not `nil` or the constant `false` is true. You'll find that the library routines use this fact consistently. For example, `IO#gets`, which returns the next line from a file, returns `nil` at end of file, enabling you to write loops such as:

```
while line = gets
  # process line
end
```

However, there's a trap here for C, C++, and Perl programmers. The number zero is *not* interpreted as a false value. Neither is a zero-length string. This can be a tough habit to break.

Defined?, And, Or, and Not

Ruby supports all the standard boolean operators and introduces the new predicate method `defined?`.

Both "`and`" and "`&&`" evaluate to true only if both operands are true. They evaluate the second operand only if the first is true (this is sometimes known as "short-circuit evaluation"). The only difference in the two forms is precedence ("**and**" binds lower than "**&&**").

Similarly, both "**or**" and "**||**" evaluate to true if either operand is true. They evaluate their second operand only if the first is false. As with "**and**", the only difference between "**or**" and "**||**" is their precedence.

Just to make life interesting, "**and**" and "**or**" have the same precedence, while "**&&**" has a higher precedence than "**||**".

"**not**" and "**!**" return the opposite of their operand (false if the operand is true, and true if the operand is false). And, yes, "**not**" and "**!**" differ only in precedence.

All these precedence rules are summarized in Table 18.4 on page 221.

The **defined?** method returns **nil** if its argument (which can be an arbitrary expression) is not defined, otherwise it returns a description of that argument. If the argument is **yield**, **defined?** returns the string "yield" if a code block is associated with the current context.

```
defined? 1              →    "expression"
defined? dummy          →    nil
defined? printf         →    "method"
defined? String         →    "constant"
defined? $&             →    "$&"
defined? $_             →    "global-variable"
defined? Math::PI       →    "constant"
defined? ( c,d = 1,2 )  →    "assignment"
defined? 42.abs         →    "method"
```

In addition to the boolean operators, Ruby objects support comparison using the methods ==, ===, <=>, =~, eql?, and **equal?** (see Table 7.1 on the next page). All but <=> are defined in class **Object** but are often overridden by descendents to provide appropriate semantics. For example, class **Array** redefines == so that two array objects are equal if they have the same number of elements and corresponding elements are equal.

Both == and =~ have negated forms, != and !~. However, these are converted by Ruby when your program is read. a != b is equivalent to !(a == b), and a !~ b is the same as !(a =~ b). This means that if you write a class that overrides == or =~ you get a working != and !~ for free. But on the flip side, this also means that you cannot define != and !~ independent of == and =~, respectively.

You can use a Ruby range as a boolean expression. A range such as **exp1..exp2** will evaluate as false until **exp1** becomes true. The range will then evaluate as true until **exp2** becomes true. Once this happens, the range resets, ready to fire again. We show some examples of this on page 84.

Finally, you can use a bare regular expression as a boolean expression. Ruby expands it to $_ =~ /re/.

Table 7.1. Common comparison operators

Operator	Meaning
==	Test for equal value.
===	Used to test equality within a **when** clause of a **case** statement.
<=>	General comparison operator. Returns −1, 0, or +1, depending on whether its receiver is less than, equal to, or greater than its argument.
<, <=, >=, >	Comparison operators for less than, less than or equal, greater than or equal, and greater than.
=~	Regular expression pattern match.
eql?	True if the receiver and argument have both the same type and equal values. 1 == 1.0 returns **true**, but 1.eql?(1.0) is **false**.
equal?	True if the receiver and argument have the same object id.

If and Unless Expressions

An `if` expression in Ruby is pretty similar to "if" statements in other languages.

```
if aSong.artist == "Gillespie" then
  handle = "Dizzy"
elsif aSong.artist == "Parker" then
  handle = "Bird"
else
  handle = "unknown"
end
```

If you lay out your `if` statements on multiple lines, you can leave off the **then** keyword.

```
if aSong.artist == "Gillespie"
  handle = "Dizzy"
elsif aSong.artist == "Parker"
  handle = "Bird"
else
  handle = "unknown"
end
```

However, if you lay your code out more tightly, the **then** keyword is necessary to separate the boolean expression from the following statements.

```
if aSong.artist == "Gillespie" then  handle = "Dizzy"
elsif aSong.artist == "Parker" then  handle = "Bird"
else  handle = "unknown"
end
```

You can have zero or more `elsif` clauses and an optional `else` clause.

As we've said before, `if` is an expression, not a statement—it returns a value. You don't have to use the value of an `if` expression, but it can come in handy.

```
handle = if aSong.artist == "Gillespie" then
           "Dizzy"
         elsif aSong.artist == "Parker" then
           "Bird"
         else
           "unknown"
         end
```

Ruby also has a negated form of the if statement:

```
unless aSong.duration > 180 then
  cost = .25
else
  cost = .35
end
```

Finally, for the C fans out there, Ruby also supports the C-style conditional expression:

```
cost = aSong.duration > 180 ? .35 : .25
```

The conditional expression returns the value of either the expression before or the expression after the colon, depending on whether the boolean expression before the question mark evaluates to **true** or **false**. In this case, if the song duration is greater than 3 minutes, the expression returns .35. For shorter songs, it returns .25. Whatever the result, it is then assigned to **cost**.

If and Unless Modifiers

Ruby shares a neat feature with Perl. Statement modifiers let you tack conditional statements onto the end of a normal statement.

```
mon, day, year = $1, $2, $3 if /(\d\d)-(\d\d)-(\d\d)/
puts "a = #{a}" if fDebug
print total unless total == 0
```

For an **if** modifier, the preceding expression will be evaluated only if the condition is true. **unless** works the other way around.

```
while gets
  next if /^#/            # Skip comments
  parseLine unless /^$/   # Don't parse empty lines
end
```

Because **if** itself is an expression, you can get really obscure with statements such as:

```
if artist == "John Coltrane"
  artist = "'Trane"
end unless nicknames == "no"
```

This path leads to the gates of madness.

Case Expressions

The Ruby `case` expression is a powerful beast: a multiway `if` on steroids.

```
case inputLine
  when "debug"
    dumpDebugInfo
    dumpSymbols

  when /p\s+(\w+)/
    dumpVariable($1)

  when "quit", "exit"
    exit

  else
    print "Illegal command: #{inputLine}"
end
```

As with `if`, `case` returns the value of the last expression executed, and you also need a `then` keyword if the expression is on the same line as the condition.

```
kind = case year
         when 1850..1889 then "Blues"
         when 1890..1909 then "Ragtime"
         when 1910..1929 then "New Orleans Jazz"
         when 1930..1939 then "Swing"
         when 1940..1950 then "Bebop"
         else                   "Jazz"
       end
```

`case` operates by comparing the target (the expression after the keyword `case`) with each of the comparison expressions after the `when` keywords. This test is done using *comparison* === *target*. As long as a class defines meaningful semantics for === (and all the built-in classes do), objects of that class can be used in case expressions.

For example, regular expressions define === as a simple pattern match.

```
case line
  when /title=(.*)/
    puts "Title is #$1"
  when /track=(.*)/
    puts "Track is #$1"
  when /artist=(.*)/
    puts "Artist is #$1"
end
```

Ruby classes are instances of class `Class`, which defines === as a test to see if the argument is an instance of the class or one of its superclasses. So (abandoning the benefits of polymorphism and bringing the gods of refactoring down around your ears), you can test the class of objects:

```
case shape
  when Square, Rectangle
    # ...
  when Circle
    # ...
  when Triangle
    # ...
  else
    # ...
end
```

Loops

Don't tell anyone, but Ruby has pretty primitive built-in looping constructs.

The `while` loop executes its body zero or more times as long as its condition is true. For example, this common idiom reads until the input is exhausted.

```
while gets
  # ...
end
```

There's also a negated form that executes the body until the condition becomes true.

```
until playList.duration > 60
  playList.add(songList.pop)
end
```

As with `if` and `unless`, both of the loops can also be used as statement modifiers.

```
a *= 2 while a < 100
a -= 10 until a < 100
```

On page 80 in the section on boolean expressions, we said that a range can be used as a kind of flip-flop, returning true when some event happens and then staying true until a second event occurs. This facility is normally used within loops. In the example that follows, we read a text file containing the first ten ordinal numbers ("first," "second," and so on) but only print the lines starting with the one that matches "third" and ending with the one that matches "fifth."

```
file = File.open("ordinal")
while file.gets
  print if /third/ .. /fifth/
end
```

produces:

```
third
fourth
fifth
```

The elements of a range used in a boolean expression can themselves be expressions. These are evaluated each time the overall boolean expression is evaluated. For example, the following code uses the fact that the variable $. contains the current input line number to display line numbers one through three and those between a match of /eig/ and /nin/.

```
file = File.open("ordinal")
while file.gets
  print if ($. == 1) || /eig/ .. ($. == 3) || /nin/
end
```

produces:

```
first
second
third
eighth
ninth
```

There's one wrinkle when **while** and **until** are used as statement modifiers. If the statement they are modifying is a **begin/end** block, the code in the block will always execute at least one time, regardless of the value of the boolean expression.

```
print "Hello\n" while false
begin
  print "Goodbye\n"
end while false
```

produces:

```
Goodbye
```

Iterators

If you read the beginning of the previous section, you might have been discouraged. "Ruby has pretty primitive built-in looping constructs," it said. Don't despair, gentle reader, for there's good news. Ruby doesn't need any sophisticated built-in loops, because all the fun stuff is implemented using Ruby iterators.

For example, Ruby doesn't have a "for" loop—at least not the kind you'd find in C, C++, and Java. Instead, Ruby uses methods defined in various built-in classes to provide equivalent, but less error-prone, functionality.

Let's look at some examples.

```
3.times do
  print "Ho! "
end
```

produces:

```
Ho! Ho! Ho!
```

It's easy to avoid fencepost and off-by-1 errors; this loop will execute three times, period. In addition to `times`, integers can loop over specific ranges by calling `downto`, `upto`, and `step`. For instance, a traditional "for" loop that runs from 0 to 9 (something like `i=0; i < 10; i++`) is written as follows.

```
0.upto(9) do |x|
  print x, " "
end
```

produces:

```
0 1 2 3 4 5 6 7 8 9
```

A loop from 0 to 12 by 3 can be written as follows.

```
0.step(12, 3) {|x| print x, " " }
```

produces:

```
0 3 6 9 12
```

Similarly, iterating over arrays and other containers is made easy using their `each` method.

```
[ 1, 1, 2, 3, 5 ].each {|val| print val, " " }
```

produces:

```
1 1 2 3 5
```

And once a class supports `each`, the additional methods in the `Enumerable` module (documented beginning on page 407 and summarized on pages 104–105) become available. For example, the `File` class provides an `each` method, which returns each line of a file in turn. Using the `grep` method in `Enumerable`, we could iterate over only those lines that meet a certain condition.

```
File.open("ordinal").grep /d$/ do |line|
  print line
end
```

produces:

```
second
third
```

Last, and probably least, is the most basic loop of all. Ruby provides a built-in iterator called `loop`.

```
loop {
  # block ...
}
```

The `loop` iterator calls the associated block forever (or at least until you break out of the loop, but you'll have to read ahead to find out how to do that).

For ... In

Earlier we said that the only built-in Ruby looping primitives were `while` and `until`. What's this "`for`" thing, then? Well, `for` is almost a lump of syntactic sugar. When you write

```
for aSong in songList
  aSong.play
end
```

Ruby translates it into something like:

```
songList.each do |aSong|
  aSong.play
end
```

The only difference between the `for` loop and the `each` form is the scope of local variables that are defined in the body. This is discussed on page 89.

You can use `for` to iterate over any object that responds to the method `each`, such as an `Array` or a `Range`.

```
for i in ['fee', 'fi', 'fo', 'fum']
  print i, " "
end
for i in 1..3
  print i, " "
end
for i in File.open("ordinal").find_all { |l| l =~ /d$/}
  print i.chomp, " "
end
```

produces:

```
fee fi fo fum 1 2 3 second third
```

As long as your class defines a sensible `each` method, you can use a `for` loop to traverse it.

```
class Periods
  def each
    yield "Classical"
    yield "Jazz"
    yield "Rock"
  end
end
periods = Periods.new
for genre in periods
  print genre, " "
end
```

produces:

```
Classical Jazz Rock
```

Break, Redo, and Next

The loop control constructs `break`, `redo`, and `next` let you alter the normal flow through a loop or iterator.

`break` terminates the immediately enclosing loop; control resumes at the statement following the block. `redo` repeats the loop from the start, but without reevaluating the condition or fetching the next element (in an iterator). `next` skips to the end of the loop, effectively starting the next iteration.

```
while gets
  next if /^\s*#/   # skip comments
  break if /^END/   # stop at end
                    # substitute stuff in backticks and try again
  redo if gsub!(/`(.*?)`/) { eval($1) }
  # process line ...
end
```

These keywords can also be used with any of the iterator-based looping mechanisms:

```
i=0
loop do
  i += 1
  next if i < 3
  print i
  break if i > 4
end
```

produces:

```
345
```

Retry

The `redo` statement causes a loop to repeat the current iteration. Sometimes, though, you need to wind the loop right back to the very beginning. The `retry` statement is just the ticket. `retry` restarts any kind of iterator loop.

```
for i in 1..100
  print "Now at #{i}. Restart? "
  retry if gets =~ /^y/i
end
```

Running this interactively, you might see

```
Now at 1. Restart? n
Now at 2. Restart? y
Now at 1. Restart? n
  . . .
```

`retry` will reevaluate any arguments to the iterator before restarting it. The online Ruby documentation has the following example of a do-it-yourself *until* loop.

```
def doUntil(cond)
  yield
  retry unless cond
end
i = 0
doUntil(i > 3) {
  print i, " "
  i += 1
}
```

produces:

```
0 1 2 3 4
```

Variable Scope and Loops

The `while`, `until`, and `for` loops are built into the language and do not introduce new scope; previously existing locals can be used in the loop, and any new locals created will be available afterward.

The blocks used by iterators (such as `loop` and `each`) are a little different. Normally, the local variables created in these blocks are not accessible outside the block.

```
[ 1, 2, 3 ].each do |x|
  y = x + 1
end
[ x, y ]
```

produces:

```
prog.rb:4: undefined local variable or method `x'
for #<Object:0x40197d08> (NameError)
```

However, if at the time the block executes a local variable already exists with the same name as that of a variable in the block, the existing local variable will be used in the block. Its value will therefore be available after the block finishes. As the following example shows, this applies both to normal variables in the block and to the block's parameters.

```
x = nil
y = nil
[ 1, 2, 3 ].each do |x|
  y = x + 1
end
[ x, y ]   →   [3, 4]
```

## Chapter 8

Exceptions, Catch, and Throw

So far we're been developing code in in Pleasantville, a wonderful place where nothing ever, ever goes wrong. Every library call succeeds, users never enter incorrect data, and resources are plentiful and cheap. Well, that's about to change. Welcome to the real world!

In the real world, errors happen. Good programs (and programmers) anticipate them and arrange to handle them gracefully. This isn't always as easy as it might be. Often the code that detects an error does not have the context to know what to do about it. For example, attempting to open a file that doesn't exist is acceptable in some circumstances and is a fatal error at other times. What's your file-handling module to do?

The traditional approach is to use return codes. The **open** method returns some specific value to say it failed. This value is then propagated back through the layers of calling routines until someone wants to take responsibility for it.

The problem with this approach is that managing all these error codes can be a pain. If a function calls **open**, then **read**, and finally **close**, and each can return an error indication, how can the function distinguish these error codes in the value it returns to *its* caller?

To a large extent, exceptions solve this problem. Exceptions let you package up information about an error into an object. That exception object is then propagated back up the calling stack automatically until the runtime system finds code that explicitly declares that it knows how to handle that type of exception.

The Exception Class

The package that contains the information about an exception is an object of class **Exception**, or one of class **Exception**'s children. Ruby predefines a tidy hierarchy of exceptions, shown in Figure 8.1 on the next page. As we'll see later, this hierarchy makes handling exceptions considerably easier.

When you need to raise an exception, you can use one of the built-in **Exception** classes, or you can create one of your own. If you create your own, you might want to make it a subclass of **StandardError** or one of its children. If you don't, your exception won't be caught by default.

Every **Exception** has associated with it a message string and a stack backtrace. If you define your own exceptions, you can add additional information.

Handling Exceptions

Our jukebox downloads songs from the Internet using a TCP socket. The basic code is simple:

```
opFile = File.open(opName, "w")
while data = socket.read(512)
  opFile.write(data)
end
```

What happens if we get a fatal error halfway through the download? We certainly don't want to store an incomplete song in the song list. "I Did It My *click*".

Let's add some exception handling code and see how it helps. We enclose the code that could raise an exception in a **begin/end** block and use **rescue** clauses to tell Ruby the types of exceptions we want to handle. In this case we're interested in trapping **SystemCallError** exceptions (and, by implication, any exceptions that are subclasses of **SystemCallError**), so that's what appears on the **rescue** line. In the error handling block, we report the error, close and delete the output file, and then reraise the exception.

```
opFile = File.open(opName, "w")
begin
  # Exceptions raised by this code will
  # be caught by the following rescue clause
  while data = socket.read(512)
    opFile.write(data)
  end

rescue SystemCallError
  $stderr.print "IO failed: " + $!
  opFile.close
  File.delete(opName)
  raise
end
```

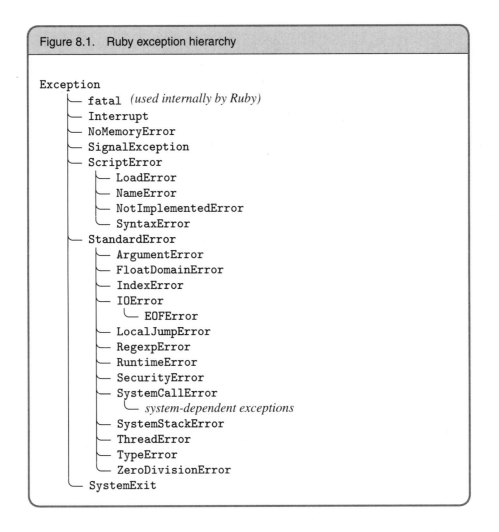

Figure 8.1. Ruby exception hierarchy

```
Exception
      ├── fatal  (used internally by Ruby)
      ├── Interrupt
      ├── NoMemoryError
      ├── SignalException
      ├── ScriptError
      │      ├── LoadError
      │      ├── NameError
      │      ├── NotImplementedError
      │      └── SyntaxError
      ├── StandardError
      │      ├── ArgumentError
      │      ├── FloatDomainError
      │      ├── IndexError
      │      ├── IOError
      │      │    └── EOFError
      │      ├── LocalJumpError
      │      ├── RegexpError
      │      ├── RuntimeError
      │      ├── SecurityError
      │      ├── SystemCallError
      │      │    └── system-dependent exceptions
      │      ├── SystemStackError
      │      ├── ThreadError
      │      ├── TypeError
      │      └── ZeroDivisionError
      └── SystemExit
```

When an exception is raised, and independent of any subsequent exception handling, Ruby places a reference to the **Exception** object associated with the exception in the global variable **$!** (the exclamation point presumably mirroring our surprise that any of *our* code could cause errors). In the previous example, we used this variable to format our error message.

After closing and deleting the file, we call **raise** with no parameters, which reraises the exception in **$!**. This is a useful technique, as it allows you to write code that filters exceptions, passing on those you can't handle to higher levels. It's almost like implementing an inheritance hierarchy for error processing.

You can have multiple **rescue** clauses in a **begin** block, and each **rescue** clause can specify multiple exceptions to catch. At the end of each rescue clause you can give

Ruby the name of a local variable to receive the matched exception. Many people find this more readable than using $! all over the place.

```
begin
  eval string
rescue SyntaxError, NameError => boom
  print "String doesn't compile: " + boom
rescue StandardError => bang
  print "Error running script: " + bang
end
```

How does Ruby decide which rescue clause to execute? It turns out that the processing is pretty similar to that used by the case statement. For each rescue clause in the begin block, Ruby compares the raised exception against each of the parameters in turn. If the raised exception matches a parameter, Ruby executes the body of the rescue and stops looking. The match is made using $!.kind_of?(*parameter*), and so will succeed if the parameter has the same class as the exception or is an ancestor of the exception. If you write a rescue clause with no parameter list, the parameter defaults to StandardError.

If no rescue clause matches, or if an exception is raised outside a begin/end block, Ruby moves up the stack and looks for an exception handler in the caller, then in the caller's caller, and so on.

Although the parameters to the rescue clause are typically the names of Exception classes, they can actually be arbitrary expressions (including method calls) that return an Exception class.

Tidying Up

Sometimes you need to guarantee that some processing is done at the end of a block of code, regardless of whether an exception was raised. For example, you may have a file open on entry to the block, and you need to make sure it gets closed as the block exits.

The ensure clause does just this. ensure goes after the last rescue clause and contains a chunk of code that will always be executed as the block terminates. It doesn't matter if the block exits normally, if it raises and rescues an exception, or if it is terminated by an uncaught exception—the ensure block will get run.

```
f = File.open("testfile")
begin
  # .. process
rescue
  # .. handle error
ensure
  f.close unless f.nil?
end
```

The `else` clause is a similar, although less useful, construct. If present, it goes after the `rescue` clauses and before any `ensure`. The body of an `else` clause is executed only if no exceptions are raised by the main body of code.

```
f = File.open("testfile")
begin
  # .. process
rescue
  # .. handle error
else
  puts "Congratulations-- no errors!"
ensure
  f.close unless f.nil?
end
```

Play It Again

Sometimes you may be able to correct the cause of an exception. In those cases, you can use the `retry` statement within a `rescue` clause to repeat the entire begin/end block. Clearly there is tremendous scope for infinite loops here, so this is a feature to use with caution (and with a finger resting lightly on the interrupt key).

As an example of code that retries on exceptions, have a look at the following, adapted from Minero Aoki's `net/smtp.rb` library.

```
@esmtp = true

begin
  # First try an extended login. If it fails because the
  # server doesn't support it, fall back to a normal login

  if @esmtp then
    @command.ehlo(helodom)
  else
    @command.helo(helodom)
  end

rescue ProtocolError
  if @esmtp then
    @esmtp = false
    retry
  else
    raise
  end
end
```

This code tries first to connect to an SMTP server using the `EHLO` command, which is not universally supported. If the connection attempt fails, the code sets the `@esmtp` variable to `false` and retries the connection. If this fails again, the exception is reraised up to the caller.

Raising Exceptions

So far we've been on the defensive, handling exceptions raised by others. It's time to turn the tables and go on the offensive. (There are those that say your gentle authors are always offensive, but that's a different book.)

You can raise exceptions in your code with the `Kernel.raise` method.

```
raise
raise "bad mp3 encoding"
raise InterfaceException, "Keyboard failure", caller
```

The first form simply reraises the current exception (or a `RuntimeError` if there is no current exception). This is used in exception handlers that need to intercept an exception before passing it on.

The second form creates a new `RuntimeError` exception, setting its message to the given string. This exception is then raised up the call stack.

The third form uses the first argument to create an exception and then sets the associated message to the second argument and the stack trace to the third argument. Typically the first argument will be either the name of a class in the `Exception` hierarchy or a reference to an object instance of one of these classes.[1] The stack trace is normally produced using the `Kernel.caller` method.

Here are some typical examples of `raise` in action.

```
raise

raise "Missing name" if name.nil?

if i >= myNames.size
  raise IndexError, "#{i} >= size (#{myNames.size})"
end

raise ArgumentError, "Name too big", caller
```

In the last example, we remove the current routine from the stack backtrace, which is often useful in library modules. We can take this further: the following code removes two routines from the backtrace.

```
raise ArgumentError, "Name too big", caller[1..-1]
```

---

1. Technically, this argument can be any object that responds to the message **exception** by returning an object such that `object.kind_of?(Exception)` is true.

Adding Information to Exceptions

You can define your own exceptions to hold any information that you need to pass out from the site of an error. For example, certain types of network errors might be transient depending on the circumstances. If such an error occurs, and the circumstances are right, you could set a flag in the exception to tell the handler that it might be worth retrying the operation.

```
class RetryException < RuntimeError
  attr :okToRetry
  def initialize(okToRetry)
    @okToRetry = okToRetry
  end
end
```

Somewhere down in the depths of the code, a transient error occurs.

```
def readData(socket)
  data = socket.read(512)
  if data.nil?
    raise RetryException.new(true), "transient read error"
  end
  # .. normal processing
end
```

Higher up the call stack, we handle the exception.

```
begin
  stuff = readData(socket)
  # .. process stuff
rescue RetryException => detail
  retry if detail.okToRetry
  raise
end
```

Catch and Throw

While the exception mechanism of **raise** and **rescue** is great for abandoning execution when things go wrong, it's sometimes nice to be able to jump out of some deeply nested construct during normal processing. This is where **catch** and **throw** come in handy.

```
catch (:done)  do
  while gets
    throw :done unless fields = split(/\t/)
    songList.add(Song.new(*fields))
  end
  songList.play
end
```

catch defines a block that is labeled with the given name (which may be a Symbol or a String). The block is executed normally until a throw is encountered.

When Ruby encounters a throw, it zips back up the call stack looking for a catch block with a matching symbol. When it finds it, Ruby unwinds the stack to that point and terminates the block. If the throw is called with the optional second parameter, that value is returned as the value of the catch. So, in the previous example, if the input does not contain correctly formatted lines, the throw will skip to the end of the corresponding catch, not only terminating the while loop but also skipping the playing of the song list.

The following example uses a throw to terminate interaction with the user if "!" is typed in response to any prompt.

```
def promptAndGet(prompt)
  print prompt
  res = readline.chomp
  throw :quitRequested if res == "!"
  return res
end
catch :quitRequested do
  name = promptAndGet("Name: ")
  age  = promptAndGet("Age:  ")
  sex  = promptAndGet("Sex:  ")
  # ..
  # process information
end
```

As this example illustrates, the throw does not have to appear within the static scope of the catch.

Chapter 9

Modules

Modules are a way of grouping together methods, classes, and constants. Modules give you two major benefits:

1. Modules provide a namespace and prevent name clashes.

2. Modules implement the mixin facility.

Namespaces

As you start to write bigger and bigger Ruby programs, you'll naturally find your-self producing chunks of reusable code—libraries of related routines that are generally applicable. You'll want to break this code out into separate files so the contents can be shared among different Ruby programs.

Often this code will be organized into classes, so you'll probably stick a class (or a set of interrelated classes) into a file.

However, there are times when you want to group things together that don't naturally form a class.

An initial approach might be to put all these things into a file and simply load that file into any program that needs it. This is the way the C language works. However, there's a problem. Say you write a set of trigonometry functions `sin`, `cos`, and so on. You stuff them all into a file, `trig.rb`, for future generations to enjoy. Meanwhile, Sally is working on a simulation of good and evil, and codes up a set of her own useful routines, including `beGood` and `sin`, and sticks them into `action.rb`. Joe, who wants to write a program to find out how many angels can dance on the head of a pin, needs to load both `trig.rb` and `action.rb` into his program. But both define a method called `sin`. Bad news.

The answer is the module mechanism. Modules define a namespace, a sandbox in which your methods and constants can play without having to worry about being stepped on by other methods and constants. The trig functions can go into one module:

```
module Trig
  PI = 3.141592654
  def Trig.sin(x)
   # ..
  end
  def Trig.cos(x)
   # ..
  end
end
```

and the good and bad action methods can go into another:

```
module Action
  VERY_BAD = 0
  BAD     = 1
  def Action.sin(badness)
    # ...
  end
end
```

Module constants are named just like class constants, with an initial uppercase letter. The method definitions look similar, too: these module methods are defined just like class methods.

If a third program wants to use these modules, it can simply load up the two files (using the Ruby `require` statement, which we discuss on page 105) and reference the qualified names.

```
require "trig"
require "action"

y = Trig.sin(Trig::PI/4)
wrongdoing = Action.sin(Action::VERY_BAD)
```

As with class methods, you call a module method by preceding its name with the module's name and a period, and you reference a constant using the module name and two colons.

Mixins

Modules have another, wonderful use. At a stroke, they pretty much eliminate the need for multiple inheritance, providing a facility called a *mixin*.

In the previous section's examples, we defined module methods, methods whose names were prefixed by the module name. If this made you think of class methods, your next thought might well be "what happens if I define instance methods within a module?" Good question. A module can't have instances, because a module isn't a class. However, you can *include* a module within a class definition. When this happens, all the module's instance methods are suddenly available as methods in the class as well. They get *mixed in*. In fact, mixed-in modules effectively behave as superclasses.

```
module Debug
  def whoAmI?
    "#{self.type.name} (\##{self.id}): #{self.to_s}"
  end
end
class Phonograph
  include Debug
  # ...
end
class EightTrack
  include Debug
  # ...
end
ph = Phonograph.new("West End Blues")
et = EightTrack.new("Surrealistic Pillow")

ph.whoAmI?   →   "Phonograph (#537677826): West End Blues"
et.whoAmI?   →   "EightTrack (#537677806): Surrealistic Pillow"
```

By including the `Debug` module, both `Phonograph` and `EightTrack` gain access to the `whoAmI?` instance method.

A couple of points about the `include` statement before we go on. First, it has nothing to do with files. C programmers use a preprocessor directive called `#include` to insert the contents of one file into another during compilation. The Ruby `include` statement simply makes a reference to a named module. If that module is in a separate file, you must use `require` to drag that file in before using `include`. Second, a Ruby `include` does not simply copy the module's instance methods into the class. Instead, it makes a reference from the class to the included module. If multiple classes include that module, they'll all point to the same thing. If you change the definition of a method within a module, even while your program is running, all classes that include that module will exhibit the new behavior.[1]

Mixins give you a wonderfully controlled way of adding functionality to classes. However, their true power comes out when the code in the mixin starts to interact with code in the class that uses it. Let's take the standard Ruby mixin `Comparable` as an example. The `Comparable` mixin can be used to add the comparison operators (`<`, `<=`, `==`, `>=`, and `>`), as well as the method `between?`, to a class. For this to work, `Comparable`

1.　Of course, we're speaking only of methods here. Instance variables are always per-object, for example.

assumes that any class that uses it defines the operator <=>. So, as a class writer, you define the one method, <=>, include `Comparable`, and get six comparison functions for free. Let's try this with our `Song` class, by making the songs comparable based on their duration. All we have to do is include the `Comparable` module and implement the comparison operator <=>.

```
class Song
  include Comparable
  def <=>(other)
    self.duration <=> other.duration
  end
end
```

We can check that the results are sensible with a few test songs.

```
song1 = Song.new("My Way",   "Sinatra", 225)
song2 = Song.new("Bicylops", "Fleck",   260)

song1 <=> song2   →   -1
song1  <   song2   →   true
song1 ==  song1   →   true
song1  >   song2   →   false
```

Finally, back on page 45 we showed an implementation of Smalltalk's `inject` function, implementing it within class `Array`. We promised then that we'd make it more generally applicable. What better way than making it a mixin module?

```
module Inject
  def inject(n)
    each do |value|
      n = yield(n, value)
    end
    n
  end
  def sum(initial = 0)
    inject(initial) { |n, value| n + value }
  end
  def product(initial = 1)
    inject(initial) { |n, value| n * value }
  end
end
```

We can then test this by mixing it into some built-in classes.

```
class Array
  include Inject
end
[ 1, 2, 3, 4, 5 ].sum      →   15
[ 1, 2, 3, 4, 5 ].product   →   120
```

```
class Range
  include Inject
end
(1..5).sum                    →    15
(1..5).product                →    120
('a'..'m').sum("Letters: ")   →    "Letters: abcdefghijklm"
```

For a more extensive example of a mixin, have a look at the documentation for the
Enumerable module, which starts on page 407.

Instance Variables in Mixins

People coming to Ruby from C++ often ask us, "What happens to instance variables
in a mixin? In C++, I have to jump through some hoops to control how variables are
shared in a multiple-inheritance hierarchy. How does Ruby handle this?"

Well, for starters, it's not really a fair question, we tell them. Remember how instance
variables work in Ruby: the first mention of an "@"-prefixed variable creates the
instance variable *in the current object,* self.

For a mixin, this means that the module that you mix into your client class (the mixee?)
may create instance variables in the client object and may use attr and friends to
define accessors for these instance variables. For instance:

```
module Notes
  attr   :concertA
  def tuning(amt)
    @concertA = 440.0 + amt
  end
end

class Trumpet
  include Notes
  def initialize(tune)
    tuning(tune)
    puts "Instance method returns #{concertA}"
    puts "Instance variable is #{@concertA}"
  end
end

# The piano is a little flat, so we'll match it
Trumpet.new(-5.3)
```

produces:

```
Instance method returns 434.7
Instance variable is 434.7
```

Not only do we have access to the methods defined in the mixin, but we get access to
the necessary instance variables as well. There's a risk here, of course, that different
mixins may use an instance variable with the same name and create a collision:

```
module MajorScales
  def majorNum
    @numNotes = 7 if @numNotes.nil?
    @numNotes # Return 7
  end
end
module PentatonicScales
  def pentaNum
    @numNotes = 5 if @numNotes.nil?
    @numNotes # Return 5?
  end
end

class ScaleDemo
  include MajorScales
  include PentatonicScales
  def initialize
    puts majorNum # Should be 7
    puts pentaNum # Should be 5
  end
end

ScaleDemo.new
```

produces:

```
7
7
```

The two bits of code that we mix in both use an instance variable named @numNotes. Unfortunately, the result is probably not what the author intended.

For the most part, mixin modules don't try to carry their own instance data around—they use accessors to retrieve data from the client object. But if you need to create a mixin that has to have its own state, ensure that the instance variables have unique names to distinguish them from any other mixins in the system (perhaps by using the module's name as part of the variable name).

Iterators and the Enumerable Module

You've probably noticed that the Ruby collection classes support a large number of operations that do various things with the collection: traverse it, sort it, and so on. You may be thinking, "Gee, it'd sure be nice if *my* class could support all these neat-o features, too!" (If you actually thought that, it's probably time to stop watching reruns of 1960s television shows.)

Well, your classes *can* support all these neat-o features, thanks to the magic of mixins and module **Enumerable**. All you have to do is write an iterator called **each**, which returns the elements of your collection in turn. Mix in **Enumerable**, and suddenly your class supports things such as `map`, `include?`, and `find_all?`. If the objects in your collection implement meaningful ordering semantics using the `<=>` method, you'll also get `min`, `max`, and `sort`.

Including Other Files

Because Ruby makes it easy to write good, modular code, you'll often find yourself producing small files containing some chunk of self-contained functionality—an interface to *x*, an algorithm to do *y*, and so on. Typically, you'll organize these files as class or module libraries.

Having produced these files, you'll want to incorporate them into your new programs. Ruby has two statements that do this.

```
load "filename.rb"
require "filename"
```

The `load` method includes the named Ruby source file every time the method is executed, whereas `require` loads any given file only once. `require` has additional functionality: it can load shared binary libraries. Both routines accept relative and absolute paths. If given a relative path (or just a plain name), they'll search every directory in the current load path (`$:`, discussed on page 142) for the file.

Files loaded using `load` and `require` can, of course, include other files, which include other files, and so on. What might *not* be obvious is that `require` is an executable statement—it may be inside an `if` statement, or it may include a string that was just built. The search path can be altered at runtime as well. Just add the directory you want to the string `$:`.

Since `load` will include the source unconditionally, you can use it to reload a source file that may have changed since the program began:

```
5.times do |i|
  File.open("temp.rb","w") { |f|
    f.puts "module Temp\ndef Temp.var() #{i}; end\nend"
  }
  load "temp.rb"
  puts Temp.var
end
```

produces:

```
0
1
2
3
4
```

## Chapter 10

Basic Input and Output

Ruby provides what at first sight looks like two separate sets of I/O routines. The first is the simple interface—we've been using it pretty much exclusively so far.

```
print "Enter your name: "
name = gets
```

There are a whole set of I/O-related methods implemented in the `Kernel` module—`gets`, `open`, `print`, `printf`, `putc`, `puts`, `readline`, `readlines`, and `test`—that make it simple and convenient to write straightforward Ruby programs. These methods typically do I/O to standard input and standard output, which makes them useful for writing filters. You'll find them documented starting on page 415.

The second way, which gives you a lot more control, is to use `IO` objects.

What Is an IO Object?

Ruby defines a single base class, `IO`, to handle input and output. This base class is subclassed by classes `File` and `BasicSocket` to provide more specialized behavior, but the principles are the same throughout. An `IO` object is a bidirectional channel between a Ruby program and some external resource.[1] There may be more to an `IO` object than meets the eye, but in the end you still simply write to it and read from it.

In this chapter, we'll be concentrating on class `IO` and its most commonly used subclass, class `File`. For more details on using the socket classes for networking, see the section beginning on page 473.

---

1.   For those who just have to know the implementation details, this means that a single `IO` object can sometimes be managing more than one operating system file descriptor. For example, if you open a pair of pipes, a single `IO` object contains both a read pipe and a write pipe.

Opening and Closing Files

As you might expect, you can create a new file object using `File.new`.

```
aFile = File.new("testfile", "r")
# ... process the file
aFile.close
```

You can create a `File` object that is open for reading, writing, or both, according to the mode string (here we opened "`testfile`" for reading with an "`r`"). The full list of allowed modes appears on page 331. You can also optionally specify file permissions when creating a file; see the description of `File.new` on page 308 for details. After opening the file, we can work with it, writing and/or reading data as needed. Finally, as responsible software citizens, we close the file, ensuring that all buffered data is written and that all related resources are freed.

But here Ruby can make life a little bit easier for you. The method `File.open` also opens a file. In regular use, it behaves just like `File.new`. However, if there's a block associated with the call, `open` behaves differently. Instead of returning a new `File` object, it instead invokes the block, passing the newly opened `File` as a parameter. When the block exits, the file is automatically closed.

```
File.open("testfile", "r") do |aFile|
# ... process the file
end
```

Reading and Writing Files

The same methods that we've been using for "simple" I/O are available for all file objects. So, `gets` reads a line from standard input, and `aFile.gets` reads a line from the file object `aFile`.

However, I/O objects enjoy an additional set of access methods, all intended to make our lives easier.

Iterators for Reading

Instead of using the usual loops to read data from an `IO` stream, you can use various iterators instead. `IO#each_byte` invokes a block with the next 8-bit byte from the `IO` object (in this case, an object of type `File`).

```
aFile = File.new("testfile")
aFile.each_byte {|ch| putc ch; putc ?. }
```

produces:

```
T.h.i.s. .i.s. .l.i.n.e. .o.n.e.
.T.h.i.s. .i.s. .l.i.n.e. .t.w.o.
.T.h.i.s. .i.s. .l.i.n.e. .t.h.r.e.e.
.A.n.d. .s.o. .o.n.......
.
```

`IO#each_line` calls the block with the next line from the file. In the next example, we'll make the original newlines visible using `String#dump`, so you can see that we're not cheating.

```
aFile.each_line {|line| puts "Got #{line.dump}" }
```

produces:

```
Got "This is line one\n"
Got "This is line two\n"
Got "This is line three\n"
Got "And so on...\n"
```

You can pass `each_line` any sequence of characters as a line separator, and it will break up the input accordingly, returning the line ending at the end of each line of data. That's why you see the "\n" characters in the output of the previous example. In the next example, we'll use "e" as the line separator.

```
aFile.each_line("e") do |line|
  puts "Got #{ line.dump }"
end
```

produces:

```
Got "This is line"
Got " one"
Got "\nThis is line"
Got " two\nThis is line"
Got " thre"
Got "e"
Got "\nAnd so on...\n"
```

If you combine the idea of an iterator with the auto-closing block feature, you get `IO.foreach`. This method takes the name of an I/O source, opens it for reading, calls the iterator once for every line in the file, and then closes the file automatically.

```
IO.foreach("testfile") { |line| puts line }
```

produces:

```
This is line one
This is line two
This is line three
And so on...
```

Or, if you prefer, you can retrieve an entire file into an array of lines:

```
arr = IO.readlines("testfile")
arr.length   →   4
arr[0]       →   "This is line one\n"
```

Don't forget that I/O is never certain in an uncertain world—exceptions will be raised on most errors, and you should be ready to catch them and take appropriate action.

Writing to Files

So far, we've been merrily calling `puts` and `print`, passing in any old object and trusting that Ruby will do the right thing (which, of course, it does). But what exactly *is* it doing?

The answer is pretty simple. With a couple of exceptions, every object you pass to `puts` and `print` is converted to a string by calling that object's `to_s` method. If for some reason the `to_s` method doesn't return a valid string, a string is created containing the object's class name and id, something like `<ClassName:0x123456>`.

The exceptions are simple, too. The `nil` object will print as the string "nil," and an array passed to `puts` will be written as if each of its elements in turn were passed separately to `puts`.

What if you want to write binary data and don't want Ruby messing with it? Well, normally you can simply use `IO#print` and pass in a string containing the bytes to be written. However, you can get at the low-level input and output routines if you really want—have a look at the documentation for `IO#sysread` and `IO#syswrite` on page 339.

And how do you get the binary data into a string in the first place? The two common ways are to poke it in byte by byte or to use `Array#pack`.

```
str = ""              →   ""
str << 1 << 2 << 3    →   "\001\002\003"

[ 4, 5, 6 ].pack("c*")   →   "\004\005\006"
```

But I Miss My C++ Iostream

Sometimes there's just no accounting for taste...

However, just as you can append an object to an **Array** using the << operator, you can also append an object to an output **IO** stream:

```
endl = "\n"
$stdout << 99 << " red balloons" << endl
```

produces:

```
99 red balloons
```

Again, the << method uses to_s to convert its arguments to strings before sending them on their merry way.

Talking to Networks

Ruby is fluent in most of the Internet's protocols, both low-level and high-level.

For those who enjoy groveling around at the network level, Ruby comes with a set of classes in the socket library (documented starting on page 473). These classes give you access to TCP, UDP, SOCKS, and Unix domain sockets, as well as any additional socket types supported on your architecture. The library also provides helper classes to make writing servers easier. Here's a simple program that gets information about the "oracle" user on our local machine using the finger protocol.

```
require 'socket'
client = TCPSocket.open('localhost', 'finger')
client.send("oracle\n", 0)    # 0 means standard packet
puts client.readlines
client.close
```

produces:

```
Login: oracle          Name: Oracle installation
Directory: /home/oracle         Shell: /bin/bash
Never logged in.
No Mail.
No Plan.
```

At a higher level, the lib/net set of library modules provides handlers for a set of application-level protocols (currently FTP, HTTP, POP, SMTP, and telnet). These are documented starting on page 486. For example, the following program lists the images that are displayed on the Pragmatic Programmer home page.

```
require 'net/http'

h = Net::HTTP.new('www.pragmaticprogrammer.com', 80)
resp, data = h.get('/index.html', nil)
if resp.message == "OK"
  data.scan(/<img src="(.*?)"/) { |x| puts x }
end
```

produces:

```
images/title_main.gif
images/dot.gif
images/dot.gif
images/dot.gif
images/dot.gif
images/dot.gif
```

## Chapter 11

Threads and Processes

Ruby gives you two basic ways to organize your program so that you can run different parts of it "at the same time." You can split up cooperating tasks *within* the program, using multiple threads, or you can split up tasks between different programs, using multiple processes. Let's look at each in turn.

Multithreading

Often the simplest way to do two things at once is by using *Ruby threads*. These are totally in-process, implemented within the Ruby interpreter. That makes the Ruby threads completely portable—there is no reliance on the operating system—but you don't get certain benefits from having native threads. You may experience thread starvation (that's where a low-priority thread doesn't get a chance to run). If you manage to get your threads deadlocked, the whole process may grind to a halt. And if some thread happens to make a call to the operating system that takes a long time to complete, all threads will hang until the interpreter gets control back. However, don't let these potential problems put you off—Ruby threads are a lightweight and efficient way to achieve parallelism in your code.

Creating Ruby Threads

Creating a new thread is pretty straightforward. Here's a simple code fragment that downloads a set of Web pages in parallel. For each request it's given, the code creates a separate thread that handles the HTTP transaction.

```
require 'net/http'
pages = %w( www.rubycentral.com
            www.awl.com
            www.pragmaticprogrammer.com
          )
threads = []
```

```
for page in pages
  threads << Thread.new(page) { |myPage|

    h = Net::HTTP.new(myPage, 80)
    puts "Fetching: #{myPage}"
    resp, data = h.get('/', nil )
    puts "Got #{myPage}:  #{resp.message}"
  }
end

threads.each { |aThread|  aThread.join }
```

produces:

```
Fetching: www.rubycentral.com
Fetching: www.awl.com
Fetching: www.pragmaticprogrammer.com
Got www.rubycentral.com:  OK
Got www.pragmaticprogrammer.com:  OK
Got www.awl.com:  OK
```

Let's look at this code in more detail, as there are a few subtle things going on.

New threads are created with the Thread.new call. It is given a block that contains the code to be run in a new thread. In our case, the block uses the net/http library to fetch the top page from each of our nominated sites. Our tracing clearly shows that these fetches are going on in parallel.

When we create the thread, we pass the required HTML page in as a parameter. This parameter is passed on to the block as myPage. Why do we do this, rather than simply using the value of the variable page within the block?

A thread shares all global, instance, and local variables that are in existence at the time the thread starts. As anyone with a kid brother can tell you, sharing isn't always a good thing. In this case, all three threads would share the variable page. The first thread gets started, and page is set to www.rubycentral.com. In the meantime, the loop creating the threads is still running. The second time around, page gets set to www.awl.com. If the first thread has not yet finished using the page variable, it will suddenly start using its new value. These bugs are difficult to track down.

However, local variables created within a thread's block are truly local to that thread—each thread will have its own copy of these variables. In our case, the variable myPage will be set at the time the thread is created, and each thread will have its own copy of the page address.

Manipulating Threads

Another subtlety occurs on the last line in the program. Why do we call join on each of the threads we created?

When a Ruby program terminates, all running threads are killed, regardless of their states. However, you can wait for a particular thread to finish by calling that thread's Thread#join method. The calling thread will block until the given thread is finished. By calling join on each of the requestor threads, you can make sure that all three requests have completed before you terminate the main program.

In addition to join, there are a few other handy routines that are used to manipulate threads. First of all, the current thread is always accessible using Thread.current. You can obtain a list of all threads using Thread.list, which returns a list of all Thread objects that are runnable or stopped. To determine the status of a particular thread, you can use Thread#status and Thread#alive?.

Also, you can adjust the priority of a thread using Thread#priority= . Higher-priority threads will run before lower-priority threads. We'll talk more about thread scheduling, and stopping and starting threads, in just a bit.

Thread Variables

As we described in the previous section, a thread can normally access any variables that are in scope when the thread is created. Variables local to the block of a thread are local to the thread, and are not shared.

But what if you need per-thread variables that can be accessed by other threads— including the main thread? Thread features a special facility that allows thread-local variables to be created and accessed by name. You simply treat the thread object as if it were a Hash, writing to elements using []= and reading them back using []. In this example, each thread records the current value of the variable count in a thread-local variable with the key mysum. (There's a race condition in this code, but we haven't talked about synchronization yet, so we'll just quietly ignore it for now.)

```
count = 0
arr = []
10.times do |i|
  arr[i] = Thread.new {
    sleep(rand(0)/10.0)
    Thread.current["mycount"] = count
    count += 1
  }
end
arr.each {|t| t.join; print t["mycount"], ", " }
puts "count = #{count}"
```

produces:

```
8, 1, 5, 7, 4, 0, 6, 3, 2, 9, count = 10
```

The main thread waits for the subthreads to finish and then prints out the value of count captured by each. Just to make it more interesting, we have each thread wait a random time before recording the value.

Threads and Exceptions

What happens if a thread raises an unhandled exception? It depends on the setting of the `abort_on_exception` flag, documented on pages 389 and 392.

If `abort_on_exception` is `false`, the default condition, an unhandled exception simply kills the current thread—all the rest continue to run. In the following example, thread number 3 blows up and fails to produce any output. However, you can still see the trace from the other threads.

```
threads = []
6.times { |i|
  threads << Thread.new(i) {
    raise "Boom!" if i == 3
    puts i
  }
}
threads.each {|t| t.join }
```

produces:

```
0
1
2
4
5
prog.rb:4: Boom! (RuntimeError)
from prog.rb:8:in `join'
from prog.rb:8
from prog.rb:8:in `each'
from prog.rb:8
```

However, set `abort_on_exception` to `true`, and an unhandled exception kills all running threads. Once thread 3 dies, no more output is produced.

```
Thread.abort_on_exception = true
threads = []
6.times { |i|
  threads << Thread.new(i) {
    raise "Boom!" if i == 3
    puts i
  }
}
threads.each {|t| t.join }
```

produces:

```
0
1
2
prog.rb:5: Boom! (RuntimeError)
from prog.rb:7:in `initialize'
from prog.rb:7:in `new'
```

```
from prog.rb:7
from prog.rb:3:in `times'
from prog.rb:3
```

Controlling the Thread Scheduler

In a well-designed application, you'll normally just let threads do their thing; building timing dependencies into a multithreaded application is generally considered to be bad form.

However, there are times when you need to control threads. Perhaps the jukebox has a thread that displays a light show. We might need to stop it temporarily when the music stops. You might have two threads in a classic producer-consumer relationship, where the consumer has to pause if the producer gets backlogged.

Class `Thread` provides a number of methods to control the thread scheduler. Invoking `Thread.stop` stops the current thread, while `Thread#run` arranges for a particular thread to be run. `Thread.pass` deschedules the current thread, allowing others to run, and `Thread#join` and `Thread#value` suspend the calling thread until a given thread finishes.

We can demonstrate these features in the following, totally pointless program.

```
t = Thread.new { Thread.pass; Thread.stop; }
t.status    →    "run"
t.run
t.status    →    "sleep"
t.run
t.status    →    false
```

However, using these primitives to achieve any kind of real synchronization is, at best, hit or miss; there will always be race conditions waiting to bite you. And when you're working with shared data, race conditions pretty much guarantee long and frustrating debugging sessions. Fortunately, threads have one additional facility—the idea of a critical section. Using this, we can built a number of secure synchronization schemes.

Mutual Exclusion

The lowest-level method of blocking other threads from running uses a global "thread critical" condition. When the condition is set to `true` (using the `Thread.critical=` method), the scheduler will not schedule any existing thread to run. However, this does not block new threads from being created and run. Certain thread operations (such as stopping or killing a thread, sleeping in the current thread, or raising an exception) may cause a thread to be scheduled even when in a critical section.

Using `Thread.critical=` directly is certainly possible, but it isn't terribly convenient. Fortunately, Ruby comes packaged with several alternatives. Of these, two of the best, class `Mutex` and class `ConditionVariable`, are available in the **thread** library module; see the documentation beginning on page 462.

The Mutex Class

`Mutex` is a class that implements a simple semaphore lock for mutually exclusive access to some shared resource. That is, only one thread may hold the lock at a given time. Other threads may choose to wait in line for the lock to become available, or may simply choose to get an immediate error indicating that the lock is not available.

A mutex is often used when updates to shared data need to be atomic. Say we need to update two variables as part of a transaction. We can simulate this in a trivial program by incrementing some counters. The updates are supposed to be atomic—the outside world should never see the counters with different values. Without any kind of mutex control, this just doesn't work.

```
count1 = count2 = 0
difference = 0
counter = Thread.new do
  loop do
    count1 += 1
    count2 += 1
  end
end
spy = Thread.new do
  loop do
    difference += (count1 - count2).abs
  end
end
sleep 1
Thread.critical = 1
count1          →    182917
count2          →    182917
difference      →    65041
```

This example shows that the "spy" thread woke up a large number of times and found the values of `count1` and `count2` inconsistent.

Fortunately we can fix this using a mutex.

```
require 'thread'
mutex = Mutex.new

count1 = count2 = 0
difference = 0
counter = Thread.new do
  loop do
    mutex.synchronize do
```

```
        count1 += 1
        count2 += 1
      end
    end
  end
  spy = Thread.new do
    loop do
      mutex.synchronize do
        difference += (count1 - count2).abs
      end
    end
  end

  sleep 1
  mutex.lock
  count1      →    20911
  count2      →    20911
  difference  →    0
```

By placing all accesses to the shared data under control of a mutex, we ensure consistency. Unfortunately, as you can see from the numbers, we also suffer quite a performance penalty.

Condition Variables

Using a mutex to protect critical data is sometimes not enough. Suppose you are in a critical section, but you need to wait for some particular resource. If your thread goes to sleep waiting for this resource, it is possible that no other thread will be able to release the resource because it cannot enter the critical section—the original process still has it locked. You need to be able to give up temporarily your exclusive use of the critical region and simultaneously tell people that you're waiting for a resource. When the resource becomes available, you need to be able to grab it *and* reobtain the lock on the critical region, all in one step.

This is where condition variables come in. A condition variable is simply a semaphore that is associated with a resource and is used within the protection of a particular mutex. When you need a resource that's unavailable, you wait on a condition variable. That action releases the lock on the corresponding mutex. When some other thread signals that the resource is available, the original thread comes off the wait and simultaneously regains the lock on the critical region.

```
require 'thread'
mutex = Mutex.new
cv = ConditionVariable.new

a = Thread.new {
  mutex.synchronize {
    puts "A: I have critical section, but will wait for cv"
    cv.wait(mutex)
    puts "A: I have critical section again! I rule!"
```

```
    }
  }
  puts "(Later, back at the ranch...)"
  b = Thread.new {
    mutex.synchronize {
      puts "B: Now I am critical, but am done with cv"
      cv.signal
      puts "B: I am still critical, finishing up"
    }
  }
  a.join
  b.join
```

produces:

```
A: I have critical section, but will wait for cv
(Later, back at the ranch...)
B: Now I am critical, but am done with cv
B: I am still critical, finishing up
A: I have critical section again! I rule!
```

For alternative implementations of synchronization mechanisms, see `monitor.rb` and `sync.rb` in the `lib` subdirectory of the distribution.

Running Multiple Processes

Sometimes you may want to split a task into several process-sized chunks—or perhaps you need to run a separate process that was not written in Ruby. Not a problem: Ruby has a number of methods by which you may spawn and manage separate processes.

Spawning New Processes

There are several ways to spawn a separate process; the easiest is to run some command and wait for it to complete. You might find yourself doing this to run some separate command or retrieve data from the host system. Ruby does this for you with the `system` and backquote methods.

```
system("tar xzf test.tgz")   →   true
result = `date`
result                       →   "Wed Sep 20 10:35:06 CDT 2000\n"
```

The method `Kernel.system` executes the given command in a subprocess; it returns `true` if the command was found and executed properly, `false` otherwise. In case of failure, you'll find the subprocess's exit code in the global variable `$?`.

One problem with `system` is that the command's output will simply go to the same destination as your program's output, which may not be what you want. To capture the standard output of a subprocess, you can use the backquotes, as with `date` in the previous example. Remember that you may need to use **String#chomp** to remove the line-ending characters from the result.

Okay, this is fine for simple cases—we can run some other process and get the return status. But many times we need a bit more control than that. We'd like to carry on a conversation with the subprocess, possibly sending it data and possibly getting some back. The method **IO.popen** does just this. The **popen** method runs a command as a subprocess and connects that subprocess's standard input and standard output to a Ruby **IO** object. Write to the **IO** object, and the subprocess can read it on standard input. Whatever the subprocess writes is available in the Ruby program by reading from the **IO** object.

For example, on our systems one of the more useful utilities is **pig**, a program that reads words from standard input and prints them in pig Latin (or igpay atinlay). We can use this when our Ruby programs need to send us output that our 5-year-olds shouldn't be able to understand.

```
pig = IO.popen("pig", "w+")
pig.puts "ice cream after they go to bed"
pig.close_write
puts pig.gets
```

produces:

```
iceway eamcray afterway eythay ogay otay edbay
```

This example illustrates both the apparent simplicity and the real-world complexities involved in driving subprocesses through pipes. The code certainly looks simple enough: open the pipe, write a phrase, and read back the response. But it turns out that the **pig** program doesn't flush the output it writes. Our original attempt at this example, which had a **pig.puts** followed by a **pig.gets**, hung forever. The **pig** program processed our input, but its response was never written to the pipe. We had to insert the **pig.close_write** line. This sends an end-of-file to **pig**'s standard input, and the output we're looking for gets flushed as **pig** terminates.

There's one more twist to **popen**. If the command you pass it is a single minus sign ("–"), **popen** will fork a new Ruby interpreter. Both this and the original interpreter will continue running by returning from the **popen**. The original process will receive an **IO** object back, while the child will receive **nil**.

```
pipe = IO.popen("-","w+")
if pipe
  pipe.puts "Get a job!"
  $stderr.puts "Child says '#{pipe.gets.chomp}'"
else
  $stderr.puts "Dad says '#{gets.chomp}'"
  puts "OK"
end
```

produces:

```
Dad says 'Get a job!'
Child says 'OK'
```

In addition to **popen**, the traditional Unix calls **Kernel.fork**, **Kernel.exec**, and **IO.pipe** are available on platforms that support them. The file-naming convention of many **IO** methods and **Kernel.open** will also spawn subprocesses if you put a "**|**" as the first character of the filename (see the introduction to class **IO** on page 329 for details). Note that you *cannot* create pipes using **File.new**; it's just for files.

Independent Children

Sometimes we don't need to be quite so hands-on: we'd like to give the subprocess its assignment and then go on about our business. Some time later, we'll check in with it to see if it has finished. For instance, we might want to kick off a long-running external sort.

```
exec("sort testfile > output.txt") if fork == nil
# The sort is now running in a child process
# carry on processing in the main program

# then wait for the sort to finish
Process.wait
```

The call to **Kernel.fork** returns a process id in the parent, and **nil** in the child, so the child process will perform the **Kernel.exec** call and run sort. Sometime later, we issue a **Process.wait** call, which waits for the sort to complete (and returns its process id).

If you'd rather be notified when a child exits (instead of just waiting around), you can set up a signal handler using **Kernel.trap** (described on page 431). Here we set up a trap on **SIGCLD**, which is the signal sent on "death of child process."

```
trap("CLD") {
  pid = Process.wait
  puts "Child pid #{pid}: terminated"
  exit
}

exec("sort testfile > output.txt") if fork == nil

# do other stuff...
```

produces:

```
Child pid 20845: terminated
```

Blocks and Subprocesses

`IO.popen` works with a block in pretty much the same way as `File.open` does. Pass `popen` a command, such as `date`, and the block will be passed an `IO` object as a parameter.

```
IO.popen ("date") { |f| puts "Date is #{f.gets}" }
```

produces:

```
Date is Wed Sep 20 10:35:06 CDT 2000
```

The `IO` object will be closed automatically when the code block exits, just as it is with `File.open`.

If you associate a block with `Kernel.fork`, the code in the block will be run in a Ruby subprocess, and the parent will continue after the block.

```
fork do
  puts "In child, pid = #$$"
  exit 99
end
pid = Process.wait
puts "Child terminated, pid = #{pid}, exit code = #{$? >> 8}"
```

produces:

```
In child, pid = 20852
Child terminated, pid = 20852, exit code = 99
```

One last thing. Why do we shift the exit code in `$?` 8 bits to the right before displaying it? This is a "feature" of Posix systems: the bottom 8 bits of an exit code contain the reason the program terminated, while the higher-order 8 bits hold the actual exit code.

## Chapter 12

When Trouble Strikes

Sad to say, it is possible to write buggy programs using Ruby. Sorry about that.

But not to worry! Ruby has several features that will help debug your programs. We'll look at these features, and then we'll show some common mistakes you can make in Ruby and how to fix them.

Ruby Debugger

Ruby comes with a debugger, which is conveniently built into the base system. You can run the debugger by invoking the interpreter with the `-r debug` option, along with any other Ruby options and the name of your script:

```
ruby -r debug [ options ] [ programfile ] [ arguments ]
```

The debugger supports the usual range of features you'd expect, including the ability to set breakpoints, to step into and step over method calls, and to display stack frames and variables.

It can also list the instance methods defined for a particular object or class, and allows you to list and control separate threads within Ruby. Table 12.1 on page 133 lists all of the commands that are available under the debugger.

If your Ruby has **readline** support enabled, you can use cursor keys to move back and forth in command history and use line editing commands to amend previous input.

To give you an idea of what the Ruby debugger is like, here is a sample session.

```
% ruby -rdebug t.rb
Debug.rb
Emacs support available.
t.rb:1:def fact(n)
(rdb:1) list 1-9
[1, 10] in t.rb
```

```
=> 1  def fact(n)
   2    if n <= 0
   3      1
   4    else
   5      n * fact(n-1)
   6    end
   7  end
   8
   9  p fact(5)
(rdb:1) b 2
Set breakpoint 1 at t.rb:2
(rdb:1) c
breakpoint 1, fact at t.rb:2
t.rb:2:  if n <= 0
(rdb:1) disp n
  1: n = 5
(rdb:1) del 1
(rdb:1) watch n==1
Set watchpoint 2
(rdb:1) c
watchpoint 2, fact at t.rb:fact
t.rb:1:def fact(n)
1: n = 1
(rdb:1) where
--> #1  t.rb:1:in 'fact'
    #2  t.rb:5:in 'fact'
    #3  t.rb:5:in 'fact'
    #4  t.rb:5:in 'fact'
    #5  t.rb:5:in 'fact'
    #6  t.rb:9
(rdb:1) del 2
(rdb:1) c
120
```

Interactive Ruby

If you want to play with Ruby, there is a facility called Interactive Ruby—irb, for short. irb is essentially a Ruby "shell" similar in concept to an operating system shell (complete with job control). It provides an environment where you can "play around" with the language in real time. You launch irb at the command prompt:

```
irb [ irb-options ] [ ruby_script ] [ options ]
```

irb will display the value of each expression as you complete it. For instance:

```
% irb
irb(main):001:0> a = 1 +
irb(main):002:0* 2 * 3 /
irb(main):003:0* 4 % 5
```

```
2
irb(main):004:0> 2+2
4
irb(main):005:0> def test
irb(main):006:1> puts "Hello, world!"
irb(main):007:1> end
nil
irb(main):008:0> test
Hello, world!
nil
irb(main):009:0>
```

irb also allows you to create subsessions, each one of which may have its own context. For example, you can create a subsession with the same (top-level) context as the original session, or create a subsession in the context of a particular class or instance. The sample session shown in Figure 12.1 on the following page is a bit longer, but shows how you can create subsessions and switch between them.

For a full description of all the commands that irb supports, see the reference beginning on page 523.

As with the debugger, if your version of Ruby was built with GNU Readline support, you can use arrow keys (as with Emacs) or vi-style key bindings to edit individual lines or to go back and reexecute or edit a previous line—just like a command shell.

irb is a great learning tool: it's very handy if you want to try out an idea quickly and see if it works.

Editor Support

Ruby is designed to read a program in one pass; this means you can pipe an entire program to Ruby's standard input and it will work just fine.

We can take advantage of this feature to run Ruby code from inside an editor. In Emacs, for instance, you can select a region of Ruby text and use the command `Meta-|` to execute Ruby. The Ruby interpreter will use the selected region as standard input and output will go to a buffer named "`*Shell Command Output*`." This feature has come in quite handy for us while writing this book—just select a few lines of Ruby in the middle of a paragraph and try it out!

You can do something similar in the vi editor using the "!" command—except that it will *replace* the program text with its output, which may or may not be what you want. Other editors have similar features.

While we are on the subject, this would probably be a good place to mention that there is a Ruby mode for Emacs included in the distribution as `misc/ruby-mode.el`. There are also several syntax-highlighting modules for vim (an enhanced version of the vi

Figure 12.1.   Sample irb session

```
% irb
irb(main):001:0> irb
irb#1(main):001:0> jobs
#0->irb on main (#<Thread:0x401bd654>: stop)
#1->irb#1 on main (#<Thread:0x401d5a28>: running)
irb#1(main):002:0> fg 0
#<IRB::Irb:@scanner=#<RubyLex:0x401ca7>,@signal_status=:IN_EVAL,
        @context=#<IRB::Context:0x401ca86c>>
irb(main):002:0> class VolumeKnob
irb(main):003:1> end
nil
irb(main):004:0> irb VolumeKnob
irb#2(VolumeKnob):001:0> def initialize
irb#2(VolumeKnob):002:1> @vol=50
irb#2(VolumeKnob):003:1> end
nil
irb#2(VolumeKnob):004:0> def up
irb#2(VolumeKnob):005:1> @vol += 10
irb#2(VolumeKnob):006:1> end
nil
irb#2(VolumeKnob):007:0> fg 0
#<IRB::Irb:@scanner=#<RubyLex:0x401ca7>,@signal_status=:IN_EVAL,
        @context=#<IRB::Context:0x401ca86c>>
irb(main):005:0> jobs
#0->irb on main (#<Thread:0x401bd654>: running)
#1->irb#1 on main (#<Thread:0x401d5a28>: stop)
#2->irb#2 on VolumeKnob (#<Thread:0x401c400c>: stop)
irb(main):006:0> VolumeKnob.instance_methods
["up"] #
irb(main):007:0> v = VolumeKnob.new
#<VolumeKnob: @vol=50>
irb(main):008:0> irb v
irb#3(#<VolumeKnob:0x401e7d40>):001:0> up
60
irb#3(#<VolumeKnob:0x401e7d40>):002:0> up
70
irb#3(#<VolumeKnob:0x401e7d40>):003:0> up
80 #
irb#3(VolumeKnob):004:0> fg 0
#<IRB::Irb:@scanner=#<RubyLex:0x401ca7>,@signal_status=:IN_EVAL,
        @context=#<IRB::Context:0x401ca86c>>
irb(main):009:0> kill 1,2,3
[1, 2, 3]
irb(main):010:0> jobs
#0->irb on main (#<Thread:0x401bd654>: running)
irb(main):011:0> exit
```

In this same irb session, we'll create a new subsession in the context of class VolumeKnob.

We can use fg 0 to switch back to the main session, take at look at all current jobs, and see what instance methods VolumeKnob defines.

Make a new VolumeKnob object, and create a new subsession with that object as the context.

Switch back to the main session, kill the subsessions, and exit.

editor), jed, and other editors available on the net as well. Check the Ruby FAQ for current locations and availability.

But It Doesn't Work!

So you've read through enough of the book, you start to write your very own Ruby program, and it doesn't work. Here's a list of common gotchas and other tips.

- Attribute setter not being called. Within an object, Ruby will parse `setter=` as an assignment to a local variable, not as a method call. Use `self.setter=` to indicate the method call.

- A parse error at the last line of the source often indicates a missing **end** keyword.

- Make sure that the type of the object you are using is what you think it is. If in doubt, use `Object#type` to check the type of an object.

- Make sure that your methods start with a lowercase letter and that classes and constants start with an uppercase letter.

- If you happen to forget a "," in an argument list—especially to print—you can produce some very odd error messages.

- Block parameters are actually local variables. If an existing local of the same name exists when the block executes, that variable will be modified by the call to the block. This may or may not be a good thing.

- Watch out for precedence, especially when using {} instead of **do/end**.

- Make sure that the open parenthesis of a method's parameter list butts up against the end of the method name with no intervening spaces.

- Output written to a terminal may be buffered. This means that you may not see a message you write immediately. In addition, if you write messages to both `$stdout` and `$stderr`, the output may not appear in the order you were expecting. Always use nonbuffered I/O (set `sync=true`) for debug messages.

- If numbers don't come out right, perhaps they're strings. Test read from a file will be a `String`, and will not be automatically converted to a number by Ruby. A call to `to_i` will work wonders. A common mistake Perl programmers make is:

  ```
  while gets
    num1, num2 = split /,/
    # ...
  end
  ```

- Unintended aliasing—if you are using an object as the key of a hash, make sure it doesn't change its hash value (or arrange to call `Hash#rehash` if it does).

- Use `trace_var` to watch when a variable changes value.

- Use the debugger.

- Use `Object#freeze`. If you suspect that some unknown portion of code is setting a variable to a bogus value, try freezing the variable. The culprit will then be caught during the attempt to modify the variable.

There's one major technique that makes writing Ruby code both easier and more fun. *Develop your applications incrementally.* Write a few lines of code, then run them. Write a few more, then run those. One of the major benefits of an untyped language is that things don't have to be complete before you use them.

But It's Too Slow!

Ruby is an interpreted, high-level language, and as such it may not perform as fast as a lower-level language such as C. In this section, we'll list some basic things you can do to improve performance; also have a look in the index under *Performance* for other pointers.

Create Locals Outside Blocks

Try defining the variables used in a block before the block executes. When iterating over a very large set of elements, you can improve execution speed somewhat by pre-declaring any iterator variables. In the first example below, Ruby has to create new x and y variables on each iteration, but in the second version it doesn't. We'll use the `benchmark` package from the Ruby Application Archive to compare the loops:

```
require "benchmark"
include Benchmark
n = 1000000
bm(12) do |test|
  test.report("normal:")    do
    n.times do |x|
      y = x + 1
    end
  end
  test.report("predefine:") do
    x = y = 0
    n.times do |x|
      y = x + 1
    end
  end
end
```

produces:

	user	system	total	real
normal:	3.470000	0.000000	3.470000	(3.493525)
predefine:	2.290000	0.000000	2.290000	(2.300784)

Use the Profiler

Ruby comes with a code profiler (documentation begins on on page 458). In and of itself, that isn't too surprising, but when you realize that the profiler is written in just about 50 lines of Ruby, that makes for a pretty impressive language.

You can add profiling to your code using the command-line option -r profile, or from within the code using require "profile". For example:

```ruby
require "profile"
class Peter
  def initialize(amt)
    @value = amt
  end

  def rob(amt)
    @value -= amt
    amt
  end
end

class Paul
  def initialize
    @value = 0
  end

  def pay(amt)
    @value += amt
    amt
  end
end

peter = Peter.new(1000)
paul = Paul.new
1000.times do
  paul.pay(peter.rob(10))
end
```

Run this, and you'll get something like the following.

% time	cumulative seconds	self seconds	calls	self ms/call	total ms/call	name
45.16	0.42	0.42	1000	0.42	0.46	Paul#pay
22.58	0.63	0.21	1000	0.21	0.27	Peter#rob
21.51	0.83	0.20	1	200.00	930.00	Fixnum#times
6.45	0.89	0.06	1000	0.06	0.06	Fixnum#-
4.30	0.93	0.04	1000	0.04	0.04	Fixnum#+
0.00	0.93	0.00	1	0.00	0.00	Peter#initialize
0.00	0.93	0.00	2	0.00	0.00	Class#inherited
0.00	0.93	0.00	1	0.00	0.00	Paul#initialize
0.00	0.93	0.00	4	0.00	0.00	Module#method_added
0.00	0.93	0.00	2	0.00	0.00	Class#new
0.00	0.93	0.00	1	0.00	930.00	#toplevel

With the profiler, you can quickly identify and fix bottlenecks. Remember to check the code without the profiler afterward, though—sometimes the slowdown the profiler introduces can mask other problems.

Ruby is a wonderfully transparent and expressive language, but it does not relieve the programmer of the need to apply common sense: creating unnecessary objects, performing unneeded work, and creating generally bloated code are wasteful in any language.

Table 12.1. Debugger commands

Command	Description
b [reak] [file:]line	Set breakpoint at given line in *file* (default current file).
b [reak] [file:]name	Set breakpoint at *method* in *file*.
b [reak]	Display breakpoints and watchpoints.
wat [ch] expr	Break when expression becomes true.
del [ete] [nnn]	Delete breakpoint *nnn* (default all).
disp [lay] expr	Display value of *nnn* every time debugger gets control.
disp [lay]	Show current displays.
undisp [lay] [nnn]	Remove display (default all).
c [ont]	Continue execution.
s [tep] nnn=1	Execute next *nnn* lines, stepping into methods.
n [ext] nnn=1	Execute next *nnn* lines, stepping over methods.
fi [nish]	Finish execution of the current function.
q [uit]	Exit the debugger.
w [here]	Display current stack frame.
f [rame]	Synonym for `where`.
l [ist] [start–end]	List source lines from start to end.
up nnn=1	Move up *nnn* levels in the stack frame.
down nnn=1	Move down *nnn* levels in the stack frame.
v [ar] g [lobal]	Display global variables.
v [ar] l [ocal]	Display local variables.
v [ar] i [stance] *obj*	Display instance variables of *obj*.
v [ar] c [onst] Name	Display constants in class or module name.
m [ethod] i [nstance] *obj*	Display instance methods of *obj*.
m [ethod] Name	Display instance methods of the class or module name.
th [read] l [ist]	List all threads.
th [read] [c[ur[rent]]]	Display status of current thread.
th [read] [c[ur[rent]]] nnn	Make thread *nnn* current and stop it.
th [read] stop nnn	Make thread *nnn* current and stop it.
th [read] resume nnn	Resume thread *nnn*.
[p] expr	Evaluate *expr* in the current context. *expr* may include assignment to variables and method invocations.
empty	A null command repeats the last command.

Part II

Ruby in Its Setting

## Chapter 13

Ruby and Its World

It's an unfortunate fact of life that our applications have to deal with the big, bad world. In this chapter, we'll look at how Ruby interacts with its environment. Microsoft Windows users will probably also want to look at platform-specific information beginning on page 165.

Command-Line Arguments

"In the beginning, was the command line."[1] Regardless of the system in which Ruby is deployed, whether it be a super high-end scientific graphics workstation or an embedded PDA device, you've got to start the Ruby interpreter somehow, and that gives us the opportunity to pass in command-line arguments.

A Ruby command line consists of three parts: options to the Ruby interpreter, optionally the name of a program to run, and optionally a set of arguments for that program.

    ruby [options] [--] [programfile] [arguments]

The Ruby options are terminated by the first word on the command line that doesn't start with a hyphen, or by the special flag "--" (two hyphens).

If no filename is present on the command line, or if the filename is a single hyphen (-), Ruby reads the program source from standard input.

Arguments for the program itself follow the program name. For example:

    % ruby -w - "Hello World"

will enable warnings, read a program from standard input, and pass it the quoted string "Hello World" as an argument.

---

1. Title of a marvelous essay by Neal Stephenson (available online at `http://www.spack.org/essays/commandline.html`).

Command-Line Options

-0[*octal*]

The number "0" flag specifies the record separator character (\0, if no digit follows). -00 indicates paragraph mode: records are separated by two successive default record separator characters. -0777 reads the entire file at once (as it is an illegal character). Sets $/.

-a Auto split mode when used with -n or -p; equivalent to executing $F = $_.split at the top of each loop iteration.

-C *directory*

Changes working directory to *directory* before executing.

-c Checks syntax only; does not execute the program.

--copyright

Prints the copyright notice and exits.

-d, --debug

Sets $DEBUG to true. This can be used by your programs to enable additional tracing.

-e '*command*'

Executes *command* as one line of Ruby source. Several -e's are allowed, and the commands are treated as multiple lines in the same program. If *programfile* is omitted when -e is present, execution stops after the -e commands have been run.

-F *pattern*

Specifies the input field separator ($;) used as the default for split() (affects -a).

-h, --help

Displays a short help screen.

-I *directories*

Specifies directories to be prepended to $LOAD_PATH ($:). Multiple -I options may be present, and multiple directories may appear following each -I. Directories are separated by a ":" on Unix-like systems and by a ";" on DOS/Windows systems.

-i [*extension*]

Edits ARGV files in place. For each file named in ARGV, anything you write to standard output will be saved back as the contents of that file. A backup copy of the file will be made if *extension* is supplied.

```
% ruby -pi.bak -e "gsub(/Perl/, 'Ruby')" *.txt
```

-K *kcode*

Specifies the code set to be used. This option is useful mainly when Ruby is used for Japanese-language processing. *kcode* may be one of: e, E for EUC; s, S for SJIS; u, U for UTF-8; or a, A, n, N for ASCII.

-l   Enables automatic line-ending processing; sets $\ to the value of $/ and chops every input line automatically.

-n   Assumes "while gets; ...; end" loop around your program. For example, a simple **grep** command might be implemented as:

```
% ruby -n -e "print if /wombat/" *.txt
```

-p   Places your program code within the loop "while gets; ...; print; end."

```
% ruby -p -e "$_.downcase!" *.txt
```

-r *library*

requires the named library before executing.

-S   Looks for the program file using **RUBYPATH** or **PATH** environment variable.

-s   Any command line switches found after the program filename, but before any filename arguments or before a --, are removed from **ARGV** and set to a global variable named for the switch. In the following example, the effect of this would be to set the variable $opt to "electric".

```
% ruby -s prog -opt=electric ./mydata
```

-T[*level*]

Sets the safe level, which among other things enables tainting checks (see page 257). Sets $SAFE.

-v, --verbose

Enables verbose mode and print the version number. In verbose mode, compilation warnings are printed. If no program filename appears on the command line, Ruby exits.

--version

Displays the Ruby version number and exits.

-w   Enables verbose mode. Unlike -v, reads program from standard input if no program files are present on the command line. We recommend running your Ruby programs with -w.

-X *directory*

Changes working directory to *directory* before executing. Same as -C *directory*.

-x [*directory*]

Strips off text before #!ruby line and changes working directory to *directory* if given.

-y, --yydebug
 Enables yacc debugging in the parser *(waaay too much information)*.

ARGV

Any command-line arguments after the program filename are available to your Ruby program in the global array **ARGV**. For instance, invoking Ruby as

```
% ruby -w ptest "Hello World" a1 1.6180
```

yields an **ARGV** array containing ["Hello World", a1, 1.6180]. There's a gotcha here for all you C programmers—**ARGV**[0] is the first argument to the program, not the program name. The name of the current program is available in the global variable $0.

Program Termination

The method **Kernel#exit** terminates your program, returning a status value to the operating system. However, unlike some languages, **exit** doesn't just terminate the program immediately. **Kernel#exit** first raises a **SystemExit** exception, which you may catch, and then performs a number of cleanup actions, including running any registered **at_exit** methods and object finalizers. See the reference for **Kernel#exit** beginning on page 419 for details.

Environment Variables

You can access operating system environment variables using the predefined variable ENV. It responds to the same methods as **Hash**.[2]

The values of some environment variables are read by Ruby when it first starts. These variables modify the behavior of the interpreter, as shown in Table 13.1 on the next page.

Writing to Environment Variables

A Ruby program may write to the ENV object, which on most systems changes the values of the corresponding environment variables. However, this change is local to the process that makes it and to any subsequently spawned child processes. This inheritance of environment variables is illustrated in the code that follows. A subprocess changes an environment variable and this change is seen in a process that it then starts. However,

---

2. **ENV** is not actually a hash, but if you need to, you can convert it into a **Hash** using **ENV#to_hash**.

Table 13.1. Environment variables used by Ruby

Variable Name	Description
RUBYOPT	Additional command-line options to Ruby; examined after real command-line options are parsed ($SAFE must be 0).
RUBYLIB	Additional search path for Ruby programs ($SAFE must be 0).
RUBYPATH	With -S option, search path for Ruby programs (defaults to PATH).
RUBYSHELL	Shell to use when spawning a process; if not set, will also check SHELL or COMSPEC.
DLN_LIBRARY_PATH	Search path for dynamically loaded modules.
RUBYLIB_PREFIX	(Windows only) Mangle the RUBYLIB search path by adding this prefix to each component.

the change is not visible to the original parent. (This just goes to prove that parents never really know what their children are doing.)

```
puts "In parent, term = #{ENV['TERM']}"
fork do
  puts "Start of child 1, term = #{ENV['TERM']}"
  ENV['TERM'] = "ansi"
  fork do
    puts "Start of child 2, term = #{ENV['TERM']}"
  end
  Process.wait
  puts "End of child 1, term = #{ENV['TERM']}"
end
Process.wait
puts "Back in parent, term = #{ENV['TERM']}"
```

produces:

```
In parent, term = xterm
Start of child 1, term = xterm
Start of child 2, term = ansi
End of child 1, term = ansi
Back in parent, term = xterm
```

Where Ruby Finds Its Modules

You use **require** or **load** to bring a library module into your Ruby program. Some of these modules are supplied with Ruby, some you installed off the Ruby Application Archive, and some you wrote yourself. How does Ruby find them?

When Ruby is built for your particular machine, it predefines a set of standard directories to hold library stuff. Where these are depends on the machine in question. You can determine this from the command line with something like:

```
% ruby -e 'puts $:.join("\n")'
```

On a typical Linux box, you'll probably find something such as:

```
/usr/local/lib/ruby/site_ruby/1.6/i686-linux
/usr/local/lib/ruby/site_ruby/1.6
/usr/local/lib/ruby/site_ruby
/usr/local/lib/ruby/1.6/i686-linux
/usr/local/lib/ruby/1.6
.
```

The `site_ruby` directories are intended to hold modules and extensions that you've added. The architecture-dependent directories (`i686-linux` in this case) hold executables and other things specific to this particular machine. All these directories are automatically included in Ruby's search for modules.

Sometimes this isn't enough. Perhaps you're working on a large project written in Ruby, and you and your colleagues have built a substantial library of Ruby code. You want everyone on the team to have access to all of this code. You have a couple of options to accomplish this. If your program runs at a safe level of zero (see Chapter 20 beginning on page 257), you can set the environment variable `RUBYLIB` to a list of one or more directories to be searched.[3] If your program is not *setuid*, you can use the command-line parameter `-I` to do the same thing.

Finally, the Ruby variable `$:` is an array of places to search for loaded files. This variable is initialized to the list of standard directories, plus any additional ones you specified using `RUBYLIB` and `-I`. You can always add additional directories to this array from within your running program.

Build Environment

When Ruby is compiled for a particular architecture, all of the relevant settings used to build it (including the architecture of the machine on which it was compiled, compiler options, source code directory, and so on) are written to the module `Config` within the library file "`rbconfig.rb`". After installation, any Ruby program can use this module to get details on how Ruby was compiled.

---

3.   The separator between entries depends on your platform. For Windows, it's a semicolon; for Unix, a colon.

```
require "rbconfig.rb"
include Config
CONFIG["host"]      →    "i686-pc-linux"
CONFIG["LDFLAGS"]   →    "-rdynamic"
```

Extension libraries use this configuration file in order to compile and link properly on any given architecture. See Chapter 17 beginning on page 171, and the reference for mkmf beginning on page 455 for details.

## Chapter 14

Ruby and the Web

Ruby is no stranger to the Internet. Not only can you write your own SMTP server, FTP daemon, or Web server in Ruby, but you can also use Ruby for more usual tasks such as CGI programming or as a replacement for PHP.

Writing CGI Scripts

You can use Ruby to write CGI scripts quite easily. To have a Ruby script generate HTML output, all you need is

```
#!/usr/bin/env ruby
print "HTTP/1.0 200 OK\r\n"
print "Content-type: text/html\r\n\r\n"
print "<html><body>Hello World!</body></html>\r\n"
```

You *could* use Ruby's regular expression features to parse incoming query strings, look up environment variables, check tags, substitute text into templates, escape special characters, format up the HTML, and print it all out.

Or, you could use class CGI.

Using cgi.rb

Class CGI provides support for writing CGI scripts. With it, you can manipulate forms, cookies, and the environment, maintain stateful sessions, and so on. It's documented in full in the reference section beginning on page 501, but we'll take a quick look at its capabilities here.

Quoting

When dealing with URLs and HTML code, you must be careful to quote certain characters. For instance, a slash character ("/") has special meaning in a URL, so it must be "escaped" if it's not part of the path name. That is, any "/" in the query portion of the URL will be translated to the string "%2F" and must be translated back to a "/" for you to use it. Space and ampersand are also special characters. To handle this, CGI provides the routines CGI.escape and CGI.unescape:

```
require 'cgi'
puts CGI.escape( "Nicholas Payton/Trumpet & Flugel Horn" )
```

produces:

```
Nicholas+Payton%2FTrumpet+%26+Flugel+Horn
```

Similarly, you may want to escape HTML special characters:

```
require 'cgi'
puts CGI.escapeHTML( '<a href="/mp3">Click Here</a>' )
```

produces:

```
&lt;a href=&quot;/mp3&quot;&gt;Click Here&lt;/a&gt;
```

To get really fancy, you can decide to escape only certain elements within a string:

```
require 'cgi'
puts CGI.escapeElement('<hr><a href="/mp3">Click Here</a><br>','A')
```

produces:

```
<hr>&lt;a href=&quot;/mp3&quot;&gt;Click Here&lt;/a&gt;<br>
```

Here only the "A" tag is escaped; other tags are left alone. Each of these methods has an "un-" version to restore the original string.

Forms

Using class CGI gives you access to HTML query parameters in two ways. Suppose we are given a URL of /cgi-bin/lookup?player=Miles%20Davis&year=1958. You can access the parameters "player" and "year" using CGI#[] directly:

```
require 'cgi'
cgi = CGI.new
cgi['player']   →   ["Miles Davis"]
cgi['year']     →   ["1958"]
```

Or, you can retrieve all parameters as a Hash:

```
require 'cgi'
cgi = CGI.new
h = cgi.params
h['player']   →   ["Miles Davis"]
```

Creating Forms and HTML

`CGI` contains a huge number of methods used to create HTML—one method per tag. In order to enable these methods, you must create a `CGI` object by calling `CGI.new`, passing in the required level of HTML. For these examples, we'll use "`html3`".

To make tag nesting easier, these methods take their content as code blocks. The code blocks should return a `String`, which will be used as the content for the tag. For this example, we've added some gratuitous newlines to make the output fit on the page.

```
require "cgi"
cgi = CGI.new("html3")   # add HTML generation methods
cgi.out{
  cgi.html{
    cgi.head{ "\n"+cgi.title{"This Is a Test"} } +
    cgi.body{ "\n"+
      cgi.form{"\n"+
        cgi.hr +
        cgi.h1 { "A Form: " } + "\n"+
        cgi.textarea("get_text") +"\n"+
        cgi.br +
        cgi.submit
      }
    }
  }
}
```

produces:

```
Content-Type: text/html
Content-Length: 302

<!DOCTYPE HTML PUBLIC "-//W3C//DTD HTML 3.2 Final//EN"><HTML><HEAD>
<TITLE>This Is a Test</TITLE></HEAD><BODY>
<FORM METHOD="post" ENCTYPE="application/x-www-form-urlencoded">
<HR><H1>A Form: </H1>
<TEXTAREA COLS="70" NAME="get_text" ROWS="10"></TEXTAREA>
<BR><INPUT TYPE="submit"></FORM></BODY></HTML>
```

This code will produce an HTML form titled "This Is a Test," followed by a horizontal rule, a level-one header, a test input area, and finally a submit button. When the submit comes back, you'll have a CGI parameter named "`get_text`" containing the text the user entered.

Cookies

You can store all kinds of interesting stuff on an unsuspecting surfer's machine using *cookies*. You can create a named cookie object and store a number of values in it. To send it down to the browser, set a "cookie" header in the call to `CGI#out`.

```
require "cgi"
cookie = CGI::Cookie.new("rubyweb", "CustID=123", "Part=ABC");
cgi = CGI.new("html3")
cgi.out( "cookie" => [cookie] ){
  cgi.html{
    "\nHTML content here"
  }
}
```

produces:

```
Content-Type: text/html
Content-Length: 86
Set-Cookie: rubyweb=CustID%3D123&Part%3DABC; path=

<!DOCTYPE HTML PUBLIC "-//W3C//DTD HTML 3.2 Final//EN"><HTML>
HTML content here</HTML>
```

The next time the user comes back to this page, you can retrieve the cookie values for CustID and Part, as shown in the HTML output.

```
require "cgi"
cgi = CGI.new("html3")
cgi.out{
  cgi.html{
    cgi.pre{
      cookie = cgi.cookies["rubyweb"]
        "\nCookies are\n" + cookie.value.join("\n")
    }
  }
}
```

produces:

```
Content-Type: text/html
Content-Length: 111

<!DOCTYPE HTML PUBLIC "-//W3C//DTD HTML 3.2 Final//EN"><HTML><PRE>
Cookies are
CustID=123
Part=ABC</PRE></HTML>
```

Sessions

Cookies by themselves still need a bit of work to be useful. What we really want is a *session:* a persistent state for some Web surfer. Sessions are handled with CGI::Session (documented beginning on page 508), which uses cookies but provides a higher-level abstraction.

```
require "cgi"
require "cgi/session"
```

```
cgi = CGI.new("html3")
sess = CGI::Session.new( cgi, "session_key" => "rubyweb",
                              "session_id"  => "9650",
                              "new_session" => true,
                              "prefix" => "web-session.")
sess["CustID"] = 123
sess["Part"] = "ABC"

cgi.out{
  cgi.html{
    "\nHTML content here"
  }
}
```

This will send a cookie to the user named "rubyweb" with a value of 9650. It will also create a disk file in $TMP/web-session.9650 with the *key, value* pairs for CustID and Part.

When the user returns, all you need is a parameter to indicate the session id. In this example, that would be rubyweb=9650. With that value in the parameters, you'll be able to retrieve the full set of saved session data.

```
require "cgi"
require "cgi/session"

cgi = CGI.new("html3")
sess = CGI::Session.new( cgi, "session_key" => "rubyweb",
                              "prefix" => "web-session.")
cgi.out{
  cgi.html{
    "\nCustomer #{sess['CustID']} orders an #{sess['Part']}"
  }
}
```

Embedding Ruby in HTML

So far we've looked at using Ruby to create HTML output, but we can turn the problem inside out; we can actually embed Ruby in an HTML document.

There are a number of packages that allow you to embed Ruby statements in some other sort of a document, especially in an HTML page. Generically, this is known as "eRuby." Specifically, there are several different implementations of eRuby, including eruby and erb. The remainder of this section will discuss eruby, written by Shugo Maeda.

Embedding Ruby in HTML is a very powerful concept—it basically gives us the equivalent of a tool such as ASP, JSP, or PHP, but with the full power of Ruby.

Using eruby

eruby acts as a filter, plain and simple. Any text within the input file is passed through untouched, with the following exceptions:

Expression	Description
<% *ruby code* %>	The Ruby code between the delimiters is replaced with its output.
<%= *ruby expression* %>	The Ruby expression between the delimiters is replaced with its value.
<%# *ruby code* %>	The Ruby code between the delimiters is ignored (useful for testing).

You invoke eruby as:

```
eruby [ options ] [ document ]
```

If the *document* is omitted, eruby will read from standard input. The command-line options for eruby are shown in Table 14.1 on the next page.

Let's look at some simple examples. We'll run the eruby executable on the following input.

```
This text is <% a = 100; puts "#{a}% Live!" %>
```

eruby substitutes the expression between the delimiters and produces

```
This text is 100% Live!
```

Using the <%= form acts as if you printed the value of the expression. For instance, the input

```
<%a = 100%>This text is almost <%=a%> degrees! Cool!
```

replaces the =a with the value of a.

```
This text is almost 100 degrees! Cool!
```

And, of course, you can embed Ruby within a more complex document type, such as HTML.

```
<!DOCTYPE HTML PUBLIC "-//W3C//DTD HTML 4.01//EN">
<html>
<head>
<title>eruby example</title>
</head>
<body>
<h1>Enumeration</h1>
<ul>
<%(1..10).each do|i|%>
```

Table 14.1. Command-line options for `eruby`

Option	Description
-d, --debug	Sets $DEBUG to `true`.
-K*kcode*	Specifies an alternate coding system (see page 139).
-M*mode*	Specifies runtime *mode*, one of:
	f filter mode
	c CGI mode (prints errors as HTML, sets $SAFE=1)
	n NPH-CGI mode (prints extra HTTP headers, sets $SAFE=1)
-n, --noheader	Disables CGI header output.
-v, --verbose	Enables verbose mode.
--version	Prints version information and exits.

```
    <li>number <%=i%></li>
<%end%>
</ul>
<h1>Environment variables</h1>
<table>
<%ENV.keys.sort.each do |key|%>
  <tr>
    <th><%=key%></th><td><%=ENV[key]%></td>
  </tr>
<%end%>
</table>
</body>
</html>
```

Installing eruby in Apache

You can set up an Apache Web server to automatically parse Ruby-embedded documents using eRuby, much in the same way that PHP does. You create Ruby-embedded files with an ".rhtml" suffix and configure the Web server to run the `eruby` executable on these documents to produce the desired HTML output.

In order to use `eruby` with the Apache Web server, you need to perform the following steps.

- Copy the `eruby` binary to the `cgi-bin` directory.

- Add the following two lines to `httpd.conf`:

    ```
    AddType application/x-httpd-eruby .rhtml
    Action application/x-httpd-eruby /cgi-bin/eruby
    ```

- If desired, you can also add or replace the `DirectoryIndex` directive such that it includes `index.rhtml`. This lets you use Ruby to create directory listings for directories that do not contain an `index.html`. For instance, the following directive would cause the embedded Ruby script `index.rhtml` to be searched for and served if neither `index.html` nor `index.shtml` existed in a directory.

```
DirectoryIndex index.html index.shtml index.rhtml
```

Of course, you could also simply use a site-wide Ruby script as well.

```
DirectoryIndex index.html index.shtml /cgi-bin/index.rb
```

And that's it! You can now write HTML documents that contain embedded Ruby to generate forms and content dynamically. Be sure to see also the Ruby `CGI` library, which is documented beginning on page 501.

Improving Performance

You can use Ruby to write CGI programs for the Web, but, as with most CGI programs, the default configuration has to start up a new copy of Ruby with every cgi-bin page access. That's expensive in terms of machine utilization and can be painfully slow for Web surfers. The Apache Web server solves this problem by allowing loadable *modules.*

Typically, these modules are dynamically loaded and become part of the running Web server process—there is no need to spawn another interpreter over and over again to service requests; the Web server *is* the interpreter.

And so we come to `mod_ruby` (available from the archives), an Apache module that links a full Ruby interpreter into the Apache Web server itself. The `README` file included with `mod_ruby` provides details on how to compile and install it.

Once installed and configured, you can run Ruby scripts just like you could without `mod_ruby`, except that now they will come up much faster.

## Chapter 15

Ruby Tk

The Ruby Application Archive contains several extensions that provide Ruby with a graphical user interface (GUI), including extensions for Tcl/Tk, GTK, OpenGL, and others.

The Tk extension is bundled in the main distribution and works on both Unix and Windows systems. To use it, you need to have Tk installed on your system. Tk is a large system, and entire books have been written about it, so we won't waste time or resources by delving too deeply into Tk itself, but instead concentrate on how to access Tk features from Ruby. You'll need one of these reference books in order to use Tk with Ruby effectively. The binding we use is closest to the Perl binding, so you probably want to get a copy of *Learning Perl/Tk* [Wal99] or *Perl/Tk Pocket Reference* [Lid98].

Tk works along a composition model—that is, you start off by creating a container widget (such as a `TkFrame` or `TkRoot`) and then create the widgets that populate it, such as buttons or labels. When you are ready to start the GUI, you invoke `Tk.mainloop`. The Tk engine then takes control of the program, displaying widgets and calling your code in response to GUI events.

Simple Tk Application

A simple Tk application in Ruby might look something like this:

```
require 'tk'
root = TkRoot.new { title "Ex1" }
TkLabel.new(root) {
  text 'Hello, World!'
  pack  { padx 15 ; pady 15; side 'left' }
}
Tk.mainloop
```

Let's look at the code a little more closely. After loading in the `tk` extension module, we create a root-level frame using `TkRoot.new`. We then make a label widget as a child of the root frame, setting several options for the label. Finally, we pack the root frame and enter the main GUI event loop.

It's a good habit to specify the root explicitly, but you could leave it out—along with the extra options—and boil this down to a three-liner:

```
require 'tk'
TkLabel.new { text 'Hello, World!' }
Tk.mainloop
```

That's all there is to it! Armed with one of the Perl/Tk books we reference at the start of this chapter, you can now produce all the sophisticated GUIs you need. But then again, if you'd like to stick around for some more details, here they come.

Widgets

Creating widgets is easy. Take the name of the widget as given in the Tk documentation and add a **Tk** to the front of it. For instance, the widgets Label, Button, and Entry become the classes **TkLabel**, **TkButton**, and **TkEntry**. You create an instance of a widget using **new**, just as you would any other object. If you don't specify a parent for a given widget, it will default to the root-level frame. We usually want to specify the parent of a given widget, along with many other options—color, size, and so on. We also need to be able to get information back from our widgets while our program is running by setting up callbacks and sharing data.

Setting Widget Options

If you look at a Tk reference manual (the one written for Perl/Tk, for example), you'll notice that options for widgets are usually listed with a hyphen—as a command-line option might be. In Perl/Tk, options are passed to a widget in a **Hash**. You can do that in Ruby as well, but you can also pass options using a code block; the name of the option is used as a method name within the block and arguments to the option appear as arguments to the method call. Widgets take a parent as the first argument, followed by an optional hash of options or the code block of options. Thus, the following two forms are equivalent.

```
TkLabel.new(parent_widget) {
  text     'Hello, World!'
  pack('padx'  => 5,
       'pady'  => 5,
       'side'  => 'left')
}
# or
TkLabel.new(parent_widget, text => 'Hello, World!').pack(...)
```

One small caution when using the code block form: the scope of variables is not what you think it is. The block is actually evaluated in the context of the widget's object, not the caller's. This means that the caller's instance variables will not be available in the block, but local variables from the enclosing scope and globals (not that you ever use *those*) will be. We'll show option passing using both methods in the examples that follow.

Distances (as in the `padx` and `pady` options in these examples) are assumed to be in pixels, but may be specified in different units using one of the suffixes "`c`" (centimeter), "`i`" (inch), "`m`" (millimeter), or "`p`" (point).

Getting Widget Data

We can get information back from widgets with callbacks and by binding variables.

Callbacks are very easy to set up. The `command` option (shown in the `TkButton` call in the example that follows) takes a `Proc` object, which will be called when the callback fires. Here we use `Kernel.proc` to convert the `{exit}` block to a `Proc`.

```
TkButton.new(bottom) {
  text "Ok"
  command proc { p mycheck.value; exit }
  pack('side'=>'left', 'padx'=>10, 'pady'=>10)
}
```

We can also bind a Ruby variable to a Tk widget's value using a `TkVariable` proxy. We show this in the following example. Notice how the `TkCheckButton` is set up; the documentation says that the `variable` option takes a *var reference* as an argument. For this, we create a Tk variable reference using `TkVariable.new`. Accessing `mycheck.value` will return the string "0" or "1" depending on whether the checkbox is checked. You can use the same mechanism for anything that supports a var reference, such as radio buttons and text fields.

```
mycheck = TkVariable.new

TkCheckButton.new(top) {
  variable mycheck
  pack('padx'=>5, 'pady'=>5, 'side' => 'left')
}
```

Setting/Getting Options Dynamically

In addition to setting a widget's options when it's created, you can reconfigure a widget while it's running. Every widget supports the `configure` method, which takes a `Hash` or a code block in the same manner as `new`. We can modify the first example to change the label text in response to a button press:

```
lbl = TkLabel.new(top) { justify 'center'
  text     'Hello, World!';
  pack('padx'=>5, 'pady'=>5, 'side' => 'top') }
TkButton.new(top) {
  text "Cancel"
  command proc { lbl.configure('text'=>"Goodbye, Cruel World!") }
  pack('side'=>'right', 'padx'=>10, 'pady'=>10)
}
```

Now when the Cancel button is pressed, the text in the label will change immediately from "Hello, World!" to "Goodbye, Cruel World!"

You can also query widgets for particular option values using cget:

```
require 'tk'
b = TkButton.new {
  text     "OK"
  justify  'left'
  border   5
}
b.cget('text')     →    "OK"
b.cget('justify')  →    "left"
b.cget('border')   →    5
```

Sample Application

Here's a slightly longer example, showing a genuine application—a "pig Latin" generator. Type in the phrase such as "Ruby rules," and the "Pig It" button will instantly translate it into pig Latin.

```
require 'tk'

class PigBox
  def pig(word)
    leadingCap = word =~ /^[A-Z]/
    word.downcase
    res = case word
      when /^[aeiouy]/
        word+"way"
      when /^([^aeiouy]+)(.*)/
        $2+$1+"ay"
      else
        word
    end
    leadingCap ? res.capitalize : res
  end

  def showPig
    @text.value = @text.value.split.collect{|w| pig(w)}.join(" ")
  end
```

```
    def initialize
      ph = { 'padx' => 10, 'pady' => 10 }      # common options
      p = proc {showPig}

      @text = TkVariable.new
      root = TkRoot.new { title "Pig" }
      top = TkFrame.new(root)
      TkLabel.new(top) {text    'Enter Text:' ; pack(ph) }
      @entry = TkEntry.new(top, 'textvariable' => @text)
      @entry.pack(ph)
      TkButton.new(top) {text 'Pig It'; command p; pack ph}
      TkButton.new(top) {text 'Exit'; command {proc exit}; pack ph}
      top.pack('fill'=>'both', 'side' =>'top')
    end
  end

  PigBox.new
  Tk.mainloop
```

Binding Events

Our widgets are exposed to the real world; they get clicked on, the mouse moves over them, the user tabs into them; all these things, and more, generate *events* that we can capture. You can create a *binding* from an event on a particular widget to a block of code, using the widget's **bind** method.

For instance, suppose we've created a button widget that displays an image. We'd like the image to change when the user's mouse is over the button.

```
  image1 = TkPhotoImage.new { file "img1.gif" }
  image2 = TkPhotoImage.new { file "img2.gif" }

  b = TkButton.new(@root) {
    image      image1
    command  proc { doit }
  }

  b.bind("Enter") { b.configure('image'=>image2) }
  b.bind("Leave") { b.configure('image'=>image1) }
```

First, we create two GIF image objects from files on disk, using **TkPhotoImage**. Next we create a button (very cleverly named "b"), which displays the image **image1**. We then bind the "Enter" event so that it dynamically changes the image displayed by the button to **image2**, and the "Leave" event to revert back to **image1**.

This example shows the simple events "Enter" and "Leave." But the named event given as an argument to **bind** can be composed of several substrings, separated with dashes, in the order *modifier-modifier-type-detail*. Modifiers are listed in the Tk reference and include **Button1**, **Control**, **Alt**, **Shift**, and so on. *Type* is the name of the event

---

Geometry Management

In the example code in this chapter, you'll see references to the widget method `pack`. That's a very important call, as it turns out—leave it off and you'll never see the widget. `pack` is a command that tells the geometry manager to place the widget according to constraints that we specify. Geometry managers recognize three commands:

Command	Placement Specification
pack	Flexible, constraint-based placement
place	Absolute position
grid	Tabular (row/column) position

As `pack` is the most commonly used command, we'll use it in our examples.

(taken from the X11 naming conventions) and includes events such as **ButtonPress**, **KeyPress**, and **Expose**. *Detail* is either a number from 1 to 5 for buttons or a keysym for keyboard input. For instance, a binding that will trigger on mouse release of button 1 while the control key is pressed could be specified as:

```
Control-Button1-ButtonRelease
```
or
```
Control-ButtonRelease-1
```

The event itself can contain certain fields such as the time of the event and the x and y positions. `bind` can pass these items to the callback, using *event field codes*. These are used like `printf` specifications. For instance, to get the x and y coordinates on a mouse move, you'd specify the call to `bind` with three parameters. The second parameter is the `Proc` for the callback, and the third parameter is the event field string.

```
canvas.bind("Motion", proc{|x, y| do_motion (x, y)}, "%x %y")
```

Canvas

Tk provides a *Canvas* widget with which you can draw and produce PostScript output. Here's a simple bit of code (adapted from the distribution) that will draw straight lines. Clicking and holding button 1 will start a line, which will be "rubber-banded" as you move the mouse around. When you release button 1, the line will be drawn in that position. Pressing button 2 on the mouse will dump out a PostScript representation of the drawing canvas, suitable for printing.

```ruby
require 'tk'

class Draw
  def do_press(x, y)
    @start_x = x
    @start_y = y
    @current_line = TkcLine.new(@canvas, x, y, x, y)
  end
  def do_motion(x, y)
    if @current_line
      @current_line.coords @start_x, @start_y, x, y
    end
  end
  def do_release(x, y)
    if @current_line
      @current_line.coords @start_x, @start_y, x, y
      @current_line.fill 'black'
      @current_line = nil
    end
  end
  def initialize(parent)
    @canvas = TkCanvas.new(parent)
    @canvas.pack
    @start_x = @start_y = 0
    @canvas.bind("1", proc{|e| do_press(e.x, e.y)})
    @canvas.bind("2", proc{ puts @canvas.postscript({}) })
    @canvas.bind("B1-Motion", proc{|x, y| do_motion(x, y)}, "%x %y")
    @canvas.bind("ButtonRelease-1",
                 proc{|x, y| do_release (x, y)}, "%x %y")
  end
end


root = TkRoot.new{ title 'Canvas' }
Draw.new(root)
Tk.mainloop
```

A few mouse clicks, and you've got an instant masterpiece:

"We couldn't find the artist, so we had to hang the picture...."

Scrolling

Unless you plan on drawing very small pictures, the previous example may not be all that useful. TkCanvas, TkListbox, and TkText can be set up to use scrollbars, so you can work on a smaller subset of the "big picture."

Communication between a scrollbar and a widget is bidirectional. Moving the scrollbar means that the widget's view has to change; but when the widget's view is changed by some other means, the scrollbar has to change as well to reflect the new position.

Since we haven't done much with lists yet, our scrolling example will use a scrolling list of text. In the following code fragment, we'll start off by creating a plain old TkListbox. Then, we'll make a TkScrollbar. The scrollbar's callback (set with command) will call the list widget's yview method, which will change the value of the visible portion of the list in the *y*-direction.

After that callback is set up, we make the inverse association: when the list feels the need to scroll, we'll set the appropriate range in the scrollbar using TkScrollbar#set. We'll use this same fragment in a fully functional program in the next section.

```
list_w = TkListbox.new(frame, 'selectmode' => 'single')

scroll_bar = TkScrollbar.new(frame,
                  'command' => proc { |*args| list_w.yview *args })

scroll_bar.pack('side' => 'left', 'fill' => 'y')

list_w.yscrollcommand(proc { |first,last|
                             scroll_bar.set(first,last) })
```

Just One More Thing

We could go on about Tk for another few hundred pages, but that's another book. The following program is our final Tk example—a simple GIF image viewer. You can select a GIF filename from the scrolling list, and a thumb nail version of the image will be displayed. There are just a *few* more things we'd like to point out.

Have you ever seen an application that creates a "busy cursor" and then forgets to reset it to normal? There's a neat trick in Ruby that will prevent this from happening. Remember how File.new uses a block to ensure that the file is closed after it is used? We can do a similar thing with the method busy, as shown in the next example.

This program also demonstrates some simple TkListbox manipulations—adding elements to the list, setting up a callback on a mouse button release,[1] and retrieving the current selection.

---

1.   You probably want the button release, not the press, as the widget gets selected on the button press.

So far, we've used `TkPhotoImage` to only display icons directly, but you can also zoom, subsample, and show portions of images as well. Here we use the subsample feature to scale down the image for viewing.

```ruby
require 'tk'

def busy
  begin
    $root.cursor "watch" # Set a watch cursor
    $root.update # Make sure it updates  the screen
    yield # Call the associated block
  ensure
    $root.cursor "" # Back to original
    $root.update
  end
end

$root = TkRoot.new {title 'Scroll List'}
frame = TkFrame.new($root)

list_w = TkListbox.new(frame, 'selectmode' => 'single')

scroll_bar = TkScrollbar.new(frame,
                    'command' => proc { |*args| list_w.yview *args })

scroll_bar.pack('side' => 'left', 'fill' => 'y')

list_w.yscrollcommand(proc { |first,last|
                            scroll_bar.set(first,last) })
list_w.pack('side'=>'left')

image_w = TkPhotoImage.new
TkLabel.new(frame, 'image' => image_w).pack('side'=>'left')
frame.pack

list_contents = Dir["screenshots/gifs/*.gif"]
list_contents.each {|x|
  list_w.insert('end',x) # Insert each file name into the list
}
list_w.bind("ButtonRelease-1") {
  index = list_w.curselection[0]
  busy {
    tmp_img = TkPhotoImage.new('file'=> list_contents[index])
    scale   = tmp_img.height / 100
    scale   = 1 if scale < 1
    image_w.copy(tmp_img, 'subsample' => [scale,scale])
    tmp_img = nil # Be sure to remove it, the
    GC.start      # image may have been large
  }
}

Tk.mainloop
```

Finally, a word about garbage collection—we happened to have a few very large GIF files lying about[2] while testing this code. We didn't want to carry these huge images around in memory any longer then necessary, so we set the image reference to `nil` and call the garbage collector immediately to remove the trash.

Translating from Perl/Tk Documentation

That's it, you're on your own now. For the most part, you can easily translate the documentation given for Perl/Tk to Ruby. But there are a few exceptions; some methods are not implemented, and there is undocumented extra functionality. Until a Ruby/Tk book comes out, your best bet is to ask on the newsgroup or read the source code.

But in general, it's pretty easy to see what's going on. Remember that options may be given as a hash, or in code block style, and the scope of the code block is within the `TkWidget` being used, not your class instance.

Object Creation

```
Perl/Tk:  $widget = $parent->Widget( [ option => value ] )
Ruby:     widget = TkWidget.new(parent, option-hash)
          widget = TkWidget.new(parent) { code block }
```

You may not need to save the returned value of the newly created widget, but it's there if you do. Don't forget to pack a widget (or use one of the other geometry calls), or it won't show up.

Options

```
Perl/Tk:  -background => color
Ruby:     'background' => color
          { background color }
```

Remember that the code block scope is different.

Variable References

```
Perl/Tk:  -textvariable => \$variable
          -textvariable => varRef
Ruby:     ref = TkVariable.new
          'textvariable' => ref
          { textvariable ref }
```

---

2. They were technical documents! Really!

Use **TkVariable** to attach a Ruby variable to a widget's value. You can then use the **value** accessors in **TkVariable** (**TkVariable#value** and **TkVariable#value=**) to affect the contents of the widget directly.

## Chapter 16

Ruby and Microsoft Windows

Ruby is written for POSIX environments, which means that it can take advantage of all of the system calls and libraries that Unix programmers are familiar with.

But there are a number of features and extensions designed to make Ruby more useful in a Microsoft Windows environment, too. In this chapter, we'll look at these features and share some secrets to using Ruby effectively under Windows.

Ruby Ports

Windows does not provide a POSIX environment by itself, so some sort of emulation library is required in order to provide the necessary functions. There are several ports of Ruby for Windows: the most commonly used one relies on the GNU Win32 environment, and is called the "cygwin32" port. The cygwin32 port works well with extension libraries, and is available on the Web as a precompiled binary. Another port, "mswin32," does not rely on cygwin. It is currently available as source code only. The remainder of this chapter will refer to the cygwin32 port.

Running Ruby Under Windows

There are two executables provided with the cygwin32 Ruby distribution: `ruby.exe` and `rubyw.exe`.

`ruby.exe` is meant to be used at a command prompt (a DOS shell), just as in the Unix version. For applications that read and write to the standard input and output, this is fine. But that also means that anytime you run `ruby.exe`, you'll get a DOS shell even if you don't want one—Windows will create a new command prompt window and display it while Ruby is running. This might not be appropriate behavior if, for example, you double-click on a Ruby script that uses a graphical interface (such as Tk), or if you are running a Ruby script as a background task, or from inside another program.

In these cases, you'll want to use `rubyw.exe`. It is the same as `ruby.exe` except that it does not provide standard in, standard out, or standard error, and does not launch a DOS shell when run.

You can set a file association[1] so that files with the extension ".rb" will automatically use `rubyw.exe`. By doing this, you can double-click on Ruby scripts and they will simply run without popping up a DOS shell.

Win32API

If you plan on doing Ruby programming that needs to access some Windows 32 API functions directly, or to use the entry points in some other DLLs, we've got good news for you—the `Win32API` extension.

The `Win32API` module is documented beginning on page 512, but here's a quick peek at how it works.

You create a `Win32API` object that represents a call to a particular DLL entry point by specifying the name of the function, the name of the DLL that contains the function, and the function signature (argument types and return type). The resulting object can then be used to make the function call.

Many of the arguments to DLL functions are binary structures of some form. `Win32API` handles this by using Ruby `String` objects to pass the binary data back and forth. You will need to pack and unpack these strings as necessary (see the example on page 512).

Windows Automation

If groveling around in the low-level Windows API doesn't interest you, Windows automation might—you can use Ruby as a client for Windows Automation thanks to a Ruby extension called `WIN32OLE`, written by Masaki Suketa. The examples in this section are taken from those provided in the `WIN32OLE` distribution.

Windows automation allows an automation controller (a client) to issue commands and queries against an automation server, such as Microsoft Excel, Word, PowerPoint, and so on.

You can execute a method of an automation server by calling a method of the same name from a `WIN32OLE` object. For instance, you can create a new `WIN32OLE` client that launches a fresh copy of Internet Explorer and commands it to visit the home page.

---

1. Using `View/Options/File types` from Explorer.

```
ie = WIN32OLE.new('InternetExplorer.Application')
ie.visible = true
ie.gohome
```

Methods that aren't known to `WIN32OLE` (such as `visible` or `gohome`) are passed on to the `WIN32OLE#invoke` method, which sends the proper commands to the server. The `WIN32OLE` reference beginning on page 509 describes the class in detail, but we'll go over a few of its features here.

Getting and Setting Properties

You can set and get *properties* from the server using normal Ruby hash notation. For example, to set the `Rotation` property in an Excel chart, you might write

```
excel = WIN32OLE.new("excel.application")
excelchart = excel.Charts.Add()
...
excelchart['Rotation'] = 45
puts excelchart['Rotation']
```

An OLE object's parameters are automatically set up as attributes of the `WIN32OLE` object. This means that you can set a parameter by assigning to an object attribute.

```
excelchart.rotation = 45
r = excelchart.rotation
```

Because these attributes are conventional Ruby accessor methods, attribute names cannot start with a capital letter. In this example, we have to use `rotation` instead of `Rotation`.

Named Arguments

Other automation client languages such as Visual Basic have the concept of *named arguments*. Suppose you had a Visual Basic routine with the signature:

```
Song(artist, title, length):    rem Visual Basic
```

Instead of calling it with all three arguments in the order specified, you could use named arguments.

```
Song title := 'Get It On':    rem Visual Basic
```

This is equivalent to the call `Song(nil, 'Get It On', nil)`.

In Ruby, you can use this feature by passing a hash with the named arguments.

```
Song.new( 'title' => 'Get It On' )
```

for each

Where Visual Basic has a "for each" statement to iterate over a collection of items in a server, a WIN32OLE object has an **each** method (which takes a block) to accomplish the same thing.

An Example

The following example, using Microsoft Excel, illustrates most of these concepts. First, we create a new WIN32OLE object attached to Excel and set some cell values. Next we select a range of cells and create a chart. We set the Type property in the excelchart object to make it a 3D chart. Next we'll loop through and change the chart rotation, 10° at a time. We'll add a few charts, and we'll use **each** to step through and print them out. Finally, we'll close down the Excel application and exit.

```ruby
require 'win32ole'

# -4100 is the value for the Excel constant xl3DColumn.
ChartTypeVal = -4100;

# Creates OLE object to Excel
excel = WIN32OLE.new("excel.application")

# Create and rotate the chart

excel['Visible'] = TRUE;
workbook = excel.Workbooks.Add();
excel.Range("a1")['Value'] = 3;
excel.Range("a2")['Value'] = 2;
excel.Range("a3")['Value'] = 1;
excel.Range("a1:a3").Select();
excelchart = workbook.Charts.Add();
excelchart['Type'] = ChartTypeVal;

30.step(180, 10) do |rot|
    excelchart['Rotation'] = rot
end

excelchart2 = workbook.Charts.Add();
excelchart3 = workbook.Charts.Add();

charts = workbook.Charts
charts.each { |i| puts i }

excel.ActiveWorkbook.Close(0);
excel.Quit();
```

Optimizing

As with most (if not all) high-level languages, it can be all too easy to churn out code that is unbearably slow, but that can be easily fixed with a little thought.

With WIN32OLE, you need to be careful with unnecessary dynamic lookups. Where possible, it is better to assign a WIN32OLE object to a variable and then reference elements from it, rather than creating a long chain of "." expressions.

For example, instead of writing

```
workbook.Worksheets(1).Range("A1").value = 1
workbook.Worksheets(1).Range("A2").value = 2
workbook.Worksheets(1).Range("A3").value = 4
workbook.Worksheets(1).Range("A4").value = 8
```

we can eliminate the common subexpressions by saving the first part of the expression to a temporary variable and then make calls from that variable:

```
worksheet = workbook.Worksheets(1)

worksheet.Range("A1").value = 1
worksheet.Range("A2").value = 2
worksheet.Range("A3").value = 4
worksheet.Range("A4").value = 8
```

## Chapter 17

Extending Ruby

It is easy to extend Ruby with new features by writing code in Ruby. Once you start adding in low-level code written in C, however, the possibilities are endless.

Extending Ruby with C is pretty easy. For instance, suppose we are building a custom Internet-ready jukebox for the Sunset Diner and Grill. It will play MP3 audio files from a hard disk or audio CDs from a CD jukebox. We want to be able to control the jukebox hardware from a Ruby program. The hardware vendor gave us a C header file and a binary library to use; our job is to construct a Ruby object that makes the appropriate C function calls.

But before we can get Ruby and C to work together, we need to see what the Ruby world looks like from the C side.[1]

Ruby Objects in C

The first thing we need to look at is how to represent and access Ruby datatypes from within C. Everything in Ruby is an object, and all variables are references to objects. In C, this means that the type of all Ruby variables is **VALUE**, which is either a pointer to a Ruby object or an immediate value (such as **Fixnum**).

This is how Ruby implements object-oriented code in C: a Ruby object is an allocated structure in memory that contains a table of instance variables and information about the class. The class itself is another object (an allocated structure in memory) that contains a table of the methods defined for that class. On this foundation hangs all of Ruby.

---

1. Much of the information in this chapter is taken from the **README.EXT** file that is included in the distribution. If you are planning on writing a Ruby extension, you may want to refer to that file for more details as well as the latest changes.

VALUE as a Pointer

When VALUE is a pointer, it is a pointer to one of the defined Ruby object structures—
you can't have a VALUE that points to an arbitrary structure. The structures for each
built-in class are defined in "ruby.h" and are named R*Classname*, as in RString and
RArray.

You can check to see what type of structure is used for a particular VALUE in a number
of ways. The macro TYPE(*obj*) will return a constant representing the C type of the
given object: T_OBJECT, T_STRING, and so on. Constants for the built-in classes are
defined in "ruby.h". Note that the *type* we are referring to here is an implementation
detail—it is not the same as the class of an object.

If you want to ensure that a value pointer points to a particular structure, you can use
the macro Check_Type, which will raise a TypeError exception if *value* is not of the
expected *type* (which is one of the constants T_STRING, T_FLOAT, and so on):

```
Check_Type(VALUE value, int type)
```

If speed is an issue, there are faster macros that check specifically for the immediate
values Fixnum and nil.

```
FIXNUM_P(value)  → non-zero if value is a Fixnum
NIL_P(value)     → non-zero if value is nil
RTEST(value)     → non-zero if value is neither nil nor false
```

Again, note that we are talking about "type" as the C structure that represents a particular built-in type. The class of an object is a different beast entirely. The class objects
for the built-in classes are stored in C global variables named rb_c*Classname* (for
instance, rb_cObject); modules are named rb_m*Modulename*.

It wouldn't be advisable to mess with the data in these structures directly, however—
you may look, but don't touch unless you are fond of debuggers. You should normally
use only the supplied C functions to manipulate Ruby data (we'll talk more about this
in just a moment).

However, in the interests of efficiency you may need to dig into these structures to
obtain data. In order to dereference members of these C structures, you have to cast
the generic VALUE to the proper structure type. ruby.h contains a number of macros
that perform the proper casting for you, allowing you to dereference structure members
easily. These macros are named R*CLASSNAME*, as in RSTRING or RARRAY. For example:

```
VALUE str, arr;
RSTRING(str)->len  → length of the Ruby string
RSTRING(str)->ptr  → pointer to string storage
RARRAY(arr)->len   → length of the Ruby array
RARRAY(arr)->capa  → capacity of the Ruby array
RARRAY(arr)->ptr   → pointer to array storage
```

VALUE as an Immediate Object

As we said above, immediate values are not pointers: `Fixnum`, `Symbol`, `true`, `false`, and `nil` are stored directly in `VALUE`.

`Fixnum` values are stored as 31-bit numbers[2] that are formed by shifting the original number left 1 bit and then setting the least significant bit (bit 0) to "1." When `VALUE` is used as a pointer to a specific Ruby structure, it is guaranteed always to have an LSB of zero; the other immediate values also have LSBs of zero. Thus, a simple bit test can tell you whether or not you have a `Fixnum`.

There are several useful conversion macros for numbers as well as other standard datatypes shown in Table 17.1 on page 176.

The other immediate values (`true`, `false`, and `nil`) are represented in C as the constants `Qtrue`, `Qfalse`, and `Qnil`, respectively. You can test `VALUE` variables against these constants directly, or use the conversion macros (which perform the proper casting).

Writing Ruby in C

One of the joys of Ruby is that you can write Ruby programs almost directly in C. That is, you can use the same methods and the same logic, but with slightly different syntax to accommodate C. For instance, here is a small, fairly boring test class written in Ruby.

```ruby
class Test
  def initialize
    @arr = Array.new
  end
  def add(anObject)
    @arr.push(anObject)
  end
end
```

The equivalent code in C should look somewhat familiar.

```c
#include "ruby.h"

static VALUE t_init(VALUE self)
{
  VALUE arr;

  arr = rb_ary_new();
  rb_iv_set(self, "@arr", arr);
```

---

2.   Or 63-bit on wider CPU architectures.

```
    return self;
  }
  static VALUE t_add(VALUE self, VALUE anObject)
  {
    VALUE arr;

    arr = rb_iv_get(self, "@arr");
    rb_ary_push(arr, anObject);
    return arr;
  }

  VALUE cTest;

  void Init_Test() {
    cTest = rb_define_class("Test", rb_cObject);
    rb_define_method(cTest, "initialize", t_init, 0);
    rb_define_method(cTest, "add", t_add, 1);
  }
```

Let's go through this example in detail, as it illustrates many of the important concepts in this chapter. First off, we need to include the header file "ruby.h" to obtain the necessary definitions.

Now look at the last function, Init_Test. Every class or module defines a C global function named Init_*Name*. This function will be called when the interpreter first loads the extension *Name* (or on startup for statically linked extensions). It is used to initialize the extension and to insinuate it into the Ruby environment. In this case, we define a new class named Test, which is a subclass of Object (represented by the external symbol rb_cObject; see "ruby.h" for others).

Next we set up add and initialize as two instance methods for class Test. The calls to rb_define_method establish a binding between the Ruby method name and the C function that will implement it, so a call to the add method in Ruby will call the C function t_add with one argument.

Similarly, when new is called for this class, Ruby will construct a basic object and then call initialize, which we have defined here to call the C function t_init with no (Ruby) arguments.

Now go back and look at the definition of initialize. Even though we said it took no arguments, there's a parameter here! In addition to any Ruby arguments, every method is passed an initial VALUE argument that contains the receiver for this method (the equivalent of self in Ruby code).

The first thing we'll do in initialize is create a Ruby array and set the instance variable @arr to point to it. Just as you would expect if you were writing Ruby source, referencing an instance variable that doesn't exist creates it.

Finally, the function t_add gets the instance variable @arr from the current object and calls Array#push to push the passed value onto that array. When accessing instance variables in this way, the @-prefix is mandatory—otherwise the variable is created, but cannot be referenced from Ruby.

Despite the extra, clunky syntax that C imposes, you're still writing in Ruby—you can manipulate objects using all of the method calls you've come to know and love, with the added advantage of being able to craft tight, fast code when needed.

WARNING: Every C function that is callable from Ruby *must* return a **VALUE**, even if it's just **Qnil**. Otherwise, a core dump (or GPF) will be the likely result.

We can use the C version of the code in Ruby simply by **require**-ing it dynamically at runtime (on most platforms).

```
require "code/ext/Test"
t = Test.new
t.add("Bill Chase")
```

Evaluating Ruby Expressions in C

If you are in the middle of some C code and you want to run an arbitrary Ruby expression without writing a bunch of C, you can always use the C version of **eval**. Suppose you have a collection of objects that need to have a flag cleared.

```
rb_eval_string("anObject.each{|x| x.clearFlag }");
```

If you just want to call a particular method (which is cheaper than **eval**-ing an entire string) you can use

```
rb_funcall(receiver, method_id, argc, ...)
```

Full descriptions of these and other commonly used C functions begin on page 189.

Sharing Data Between Ruby and C

We've covered enough of the basics now to return to our jukebox example—interfacing C code with Ruby and sharing data and behavior between the two worlds.

Directly Sharing Variables

Although you could maintain a C version of some variable along with a separate Ruby version of that variable, and struggle to keep the two in sync,[3] it would be much better to share a variable directly between Ruby and C. You can share global variables by

---

3. A clear violation of the *DRY*–Don't Repeat Yourself—principle described in our book *The Pragmatic Programmer* [HT00].

Table 17.1. C/Ruby datatype conversion functions and macros

C Datatypes to Ruby Objects:

INT2NUM(*int*)	→ *Fixnum* or *Bignum*
INT2FIX(*int*)	→ *Fixnum* (faster)
INT2NUM(*long* or *int*)	→ *Fixnum* or *Bignum*
INT2FIX(*long* or *int*)	→ *Fixnum* (faster)
CHR2FIX(*char*)	→ *Fixnum*
rb_str_new2(*char **)	→ *String*
rb_float_new(*double*)	→ *Float*

Ruby Objects to C Datatypes:

int	NUM2INT(*Numeric*)	(Includes type check)
int	FIX2INT(*Fixnum*)	(Faster)
unsigned int	NUM2UINT(*Numeric*)	(Includes type check)
unsigned int	FIX2UINT(*Fixnum*)	(Includes type check)
long	NUM2LONG(*Numeric*)	(Includes type check)
long	FIX2LONG(*Fixnum*)	(Faster)
unsigned long	NUM2ULONG(*Numeric*)	(Includes type check)
char	NUM2CHR(*Numeric* or *String*)	(Includes type check)
char *	STR2CSTR(*String*)	
char *	rb_str2cstr(*String*, int *length)	Returns length as well
double	NUM2DBL(*Numeric*)	

creating a Ruby object on the C side and then binding its address to a Ruby global variable. In this case, the $ prefix is optional, but it helps clarify that this is a global variable.

```
VALUE hardware_list;
hardware_list = rb_ary_new();
rb_define_variable("$hardware", &hardware_list);
...
rb_ary_push(hardware_list, rb_str_new2("DVD"));
rb_ary_push(hardware_list, rb_str_new2("CDPlayer1"));
rb_ary_push(hardware_list, rb_str_new2("CDPlayer2"));
```

The Ruby side can then access the C variable `hardware_list` as `$hardware`:

```
$hardware  →  ["DVD", "CDPlayer1", "CDPlayer2"]
```

You can also create *hooked* variables that will call a specified function when the variable is accessed, and *virtual* variables that only call the hooks—no actual variable is involved. See the API section that begins on page 192 for details.

If you create a Ruby object from C and store it in a C global variable *without* exporting it to Ruby, you must at least tell the garbage collector about it, lest ye be reaped inadvertently:

```
VALUE obj;
obj = rb_ary_new();
rb_global_variable(obj);
```

Wrapping C Structures

Now on to the *really* fun stuff. We've got the vendor's library that controls the audio CD jukebox units, and we're ready to wire it into Ruby. The vendor's header file looks like this:

```
typedef struct _cdjb {
  int statusf;
  int request;
  void *data;
  char pending;
  int unit_id;
  void *stats;
} CDJukebox;

// Allocate a new CDPlayer structure and bring it online
CDJukebox *CDPlayerNew(int unit_id);

// Deallocate when done (and take offline)
void CDPlayerDispose(CDJukebox *rec);

// Seek to a disc, track and notify progress
void CDPlayerSeek(CDJukebox *rec,
                  int disc,
                  int track,
                  void (*done)(CDJukebox *rec, int percent));
// ... others...
// Report a statistic
double CDPlayerAvgSeekTime(CDJukebox *rec);
```

This vendor has its act together; while the vendor might not admit it, the code is written with an object-oriented flavor. We don't know what all those fields mean within the CDJukeBox structure, but that's okay—we can treat it as an opaque pile of bits. The vendor's code knows what to do with it, we just have to carry it around.

Anytime you have a C-only structure that you would like to handle as a Ruby object, you should wrap it in a special, internal Ruby class called DATA (type T_DATA). There are two macros to do this wrapping, and one to retrieve your structure back out again.

API: C Datatype Wrapping

```
VALUE Data_Wrap_Struct( VALUE class, void (*mark)(),
                        void (*free)(), void *ptr )
```
> Wraps the given C datatype *ptr*, registers the two garbage collection routines (see below), and returns a VALUE pointer to a genuine Ruby object. The C type of the resulting object is `T_DATA` and its Ruby class is *class*.

```
VALUE Data_Make_Struct( VALUE class, c-type, void (*mark)(),
                        void (*free)(), c-type * )
```
> Allocates a structure of the indicated type first, then proceeds as `Data_Wrap_Struct`. *c-type* is the name of the C datatype that you're wrapping, not a variable of that type.

```
Data_Get_Struct( VALUE obj, c-type, c-type * )
```
> Returns the original pointer. This macro is a type-safe wrapper around the macro `DATA_PTR(obj)`, which evaluates the pointer.

The object created by `Data_Wrap_Struct` is a normal Ruby object, except that it has an additional C datatype that can't be accessed from Ruby. As you can see in Figure 17.1 on the next page, this C datatype is separate from any instance variables that the object contains. But since it's a separate thing, how do you get rid of it when the garbage collector claims this object? What if you have to release some resource (close some file, clean up some lock or IPC mechanism, and so on)?

In order to participate in garbage collection, you need to define a routine to free your structure, and possibly a routine to mark any references from your structure to other structures. Both routines take a void pointer. These routines are used by Ruby's mark-and-sweep garbage collector. The *mark* routine will be called by the garbage collector during its "mark" phase. If your structure references other Ruby objects, then your mark function needs to identify these objects using `rb_gc_mark(value)`. If the structure doesn't reference other Ruby objects, you can simply pass 0 as a function pointer.

When the object needs to be disposed of, the garbage collector will call the *free* routine to free it. If you have allocated any memory yourself (for instance, by using `Data_Make_Struct`), you'll need to pass a free function—even if it's just the standard C library's `free` routine. For complex structures that you have allocated, your free function may need to traverse the structure to free all the allocated memory.

First a simple example, without any special handling. Given the structure definition

```
typedef struct mp3info {
  char *title;
  char *artist;
  int  genre;
} MP3Info;
```

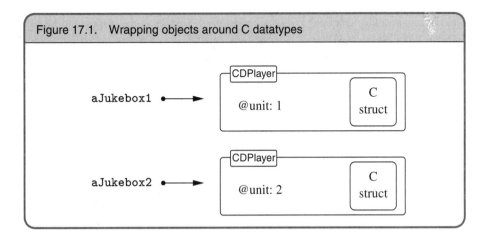

Figure 17.1.   Wrapping objects around C datatypes

we can create a structure, populate it, and wrap it as an object.[4]

```
MP3Info *p;
VALUE info;

p = ALLOC(MP3Info);
p->artist = "Maynard Ferguson";
p->title = "Chameleon";
...
info = Data_Wrap_Struct(cTest, 0, free, p);
```

info is a **VALUE** type, a genuine Ruby object of class **Test** (represented in C by the built-in type **T_DATA**). You can push it onto an array, hold a reference to it in an object, and so on. At some later point in the code, we may want to access this structure again, given the **VALUE**:

```
VALUE doit(VALUE info)
  MP3Info *p;
  Data_Get_Struct(info, MP3Info, p);
  ...
  p->artist    → "Maynard Ferguson"
  p->title     → "Chameleon"
  ...
```

In order to follow convention, however, you may need a few more things: support for an **initialize** method, and a "C-constructor." If you were writing Ruby source, you'd

---

4.   We cheat a bit in this example. Our **MP3Info** structure has a couple of **char** pointers in it. In our code we initialize them from two static strings. This means that we don't have to free these strings when the **MP3Info** structure is freed. If we'd allocated these strings dynamically, we'd have to write a free method to dispose of them.

allocate and initialize an object by calling **new**. In C extensions, the corresponding call is **Data_Make_Struct**. However, although this allocates memory for the object, it does *not* automatically call an **initialize** method; you need to do that yourself:

```
info = Data_Make_Struct(cTest, MP3Info, 0, free, one);
rb_obj_call_init(info, argc, argv);
```

This has the benefit of allowing subclasses in Ruby to override or augment the basic **initialize** in your class. Within **initialize**, it is allowable (but not necessarily advisable) to alter the existing data pointer, which may be accessed directly with **DATA_PTR(obj)**.

And finally, you may want to define a "C-constructor"—that is, a globally available C function that will create the object in one convenient call. You can use this function within your own code or allow other extension libraries to use it. All of the built-in classes support this idea with functions such as **rb_str_new**, **rb_ary_new**, and so on. We can make our own:

```
VALUE mp3_info_new() {
  VALUE info;
  MP3Info *one;
  info = Data_Make_Struct(cTest, MP3Info, 0, free, one);
  ...
  rb_obj_call_init(info, 0, 0);
  return info;
}
```

An Example

Okay, now we're ready for a full-size example. Given our vendor's header file above, we write the following code.

```
#include "ruby.h"
#include "cdjukebox.h"

VALUE cCDPlayer;

static void cd_free(void *p) {
  CDPlayerDispose(p);
}

static void progress(CDJukebox *rec, int percent)
{
  if (rb_block_given_p()) {
    if (percent > 100) percent = 100;
    if (percent < 0) percent = 0;
    rb_yield(INT2FIX(percent));
  }
}
```

```
static VALUE
cd_seek(VALUE self, VALUE disc, VALUE track)
{
  CDJukebox *ptr;
  Data_Get_Struct(self, CDJukebox, ptr);

  CDPlayerSeek(ptr,
               NUM2INT(disc),
               NUM2INT(track),
               progress);
  return Qnil;
}
static VALUE
cd_seekTime(VALUE self)
{
  double tm;
  CDJukebox *ptr;
  Data_Get_Struct(self, CDJukebox, ptr);
  tm = CDPlayerAvgSeekTime(ptr);
  return rb_float_new(tm);
}
static VALUE
cd_unit(VALUE self)
{
  return rb_iv_get(self, "@unit");
}
static VALUE
cd_init(VALUE self, VALUE unit)
{
  rb_iv_set(self, "@unit", unit);
  return self;
}
VALUE cd_new(VALUE class, VALUE unit)
{
  VALUE argv[1];
  CDJukebox *ptr = CDPlayerNew(NUM2INT(unit));
  VALUE tdata = Data_Wrap_Struct(class, 0, cd_free, ptr);
  argv[0] = unit;
  rb_obj_call_init(tdata, 1, argv);
  return tdata;
}
void Init_CDJukebox() {
  cCDPlayer = rb_define_class("CDPlayer", rb_cObject);
  rb_define_singleton_method(cCDPlayer, "new", cd_new, 1);
  rb_define_method(cCDPlayer, "initialize", cd_init, 1);
  rb_define_method(cCDPlayer, "seek", cd_seek, 2);
  rb_define_method(cCDPlayer, "seekTime", cd_seekTime, 0);
  rb_define_method(cCDPlayer, "unit", cd_unit, 0);
}
```

Now we have the ability to control our jukebox from Ruby in a nice, object-oriented manner:

```
require "code/ext/CDJukebox"
p = CDPlayer.new(1)
puts "Unit is #{p.unit}"
p.seek(3, 16) {|x| puts "#{x}% done" }
puts "Avg. time was #{p.seekTime} seconds"
```

produces:

```
Unit is 1
26% done
79% done
100% done
Avg. time was 1.2 seconds
```

This example demonstrates most of what we've talked about so far, with one additional neat feature. The vendor's library provided a callback routine—a function pointer that is called every so often while the hardware is grinding its way to the next disc. We've set that up here to run a code block passed as an argument to **seek**. In the **progress** function, we check to see if there is an iterator in the current context and, if there is, run it with the current percent done as an argument.

Memory Allocation

You may sometimes need to allocate memory in an extension that won't be used for object storage—perhaps you've got a giant bitmap for a Bloom filter, or an image, or a whole bunch of little structures that Ruby doesn't use directly.

In order to work correctly with the garbage collector, you should use the following memory allocation routines. These routines do a little bit more work than the standard **malloc**. For instance, if **ALLOC_N** determines that it cannot allocate the desired amount of memory, it will invoke the garbage collector to try to reclaim some space. It will raise a **NoMemError** if it can't or if the requested amount of memory is invalid.

API: Memory Allocation

type * ALLOC_N(*c-type*, n)

> Allocates *n c-type* objects, where *c-type* is the literal name of the C type, not a variable of that type.

type * ALLOC(*c-type*)

> Allocates a *c-type* and casts the result to a pointer of that type.

```
REALLOC_N( var, c-type, n )
```
Reallocates *n c-type*s and assigns the result to *var*, a pointer to a *c-type*.

```
type * ALLOCA_N( c-type, n )
```
Allocates memory for *n* objects of *c-type* on the stack—this memory will be automatically freed when the function that invokes ALLOCA_N returns.

Creating an Extension

Having written the source code for an extension, we now need to compile it so Ruby can use it. We can either do this as a shared object, which is dynamically loaded at runtime, or statically link the extension into the main Ruby interpreter itself. The basic procedure is the same:

- Create the C source code file(s) in a given directory.
- Create extconf.rb.
- Run extconf.rb to create a Makefile for the C files in this directory.
- Run make.
- Run make install.

Creating a Makefile with extconf.rb

Figure 17.2 on the following page shows the overall workflow when building an extension. The key to the whole process is the extconf.rb program which you, as a developer, create. In extconf.rb, you write a simple program that determines what features are available on the user's system and where those features may be located. Executing extconf.rb builds a customized Makefile, tailored for both your application and the system on which it's being compiled. When you run the make command against this Makefile, your extension is built and (optionally) installed.

The simplest extconf.rb may be just two lines long, and for many extensions this is sufficient.

```
require 'mkmf'
create_makefile("Test")
```

The first line brings in the mkmf library module (documented beginning on page 455). This contains all the commands we'll be using. The second line creates a Makefile for an extension called "Test." (Note that "Test" is the name of the extension; the makefile will always be called "Makefile.") Test will be built from all the C source files in the current directory.

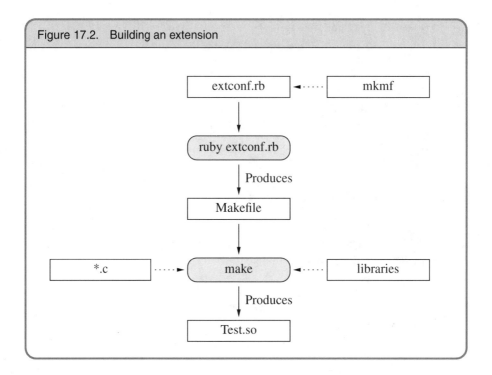

Figure 17.2. Building an extension

Let's say that we run this `extconf.rb` program in a directory containing a single source file, `main.c`. The result is a `Makefile` that will build our extension. On our system, this contains the following commands.

```
gcc -fPIC -I/usr/local/lib/ruby/1.6/i686-linux -g -O2  \
  -c main.c -o main.o
gcc -shared -o Test.so main.o -lc
```

The result of this compilation is `Test.so`, which may be dynamically linked into Ruby at runtime with "`require`". See how the mkmf commands have located platform-specific libraries and used compiler-specific options automatically. Pretty neat, eh?

Although this basic program works for many simple extensions, you may have to do some more work if your extension needs header files or libraries that aren't included in the default compilation environment, or if you conditionally compile code based on the presence of libraries or functions.

A common requirement is to specify nonstandard directories where include files and libraries may be found. This is a two-step process. First, your `extconf.rb` should contain one or more `dir_config` commands. This specifies a tag for a set of directories. Then, when you run the `extconf.rb` program, you tell mkmf where the corresponding physical directories are on the current system.

If `extconf.rb` contains the line `dir_config(`*name*`)`, then you give the location of the corresponding directories with the command-line options:

`--with-`*name*`-include=`*directory*
> Add *directory*/`include` to the compile command.

`--with-`*name*`-lib=`*directory*
> Add *directory*/`lib` to the link command.

If (as is common) your include and library directories are both subdirectories of some other directory, and (as is also common) they're called `include` and `lib`, you can take a shortcut:

`--with-`*name*`-dir=`*directory*
> Add *directory*/`lib` and *directory*/`include` to the link command and compile command, respectively.

There's a twist here. As well as specifying all these `--with` options when you run `extconf.rb`, you can also use the `--with` options that were specified when Ruby was built for your machine. This means you can find out the locations of libraries that are used by Ruby itself.

To make all this concrete, lets say you need to use libraries and include files for the CD jukebox we're developing. Your `extconf.rb` program might contain

```
require 'mkmf'
dir_config('cdjukebox')
# .. more stuff
create_makefile("CDJukeBox")
```

You'd then run `extconf.rb` with something like:

```
% ruby extconf.rb --with-cdjukebox-dir=/usr/local/cdjb
```

The generated `Makefile` would assume that the libraries were in `/usr/local/cdjb/lib` and the include files were in `/usr/local/cdjb/include`.

The `dir_config` command adds to the list of places to search for libraries and include files. It does not, however, link the libraries into your application. To do that, you'll need to use one or more `have_library` or `find_library` commands.

`have_library` looks for a given entry point in a named library. If it finds the entry point, it adds the library to the list of libraries to be used when linking your extension. `find_library` is similar, but allows you to specify a list of directories to search for the library.

```
require 'mkmf'
dir_config('cdjukebox')
have_library('cdjb', 'CDPlayerNew')
create_makefile("CDJukeBox")
```

On some platforms, a popular library may be in one of several places. The X Window system, for example, is notorious for living in different directories on different systems. The `find_library` command will search a list of supplied directories to find the right one (this is different from `have_library`, which uses only configuration information for the search). For example, to create a `Makefile` that uses X Windows and a jpeg library, `extconf.rb` might contain

```
require 'mkmf'

if have_library("jpeg","jpeg_mem_init") and
   find_library("X11", "XOpenDisplay", "/usr/X11/lib",
                "/usr/X11R6/lib", "/usr/openwin/lib")
then
    create_makefile("XThing")
else
    puts "No X/JPEG support available"
end
```

We've added some additional functionality to this program. All of the `mkmf` commands return `false` if they fail. This means that we can write an `extconf.rb` that generates a `Makefile` only if everything it needs is present. The Ruby distribution does this so that it will try to compile only those extensions that are supported on your system.

You also may want your extension code to be able to configure the features it uses depending on the target environment. For example, our CD jukebox may be able to use a high-performance MP3 decoder if the end user has one installed. We can check by looking for its header file.

```
require 'mkmf'
dir_config('cdjukebox')
have_library('cdjb', 'CDPlayerNew')
have_header('hp_mp3.h')
create_makefile("CDJukeBox")
```

We can also check to see if the target environment has a particular function in any of the libraries we'll be using. For example, the `setpriority` call would be useful but isn't always available. We can check for it with:

```
require 'mkmf'
dir_config('cdjukebox')
have_func('setpriority')
create_makefile("CDJukeBox")
```

Both `have_header` and `have_func` define preprocessor constants if they find their targets. The names are formed by converting the target name to uppercase and prepending "HAVE_". Your C code can take advantage of this using constructs such as:

```
#if defined(HAVE_HP_MP3_H)
#  include <hp_mp3.h>
#endif
```

```
#if defined(HAVE_SETPRIORITY)
  err = setpriority(PRIOR_PROCESS, 0, -10)
#endif
```

If you have special requirements that can't be met with all these `mkmf` commands, your program can directly add to the global variables `$CFLAGS` and `$LFLAGS`, which are passed to the compiler and linker, respectively.

Static Linking

Finally, if your system doesn't support dynamic linking, or if you have an extension module that you want to have statically linked into Ruby itself, edit the file `ext/Setup` in the distribution and add your directory to the list of extensions in the file, then rebuild Ruby. The extensions listed in `Setup` will be statically linked into the Ruby executable. If you want to disable any dynamic linking, and link all extensions statically, edit `ext/Setup` to contain the following option.

```
option nodynamic
```

Embedding a Ruby Interpreter

In addition to extending Ruby by adding C code, you can also turn the problem around and embed Ruby itself within your application. Here's an example.

```
#include "ruby.h"
main() {
  /* ... our own application stuff ... */
  ruby_init();
  ruby_script("embedded");
  rb_load_file("start.rb");
  while (1) {
    if (need_to_do_ruby) {
      ruby_run();
    }
    /* ... run our app stuff */
  }
}
```

To initialize the Ruby interpreter, you need to call `ruby_init()`. But on some platforms, you may need to take special steps before that:

```
#if defined(NT)
  NtInitialize(&argc, &argv);
#endif
#if defined(__MACOS__) && defined(__MWERKS__)
  argc = ccommand(&argv);
#endif
```

See `main.c` in the Ruby distribution for any other special defines or setup needed for your platform.

API: Embedded Ruby API

`void ruby_init( )`

> Sets up and initializes the interpreter. This function should be called before any other Ruby-related functions.

`void ruby_options( int argc, char **argv )`

> Gives the Ruby interpreter the command-line options.

`void ruby_script( char *name )`

> Sets the name of the Ruby script (and `$0`) to *name*.

`void rb_load_file( char *file )`

> Loads the given file into the interpreter.

`void ruby_run( )`

> Runs the interpreter.

You need to take some special care with exception handling; any Ruby calls you make at this top level should be protected to catch exceptions and handle them cleanly. `rb_protect`, `rb_rescue`, and related functions are documented on page 194.

For an example of embedding a Ruby interpreter within another program, see also `eruby`, which is described beginning on page 149.

Bridging Ruby to Other Languages

So far, we've discussed extending Ruby by adding routines written in C. However, you can write extensions in just about any language, as long as you can bridge the two languages with C. Almost anything is possible, including awkward marriages of Ruby and C++, Ruby and Java, and so on.

But you may be able to accomplish the same thing without resorting to C code. For example, you could bridge to other languages using middleware such as CORBA or COM. See the section on Windows automation beginning on page 166 for more details.

Ruby C Language API

Last, but by no means least, here are several C-level functions that you may find useful when writing an extension.

Some functions require an ID: you can obtain an ID for a string by using `rb_intern` and reconstruct the name from an ID by using `rb_id2name`.

As most of these C functions have Ruby equivalents that are already described in detail elsewhere in this book, the descriptions here will be brief.

Also note that the following listing is not complete. There are many more functions available—too many to document them all, as it turns out. If you need a method that you can't find here, check "`ruby.h`" or "`intern.h`" for likely candidates. Also, at or near the bottom of each source file is a set of method definitions that describe the binding from Ruby methods to C functions. You may be able to call the C function directly, or search for a wrapper function that calls the function you are looking for. The following list, based on the list in **README.EXT**, shows the main source files in the interpreter.

Ruby Language Core
class.c, error.c, eval.c, gc.c, object.c, parse.y, variable.c

Utility Functions
dln.c, regex.c, st.c, util.c

Ruby Interpreter
dmyext.c, inits.c, keywords main.c, ruby.c, version.c

Base Library
array.c, bignum.c, compar.c, dir.c, enum.c, file.c, hash.c, io.c, marshal.c, math.c, numeric.c, pack.c, prec.c, process.c, random.c, range.c, re.c, signal.c, sprintf.c, string.c, struct.c, time.c

API: Defining Objects

`VALUE rb_define_class( char *name, VALUE superclass )`
Defines a new class at the top level with the given *name* and *superclass* (for class `Object`, use `rb_cObject`).

`VALUE rb_define_module( char *name )`
Defines a new module at the top level with the given *name*.

`VALUE rb_define_class_under( VALUE under, char *name,`
`                            VALUE superclass )`
Defines a nested class under the class or module *under*.

```
VALUE rb_define_module_under( VALUE under, char *name )
```
   Defines a nested module under the class or module *under*.

```
void rb_include_module( VALUE parent, VALUE module )
```
   Includes the given *module* into the class or module *parent*.

```
void rb_extend_object( VALUE obj, VALUE module )
```
   Extends *obj* with *module*.

```
VALUE rb_require( const char *name )
```
   Equivalent to "**require** *name*." Returns **Qtrue** or **Qfalse**.

API: Defining Methods

In some of the function definitions that follow, the parameter *argc* specifies how many arguments a Ruby method takes. It may have the following values.

argc	**Function prototype**
0..17	`VALUE func(VALUE self, VALUE arg...)`
	The C function will be called with this many actual arguments.
−1	`VALUE func(int argc, VALUE *argv, VALUE self)`
	The C function will be given a variable number of arguments passed as a C array.
−2	`VALUE func(VALUE self, VALUE args)`
	The C function will be given a variable number of arguments passed as a Ruby array.

In a function that has been given a variable number of arguments, you can use the C function **rb_scan_args** to sort things out (see below).

```
void rb_define_method( VALUE classmod, char *name;
                       VALUE(*func)(), int argc )
```
   Defines an instance method in the class or module *classmod* with the given *name*, implemented by the C function *func* and taking *argc* arguments.

```
void rb_define_module_function( VALUE classmod, char *name;
                                VALUE(*func)(), int argc) )
```
   Defines a method in class *classmod* with the given *name*, implemented by the C function *func* and taking *argc* arguments.

```
void rb_define_global_function( char *name, VALUE(*func)(),
                                int argc )
```
Defines a global function (a private method of `Kernel`) with the given *name*, implemented by the C function *func* and taking *argc* arguments.

```
void rb_define_singleton_method( VALUE classmod, char *name,
                                 VALUE(*func)(), int argc )
```
Defines a singleton method in class *classmod* with the given *name*, implemented by the C function *func* and taking *argc* arguments.

```
int rb_scan_args( int argcount, VALUE *argv, char *fmt, ... )
```
Scans the argument list and assigns to variables similar to `scanf`: *fmt* is a string containing zero, one, or two digits followed by some flag characters. The first digit indicates the count of mandatory arguments; the second is the count of optional arguments. A "*" means to pack the rest of the arguments into a Ruby array. A "&" means that an attached code block will be taken and assigned to the given variable (if no code block was given, `Qnil` will be assigned). After the *fmt* string, pointers to `VALUE` are given (as with `scanf`) to which the arguments are assigned.

```
VALUE name, one, two, rest;
rb_scan_args(argc, argv, "12", &name, &one, &two);
rb_scan_args(argc, argv, "1*", &name, &rest);
```

```
void rb_undef_method( VALUE classmod, const char *name )
```
Undefines the given method *name* in the given *classmod* class or module.

```
void rb_define_alias( VALUE classmod, const char *newname,
                      const char *oldname )
```
Defines an alias for *oldname* in class or module *classmod*.

API: Defining Variables and Constants

```
void rb_define_const( VALUE classmod, char *name, VALUE value )
```
Defines a constant in the class or module *classmod*, with the given *name* and *value*.

```
void rb_define_global_const( char *name, VALUE value )
```
Defines a global constant with the given *name* and *value*.

```
void rb_define_variable( const char *name, VALUE *object )
```
Exports the address of the given *object* that was created in C to the Ruby namespace as *name*. From Ruby, this will be a global variable, so *name* should start with a leading dollar sign. Be sure to honor Ruby's rules for allowed variable names; illegally named variables will not be accessible from Ruby.

```
void rb_define_class_variable( VALUE class, const char *name,
                               VALUE val )
```
Defines a class variable *name* (which must be specified with a "@@" prefix) in the given *class*, initialized to *value*.

```
void rb_define_virtual_variable( const char *name,
                                 VALUE(*getter)(),
                                 void(*setter)() )
```
Exports a virtual variable to Ruby namespace as the global $*name*. No actual storage exists for the variable; attempts to get and set the value will call the given functions with the prototypes:

```
VALUE getter(ID id, VALUE *data,
             struct global_entry *entry);
void setter(VALUE value, ID id, VALUE *data,
            struct global_entry *entry);
```

You will likely not need to use the *entry* parameter and can safely omit it from your function declarations.

```
void rb_define_hooked_variable( const char *name,
                                VALUE *variable,
                                VALUE(*getter)(),
                                void(*setter)() )
```
Defines functions to be called when reading or writing to *variable*. See also `rb_define_virtual_variable`.

```
void rb_define_readonly_variable( const char *name,
                                  VALUE *value )
```
Same as `rb_define_variable`, but read-only from Ruby.

```
void rb_define_attr( VALUE variable, const char *name,
                     int read, int write )
```
Creates accessor methods for the given *variable*, with the given *name*. If *read* is nonzero, create a read method; if *write* is nonzero, create a write method.

```
void rb_global_variable( VALUE *obj )
```
Registers the given address with the garbage collector.

API: Calling Methods

VALUE rb_funcall(VALUE recv, ID id, int argc, ...)

>Invokes the method given by *id* in the object *recv* with the given number of arguments *argc* and the arguments themselves (possibly none).

VALUE rb_funcall2(VALUE recv, ID id, int argc, VALUE *args)

>Invokes the method given by *id* in the object *recv* with the given number of arguments *argc* and the arguments themselves given in the C array *args*.

VALUE rb_funcall3(VALUE recv, ID id, int argc, VALUE *args)

>Same as **rb_funcall2**, but will not call private methods.

VALUE rb_apply(VALUE recv, ID name, int argc, VALUE args)

>Invokes the method given by *id* in the object *recv* with the given number of arguments *argc* and the arguments themselves given in the Ruby **Array** *args*.

ID rb_intern(char *name)

>Returns an **ID** for a given *name*. If the name does not exist, a symbol table entry will be created for it.

char * rb_id2name(ID id)

>Returns a name for the given *id*.

VALUE rb_call_super(int argc, VALUE *args)

>Calls the current method in the superclass of the current object.

API: Exceptions

void rb_raise(VALUE exception, const char *fmt, ...)

>Raises an *exception*. The given string *fmt* and remaining arguments are interpreted as with **printf**.

void rb_fatal(const char *fmt, ...)

>Raises a **Fatal** exception, terminating the process. No rescue blocks are called, but ensure blocks will be called. The given string *fmt* and remaining arguments are interpreted as with **printf**.

```
void rb_bug( const char *fmt, ... )
```
Terminates the process immediately—no handlers of any sort will be called. The given string *fmt* and remaining arguments are interpreted as with `printf`. You should call this function only if a fatal bug has been exposed. You don't write fatal bugs, do you?

```
void rb_sys_fail( const char *msg )
```
Raises a platform-specific exception corresponding to the last known system error, with the given *msg*.

```
VALUE rb_rescue( VALUE (*body)(), VALUE args, VALUE(*rescue)(),
          VALUE rargs )
```
Executes *body* with the given *args*. If a `StandardError` exception is raised, then execute *rescue* with the given *rargs*.

```
VALUE rb_ensure( VALUE(*body)(), VALUE args, VALUE(*ensure)(),
          VALUE eargs )
```
Executes *body* with the given *args*. Whether or not an exception is raised, execute *ensure* with the given *rargs* after *body* has completed.

```
VALUE rb_protect( VALUE (*body)(), VALUE args, int *result )
```
Executes *body* with the given *args* and returns nonzero in *result* if any exception was raised.

```
void rb_notimplement( )
```
Raises a `NotImpError` exception to indicate that the enclosed function is not implemented yet, or not available on this platform.

```
void rb_exit( int status )
```
Exits Ruby with the given *status*. Raises a `SystemExit` exception and calls registered exit functions and finalizers.

```
void rb_warn( const char *fmt, ... )
```
Unconditionally issues a warning message to standard error. The given string *fmt* and remaining arguments are interpreted as with `printf`.

```
void rb_warning( const char *fmt, ... )
```
Conditionally issues a warning message to standard error if Ruby was invoked with the -w flag. The given string *fmt* and remaining arguments are interpreted as with `printf`.

API: Iterators

```
void rb_iter_break( )
```
>Breaks out of the enclosing iterator block.

```
VALUE rb_each( VALUE obj )
```
>Invokes the each method of the given *obj*.

```
VALUE rb_yield( VALUE arg )
```
>Transfers execution to the iterator block in the current context, passing *arg* as an argument. Multiple values may be passed in an array.

```
 int rb_block_given_p( )
```
>Returns true if yield would execute a block in the current context—that is, if a code block was passed to the current method and is available to be called.

```
VALUE rb_iterate( VALUE (*method)(), VALUE args,
                VALUE (*block)(), VALUE arg2 )
```
>Invokes *method* with argument *args* and block *block*. A yield from that method will invoke *block* with the argument given to yield, and a second argument *arg2*.

```
VALUE rb_catch( const char *tag, VALUE (*proc)(), VALUE value )
```
>Equivalent to Ruby catch.

```
void rb_throw( const char *tag , VALUE value )
```
>Equivalent to Ruby throw.

API: Accessing Variables

```
VALUE rb_iv_get( VALUE obj, char *name )
```
>Returns the instance variable *name* (which must be specified with a "@" prefix) from the given *obj*.

```
VALUE rb_ivar_get( VALUE obj, ID name )
```
>Returns the instance variable *name* from the given *obj*.

```
VALUE rb_iv_set( VALUE obj, char *name, VALUE value )
```
>Sets the value of the instance variable *name* (which must be specified with a "@" prefix) in the given *obj* to *value*. Returns *value*.

```
VALUE rb_ivar_set( VALUE obj, ID name, VALUE value )
```
>Sets the value of the instance variable *name* in the given *obj* to *value*. Returns *value*.

VALUE rb_gv_set(const char *name, VALUE value)

> Sets the global variable *name* (the "**$**" prefix is optional) to *value*. Returns *value*.

VALUE rb_gv_get(const char *name)

> Returns the global variable *name* (the "**$**" prefix is optional).

void rb_cvar_set(VALUE class, ID name, VALUE val)

> Sets the class variable *name* in the given *class* to *value*.

VALUE rb_cvar_get(VALUE class, ID name)

> Returns the class variable *name* from the given *class*.

int rb_cvar_defined(VALUE class, ID name)

> Returns **Qtrue** if the given class variable *name* has been defined for *class*; otherwise, returns **Qfalse**.

void rb_cv_set(VALUE class, const char *name, VALUE val)

> Sets the class variable *name* (which must be specified with a "**@@**" prefix) in the given *class* to *value*.

VALUE rb_cv_get(VALUE class, const char *name)

> Returns the class variable *name* (which must be specified with a "**@@**" prefix) from the given *class*.

API: Object Status

OBJ_TAINT(VALUE obj)

> Marks the given *obj* as tainted.

int OBJ_TAINTED(VALUE obj)

> Returns nonzero if the given *obj* is tainted.

OBJ_FREEZE(VALUE obj)

> Marks the given *obj* as frozen.

int OBJ_FROZEN(VALUE obj)

> Returns nonzero if the given *obj* is frozen.

Check_SafeStr(VALUE str)

> Raises **SecurityError** if current safe level > 0 and *str* is tainted, or a **TypeError** if *str* is not a **T_STRING**.

int rb_safe_level( )

> Returns the current safe level.

```
void rb_secure( int level )
```
> Raises `SecurityError` if *level* <= current safe level.

```
void rb_set_safe_level( int newlevel )
```
> Sets the current safe level to *newlevel*.

API: Commonly Used Methods

```
VALUE rb_ary_new( )
```
> Returns a new `Array` with default size.

```
VALUE rb_ary_new2( long length )
```
> Returns a new `Array` of the given *length*.

```
VALUE rb_ary_new3( long length, ... )
```
> Returns a new `Array` of the given *length* and populated with the remaining arguments.

```
VALUE rb_ary_new4( long length, VALUE *values )
```
> Returns a new `Array` of the given *length* and populated with the C array *values*.

```
void rb_ary_store( VALUE self, long index, VALUE value )
```
> Stores *value* at *index* in array *self*.

```
VALUE rb_ary_push( VALUE self, VALUE value )
```
> Pushes *value* onto the end of array *self*. Returns *value*.

```
VALUE rb_ary_pop( VALUE self )
```
> Removes and returns the last element from the array *self*.

```
VALUE rb_ary_shift( VALUE self )
```
> Removes and returns the first element from the array *self*.

```
VALUE rb_ary_unshift( VALUE self, VALUE value )
```
> Pushes *value* onto the front of array *self*. Returns *value*.

```
VALUE rb_ary_entry( VALUE self, long index )
```
> Returns array *self*'s element at *index*.

```
int rb_respond_to( VALUE self, ID method )
```
> Returns nonzero if *self* responds to *method*.

```
VALUE rb_thread_create( VALUE (*func)(), void *data )
```
> Runs *func* in a new thread, passing *data* as an argument.

VALUE rb_hash_new( )
> Returns a new, empty **Hash**.

VALUE rb_hash_aref(VALUE self, VALUE key)
> Returns the element corresponding to *key* in *self*.

VALUE rb_hash_aset(VALUE self, VALUE key, VALUE value)
> Sets the value for *key* to *value* in *self*. Returns *value*.

VALUE rb_obj_is_instance_of(VALUE obj, VALUE klass)
> Returns **Qtrue** if *obj* is an instance of *klass*.

VALUE rb_obj_is_kind_of(VALUE obj, VALUE klass)
> Returns **Qtrue** if *klass* is the class of *obj* or *class* is one of the super-classes of the class of *obj*.

VALUE rb_str_new(const char *src, long length)
> Returns a new **String** initialized with *length* characters from *src*.

VALUE rb_str_new2(const char *src)
> Returns a new **String** initialized with the null-terminated C string *src*.

VALUE rb_str_dup(VALUE str)
> Returns a new **String** object duplicated from *str*.

VALUE rb_str_cat(VALUE self, const char *src, long length)
> Concatenates *length* characters from *src* onto the **String** *self*. Returns *self*.

VALUE rb_str_concat(VALUE self, VALUE other)
> Concatenates *other* onto the **String** *self*. Returns *self*.

VALUE rb_str_split(VALUE self, const char *delim)
> Returns an array of **String** objects created by splitting *self* on *delim*.

Part III

Ruby Crystallized

## Chapter 18

The Ruby Language

This chapter is a bottom-up look at the Ruby language. Unlike the previous tutorial, here we're concentrating on presenting facts, rather than motivating some of the language design features. We also ignore the built-in classes and modules where possible. These are covered in depth starting on page 279.

If the content of this chapter looks familiar, it's because it should; we've covered just about all of this in the earlier tutorial chapters. Consider this chapter to be a self-contained reference to the core Ruby language.

Source Layout

Ruby programs are written in 7-bit ASCII.[1]

Ruby is a line-oriented language. Ruby expressions and statements are terminated at the end of a line unless the statement is obviously incomplete—for example if the last token on a line is an operator or comma. A semicolon can be used to separate multiple expressions on a line. You can also put a backslash at the end of a line to continue it onto the next. Comments start with '#' and run to the end of the physical line. Comments are ignored during compilation.

```
a = 1
b = 2; c = 3
d = 4 + 5 +      # no '\' needed
    6 + 7
e = 8 + 9   \
    + 10         # '\' needed
```

---

1. Ruby also has extensive support for Kanji, using the EUC, SJIS, or UTF-8 coding system. If a code set other than 7-bit ASCII is used, the KCODE option must be set appropriately, as shown on page 139.

Physical lines between a line starting with =begin and a line starting with =end are ignored by the compiler and may be used for embedded documentation (see Appendix A, which begins on page 517).

Ruby reads its program input in a single pass, so you can pipe programs to the compiler's stdin.

```
echo 'print "Hello\n"' | ruby
```

If the compiler comes across a line anywhere in the source containing just "_ _END_ _", with no leading or trailing whitespace, it treats that line as the end of the program—any subsequent lines will not be compiled. However, these lines can be read into the running program using the global IO object DATA, described on page 219.

BEGIN and END Blocks

Every Ruby source file can declare blocks of code to be run as the file is being loaded (the BEGIN blocks) and after the program has finished executing (the END blocks).

```
BEGIN {
    begin code
}

END {
    end code
}
```

A program may include multiple BEGIN and END blocks. BEGIN blocks are executed in the order they are encountered. END blocks are executed in reverse order.

General Delimited Input

There are alternative forms of literal strings, arrays, regular expressions, and shell commands that are specified using a generalized delimited syntax. All these literals start with a percent character, followed by a single character that identifies the literal's type. These characters are summarized in Table 18.1 on the next page; the actual literals are described in the corresponding sections later in this chapter.

Following the type character is a delimiter, which can be any character. If the delimiter is one of the characters "(", "[", "{", or "<", the literal consists of the characters up to the matching closing delimiter, taking account of nested delimiter pairs. For all other delimiters, the literal comprises the characters up to the next occurrence of the delimiter character.

```
%q/this is a string/
%q-string-
%q(a (nested) string)
```

Table 18.1. General delimited input

Type	Meaning	See Page
%q	Single-quoted string	204
%Q, %	Double-quoted string	204
%w	Array of tokens	206
%r	Regular expression pattern	207
%x	Shell command	220

Delimited strings may continue over multiple lines.

```
%q{def fred(a)
      a.each { |i| puts i }
   end}
```

The Basic Types

The basic types in Ruby are numbers, strings, arrays, hashes, ranges, symbols, and regular expressions.

Integer and Floating Point Numbers

Ruby integers are objects of class `Fixnum` or `Bignum`. `Fixnum` objects hold integers that fit within the native machine word minus 1 bit. Whenever a `Fixnum` exceeds this range, it is automatically converted to a `Bignum` object, whose range is effectively limited only by available memory. If an operation with a `Bignum` result has a final value that will fit in a `Fixnum`, the result will be returned as a `Fixnum`.

Integers are written using an optional leading sign, an optional base indicator (0 for octal, `0x` for hex, or `0b` for binary), followed by a string of digits in the appropriate base. Underscore characters are ignored in the digit string.

You can get the integer value corresponding to an ASCII character by preceding that character with a question mark. Control and meta combinations of characters can also be generated using ?\C-*x*, ?\M-*x*, and ?\M-\C-*x*. The control version of `ch` is `ch & 0x9f`, and the meta version is `ch | 0x80`. The integer value of the backslash characters is ?\\.

```
123456                    # Fixnum
123_456                   # Fixnum (underscore ignored)
-543                      # Negative Fixnum
123_456_789_123_345_789   # Bignum
0xaabb                    # Hexadecimal
```

```
0377                # Octal
-0b1010             # Binary (negated)
0b001_001           # Binary
?a                  # character code
?A                  # upper case
?\C-a               # control a = A - 0x40
?\C-A               # case ignored for control chars
?\M-a               # meta sets bit 7
?\M-\C-a            # meta and control a
```

A numeric literal with a decimal point and/or an exponent is turned into a `Float` object, corresponding to the native architecture's `double` data type. You must follow the decimal point with a digit, as `1.e3` tries to invoke the method e3 in class `Fixnum`.

```
12.34       →    12.34
-.1234e2    →    -12.34
1234e-2     →    12.34
```

Strings

Ruby provides a number of mechanisms for creating literal strings. Each generates objects of type `String`. The different mechanisms vary in terms of how a string is delimited and how much substitution is done on the literal's content.

Single-quoted string literals (*'stuff'* and *%q/stuff/*) undergo the least substitution. Both convert the sequence \\ into a single backslash, and the form with single quotes converts \' into a single quote.

```
'hello'                     →    hello
'a backslash \'\\\''        →    a backslash '\'
%q/simple string/           →    simple string
%q(nesting (really) works)  →    nesting (really) works
%q no_blanks_here ;         →    no_blanks_here
```

Double-quoted strings (*"stuff"*, *%Q/stuff/*, and *%/stuff/*) undergo additional substitutions, shown in Table 18.2 on the facing page.

```
a   = 123
"\123mile"                      →    Smile
"Say \"Hello\""                 →    Say "Hello"
%Q!"I said 'nuts'," I said!     →    "I said 'nuts'," I said
%Q{Try #{a + 1}, not #{a - 1}}  →    Try 124, not 122
%<Try #{a + 1}, not #{a - 1}>   →    Try 124, not 122
"Try #{a + 1}, not #{a - 1}"    →    Try 124, not 122
```

Strings can continue across multiple input lines, in which case they will contain newline characters. It is also possible to use *here documents* to express long string literals. Whenever Ruby parses the sequence <<*identifier* or <<*quoted string*, it replaces it with a string literal built from successive logical input lines. It stops building the string when it finds a line that starts with the identifier or the *quoted string*. You can put a minus

Table 18.2. Substitutions in double-quoted strings

`\a`	Bell/alert (0x07)	`\nnn`	Octal *nnn*
`\b`	Backspace (0x08)	`\xnn`	Hex *nn*
`\e`	Escape (0x1b)	`\cx`	Control-*x*
`\f`	Formfeed (0x0c)	`\C-x`	Control-*x*
`\n`	Newline (0x0a)	`\M-x`	Meta-*x*
`\r`	Return (0x0d)	`\M-\C-x`	Meta-control-*x*
`\s`	Space (0x20)	`\x`	*x*
`\t`	Tab (0x09)	`#{expr}`	Value of *expr*
`\v`	Vertical tab (0x0b)		

sign immediately after the `<<` characters, in which case the terminator can be indented from the left margin. If a quoted string was used to specify the terminator, its quoting rules will be applied to the here document; otherwise, double-quoting rules apply.

```
a = 123
print <<HERE
Double quoted \
here document.
Sum = #{a + 1}
HERE

print <<-'THERE'
    This is single quoted.
    The above used #{a + 1}
    THERE
```

produces:

```
Double quoted here document.
Sum = 124
    This is single quoted.
    The above used #{a + 1}
```

Adjacent single- and double-quoted strings in the input are concatenated to form a single **String** object.

```
'Con' "cat" 'en' "ate"    →    "Concatenate"
```

Strings are stored as sequences of 8-bit bytes,[2] and each byte may contain any of the 256 8-bit values, including null and newline. The substitution mechanisms in Table 18.2 allow nonprinting characters to be inserted conveniently and portably.

---

2.   For use in Japan, the `jcode` library supports a set of operations of strings written with EUC, SJIS, or UTF-8 encoding. The underlying string, however, is still accessed as a series of bytes.

Every time a string literal is used in an assignment or as a parameter, a new **String** object is created.

```
for i in 1..3
  print 'hello'.id, " "
end
```

produces:

```
537679256 537679226 537679196
```

The documentation for class **String** starts on page 368.

Ranges

Outside the context of a conditional expression, *expr..expr* and *expr...expr* construct **Range** objects. The two-dot form is an inclusive range; the one with three dots is a range that excludes its last element. See the description of class **Range** on page 364 for details. Also see the description of conditional expressions on page 224 for other uses of ranges.

Arrays

Literals of class **Array** are created by placing a comma-separated series of object references between square brackets. A trailing comma is ignored.

```
arr = [ fred, 10, 3.14, "This is a string", barney("pebbles"), ]
```

Arrays of strings can be constructed using a shortcut notation, **%w**, which extracts space-separated tokens into successive elements of the array. A space can be escaped with a backslash. This is a form of general delimited input, described on pages 202–203.

```
arr = %w( fred wilma barney betty great\ gazoo )
arr  →  ["fred", "wilma", "barney", "betty", "great gazoo"]
```

Hashes

A literal Ruby **Hash** is created by placing a list of key/value pairs between braces, with either a comma or the sequence => between the key and the value. A trailing comma is ignored.

```
colors = { "red"   => 0xf00,
           "green" => 0x0f0,
           "blue"  => 0x00f
         }
```

There is no requirement for the keys and/or values in a particular hash to have the same type.

Requirements for a Hash Key

The only restriction for a hash key is that it must respond to the message **hash** with a hash value, and the hash value for a given key must not change. This means that certain classes (such as **Array** and **Hash**, as of this writing) can't conveniently be used as keys, because their hash values can change based on their contents.

If you keep an external reference to an object that is used as a key, and use that reference to alter the object and change its hash value, the hash lookup based on that key may not work.

Because strings are the most frequently used keys, and because string contents are often changed, Ruby treats string keys specially. If you use a **String** object as a hash key, the hash will duplicate the string internally and will use that copy as its key. Any changes subsequently made to the original string will not affect the hash.

If you write your own classes and use instances of them as hash keys, you need to make sure that either (a) the hashes of the key objects don't change once the objects have been created or (b) you remember to call the **Hash#rehash** method to reindex the hash whenever a key hash *is* changed.

Symbols

A Ruby symbol is the internal representation of a name. You construct the symbol for a name by preceding the name with a colon. A particular name will always generate the same symbol, regardless of how that name is used within the program.

```
:Object
:myVariable
```

Other languages call this process "interning," and call symbols "atoms."

Regular Expressions

Regular expression literals are objects of type **Regexp**. They can be created by explicitly calling the **Regexp.new** constructor, or by using the literal forms, */pattern/* and **%r**{*pattern*}. The **%r** construct is a form of general delimited input (described on pages 202–203).

```
/pattern/
/pattern/ options
%r{pattern}
%r{pattern} options
Regexp.new( 'pattern' [ , options ] )
```

Regular Expression Options

A regular expression may include one or more options that modify the way the pattern matches strings. If you're using literals to create the `Regexp` object, then the options comprise one or more characters placed immediately after the terminator. If you're using `Regexp.new`, the options are constants used as the second parameter of the constructor.

i *Case Insensitive.* The pattern match will ignore the case of letters in the pattern and string. Matches are also case-insensitive if the global variable `$=` is set.

o *Substitute Once.* Any `#...` substitutions in a particular regular expression literal will be performed just once, the first time it is evaluated. Otherwise, the substitutions will be performed every time the literal generates a `Regexp` object.

m *Multiline Mode.* Normally, "." matches any character except a newline. With the `/m` option, "." matches any character.

x *Extended Mode.* Complex regular expressions can be difficult to read. The 'x' option allows you to insert spaces, newlines, and comments in the pattern to make it more readable.

Regular Expression Patterns

regular characters

All characters except ., |, (,), [, \, ^, {, +, $, *, and ? match themselves. To match one of these characters, precede it with a backslash.

^

Matches the beginning of a line.

$

Matches the end of a line.

\A

Matches the beginning of the string.

\z

Matches the end of the string.

\Z

Matches the end of the string *unless* the string ends with a "\n", in which case it matches just before the "\n".

\b, \B

Match word boundaries and nonword boundaries respectively.

[*characters*]

A character class matches any single character between the brackets. The characters |, (,), [, ^, $, *, and ?, which have special meanings elsewhere in patterns, lose their special significance between brackets. The sequences \\nnn, \\xnn, \cx, \C-x, \M-x, and \M-\C-x have the meanings shown in Table 18.2 on page 205. The sequences \d, \D, \s, \S, \w, and \W are abbreviations for groups of characters, as shown in Table 5.1 on page 62. The sequence c_1-c_2 represents all the characters between c_1 and c_2, inclusive. Literal] or - characters must appear immediately after the opening bracket. An uparrow (^) immediately following the opening bracket negates the sense of the match—the pattern matches any character that isn't in the character class.

\d, \s, \w   Are abbreviations for character classes that match digits, whitespace, and word characters, respectively. \D, \S, and \W match characters that are not digits, whitespace, or word characters. These abbreviations are summarized in Table 5.1 on page 62.

. (period)   Appearing outside brackets, matches any character except a newline. (With the /m option, it matches newline, too).

re*   Matches zero or more occurrences of *re*.

re+   Matches one or more occurrences of *re*.

re{m,n}   Matches at least "m" and at most "n" occurrences of *re*.

re?   Matches zero or one occurrence of *re*. The *, +, and {m,n} modifiers are greedy by default. Append a question mark to make them minimal.

re1|re2   Matches either *re1* or *re2*. | has a low precedence.

(...)   Parentheses are used to group regular expressions. For example, the pattern /abc+/ matches a string containing an "a," a "b," and one or more "c"s. /(abc)+/ matches one or more sequences of "abc". Parentheses are also used to collect the results of pattern matching. For each opening parenthesis, Ruby stores the result of the partial match between it and the corresponding closing parenthesis as successive groups. Within the same pattern, \1 refers to the match of the first group, \2 the second group, and so on. Outside the pattern, the special variables $1, $2, and so on, serve the same purpose.

Substitutions

#{...}   Performs an expression substitution, as with strings. By default, the substitution is performed each time a regular expression literal is evaluated. With the /o option, it is performed just the first time.

\0, \1, \2, ... \9, \&, \`, \', \+
    Substitutes the value matched by the *n*th grouped subexpression, or by the entire match, pre- or postmatch, or the highest group.

Extensions

In common with Perl and Python, Ruby regular expressions offer some extensions over traditional Unix regular expressions. All the extensions are entered between the characters (? and). The parentheses that bracket these extensions are groups, but they do not generate backreferences: they do not set the values of \1 and $1 etc.

(?# comment)

Inserts a comment into the pattern. The content is ignored during pattern matching.

(?:re)

Makes *re* into a group without generating backreferences. This is often useful when you need to group a set of constructs but don't want the group to set the value of **$1** or whatever. In the example that follows, both patterns match a date with either colons or spaces between the month, day, and year. The first form stores the separator character in **$2** and **$4**, while the second pattern doesn't store the separator in an external variable.

```
date = "12/25/01"
date =~ %r{(\d+)(/|:)(\d+)(/|:)(\d+)}
[$1,$2,$3,$4,$5]    →    ["12", "/", "25", "/", "01"]
date =~ %r{(\d+)(?:/|:)(\d+)(?:/|:)(\d+)}
[$1,$2,$3]          →    ["12", "25", "01"]
```

(?=re)

Matches *re* at this point, but does not consume it (also known charmingly as "zero-width positive lookahead"). This lets you look forward for the context of a match without affecting **$&**. In this example, the **scan** method matches words followed by a comma, but the commas are not included in the result.

```
str = "red, white, and blue"
str.scan(/[a-z]+(?=,)/)    →    ["red", "white"]
```

(?!re)

Matches if *re* does not match at this point. Does not consume the match (zero-width negative lookahead). For example, /hot(?!dog)(\w+)/ matches any word that contains the letters "hot" that aren't followed by "dog", returning the end of the word in **$1**.

(?>re)

Nests an independent regular expression within the first regular expression. This expression is anchored at the current match position. If it consumes characters, these will no longer be available to the higher-level regular expression. This construct therefore inhibits backtracking, which can be a performance enhancement. For example, the pattern /a.*b.*a/ takes exponential time when matched against a string containing an "a" followed by a number of "b"s, but with no trailing "a." However, this can be avoided by using a nested regular expression /a(?>.*b).*a/. In this form, the nested expression consumes all the the input string up to the last possible "b" character. When the check for a trailing "a" then fails, there is no need to backtrack, and the pattern match fails promptly.

```
require "benchmark"
include Benchmark
str = "a" + ("b" * 5000)
```

```
bm(8) do |test|
  test.report("Normal:") { str =~ /a.*b.*a/ }
  test.report("Nested:") { str =~ /a(?>.*b).*a/ }
end
```

produces:

```
                 user     system      total        real
Normal:      2.240000   0.010000   2.250000 (   2.592112)
Nested:      0.000000   0.000000   0.000000 (   0.000873)
```

(?imx)	Turns on the corresponding "i," "m," or "x" option. If used inside a group, the effect is limited to that group.
(?-imx)	Turns off the "i," "m," or "x" option.
(?imx:*re*)	Turns on the "i," "m," or "x" option for *re*.
(?-imx:*re*)	Turns off the "i," "m," or "x" option for *re*.

Names

Ruby names are used to refer to constants, variables, methods, classes, and modules. The first character of a name helps Ruby to distinguish its intended use. Certain names, listed in Table 18.3 on the next page, are reserved words and should not be used as variable, method, class, or module names.

In these descriptions, *lowercase letter* means the characters "a" though "z", as well as "_", the underscore. *Uppercase letter* means "A" though "Z," and *digit* means "0" through "9." *Name characters* means any combination of upper- and lowercase letters and digits.

A local variable name consists of a lowercase letter followed by name characters.

```
fred  anObject  _x  three_two_one
```

An instance variable name starts with an "at" sign ("@") followed by an upper- or lowercase letter, optionally followed by name characters.

```
@name  @_  @Size
```

A class variable name starts with two "at" signs ("@@") followed by an upper- or lowercase letter, optionally followed by name characters.

```
@@name  @@_  @@Size
```

A constant name starts with an uppercase letter followed by name characters. Class names and module names are constants, and follow the constant naming conventions. By convention, constant variables are normally spelled using uppercase letters and underscores throughout.

Table 18.3. Reserved words

__FILE__	and	def	end	in	or	self	unless
__LINE__	begin	defined?	ensure	module	redo	super	until
BEGIN	break	do	false	next	rescue	then	when
END	case	else	for	nil	retry	true	while
alias	class	elsif	if	not	return	undef	yield

```
module Math
  PI = 3.1415926
end
class BigBlob
```

Global variables, and some special system variables, start with a dollar sign ("$") followed by name characters. In addition, there is a set of two-character variable names in which the second character is a punctuation character. These predefined variables are listed starting on page 216. Finally, a global variable name can be formed using "$-" followed by *any* single character.

```
$params $PROGRAM $! $_ $-a $-.
```

Method names are described in the section beginning on page 227.

Variable/Method Ambiguity

When Ruby sees a name such as "a" in an expression, it needs to determine if it is a local variable reference or a call to a method with no parameters. To decide which is the case, Ruby uses a heuristic. As Ruby reads a source file, it keeps track of symbols that have been assigned to. It assumes that these symbols are variables. When it subsequently comes across a symbol that might be either a variable or a method call, it checks to see if it has seen a prior assignment to that symbol. If so, it treats the symbol as a variable; otherwise it treats it as a method call. As a somewhat pathological case of this, consider the following code fragment, submitted by Clemens Hintze.

```
def a
  print "Function 'a' called\n"
  99
end

for i in 1..2
  if i == 2
    print "a=", a, "\n"
  else
    a = 1
    print "a=", a, "\n"
  end
end
```

produces:

```
a=1
Function 'a' called
a=99
```

During the parse, Ruby sees the use of "a" in the first print statement and, as it hasn't yet seen any assignment to "a," assumes that it is a method call. By the time it gets to the second print statement, though, it *has* seen an assignment, and so treats "a" as a variable.

Note that the assignment does not have to be executed—Ruby just has to have seen it. This program does not raise an error.

```
a = 1 if false; a
```

Variables and Constants

Ruby variables and constants hold references to objects. Variables themselves do not have an intrinsic type. Instead, the type of a variable is defined solely by the messages to which the object referenced by the variable responds.[3]

A Ruby *constant* is also a reference to an object. Constants are created when they are first assigned to (normally in a class or module definition). Ruby, unlike less flexible languages, lets you alter the value of a constant, although this will generate a warning message.

```
MY_CONST = 1
MY_CONST = 2   # generates a warning
```

produces:

```
prog.rb:2: warning: already initialized constant MY_CONST
```

Note that although constants should not be changed, you can alter the internal states of the objects they reference.

```
MY_CONST = "Tim"
MY_CONST[0] = "J"   # alter string referenced by constant
MY_CONST   →   "Jim"
```

Assignment potentially *aliases* objects, giving the same object different names.

---

3.   When we say that a variable is not typed, we mean that any given variable can at different times hold references to objects of many different types.

Scope of Constants and Variables

Constants defined within a class or module may be accessed unadorned anywhere within the class or module. Outside the class or module, they may be accessed using the scope operator, "::" prefixed by an expression that returns the appropriate class or module object. Constants defined outside any class or module may be accessed unadorned or by using the scope operator "::" with no prefix. Constants may not be defined in methods.

```
OUTER_CONST = 99
class Const
  def getConst
    CONST
  end
  CONST = OUTER_CONST + 1
end
Const.new.getConst    →    100
Const::CONST          →    100
::OUTER_CONST         →    99
```

Global variables are available throughout a program. Every reference to a particular global name returns the same object. Referencing an uninitialized global variable returns `nil`.

Class variables are available throughout a class or module body. Class variables must be initialized before use. A class variable is shared among all instances of a class and is available within the class itself.

```
class Song
  @@count = 0
  def initialize
    @@count += 1
  end
  def Song.getCount
    @@count
  end
end
```

Class variables belong to the innermost enclosing class or module. Class variables used at the top level are defined in `Object`, and behave like global variables. Class variables defined within singleton methods belong to the receiver if the receiver is a class or a module; otherwise, they belong to the class of the receiver.

```
class Holder
  @@var = 99
  def Holder.var=(val)
    @@var = val
  end
end

a = Holder.new
```

```
def a.var
  @@var
end

Holder.var = 123
a.var   →   123
```

Instance variables are available within instance methods throughout a class body. Referencing an uninitialized instance variable returns `nil`. Each instance of a class has a unique set of instance variables. Instance variables are not available to class methods.

Local variables are unique in that their scopes are statically determined but their existence is established dynamically.

A local variable is created dynamically when it is first assigned a value during program execution. However, the scope of a local variable is statically determined to be: the immediately enclosing block, method definition, class definition, module definition, or top-level program. Referencing a local variable that is in scope but that has not yet been created generates a `NameError` exception.

Local variables with the same name are different variables if they appear in disjoint scopes.

Method parameters are considered to be variables local to that method.

Block parameters are assigned values when the block is invoked.

```
a = [ 1, 2, 3 ]
a.each { |i|  puts i  } # i local to block
a.each { |$i| puts $i } # assigns to global $i
a.each { |@i| puts @i } # assigns to instance variable @i
a.each { |I|  puts I  } # generates warning assigning to constant
a.each { |b.meth| }     # invokes meth= in object b
sum = 0
var = nil
a.each { |var| sum += var } # uses sum and var from enclosing scope
```

If a local variable (including a block parameter) is first assigned in a block, it is local to the block. If instead a variable of the same name is already established at the time the block executes, the block will inherit that variable.

A block takes on the set of local variables in existence at the time that it is created. This forms part of its binding. Note that although the binding of the variables is fixed at this point, the block will have access to the *current* values of these variables when it executes. The binding preserves these variables even if the original enclosing scope is destroyed.

The bodies of `while`, `until`, and `for` loops are part of the scope that contains them; previously existing locals can be used in the loop, and any new locals created will be available outside the bodies afterward.

Predefined Variables

The following variables are predefined in the Ruby interpreter. In these descriptions, the notation [r/o] indicates that the variables are read-only; an error will be raised if a program attempts to modify a read-only variable. After all, you probably don't want to change the meaning of **true** halfway through your program (except perhaps if you're a politician). Entries marked [thread] are thread local.

Many global variables look something like Snoopy swearing: **$_**, **$!**, **$&**, and so on. This is for "historical" reasons, as most of these variable names come from Perl. If you find memorizing all this punctuation difficult, you might want to have a look at the library file called "English," documented on page 449, which gives the commonly used global variables more descriptive names.

In the tables of variables and constants that follow, we show the variable name, the type of the referenced object, and a description.

Exception Information

$!	Exception	The exception object passed to **raise**. [thread]
$@	Array	The stack backtrace generated by the last exception. See **Kernel#caller** on page 417 for details. [thread]

Pattern Matching Variables

These variables are all set to **nil** after an unsuccessful pattern match.

$&	String	The string matched by the last successful pattern match. This variable is local to the current scope. [r/o, thread]
$+	String	The contents of the highest-numbered group matched in the last successful pattern match. Thus, in **"cat" =~/(c|a)(t|z)/**, **$+** will be set to "t". This variable is local to the current scope. [r/o, thread]
$`	String	The string preceding the match in the last successful pattern match. This variable is local to the current scope. [r/o, thread]
$'	String	The string following the match in the last successful pattern match. This variable is local to the current scope. [r/o, thread]
$=	Object	If set to any value apart from **nil** or **false**, all pattern matches will be case insensitive, string comparisons will ignore case, and string hash values will be case insensitive.
$1...$9	String	The contents of successive groups matched in the last successful pattern match. In **"cat" =~/(c|a)(t|z)/**, **$1** will be set to "a" and **$2** to "t". This variable is local to the current scope. [r/o, thread]
$~	MatchData	An object that encapsulates the results of a successful pattern match. The variables **$&**, **$`**, **$'**, and **$1..$9** are all derived from **$~**. Assigning to **$~** changes the values of these derived variables. This variable is local to the current scope. [thread]

Input/Output Variables

$/	String	The input record separator (newline by default). This is the value that routines such as `Kernel#gets` use to determine record boundaries. If set to `nil`, `gets` will read the entire file.
$-0	String	Synonym for $/.
$\	String	The string appended to the output of every call to methods such as `Kernel#print` and `IO#write`. The default value is `nil`.
$,	String	The separator string output between the parameters to methods such as `Kernel#print` and `Array#join`. Defaults to `nil`, which adds no text.
$.	Fixnum	The number of the last line read from the current input file.
$;	String	The default separator pattern used by `String#split`. May be set from the command line using the `-F` flag.
$<	Object	An object that provides access to the concatenation of the contents of all the files given as command-line arguments, or `$stdin` (in the case where there are no arguments). `$<` supports methods similar to a `File` object: `binmode, close, closed?, each, each_byte, each_line, eof, eof?, file, filename, fileno, getc, gets, lineno, lineno=, pos, pos=, read, readchar, readline, readlines, rewind, seek, skip, tell, to_a, to_i, to_io, to_s,` along with the methods in `Enumerable`. The method `file` returns a `File` object for the file currently being read. This may change as `$<` reads through the files on the command line. [r/o]
$>	IO	The destination of output for `Kernel#print` and `Kernel#printf`. The default value is `$stdout`.
$_	String	The last line read by `Kernel#gets` or `Kernel#readline`. Many string-related functions in the `Kernel` module operate on `$_` by default. The variable is local to the current scope. [thread]
$defout	IO	Synonym for $>.
$-F	String	Synonym for $;.
$stderr	IO	The current standard error output.
$stdin	IO	The current standard input.
$stdout	IO	The current standard output.

Execution Environment Variables

$0	String	The name of the top-level Ruby program being executed. Typically this will be the program's filename. On some operating systems, assigning to this variable will change the name of the process reported (for example) by the `ps(1)` command.
$*	Array	An array of strings containing the command-line options from the invocation of the program. Options used by the Ruby interpreter will have been removed. [r/o]
$"	Array	An array containing the filenames of modules loaded by `require`. [r/o]

$$	Fixnum	The process number of the program being executed. [r/o]
$?	Fixnum	The exit status of the last child process to terminate. [r/o, thread]
$:	Array	An array of strings, where each string specifies a directory to be searched for Ruby scripts and binary extensions used by the **load** and **require** methods. The initial value is the value of the arguments passed via the **-I** command-line option, followed by an installation-defined standard library location, followed by the current directory ("."). This variable may be set from within a program to alter the default search path; typically, programs use **$: << dir** to append **dir** to the path. [r/o]
$-a	Object	True if the **-a** option is specified on the command line. [r/o]
$-d	Object	Synonym for **$DEBUG**.
$DEBUG	Object	Set to **true** if the **-d** command-line option is specified.
__FILE__	String	The name of the current source file. [r/o]
$F	Array	The array that receives the split input line if the **-a** command-line option is used.
$FILENAME	String	The name of the current input file. Equivalent to **$<.filename**. [r/o]
$-i	String	If in-place edit mode is enabled (perhaps using the **-i** command-line option), **$-i** holds the extension used when creating the backup file. If you set a value into **$-i**, enables in-place edit mode. See page 138.
$-I	Array	Synonym for **$:**. [r/o]
$-K	String	Sets the multibyte coding system for strings and regular expressions. Equivalent to the **-K** command-line option. See page 139.
$-l	Object	Set to **true** if the **-l** option (which enables line-end processing) is present on the command line. See page 139. [r/o]
__LINE__	String	The current line number in the source file. [r/o]
$LOAD_PATH	Array	A synonym for **$:**. [r/o]
$-p	Object	Set to **true** if the **-p** option (which puts an implicit **while gets ... end** loop around your program) is present on the command line. See page 139. [r/o]
$SAFE	Fixnum	The current safe level (see page 258). This variable's value may never be reduced by assignment. [thread]
$VERBOSE	Object	Set to **true** if the **-v**, **--version**, or **-w** option is specified on the command line. Setting this option to **true** causes the interpreter and some library routines to report additional information.
$-v	Object	Synonym for **$VERBOSE**.
$-w	Object	Synonym for **$VERBOSE**.

Standard Objects

ARGF	Object	A synonym for **$<**.
ARGV	Array	A synonym for **$***.
ENV	Object	A hash-like object containing the program's environment variables. An instance of class **Object**, ENV implements the full set of **Hash** methods. Used to query and set the value of an environment variable, as in **ENV["PATH"]** and **ENV['term']="ansi"**.
false	FalseClass	Singleton instance of class **FalseClass**. [r/o]
nil	NilClass	The singleton instance of class **NilClass**. The value of uninitialized instance and global variables. [r/o]
self	Object	The receiver (object) of the current method. [r/o]
true	TrueClass	Singleton instance of class **TrueClass**. [r/o]

Global Constants

The following constants are defined by the Ruby interpreter.

DATA	IO	If the the main program file contains the directive **__END__**, then the constant **DATA** will be initialized so that reading from it will return lines following **__END__** from the source file.
FALSE	FalseClass	Synonym for **false**.
NIL	NilClass	Synonym for **nil**.
RUBY_PLATFORM	String	The identifier of the platform running this program. This string is in the same form as the platform identifier used by the GNU configure utility (which is not a coincidence).
RUBY_RELEASE_DATE	String	The date of this release.
RUBY_VERSION	String	The version number of the interpreter.
STDERR	IO	The actual standard error stream for the program. The initial value of **$stderr**.
STDIN	IO	The actual standard input stream for the program. The initial value of **$stdin**.
STDOUT	IO	The actual standard output stream for the program. The initial value of **$stdout**.
TOPLEVEL_BINDING	Binding	A **Binding** object representing the binding at Ruby's top level—the level where programs are initially executed.
TRUE	TrueClass	Synonym for **true**.

Expressions

Single Terms

Single terms in an expression may be any of the following.

- **Literal**. Ruby literals are numbers, strings, arrays, hashes, ranges, symbols, and regular expressions. There are described starting on page 203.

- **Shell Command**. A shell command is a string enclosed in backquotes, or in a general delimited string (page 202) starting with **%x**. The value of the string is the standard output of running the command represented by the string under the host operating system's standard shell. The execution also sets the **$?** variable with the command's exit status.

  ```
  filter = "*.c"
  files = `ls #{filter}`
  files = %x{ls #{filter}}
  ```

- **Symbol Generator**. A `Symbol` object is created by prefixing an operator, variable, constant, method, class, or module name with a colon. The symbol object will be unique for each different name but does not refer to a particular instance of the name, so the symbol for (say) `:fred` will be the same regardless of context. A symbol is similar to the concept of atoms in other high-level languages.

- **Variable Reference** or **Constant Reference**. A variable is referenced by citing its name. Depending on scope (see page 214), a constant is referenced either by citing its name or by qualifying the name, using the name of the class or module containing the constant and the scope operator ("::").

  ```
  barney    # variable reference
  APP_NAMR  # constant reference
  Math::PI  # qualified constant reference
  ```

- **Method Invocation**. The various ways of invoking a method are described starting on page 229.

Operator Expressions

Expressions may be combined using operators. Table 18.4 on the facing page lists the Ruby operators in precedence order. The operators with a ✓ in the *method* column are implemented as methods, and may be overridden.

More on Assignment

The assignment operator assigns one or more *rvalues* to one or more *lvalues*. What is meant by assignment depends on each individual lvalue.

Table 18.4. Ruby operators (high to low precedence)

Method	Operator	Description
✓	[ ] [ ]=	Element reference, element set
✓	**	Exponentiation
✓	! ~ + -	Not, complement, unary plus and minus (method names for the last two are +@ and -@)
✓	* / %	Multiply, divide, and modulo
✓	+ -	Plus and minus
✓	>> <<	Right and left shift
✓	&	Bitwise 'and'
✓	^ |	Bitwise exclusive 'or' and regular 'or'
✓	<= < > >=	Comparison operators
✓	<=> == === != =~ !~	Equality and pattern match operators (!= and !~ may not be defined as methods)
	&&	Logical 'and'
	||	Logical 'or'
	.. ...	Range (inclusive and exclusive)
	? :	Ternary if-then-else
	= %= ~= /= -= += |= &= >>= <<= *= &&= ||= **=	Assignment
✓	defined?	Check if symbol defined
	not	Logical negation
	or and	Logical composition
	if unless while until	Expression modifiers
	begin/end	Block expression

If an lvalue is a variable or constant name, that variable or constant receives a reference to the corresponding rvalue.

```ruby
a, b, c = 1, "cat", [ 3, 4, 5 ]
```

If the lvalue is an object attribute, the corresponding attribute setting method will be called in the receiver, passing as a parameter the rvalue.

```ruby
anObj = A.new
anObj.value = "hello"   # equivalent to anObj.value=("hello")
```

If the lvalue is an array element reference, Ruby calls the element assignment operator ("[]=") in the receiver, passing as parameters any indices that appear between the brackets followed by the rvalue. This is illustrated in Table 18.5 on the next page.

Table 18.5. Mapping from element reference to method call

Element Reference	Actual Method Call
`anObj[] = "one"`	`anObj.[]=("one")`
`anObj[1] = "two"`	`anObj.[]=(1, "two")`
`anObj["a", /^cat/] = "three"`	`anObj.[]=("a", /^cat/, "three")`

Parallel Assignment

An assignment expression may have one or more lvalues and one or more rvalues. This section explains how Ruby handles assignment with different combinations of arguments.

1. If the last rvalue is prefixed with an asterisk and is an object of class **Array**, the rvalue is replaced with the elements of the array, with each element forming its own rvalue.

2. If the assignment contains multiple lvalues and one rvalue, the rvalue is converted into an **Array**, and this array is expanded into a set of rvalues as described in (1).

3. Successive rvalues are assigned to the lvalues. This assignment effectively happens in parallel, so that (for example) `a,b=b,a` swaps the values in "a" and "b."

4. If there are more lvalues than rvalues, the excess will have **nil** assigned to them.

5. If there are more rvalues that lvalues, the excess will be ignored.

6. These rules are modified slightly if the last lvalue is preceded with an asterisk. This lvalue will always receive an array during the assignment. The array will consist of whatever rvalue would normally have been assigned to this lvalue, followed by the excess rvalues (if any).

7. If an lvalue is a parenthesized list, it is treated as a nested assignment statement, and the list is assigned from the corresponding rvalue as described by these rules.

The tutorial has examples starting on page 77.

Block Expressions

```
begin
  body
end
```

Expressions may be grouped between **begin** and **end**. The value of the block expression is the value of the last expression executed.

Block expressions also play a role in exception handling, which is discussed starting on page 237.

Boolean Expressions

Boolean expressions evaluate to a truth value. Some Ruby constructs (particularly ranges) behave differently when evaluated in a boolean expression.

Truth Values

Ruby predefines the globals `false` and `nil`. Both of these values are treated as being false in a boolean context. All other values are treated as being true.

And, Or, Not, and Defined?

The `and` and `&&` operators evaluate their first operand. If false, the expression returns false; otherwise, the expression returns the value of the second operand.

```
expr1   and   expr2
expr1   &&    expr2
```

The `or` and `||` operators evaluate their first operand. If true, the expression returns true; otherwise, the expression returns the value of the second operand.

```
expr1   or   expr2
expr1   ||   expr2
```

The `not` and `!` operators evaluate their operand. If true, the expression returns false. If false, the expression returns true.

The word forms of these operators (`and`, `or`, and `not`) have a lower precedence than the corresponding symbol forms (`&&`, `||`, and `!`). See Table 18.4 on page 221 for details.

The `defined?` operator returns `nil` if its argument, which can be an arbitrary expression, is not defined. Otherwise, it returns a description of that argument. For examples, see page 80 in the tutorial.

Comparison Operators

The Ruby syntax defines the comparison operators ==, ===, <=>, <, <=, >, >=, =~, and the standard methods `eql?` and `equal?` (see Table 7.1 on page 81). All of these operators are implemented as methods. Although the operators have intuitive meaning, it is up to the classes that implement them to produce meaningful comparison semantics. The library reference starting on page 279 describes the comparison semantics for the built-in classes. The module `Comparable` provides support for implementing the operators ==, <=>, <, <=, >, and >= in terms of <=>. The operator === is used in `case` expressions, described on page 225.

Both == and =~ have negated forms, != and !~. Ruby converts these during syntax analysis: a != b is mapped to !(a == b), and a !~ b is mapped to !(a =~ b). There are no methods corresponding to != and !~.

Ranges in Boolean Expressions

```
if   expr1 .. expr2
while   expr1 ... expr2
```

A range used in a boolean expression acts as a flip-flop. It has two states, set and unset, and is initially unset. On each call, the range cycles through the state machine shown in Figure 18.1 on the facing page. The range returns `true` if it is in the set state at the end of the call, and `false` otherwise.

The two-dot form of a range behaves slightly differently than the three-dot form. When the two-dot form first makes the transition from unset to set, it immediately evaluates the end condition and makes the transition accordingly. This means that if *expr1* and *expr2* both evaluate to `true` on the same call, the two-dot form will finish the call in the unset state. However, it still returns `true` for this call.

The difference is illustrated by the following code:

```
a = (11..20).collect {|i| (i%4 == 0)..(i%3 == 0) ? i : nil}
a   →   [nil, 12, nil, nil, nil, 16, 17, 18, nil, 20]

a = (11..20).collect {|i| (i%4 == 0)...(i%3 == 0) ? i : nil}
a   →   [nil, 12, 13, 14, 15, 16, 17, 18, nil, 20]
```

Regular Expressions in Boolean Expressions

If a single regular expression appears as a boolean expression, it is matched against the current value of the variable `$_`.

```
if /re/ ...
```

is equivalent to

```
if $_ =~ /re/ ...
```

If and Unless Expressions

```
if boolean-expression [ then ]
   body
elsif boolean-expression [ then ]
   body
else
   body
end
```

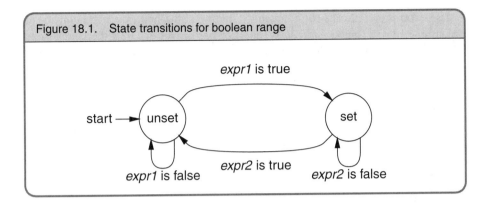

Figure 18.1. State transitions for boolean range

```
unless boolean-expression [ then ]
   body
else
   body
end
```

The **then** keyword separates the body from the condition. It is not required if the body starts on a new line. The value of an **if** or **unless** expression is the value of the last expression evaluated in whichever body is executed.

If and Unless Modifiers

```
expression if       boolean-expression
expression unless boolean-expression
```

evaluates *expression* only if *boolean-expression* is **true** (**false** for **unless**).

Ternary Operator

```
boolean-expression ? expr1 : expr2
```

returns *expr1* if *boolean expression* is true and *expr2* otherwise.

Case Expressions

```
case target
  when comparison [, comparison ]... [ then ]
     body
  when comparison [, comparison ]... [ then ]
     body
  ...
[ else
     body ]
  end
```

A case expression searches for a match by starting at the first (top left) comparison, performing *comparison* === *target*. When a comparison returns true, the search stops, and the body associated with the comparison is executed. `case` then returns the value of the last expression executed. If no *comparison* matches: if an `else` clause is present, its body will be executed; otherwise, `case` silently returns `nil`.

The `then` keyword separates the `when` comparisons from the bodies, and is not needed if the body starts on a new line.

Loops

```
while boolean-expression [ do ]
   body
end
```

executes *body* zero or more times as long as *boolean-expression* is true.

```
until boolean-expression [ do ]
   body
end
```

executes *body* zero or more times as long as *boolean-expression* is false.

In both forms, the `do` separates *boolean-expression* from the *body*, and may be omitted when the body starts on a new line.

```
for name [, name ]... in expression [ do ]
   body
end
```

The `for` loop is executed as if it were the following `each` loop, except that local variables defined in the body of the `for` loop will be available outside the loop, while those defined within an iterator block will not.

```
expression.each do | name [, name ]... |
   body
end
```

`loop`, which iterates its associated block, is not a language construct—it is a method in module `Kernel`.

While and Until Modifiers

```
expression while boolean-expression
expression until boolean-expression
```

If *expression* is anything other than a `begin/end` block, executes *expression* zero or more times while *boolean-expression* is `true` (`false` for `until`).

If *expression* is a `begin/end` block, the block will always be executed at least one time.

Break, Redo, Next, and Retry

`break`, `redo`, `next`, and `retry` alter the normal flow through a `while`, `until`, `for`, or iterator controlled loop.

`break` terminates the immediately enclosing loop—control resumes at the statement following the block. `redo` repeats the loop from the start, but without reevaluating the condition or fetching the next element (in an iterator). `next` skips to the end of the loop, effectively starting the next iteration. `retry` restarts the loop, reevaluating the condition.

Method Definition

```
def defname [ ( [ arg [ =val ], ... ] [ , *vararg ] [ , &blockarg ] ) ]
   body
end
```

defname defines both the name of the method and optionally the context in which it is valid.

```
defname   ←   methodname
              expr.methodname
```

A *methodname* is either a redefinable operator (see Table 18.4 on page 221) or a name. If *methodname* is a name, it should start with a lowercase letter (or underscore) optionally followed by upper- and lowercase letters, underscores, and digits. A *methodname* may optionally end with a question mark ("?"), exclamation point ("!"), or equals sign ("="). The question mark and exclamation point are simply part of the name. The equals sign is also part of the name but additionally signals that this method is an attribute setter (described on page 25).

A method definition using an unadorned method name within a class or module definition creates an instance method. An instance method may be invoked only by sending its name to a receiver that is an instance of the class that defined it (or one of that class's subclasses).

Outside a class or module definition, a definition with an unadorned method name is added as a private method to class `Object`, and hence may be called in any context without an explicit receiver.

A definition using a method name of the form *expr.methodname* creates a method associated with the object that is the value of the expression; the method will be callable only by supplying the object referenced by the expression as a receiver. Other Ruby documentation calls these methods *singleton methods*.

```
class MyClass
  def MyClass.method      # definition
  end
end
MyClass.method            # call

anObject = Object.new
def anObject.method       # definition
end
anObject.method           # call

  def (1.class).fred      # receiver may be an expression
  end
Fixnum.fred               # call
```

Method definitions may not contain class, module, or instance method definitions. They may contain nested singleton method definitions.

Method Arguments

A method definition may have zero or more regular arguments, an optional array argument, and an optional block argument. Arguments are separated by commas, and the argument list may be enclosed in parentheses.

A regular argument is a local variable name, optionally followed by an equals sign and an expression giving a default value. The expression is evaluated at the time the method is called. The expressions are evaluated from left to right. An expression may reference a parameter that precedes it in the argument list.

```
def options(a=99, b=a+1)
  [ a, b ]
end
options          →   [99, 100]
options 1        →   [1, 2]
options 2, 4     →   [2, 4]
```

The optional array argument must follow any regular arguments and may not have a default. When the method is invoked, Ruby sets the array argument to reference a new object of class **Array**. If the method call specifies any parameters in excess of the regular argument count, all these extra parameters will be collected into this newly created array.

```
def varargs(a, *b)
  [ a, b ]
end
varargs 1         →   [1, []]
varargs 1, 2      →   [1, [2]]
varargs 1, 2, 3   →   [1, [2, 3]]
```

If an array argument follows arguments with default values, parameters will first be used to override the defaults. The remainder will then be used to populate the array.

```
def mixed(a, b=99, *c)
  [ a, b, c]
end
mixed 1              →   [1, 99, []]
mixed 1, 2           →   [1, 2, []]
mixed 1, 2, 3        →   [1, 2, [3]]
mixed 1, 2, 3, 4     →   [1, 2, [3, 4]]
```

The optional block argument must be the last in the list. Whenever the method is called, Ruby checks for an associated block. If a block is present, it is converted to an object of class `Proc` and assigned to the block argument. If no block is present, the argument is set to `nil`.

Invoking a Method

```
[ receiver. ] name [ parameters ] [ block ]
[ receiver:: ] name [ parameters ] [ block ]

parameters  ←  ( [ param, ... ] [ , hashlist ] [ *array ] [ &aProc ] )

    block   ←  { blockbody }
               do blockbody end
```

Initial parameters are assigned to the actual arguments of the method. Following these parameters may be a list of *key => value* pairs. These pairs are collected into a single new `Hash` object and passed as a single parameter.

Following these parameters may be a single parameter prefixed with an asterisk. If this parameter is an array, Ruby replaces it with zero or more parameters corresponding to the elements of the array.

```
def regular(a, b, *c)
  # ..
end
regular 1, 2, 3, 4
regular(1, 2, 3, 4)
regular(1, *[2, 3, 4])
```

A block may be associated with a method call using either a literal block (which must start on the same source line as the last line of the method call) or a parameter containing a reference to a `Proc` or `Method` object prefixed with an ampersand character. Regardless of the presence of a block argument, Ruby arranges for the value of the global function `Kernel.block_given?` to reflect the availability of a block associated with the call.

```
aProc   = proc { 99 }
anArray = [ 98, 97, 96 ]

def block
  yield
end
block { }
block do
      end
block(&aProc)

def all(a, b, c, *d, &e)
  puts "a = #{a}"
  puts "b = #{b}"
  puts "c = #{c}"
  puts "d = #{d}"
  puts "block = #{yield(e)}"
end

all('test', 1 => 'cat', 2 => 'dog', *anArray, &aProc)
```

produces:

```
a = test
b = {1=>"cat", 2=>"dog"}
c = 98
d = [97, 96]
block = 99
```

A method is called by passing its name to a receiver. If no receiver is specified, `self` is assumed. The receiver checks for the method definition in its own class and then sequentially in its ancestor classes. The instance methods of included modules act as if they were in anonymous superclasses of the class that includes them. If the method is not found, Ruby invokes the method `method_missing` in the receiver. The default behavior defined in `Kernel.method_missing` is to report an error and terminate the program.

When a receiver is explicitly specified in a method invocation, it may be separated from the method name using either a period "`.`" or two colons "`::`". The only difference between these two forms occurs if the method name starts with an uppercase letter. In this case, Ruby will assume that a `receiver::Thing` method call is actually an attempt to access a constant called `Thing` in the receiver *unless* the method invocation has a parameter list between parentheses.

```
Foo.Bar()     #  method call
Foo.Bar       #  method call
Foo::Bar()    #  method call
Foo::Bar      #  constant access
```

The return value of a method is the value of the last expression executed.

```
return [ expr, ... ]
```

A `return` expression immediately exits a method. The value of a `return` is `nil` if it is called with no parameters, the value of its parameter if it is called with one parameter, or an array containing all of its parameters if it is called with more than one parameter.

super

```
super  [  (  [ param,  ... ] [ *array ] )  ]  [ block ]
```

Within the body of a method, a call to `super` acts just like a call to that original method, except that the search for a method body starts in the superclass of the object that was found to contain the original method. If no parameters (and no parentheses) are passed to `super`, the original method's parameters will be passed; otherwise, the parameters to `super` will be passed.

Operator Methods

```
expr1  operator
operator  expr1
expr1  operator  expr2
```

If the operator in an operator expression corresponds to a redefinable method (see the Table 18.4 on page 221), Ruby will execute the operator expression as if it had been written

```
(expr1) . operator(expr2)
```

Attribute Assignment

```
receiver. attrname = rvalue
```

When the form *receiver.attrname* appears as an lvalue, Ruby invokes a method named *attrname=* in the receiver, passing *rvalue* as a single parameter.

Element Reference Operator

```
receiver[ expr [, expr ]... ]
receiver[ expr [, expr ]... ] = rvalue
```

When used as an rvalue, element reference invokes the method `[]` in the receiver, passing as parameters the expressions between the brackets.

When used as an lvalue, element reference invokes the method `[]=` in the receiver, passing as parameters the expressions between the brackets, followed by the *rvalue* being assigned.

Aliasing

```
alias newName oldName
```

creates a new name that refers to an existing method, operator, global variable, or regular expression backreference ($&, $', $', and $+). Local variables, instance variables,
class variables, and constants may not be aliased. The parameters to **alias** may be
names or symbols.

```
class Fixnum
  alias plus +
end
1.plus(3)          →    4

alias $prematch $`
"string" =~ /i/    →    3
$prematch          →    "str"

alias :cmd :`
cmd "date"         →    "Wed Sep 20 10:35:11 CDT 2000\n"
```

When a method is aliased, the new name refers to a copy of the original method's body.
If the method is subsequently redefined, the aliased name will still invoke the original
implementation.

```
def meth
  "original method"
end

alias original meth

def meth
  "new and improved"
end
meth       →    "new and improved"
original   →    "original method"
```

Class Definition

```
class classname   [ < superexpr ]
  body
end

class << anObject
  body
end
```

A Ruby class definition creates or extends an object of class **Class** by executing the
code in *body*. In the first form, a named class is created or extended. The resulting

`Class` object is assigned to a global constant named *classname*. This name should start with an uppercase letter. In the second form, an anonymous (singleton) class is associated with the specific object.

If present, *superexpr* should be an expression that evaluates to a `Class` object that will be installed as the superclass of the class being defined. If omitted, it defaults to class `Object`.

Within *body*, most Ruby expressions are simply executed as the definition is read. However:

- Method definitions will register the methods in a table in the class object.

- Nested class and module definitions will be stored in constants within the class, not as global constants. These nested classes and modules can be accessed from outside the defining class using "`::`" to qualify their names.

```
module NameSpace
  class Example
    CONST = 123
  end
end
obj = NameSpace::Example.new
a = NameSpace::Example::CONST
```

- The `Module#include` method will add the named modules as anonymous superclasses of the class being defined.

It is worth emphasizing that a class definition is executable code. Many of the directives used in class definition (such as `attr` and `include`) are actually simply private instance methods of class `Module` (documented starting on page 348).

Chapter 19, which begins on page 241, describes in more detail how `Class` objects interact with the rest of the environment.

Creating Objects from Classes

obj = *classexpr*.`new` [([*args*, ...])]

Class `Class` defines the instance method `Class#new`, which:

- Creates an object of the class of the receiver (*classexpr* in the syntax example).

- Sets that object's type to be the receiver.

- Invokes the instance method `initialize` in the newly created object, passing it any arguments originally passed to `new`.

If a class definition overrides the class method `new` without calling `super`, no objects of that class can be created.

Class Attribute Declarations

Class attribute declarations are technically not part of the Ruby language: they are simply methods defined in class `Module` that create accessor methods automatically.

```
class name
  attr attribute   [ , writable ]
  attr_reader      attribute [, attribute ]...
  attr_writer      attribute [, attribute ]...
  attr_accessor    attribute [, attribute ]...
end
```

Module Definitions

```
module name
   body
end
```

A module is basically a class that cannot be instantiated. Like a class, its body is executed during definition and the resulting `Module` object is stored in a constant. A module may contain class and instance methods and may define constants and class variables. As with classes, module methods are invoked using the `Module` object as a receiver, and constants are accessed using the "`::`" scope resolution operator.

```
module Mod
  CONST = 1
  def Mod.method1    # module method
    CONST + 1
  end
end

Mod::CONST    →   1
Mod.method1   →   2
```

Mixins—Including Modules

```
class|module name
   include expr
end
```

A module may be included within the definition of another module or class using the `include` method. The module or class definition containing the `include` gains access to the constants, class variables, and instance methods of the module it includes.

If a module is included within a class definition, the module's constants, class variables, and instance methods are effectively bundled into an anonymous (and inaccessible) superclass for that class. In particular, objects of the class will respond to messages sent to the module's instance methods.

A module may also be included at the top level, in which case the module's constants, class variables, and instance methods become available at the top level.

Module Functions

Although `include` is useful for providing mixin functionality, it is also a way of bringing the constants, class variables, and instance methods of a module into another namespace. However, functionality defined in an instance method will not be available as a module method.

```
module Math
  def sin(x)
    #
  end
end

# Only way to access Math.sin is...
include Math
sin(1)
```

The method `Module#module_function` solves this problem by taking one or more module instance methods and copying their definitions into corresponding module methods.

```
module Math
  def sin(x)
    #
  end
  module_function :sin
end

Math.sin(1)
include Math
sin(1)
```

The instance method and module method are two different methods: the method definition is copied by `module_function`, not aliased.

Access Control

Ruby defines three levels of protection for module and class constants and methods:

- **Public**. Accessible to anyone.

- **Protected**. Can be invoked only by objects of the defining class and its subclasses.

- **Private**. Can be called only in functional form (that is, with an implicit `self` as the receiver). Private methods therefore can be called only in the defining class and by direct descendents within the same object.

```
private     [ aSymbol, ... ]
protected   [ aSymbol, ... ]
public      [ aSymbol, ... ]
```

Each function can be used in two different ways.

1. If used with no arguments, the three functions set the default access control of subsequently defined methods.

2. With arguments, the functions set the access control of the named methods and constants.

Access control is enforced when a method is invoked.

Blocks, Closures, and Proc Objects

A code block is a set of Ruby statements and expressions between braces or a do/end pair. The block may start with an argument list between vertical bars. A code block may appear only immediately after a method invocation. The start of the block must be on the same logical line as the end of the invocation.

```
invocation  do  | a1, a2, ... |
end

invocation  {    | a1, a2, ... |
}
```

Braces have a high precedence; do has a low precedence. If the method invocation has parameters that are not enclosed in parentheses, the brace form of a block will bind to the last parameter, not to the overall invocation. The do form will bind to the invocation.

Within the body of the invoked method, the code block may be called using the `yield` method. Parameters passed to the `yield` will be assigned to arguments in the block using the rules of parallel assignment described starting on page 222. The return value of the `yield` is the value of the last expression evaluated in the block.

A code block remembers the environment in which it was defined, and it uses that environment whenever it is called.

Proc Objects

Code blocks are converted into objects of class `Proc` using the methods `Proc.new` and `Kernel#proc`, or by associating the block with a method's block argument.

The `Proc` constructor takes an associated block and wraps it with enough context to be able to re-create the block's environment when it is subsequently called. The `Proc#call` instance method then allows you to invoke the original block, optionally passing in parameters. The code in the block (and the associated closure) remains available for the lifetime of the **Proc** object.

If the last argument in a method's argument list is prefixed with an ampersand ("&"), any block associated with calls to that method will be converted to a **Proc** object and assigned to that parameter.

Exceptions

Ruby exceptions are objects of class **Exception** and its descendents (a full list of the built-in exceptions is given in Figure 22.1 on page 303).

Raising Exceptions

The **Kernel.raise** method raises an exception.

```
raise
raise aString
raise thing [ , aString [ aStackTrace ] ]
```

The first form reraises the exception in **$!** or a new **RuntimeError** if **$!** is **nil**. The second form creates a new **RuntimeError** exception, setting its message to the given string. The third form creates an exception object by invoking the method **exception** on its first argument. It then sets this exception's message and backtrace to its second and third arguments. Class **Exception** and objects of class **Exception** contain factory methods called **exception**, so an exception class name or instance can be used as the first parameter to **raise**.

When an exception is raised, Ruby places a reference to the **Exception** object in the global variable **$!**.

Handling Exceptions

Exceptions may be handled within the scope of a **begin/end** block.

```
begin
    code...
    code...
[ rescue  [ parm, ... ] [ => var ] [ then ]
    error handling code... , ... ]
[ else
    no exception code... ]
[ ensure
    always executed code... ]
  end
```

A block may have multiple **rescue** clauses, and each **rescue** clause may specify zero or more parameters. A **rescue** clause with no parameter is treated as if it had a parameter of **StandardError**.

When an exception is raised, Ruby scans up the call stack until it finds an enclosing **begin/end** block. For each **rescue** clause in that block, Ruby compares the raised exception against each of the rescue clause's parameters in turn; each parameter is tested using $!.kind_of?(*parameter*). If the raised exception matches a **rescue** parameter, Ruby executes the body of the **rescue** and stops looking. If a matching **rescue** clause ends with => and a variable name, the variable is set to $!.

Although the parameters to the **rescue** clause are typically the names of **Exception** classes, they can actually be arbitrary expressions (including method calls) that return an appropriate class.

If no rescue clause matches the raised exception, Ruby moves up the stack frame looking for a higher-level **begin/end** block that matches. If an exception propagates to the top level without being rescued, the program terminates with a message.

If an **else** clause is present, its body is executed if no exceptions were raised in *initial code*. Exceptions raised during the execution of the **else** clause are not captured by **rescue** clauses in the same block as the **else**.

If an **ensure** clause is present, its body is always executed as the block is exited (even if an uncaught exception is in the process of being propagated).

Retrying a Block

The **retry** statement can be used within a **rescue** clause to restart the enclosing **begin/end** block from the beginning.

Catch and Throw

The method **Kernel.catch** executes its associated block.

```
catch ( aSymbol | aString )  do
   block...
end
```

The method **Kernel.throw** interrupts the normal processing of statements.

```
throw( aSymbol | aString [ , anObject ] )
```

When a **throw** is executed, Ruby searches up the call stack for the first **call** block with a matching symbol or string. If it is found, the search stops, and execution resumes past the end of the **catch**'s block. If the **throw** was passed a second parameter, that value is returned as the value of the `catch`. Ruby honors the `ensure` clauses of any block expressions it traverses while looking for a corresponding `catch`.

If no `catch` block matches the `throw`, Ruby raises a `NameError` exception at the location of the `throw`.

## Chapter 19

Classes and Objects

Classes and objects are obviously central to Ruby, but at first sight they can seem a little confusing. There seem to be a lot of concepts: classes, objects, class objects, instance methods, class methods, and singleton classes. In reality, however, Ruby has just a single underlying class and object structure, which we'll discuss in this chapter. In fact, the basic model is so simple, we can describe it in a single paragraph.

A Ruby object has three components: a set of flags, some instance variables, and an associated class. A Ruby class is an object of class `Class`, which contains all the object things plus a list of methods and a reference to a superclass (which is itself another class). All method calls in Ruby nominate a receiver (which is by default `self`, the current object). Ruby finds the method to invoke by looking at the list of methods in the receiver's class. If it doesn't find the method there, it looks in the superclass, and then in the superclass's superclass, and so on. If the method cannot be found in the receiver's class or any of its ancestors, Ruby invokes the method `method_missing` on the original receiver.

And that's it—the entire explanation. On to the next chapter.

"But wait," you cry, "I spent good money on this chapter. What about all this other stuff—singleton classes, class methods, and so on. How do they work?"

Good question.

How Classes and Objects Interact

All class/object interactions are explained using the simple model given above: objects reference classes, and classes reference zero or more superclasses. However, the implementation details can get a tad tricky.

We've found that the simplest way of visualizing all this is to draw the actual objects that Ruby implements. So, in the following pages we'll look at all the possible combinations of classes and objects. Note that these are not class diagrams in the UML sense; we're showing structures in memory and pointers between them.

Your Basic, Everyday Object

Let's start by looking at an object created from a simple class. Figure 19.1 on the facing page shows the object, `lucille`, its class, `Guitar`, and that class's superclass, `Object`. Notice how the object's class reference (called `klass` for historical reasons that really bug Andy) points to the class object, and how the `super` pointer from that class references the parent class.

If we invoke the method `lucille.play()`, Ruby goes to the receiver, `lucille`, and follows the `klass` reference to the class object for `Guitar`. It searches the method table, finds `play`, and invokes it.

If instead we call `lucille.display()`, Ruby starts off the same way, but cannot find `display` in the method table in class `Guitar`. It then follows the `super` reference to `Guitar`'s superclass, `Object`, where it finds and executes the method.

What's the Meta?

Astute readers (yup, that's all of you) will have noticed that the `klass` members of `Class` objects point to nothing meaningful in Figure 19.1. We now have all the information we need to work out what they *should* reference.

When you say `lucille.play()`, Ruby follows `lucille`'s `klass` pointer to find a class object in which to search for methods. So what happens when you invoke a class method, such as `Guitar.strings(...)`? Here the receiver is the class object itself, `Guitar`. So, to be consistent, we need to stick the methods in some other class, referenced from `Guitar`'s `klass` pointer. This new class will contain all of `Guitar`'s class methods. It's called a *metaclass*. We'll denote the metaclass of `Guitar` as `Guitar'`. But that's not the whole story. Because `Guitar` is a subclass of `Object`, its metaclass `Guitar'` will be a subclass of `Object`'s metaclass, `Object'`. In Figure 19.2 on page 244, we show these additional metaclasses.

When Ruby executes `Guitar.strings()`, it follows the same process as before: it goes to the receiver, class `Guitar`, follows the `klass` reference to class `Guitar'`, and finds the method.

Finally, note that an "S" has crept into the flags in class `Guitar'`. The classes that Ruby creates automatically are marked internally as *singleton classes*. Singleton classes are treated slightly differently within Ruby. The most obvious difference from the outside is that they are effectively invisible: they will never appear in a list of objects returned from methods such as `Module#ancestors` or `ObjectSpace.each_object`.

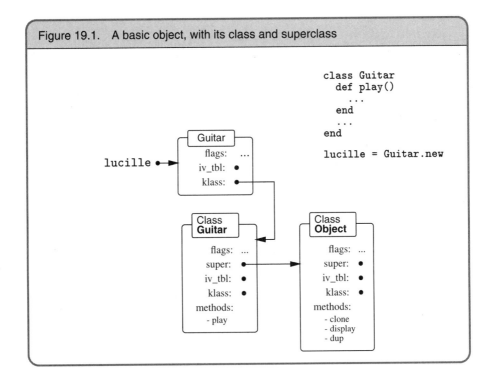

Figure 19.1.   A basic object, with its class and superclass

Object-Specific Classes

Ruby allows you to create a class tied to a particular object. In the following example, we create two **String** objects. We then associate an anonymous class with one of them, overriding one of the methods in the object's base class and adding a new method.

```
a = "hello"
b = a.dup

class <<a
  def to_s
    "The value is '#{self}'"
  end
  def twoTimes
    self + self
  end
end

a.to_s       →   "The value is 'hello'"
a.twoTimes   →   "hellohello"
b.to_s       →   "hello"
```

This example uses the "**class** <<*obj*" notation, which basically says "build me a new class just for object *obj*." We could also have written it as:

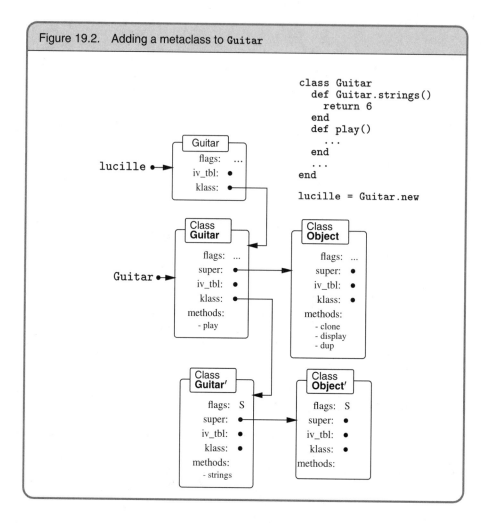

Figure 19.2.   Adding a metaclass to `Guitar`

```
a = "hello"
b = a.dup
def a.to_s
  "The value is '#{self}'"
end
def a.twoTimes
  self + self
end

a.to_s      →   "The value is 'hello'"
a.twoTimes  →   "hellohello"
b.to_s      →   "hello"
```

The effect is the same in both cases: a class is added to the object "**a**". This gives us a strong hint about the Ruby implementation: a singleton class is created and inserted as **a**'s direct class. **a**'s original class, **String**, is made this singleton's superclass. The before and after pictures are shown in Figure 19.3 on the following page.

Ruby performs a slight optimization with these singleton classes. If an object's **klass** reference already points to a singleton class, a new one will not be created. This means that the first of the two method definitions in the previous example will create a singleton class, but the second will simply add a method to it.

Mixin Modules

When a class includes a module, that module's instance methods become available as instance methods of the class. It's almost as if the module becomes a superclass of the class that uses it. Not surprisingly, that's about how it works. When you include a module, Ruby creates an anonymous proxy class that references that module, and inserts that proxy as the direct superclass of the class that did the including. The proxy class contains references to the instance variables and methods of the module. This is important: the same module may be included in many different classes, and will appear in many different inheritance chains. However, thanks to the proxy class, there is still only one underlying module: change a method definition in that module, and it will change in all classes that include that module, both past and future.

```
module SillyModule
  def hello
    "Hello."
  end
end
class SillyClass
  include SillyModule
end
s = SillyClass.new
s.hello   →   "Hello."

module SillyModule
  def hello
    "Hi, there!"
  end
end
s.hello   →   "Hi, there!"
```

The relationship between classes and the modules they include is shown in Figure 19.4 on page 247.

If a module itself includes other modules, a chain of proxy classes will be added to any class that includes that module, one proxy for each module that is directly or indirectly included.

Figure 19.3.   Adding a singleton class to an object

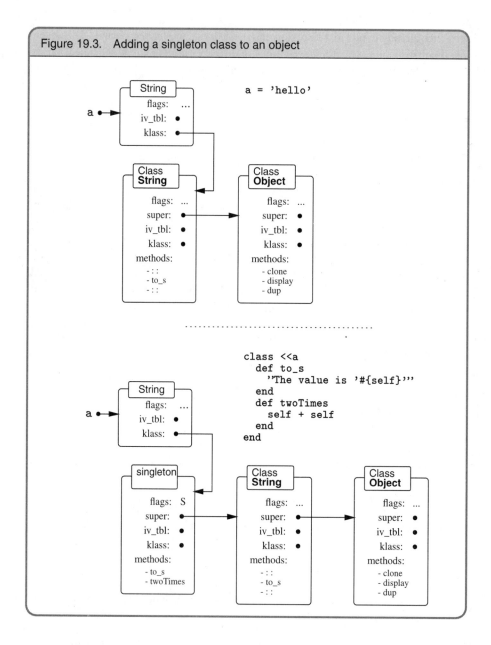

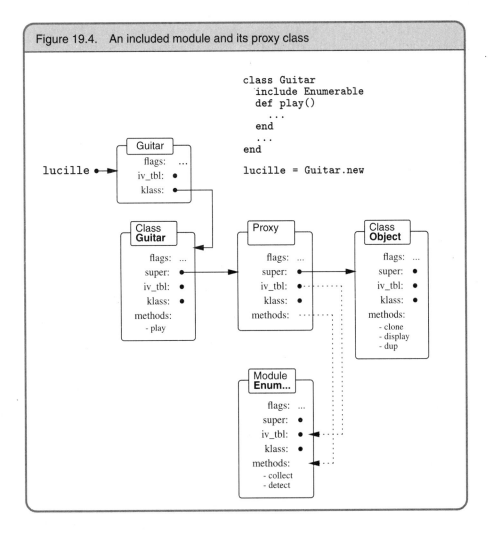

Figure 19.4. An included module and its proxy class

Extending Objects

Just as you can define an anonymous class for an object using "`class <<obj`", you can mix a module into an object using `Object#extend`. For example:

```
module Humor
  def tickle
    "hee, hee!"
  end
end

a = "Grouchy"
a.extend Humor
a.tickle   →   "hee, hee!"
```

There is an interesting trick with `extend`. If you use it within a class definition, the module's methods become class methods.

```ruby
module Humor
  def tickle
    "hee, hee!"
  end
end

class Grouchy
  include Humor
  extend  Humor
end

Grouchy.tickle   →   "hee, hee!"
a = Grouchy.new
a.tickle         →   "hee, hee!"
```

This is because calling `extend` is equivalent to `self.extend`, so the methods are added to `self`, which in a class definition is the class itself.

Class and Module Definitions

Having exhausted the combinations of classes and objects, we can (thankfully) get back to programming by looking at the nuts and bolts of class and module definitions.

In languages such as C++ and Java, class definitions are processed at compile time: the compiler loads up symbol tables, works out how much storage to allocate, constructs dispatch tables, and does all those other obscure things we'd rather not think too hard about.

Ruby is different. In Ruby, class and module definitions are executable code. Although parsed at compile time, the classes and modules are created at runtime, when the definition is encountered. (The same is also true of method definitions.) This allows you to structure your programs far more dynamically than in most conventional languages. You can make decisions once, when the class is being defined, rather than each time that objects of the class are used. The class in the following example decides as it is being defined what version of a decryption routine to create.

```ruby
class MediaPlayer
  include Tracing if $DEBUGGING

  if ::EXPORT_VERSION
    def decrypt(stream)
      raise "Decryption not available"
    end
  else
    def decrypt(stream)
```

```
      # ...
    end
  end

end
```

If class definitions are executable code, this implies that they execute in the context of some object: `self` must reference *something*. Let's find out what it is.

```
·class Test
  puts "Type of self = #{self.type}"
  puts "Name of self = #{self.name}"
end
```

produces:

```
Type of self = Class
Name of self = Test
```

This means that a class definition is executed with that class as the current object. Referring back to the section about metaclasses on page 242, we can see that this means that methods in the metaclass and its superclasses will be available during the execution of the method definition. We can check this out.

```
class Test
  def Test.sayHello
    puts "Hello from #{name}"
  end
  sayHello
end
```

produces:

```
Hello from Test
```

In this example we define a class method, `Test.sayHello`, and then call it in the body of the class definition. Within `sayHello`, we call `name`, an instance method of class `Module`. Because `Module` is an ancestor of `Class`, its instance methods can be called without an explicit receiver within a class definition.

In fact, many of the directives that you use when defining a class or module, things such as `alias_method`, `attr`, and `public`, are simply methods in class `Module`. This opens up some interesting possibilities—you can extend the functionality of class and module definitions by writing Ruby code. Let's look at a couple of examples.

As a first example, let's look at adding a basic documentation facility to modules and classes. This would allow us to associate a string with modules and classes that we write, a string that is accessible as the program is running. We'll choose a simple syntax.

```
class Example
  doc "This is a sample documentation string"
  # .. rest of class
end
```

We need to make doc available to any module or class, so we need to make it an instance method of class Module.

```
class Module
  @@docs = Hash.new(nil)
  def doc(str)
    @@docs[self.name] = str
  end

  def Module::doc(aClass)
    # If we're passed a class or module, convert to string
    # ('<=' for classes checks for same class or subtype)
    aClass = aClass.name if aClass.type <= Module
    @@docs[aClass] || "No documentation for #{aClass}"
  end
end

class Example
  doc "This is a sample documentation string"
  # .. rest of class
end

module Another
  doc <<-edoc
    And this is a documentation string
    in a module
  edoc
  # rest of module
end

puts Module::doc(Example)
puts Module::doc("Another")
```

produces:

```
This is a sample documentation string
        And this is a documentation string
        in a module
```

The second example is a performance enhancement based on Tadayoshi Funaba's date module (described beginning on page 443). Say we have a class that represents some underlying quantity (in this case, a date). The class may have many attributes that present the same underlying date in different ways: as a Julian day number, as a string, as a [year, month, day] triple, and so on. Each value represents the same date and may involve a fairly complex calculation to derive. We therefore would like to calculate each attribute only once, when it is first accessed.

The manual way would be to add a test to each accessor:

```
class ExampleDate
  def initialize(dayNumber)
    @dayNumber = dayNumber
  end
```

```
    def asDayNumber
      @dayNumber
    end

    def asString
      unless @string
        # complex calculation
        @string = result
      end
      @string
    end

    def asYMD
      unless @ymd
        # another calculation
        @ymd = [ y, m, d ]
      end
      @ymd
    end
    # ...
  end
```

This is a clunky technique—let's see if we can come up with something sexier.

What we're aiming for is a directive that indicates that the body of a particular method should be invoked only once. The value returned by that first call should be cached. Thereafter, calling that same method should return the cached value without reevaluating the method body again. This is similar to Eiffel's **once** modifier for routines. We'd like to be able to write something like:

```
  class ExampleDate
    def asDayNumber
      @dayNumber
    end

    def asString
      # complex calculation
    end

    def asYMD
      # another calculation
      [ y, m, d ]
    end

    once :asString, :asYMD
  end
```

We can use **once** as a directive by writing it as a class method of **ExampleDate**, but what should it look like internally? The trick is to have it rewrite the methods whose names it is passed. For each method, it creates an alias for the original code, then creates a new method with the same name. This new method does two things. First, it invokes the original method (using the alias) and stores the resulting value in an instance variable. Second, it redefines itself, so that on subsequent calls it simply returns the value of the instance variable directly. Here's Tadayoshi Funaba's code, slightly reformatted.

```
def ExampleDate.once(*ids)
  for id in ids
    module_eval <<-"end_eval"
      alias_method :__#{id.to_i}__, #{id.inspect}
      def #{id.id2name}(*args, &block)
        def self.#{id.id2name}(*args, &block)
          @__#{id.to_i}__
        end
        @__#{id.to_i}__ = __#{id.to_i}__(*args, &block)
      end
    end_eval
  end
end
```

This code uses `module_eval` to execute a block of code in the context of the calling module (or, in this case, the calling class). The original method is renamed _nnn_, where the _nnn_ part is the integer representation of the method name's symbol id. The code uses the same name for the caching instance variable. The bulk of the code is a method that dynamically redefines itself. Note that this redefinition uses the fact that methods may contain nested singleton method definitions, a clever trick.

Understand this code, and you'll be well on the way to true Ruby mastery.

However, we can take it further. Look in the `date` module, and you'll see method `once` written slightly differently.

```
class Date
  class << self
    def once(*ids)
      # ...
    end
  end
  # ...
end
```

The interesting thing here is the inner class definition, "`class << self`". This defines a class based on the object `self`, and `self` happens to be the class object for `Date`. The result? Every method within the inner class definition is automatically a class method of `Date`.

The `once` feature is generally applicable—it should work for any class. If you took `once` and made it a private instance method of class `Module`, it would be available for use in any Ruby class.

Class Names Are Constants

We've said that when you invoke a class method, all you're doing is sending a message to the `Class` object itself. When you say something such as `String.new("gumby")`, you're sending the message `new` to the object that is class `String`. But how does Ruby know to do this? After all, the receiver of a message should be an object reference, which implies that there must be a constant called "String" somewhere containing a reference to the `String` object.[1] And in fact, that's exactly what happens. All the built-in classes, along with the classes you define, have a corresponding global constant with the same name as the class. This is both straightforward and subtle. The subtlety comes from the fact that there are actually two things named (for example) `String` in the system. There's a *constant* that references an object of class `String`, and there's the object itself.

The fact that class names are just constants means that you can treat classes just like any other Ruby object: you can copy them, pass them to methods, and use them in expressions.

```
def factory(klass, *args)
  klass.new(*args)
end

factory(String, "Hello")            →    "Hello"
factory(Dir,    ".")                →    #<Dir:0x4018a2e8>

flag = true
(flag ? Array : Hash)[1, 2, 3, 4]   →    [1, 2, 3, 4]
flag = false
(flag ? Array : Hash)[1, 2, 3, 4]   →    {1=>2, 3=>4}
```

Top-Level Execution Environment

Many times in this book we've claimed that everything in Ruby is an object. However, there's one thing that we've used time and time again that appears to contradict this—the top-level Ruby execution environment.

```
puts "Hello, World"
```

Not an object in sight. We may as well be writing some variant of Fortran or QW-Basic. But dig deeper, and you'll come across objects and classes lurking in even the simplest code.

---

1.   It will be a constant, not a variable, because "String" starts with an uppercase letter.

We know that the literal `"Hello, World"` generates a Ruby **String**, so there's one object. We also know that the bare method call to **puts** is effectively the same as `self.puts`. But what is "self"?

```
self.type   →   Object
```

At the top level, we're executing code in the context of some predefined object. When we define methods, we're actually creating (private) singleton methods for this object. Instance variables belong to this object. And because we're in the context of **Object**, we can use all of **Object**'s methods (including those mixed-in from **Kernel**) in function form. This explains why we can call **Kernel** methods such as **puts** at the top level (and indeed throughout Ruby): these methods are part of every object.

Inheritance and Visibility

There's one last wrinkle to class inheritance, and it's fairly obscure.

Within a class definition, you can change the visibility of a method in an ancestor class. For example, you can do something like:

```
class Base
  def aMethod
    puts "Got here"
  end
  private :aMethod
end

class Derived1 < Base
  public :aMethod
end

class Derived2 < Base
end
```

In this example, you would be able to invoke **aMethod** in instances of class **Derived1**, but not via instances of **Base** or **Derived2**.

So how does Ruby pull off this feat of having one method with two different visibilities? Simply put, it cheats.

If a subclass changes the visibility of a method in a parent, Ruby effectively inserts a hidden proxy method in the subclass that invokes the original method using **super**. It then sets the visibility of that proxy to whatever you requested. This means that the code:

```
class Derived1 < Base
  public :aMethod
end
```

is effectively the same as:

```
class Derived1 < Base
  def aMethod(*args)
    super
  end
  public :aMethod
end
```

The call to `super` can access the parent's method regardless of its visibility, so the rewrite allows the subclass to override its parent's visibility rules. Pretty scary, eh?

Freezing Objects

There are times when you've worked hard to make your object exactly right, and you'll be damned if you'll let anyone just change it. Perhaps you need to pass some kind of opaque object between two of your classes via some third-party object, and you want to make sure it arrives unmodified. Perhaps you want to use an object as a hash key, and need to make sure that no one modifies it while it's being used. Perhaps something is corrupting one of your objects, and you'd like Ruby to raise an exception as soon as the change occurs.

Ruby provides a very simple mechanism to help with this. Any object can be *frozen* by invoking `Object#freeze`. A frozen object may not be modified: you can't change its instance variables (directly or indirectly), you can't associate singleton methods with it, and, if it is a class or module, you can't add, delete, or modify its methods. Once frozen, an object stays frozen: there is no `Object#thaw`. You can test to see if an object is frozen using `Object#frozen?`.

What happens when you copy a frozen object? That depends on the method you use. If you call an object's `clone` method, the entire object state (including whether it is frozen) is copied to the new object. On the other hand, `dup` typically copies only the object's contents—the new copy will not inherit the frozen status.

```
str1 = "hello"
str1.freeze    →    "hello"
str1.frozen?   →    true
str2 = str1.clone
str2.frozen?   →    true
str3 = str1.dup
str3.frozen?   →    false
```

Although freezing objects may initially seem like a good idea, you might want to hold off doing it until you come across a real need. Freezing is one of those ideas that looks essential on paper but isn't used much in practice.

## Chapter 20

Locking Ruby in the Safe

Walter Webcoder has a great idea for a portal site: The Web Arithmetic Page. Surrounded by all sorts of cool mathematical links and banner ads that will make him rich is a simple central frame, containing a text field and a button. Users type an arithmetic expression into the field, press the button, and the answer is displayed. All the world's calculators become obsolete overnight, and Walter cashes in and retires to devote his life to his collection of car license plate numbers.

Implementing the calculator is easy, thinks Walter. He accesses the contents of the form field using Ruby's CGI library, and uses the `eval` method to evaluate the string as an expression.

```
require 'cgi'

cgi = CGI::new("html4")

# Fetch the value of the form field "expression"
expr = cgi["expression"].to_s

begin
  result = eval(expr)
rescue Exception => detail
  # handle bad expressions
end

# display result back to user...
```

Roughly seven seconds after Walter puts the application online, a twelve-year-old from Waxahachie with glandular problems and no real life types "`system("rm *")`" into the form and, like his application, Walter's dreams come tumbling down.

Walter learned an important lesson: *All external data is dangerous. Don't let it close to interfaces that can modify your system.* In this case, the content of the form field was the external data, and the call to `eval` was the security breach.

Fortunately, Ruby provides support for reducing this risk. All information from the outside world can be marked as *tainted*. When running in a safe mode, potentially dangerous methods will raise a `SecurityError` if passed a tainted object.

Safe Levels

The variable $SAFE determines Ruby's level of paranoia. Table 20.1 on page 261 gives details of the checks performed at each safe level.

$SAFE	Constraints
0	No checking of the use of externally supplied (tainted) data is performed. This is Ruby's default mode.
≥ 1	Ruby disallows the use of tainted data by potentially dangerous operations.
≥ 2	Ruby prohibits the loading of program files from globally writable locations.
≥ 3	All newly created objects are considered tainted.
≥ 4	Ruby effectively partitions the running program in two. Nontainted objects may not be modified. Typically, this will be used to create a sandbox: the program sets up an environment using a lower $SAFE level, then resets $SAFE to 4 to prevent subsequent changes to that environment.

The default value of $SAFE is zero under most circumstances. However, if a Ruby script is run *setuid* or *setgid*,[1] its safe level is automatically set to 1. The safe level may also be set using the -T command-line option, and by assigning to $SAFE within the program. It is not possible to lower the value of $SAFE by assignment.

The current value of $SAFE is inherited when new threads are created. However, within each thread, the value of $SAFE may be changed without affecting the value in other threads. This facility may be used to implement secure "sandboxes," areas where external code may run safely without risking the rest of your application or system. Do this by wrapping code that you load from a file in its own, anonymous module. This will protect your program's namespace from any unintended alteration.

```
f=open(fileName,"w")
f.print ...    # write untrusted program into file.
f.close
Thread.start {
  $SAFE = 4
  load(fileName, true)
}
```

With a $SAFE level of 4, you can load *only* wrapped files. See Kernel.load on page 421 for details.

---

1. A Unix script may be flagged to be run under a different user or group id than the person running it. This allows the script to have privileges that the user does not have; the script can access resources that the user would otherwise be prohibited from using. These scripts are called *setuid* or *setgid*.

Tainted Objects

Any Ruby object derived from some external source (for example, a string read from a file, or an environment variable) is automatically marked as being tainted. If your program uses a tainted object to derive a new object, then that new object will also be tainted, as shown in the code below. Any object with external data somewhere in its past will be tainted. This tainting process is performed regardless of the current safe level. You can inspect the tainted status of an object using Object#tainted?.

```
# internal data                         # external data
# =============                         # =============
x1 = "a string"                         y1 = ENV["HOME"]
x1.tainted?        →    false           y1.tainted?        →    true

x2 = x1[2, 4]                           y2 = y1[2, 4]
x2.tainted?        →    false           y2.tainted?        →    true

x1 =~ /([a-z])/    →    0               y1 =~ /([a-z])/    →    1
$1.tainted?        →    false           $1.tainted?        →    true
```

You can force any object to become tainted by invoking its taint method. If the safe level is less than 3, you can remove the taint from an object by invoking untaint.[2] This is clearly not something to do lightly.

Clearly, Walter should have run his CGI script at a safe level of 1. This would have raised an exception when the program tried to pass form data to eval. Once this had happened, Walter would have had a number of choices. He could have choosen to implement a proper expression parser, bypassing the risks inherent in using eval. However, being lazy, it's more likely he'd have performed some simple sanity check on the form data, and untaint it if it looked innocuous.

```
require 'cgi';

$SAFE = 1

cgi = CGI::new("html4")

expr = cgi["field"].to_s

if expr =~ %r{^[-+*/\d\seE.()]*$}
  expr.untaint
  result = eval(expr)
  # display result back to user...
else
  # display error message...
end
```

---

2.   There are also some devious ways of doing this without using untaint. We'll leave it up to your darker side to find them.

Personally, we think Walter's still taking undue risks. We'd probably prefer to see a real parser here, but implementing one here has nothing to teach us about tainting, so we'll move on.

And remember—it's a dangerous world out there. Be careful.

Table 20.1. Definition of the safe levels

$SAFE >= 1

- The environment variables **RUBYLIB** and **RUBYOPT** are not processed, and the current directory is not added to the path.
- The command-line options **-e**, **-i**, **-I**, **-r**, **-s**, **-S**, and **-x** are not allowed.
- Can't start processes from **$PATH** if any directory in it is world-writable.
- Can't manipulate or chroot to a directory whose name is a tainted string.
- Can't glob tainted strings.
- Can't eval tainted strings.
- Can't load or require a file whose name is a tainted string.
- Can't manipulate or query the status of a file or pipe whose name is a tainted string.
- Can't execute a system command or exec a program from a tainted string.
- Can't pass **trap** a tainted string.

$SAFE >= 2

- Can't change, make, or remove directories, or use chroot.
- Can't load a file from a world-writable directory.
- Can't load a file from a tainted filename starting with ~.
- Can't use **File#chmod**, **File#chown**, **File#lstat**, **File.stat**, **File#truncate**, **File.umask**, **File#flock**, **IO#ioctl**, **IO#stat**, **Kernel#fork**, **Kernel#syscall**, **Kernel#trap**. **Process.setpgid**, **Process.setsid**, **Process.setpriority**, or **Process.egid=**.
- Can't handle signals using **trap**.

$SAFE >= 3

- All objects are created tainted.
- Can't untaint objects.

$SAFE >= 4

- Can't modify a nontainted array, hash, or string.
- Can't modify a global variable.
- Can't access instance variables of nontainted objects.
- Can't change an environment variable.
- Can't close or reopen nontainted files.
- Can't freeze nontainted objects.
- Can't change visibility of methods (private/public/protected).
- Can't make an alias in a nontainted class or module.
- Can't get meta information (such as method or variable lists).
- Can't define, redefine, remove, or undef a method in a nontainted class or module.
- Can't modify **Object**.
- Can't remove instance variables or constants from nontainted objects.
- Can't manipulate threads, terminate a thread other than the current, or set **abort_on_exception**.
- Can't have thread local variables.
- Can't raise an exception in a thread with a lower **$SAFE** value.
- Can't move threads between ThreadGroups.
- Can't invoke **exit**, **exit!**, or **abort**.
- Can load only wrapped files, and can't include modules in nontainted classes and modules.
- Can't convert symbol identifiers to object references.
- Can't write to files or pipes.
- Can't use **autoload**.
- Can't taint objects.

## Chapter 21

Reflection, ObjectSpace, and Distributed Ruby

One of the many advantages of dynamic languages such as Ruby is the ability to *introspect*—to examine aspects of the program from within the program itself. Java, for one, calls this feature *reflection*.

The word "reflection" conjures up an image of looking at oneself in the mirror—perhaps investigating the relentless spread of that bald spot on the top of one's head. That's a pretty apt analogy: we use reflection to examine parts of our programs that aren't normally visible from where we stand.

In this deeply introspective mood, while we are contemplating our navels and burning incense (being careful not to swap the two tasks), what can we learn about our program? We might discover:

- what objects it contains,
- the current class hierarchy,
- the contents and behaviors of objects, and
- information on methods.

Armed with this information, we can look at particular objects and decide which of their methods to call at runtime—even if the class of the object didn't exist when we first wrote the code. We can also start doing clever things, perhaps modifying the program as it's running.

Sound scary? It needn't be. In fact, these reflection capabilities let us do some very useful things. Later in this chapter we'll look at distributed Ruby and marshaling, two reflection-based technologies that let us send objects around the world and through time.

Looking at Objects

Have you ever craved the ability to traverse *all* the living objects in your program? We have! Ruby lets you perform this trick with `ObjectSpace.each_object`. We can use it to do all sorts of neat tricks.

For example, to iterate over all objects of type `Numeric`, you'd write the following.

```
a = 102.7
b = 95.1
ObjectSpace.each_object(Numeric) {|x| p x }
```

produces:

```
95.1
102.7
2.718281828
3.141592654
```

Hey, where did those last two numbers come from? We didn't define them in our program. If you look on page 433, you'll see that the `Math` module defines constants for *e* and π; since we are examining *all* living objects in the system, these turn up as well.

However, there is a catch. Let's try the same example with different numbers.

```
a = 102
b = 95
ObjectSpace.each_object(Numeric) {|x| p x }
```

produces:

```
2.718281828
3.141592654
```

Neither of the `Fixnum` objects we created showed up. That's because `ObjectSpace` doesn't know about objects with immediate values: `Fixnum`, `true`, `false`, and `nil`.

Looking Inside Objects

Once you've found an interesting object, you may be tempted to find out just what it can do. Unlike static languages, where a variable's type determines its class, and hence the methods it supports, Ruby supports liberated objects. You really cannot tell exactly what an object can do until you look under its hood.[1]

For instance, we can get a list of all the methods to which an object will respond.

---

1.   Or under its bonnet, for objects created to the east of the Atlantic.

```
r = 1..10 # Create a Range object
list = r.methods
list.length    →    60
list[0..3]    →    ["size", "length", "exclude_end?", "inspect"]
```

Or, we can check to see if an object supports a particular method.

```
r.respond_to?("frozen?")    →    true
r.respond_to?("hasKey")     →    false
"me".respond_to?("==")      →    true
```

We can determine our object's class and its unique object id, and test its relationship to other classes.

```
num = 1
num.id                         →    3
num.class                      →    Fixnum
num.kind_of? Fixnum            →    true
num.kind_of? Numeric           →    true
num.instance_of? Fixnum        →    true
num.instance_of? Numeric       →    false
```

Looking at Classes

Knowing about objects is one part of reflection, but to get the whole picture, you also need to be able to look at classes—the methods and constants that they contain.

Looking at the class hierarchy is easy. You can get the parent of any particular class using **Class#superclass**. For classes *and* modules, **Module#ancestors** lists both superclasses and mixed-in modules.

```
klass = Fixnum
begin
  print klass
  klass = klass.superclass
  print " < " if klass
end while klass
puts
p Fixnum.ancestors
```

produces:

```
Fixnum < Integer < Numeric < Object
[Fixnum, Integer, Precision, Numeric, Comparable, Object, Kernel]
```

If you want to build a complete class hierarchy, just run that code for every class in the system. We can use **ObjectSpace** to iterate over all **Class** objects:

```
ObjectSpace.each_object(Class) do |aClass|
  # ...
end
```

Looking Inside Classes

We can find out a bit more about the methods and constants in a particular object. Instead of just checking to see whether the object responds to a given message, we can ask for methods by access level, we can ask for just singleton methods, and we can have a look at the object's constants.

```
class Demo
  private
    def privMethod
    end
  protected
    def protMethod
    end
  public
    def pubMethod
    end

  def Demo.classMethod
  end

  CONST = 1.23
end
```

```
Demo.private_instance_methods          →    ["privMethod"]
Demo.protected_instance_methods        →    ["protMethod"]
Demo.public_instance_methods           →    ["pubMethod"]
Demo.singleton_methods                 →    ["classMethod"]
Demo.constants - Demo.superclass.constants   →    ["CONST"]
```

`Module.constants` returns *all* the constants available via a module, including constants from the module's superclasses. We're not interested in those just at the moment, so we'll subtract them from our list.

Given a list of method names, we might now be tempted to try calling them. Fortunately, that's easy with Ruby.

Calling Methods Dynamically

C and Java programmers often find themselves writing some kind of dispatch table: functions which are invoked based on a command. Think of a typical C idiom where you have to translate a string to a function pointer:

```
typedef struct {
  char *name;
  void (*fptr)();
} Tuple;

Tuple list[]= {
```

```
      { "play",   fptr_play },
      { "stop",   fptr_stop },
      { "record", fptr_record },
      { 0, 0 },
};

...

void dispatch(char *cmd) {
  int i = 0;
  for (; list[i].name; i++) {
    if (strncmp(list[i].name,cmd,strlen(cmd)) == 0) {
      list[i].fptr();
      return;
    }
  }
  /* not found */
}
```

In Ruby, you can do all this in one line. Stick all your command functions into a class, create an instance of that class (we called it **commands**), and ask that object to execute a method called the same name as the command string.

```
commands.send(commandString)
```

Oh, and by the way, it does much more than the C version—it's dynamic. The Ruby version will find new methods added at runtime just as easily.

You don't have to write special command classes for **send**: it works on any object.

```
"John Coltrane".send(:length)              →   13
"Miles Davis".send("sub", /iles/, '.')   →   "M. Davis"
```

Another way of invoking methods dynamically uses **Method** objects. A **Method** object is like a **Proc** object: it represents a chunk of code and a context in which it executes. In this case, the code is the body of the method, and the context is the object that created the method. Once we have our **Method** object, we can execute it sometime later by sending it the message **call**.

```
trane = "John Coltrane".method(:length)
miles = "Miles Davis".method("sub")

trane.call                 →   13
miles.call(/iles/, '.')    →   "M. Davis"
```

You can pass the **Method** object around as you would any other object, and when you invoke **Method#call**, the method is run just as if you had invoked it on the original object. It's like having a C-style function pointer but in a fully object-oriented style.

You can also use **Method** objects with iterators.

```
def double(a)
  2*a
end

mObj = method(:double)

[ 1, 3, 5, 7 ].collect(&mObj)   →   [2, 6, 10, 14]
```

As good things come in threes, here's yet another way to invoke methods dynamically. The `eval` method (and its variations such as `class_eval`, `module_eval`, and `instance_eval`) will parse and execute an arbitrary string of legal Ruby source code.

```
trane = %q{"John Coltrane".length}
miles = %q{"Miles Davis".sub(/iles/, '.')}

eval trane   →   13
eval miles   →   "M. Davis"
```

When using `eval`, it can be helpful to state explicitly the context in which the expression should be evaluated, rather than using the current context. You can obtain a context by calling `Kernel#binding` at the desired point.

```
class CoinSlot
  def initialize(amt=Cents.new(25))
    @amt = amt
    $here = binding
  end
end

a = CoinSlot.new
eval "puts @amt", $here
eval "puts @amt"
```

produces:

```
$0.25USD
nil
```

The first `eval` evaluates `@amt` in the context of the instance of class `CoinSlot`. The second `eval` evaluates `@amt` in the context of `Object`, where the instance variable `@amt` is not defined.

Performance Considerations

As we've seen in this section, there are several ways to invoke an arbitrary method of some object: `Object#send`, `Method#call`, and the various flavors of `eval`.

You may prefer to use any one of these techniques depending on your needs, but be aware that `eval` is significantly slower than the others (or, for optimistic readers, `send` and `call` are significantly faster than `eval`).

```
require "benchmark"    # from the Ruby Application Archive
include Benchmark

test = "Stormy Weather"
m = test.method(:length)
n = 100000

bm(12) {|x|
  x.report("call") { n.times { m.call } }
  x.report("send") { n.times { test.send(:length) } }
  x.report("eval") { n.times { eval "test.length" } }
}
```

produces:

	user	system	total	real
call	0.180000	0.000000	0.180000	(0.189134)
send	0.180000	0.000000	0.180000	(0.206625)
eval	2.030000	0.060000	2.090000	(2.424624)

System Hooks

A *hook* is a technique that lets you trap some Ruby event, such as object creation.

The simplest hook technique in Ruby is to intercept calls to methods in system classes. Perhaps you want to log all the operating system commands your program executes. Simply rename the method `Kernel.system`[2] and substitute it with one of your own that both logs the command and calls the original `Kernel` method.

```
module Kernel
  alias_method :old_system, :system
  def system(*args)
    result = old_system(*args)
    puts "system(#{args.join(', ')}) returned #{result}"
    result
  end
end

system("date")
system("kangaroo", "-hop 10", "skippy")
```

produces:

```
Wed Sep 20 10:35:15 CDT 2000
system(date) returned true
system(kangaroo, -hop 10, skippy) returned false
```

---

2.   This Eiffel-inspired idiom of renaming a feature and redefining a new one is very useful, but be aware that it can cause problems. If a subclass does the same thing, and renames the methods using the same names, you'll end up with an infinite loop. You can avoid this by aliasing your methods to a unique symbol name or by using a consistent naming convention.

A more powerful hook is catching objects as they are created. If you can be present when every object is born, you can do all sorts of interesting things: you can wrap them, add methods to them, remove methods from them, add them to containers to implement persistence, you name it. We'll show a simple example here: we'll add a timestamp to every object as it's created.

One way to hook object creation is to do our method renaming trick on `Class#new`, the method that's called to allocate space for a new object. The technique isn't perfect—some built-in objects, such as literal strings, are constructed without calling `new`—but it'll work just fine for objects we write.

```
class Class
  alias_method :old_new,  :new
  def new(*args)
    result = old_new(*args)
    result.timestamp = Time.now
    return result
  end
end
```

We'll also need to add a timestamp attribute to every object in the system. We can do this by hacking class `Object` itself.

```
class Object
  def timestamp
    return @timestamp
  end
  def timestamp=(aTime)
    @timestamp = aTime
  end
end
```

Finally, we can run a test. We'll create a couple of objects a few seconds apart and check their timestamps.

```
class Test
end

obj1 = Test.new
sleep 2
obj2 = Test.new

obj1.timestamp   →   Wed Sep 20 10:35:15 CDT 2000
obj2.timestamp   →   Wed Sep 20 10:35:17 CDT 2000
```

All this method renaming is fine, and it really does work. However, there are other, more refined ways to get inside a running program. Ruby provides several callback methods that let you trap certain events in a controlled way.

Runtime Callbacks

You can be notified whenever one of the following events occurs:

Event	Callback Method
Adding an instance method	`Module#method_added`
Adding a singleton method	`Kernel.singleton_method_added`
Subclassing a class	`Class#inherited`
Mixing in a module	`Module#extend_object`

These techniques are all illustrated in the library descriptions for each callback method. At runtime, these methods will be called by the system when the specified event occurs. By default, these methods do nothing. If you want to be notified when one of these events happens, just define the callback method, and you're in.

Keeping track of method creation and class and module usage lets you build an accurate picture of the dynamic state of your program. This can be important. For example, you may have written code that wraps all the methods in a class, perhaps to add transactional support or to implement some form of delegation. This is only half the job: the dynamic nature of Ruby means that users of this class could add new methods to it at any time. Using these callbacks, you can write code that wraps these new methods as they are created.

Tracing Your Program's Execution

While we're having fun reflecting on all the objects and classes in our programs, let's not forget about the humble statements that make our code actually do things. It turns out that Ruby lets us look at these statements, too.

First, you can watch the interpreter as it executes code. `set_trace_func` executes a `Proc` with all sorts of juicy debugging information whenever a new source line is executed, methods are called, objects are created, and so on. There's a full description on page 426, but here's a taste.

```ruby
class Test
  def test
    a = 1
    b = 2
  end
end

set_trace_func proc { |event, file, line, id, binding, classname|
  printf "%8s %s:%-2d %10s %8s\n", event, file, line, id, classname
}
t = Test.new
t.test
```

produces:

```
     line prog.rb:11                       false
   c-call prog.rb:11            new        Class
   c-call prog.rb:11 initialize            Object
 c-return prog.rb:11 initialize            Object
 c-return prog.rb:11            new        Class
     line prog.rb:12                       false
     call prog.rb:2             test       Test
     line prog.rb:3             test       Test
     line prog.rb:4             test       Test
   return prog.rb:4             test       Test
```

There's also a method `trace_var` (described on page 431) that lets you add a hook to a global variable; whenever an assignment is made to the global, your `Proc` object is invoked.

How Did We Get Here?

A fair question, and one we ask ourselves regularly. Mental lapses aside, in Ruby at least you can find out exactly "how you got there" by using the method `caller`, which returns an `Array` of `String` objects representing the current call stack.

```ruby
def catA
  puts caller.join("\n")
end
def catB
  catA
end
def catC
  catB
end
catC
```

produces:

```
prog.rb:5:in `catB'
prog.rb:8:in `catC'
prog.rb:10
```

Once you've figured out how you got there, where you go next is up to you.

Marshaling and Distributed Ruby

Java features the ability to *serialize* objects, letting you store them somewhere and reconstitute them when needed. You might use this facility, for instance, to save a tree of objects that represent some portion of application state—a document, a CAD drawing, a piece of music, and so on.

Ruby calls this kind of serialization *marshaling*.[3] Saving an object and some or all of its components is done using the method `Marshal.dump`. Typically, you will dump an entire object tree starting with some given object. Later on, you can reconstitute the object using `Marshal.load`.

Here's a short example. We have a class `Chord` that holds a collection of musical notes. We'd like to save away a particularly wonderful chord so our grandchildren can load it into Ruby Version 23.5 and savor it, too. Let's start off with the classes for `Note` and `Chord`.

```
class Note
  attr :value
  def initialize(val)
    @value = val
  end
  def to_s
    @value.to_s
  end
end
class Chord
  def initialize(arr)
    @arr = arr
  end
  def play
    @arr.join('-')
  end
end
```

Now we'll create our masterpiece, and use `Marshal.dump` to save a serialized version of it to disk.

```
c = Chord.new( [ Note.new("G"),  Note.new("Bb"),
                 Note.new("Db"), Note.new("E") ] )

File.open("posterity", "w+") do |f|
  Marshal.dump(c, f)
end
```

Finally, our grandchildren read it in, and are transported by our creation's beauty.

```
File.open("posterity") do |f|
  chord = Marshal.load(f)
end

chord.play   →   "G-Bb-Db-E"
```

---

3. Think of railroad marshaling yards where individual cars are assembled in sequence into a complete train, which is then dispatched somewhere.

Custom Serialization Strategy

Not all objects can be dumped: bindings, procedure objects, instances of class IO, and singleton objects cannot be saved outside of the running Ruby environment (a TypeError will be raised if you try). Even if your object doesn't contain one of these problematic objects, you may want to take control of object serialization yourself.

Marshal provides the hooks you need. In the objects that require custom serialization, simply implement two methods: an instance method called _dump, which writes the object out to a string, and a class method called _load, which reads a string that you'd previously created and converts it into a new object.

For instance, here is a sample class that defines its own serialization. For whatever reasons, Special doesn't want to save one of its internal data members, "@volatile".

```
class Special
  def initialize(valuable)
    @valuable = valuable
    @volatile = "Goodbye"
  end

  def _dump(depth)
    @valuable.to_str
  end

  def Special._load(str)
    result = Special.new(str);
  end

  def to_s
    "#{@valuable} and #{@volatile}"
  end
end

a = Special.new("Hello, World")
data = Marshal.dump(a)
obj = Marshal.load(data)
puts obj
```

produces:

```
Hello, World and Goodbye
```

For more details, see the reference section on Marshal beginning on page 432.

Distributed Ruby

Since we can serialize an object or a set of objects into a form suitable for out-of-process storage, we can use this capability for the *transmission* of objects from one process to another. Couple this capability with the power of networking, and *voilà*: you have a distributed object system. To save you the trouble of having to write the code, we suggest downloading Masatoshi Seki's Distributed Ruby library (drb) from the RAA.

Using drb, a Ruby process may act as a server, as a client, or as both. A drb server acts as a source of objects, while a client is a user of those objects. To the client, it appears that the objects are local, but in reality the code is still being executed remotely.

A server starts a service by associating an object with a given port. Threads are created internally to handle incoming requests on that port, so remember to join the drb thread before exiting your program.

```ruby
require 'drb'

class TestServer
  def doit
    "Hello, Distributed World"
  end
end

aServerObject = TestServer.new
DRb.start_service('druby://localhost:9000', aServerObject)
DRb.thread.join # Don't exit just yet!
```

A simple drb client simply creates a local drb object and associates it with the object on the remote server; the local object is a proxy.

```ruby
require 'drb'
DRb.start_service()
obj = DRbObject.new(nil, 'druby://localhost:9000')
# Now use obj
p obj.doit
```

The client connects to the server and calls the method `doit`, which returns a string that the client prints out:

```
"Hello, Distributed World"
```

The initial `nil` argument to `DRbObject` indicates that we want to attach to a new distributed object. We could also use an existing object.

Ho hum, you say. This sounds like Java's RMI, or CORBA, or whatever. Yes, it is a functional distributed object mechanism—but it is written in just 200 lines of Ruby code. No C, nothing fancy, just plain old Ruby code. Of course, there's no naming service or trader service, or anything like you'd see in CORBA, but it is simple and reasonably fast. On the 233MHz test system, this sample code runs at about 50 remote message calls per second.

And, if you like the look of Sun's JavaSpaces, the basis of their JINI architecture, you'll be interested to know that drb is distributed with a short module that does the same kind of thing. JavaSpaces is based on a technology called Linda. To prove that its Japanese author has a sense of humor, Ruby's version of Linda is known as "rinda."

Compile Time? Runtime? Anytime!

The important thing to remember about Ruby is that there isn't a big difference between "compile time" and "runtime." It's all the same. You can add code to a running process. You can redefine methods on the fly, change their scope from `public` to `private`, and so on. You can even alter basic types, such as `Class` and `Object`.

Once you get used to this flexibility, it is hard to go back to a static language such as C++, or even to a half-static language such as Java.

But then, why would you want to?

Part IV

Ruby Library Reference

## Chapter 22

Built-in Classes

This chapter documents the classes built into the standard Ruby language. They are available to every Ruby program automatically; no **require** required. This section does not contain the various predefined variables and constants; these are listed starting on page 216.

In the descriptions that follow, we show sample invocations for each method.

---

new String.new(*aString*) → *aNewString*

This description shows a class method that is called as `String.new`. The italic parameter indicates that a single `String` object is passed, and the arrow indicates that another `String` object is returned from the method. Because this return value has a different name than that of the parameter, it represents a different object.

When we illustrate instance methods, we show a sample call with a dummy object name in italics as the receiver:

---

each *str*.each(*aString=$/*) {| *rec* | *block* } → *str*

The parameter to `String#each` is shown to have a default value; call **each** with no parameter, and the value of `$/` will be used. This method is an iterator, so the call is followed by a block. `String#each` returns its receiver, so the receiver's name (*str* in this case) appears again after the arrow.

Some methods have optional parameters. We show these parameters between angle brackets, ⟨ *xxx* ⟩. (Additionally, we use the notation ⟨ *xxx* ⟩* to indicate zero or more occurrences of *xxx*, and ⟨ *xxx* ⟩+ to indicate one or more occurrences of *xxx*.)

---

index *self*.index(*aString* ⟨ , *aFixnum* ⟩) → *aFixnum* or `nil`

Finally, for methods that can be called in several different forms, we list each form on a separate line.

Alphabetical Listing

Standard classes are listed alphabetically, followed in the next chapter by the standard modules. Within each, we list the class (or module) methods, followed by the instance methods.

Array (page 282): *Class:* [ ], new. *Instance:* &, *, +, −, <<, <=>, ==, ===, [ ], [ ]=, |, assoc, at, clear, collect, collect!, compact, compact!, concat, delete, delete_at, delete_if, each, each_index, empty?, eql?, fill, first, flatten, flatten!, include?, index, indexes, indices, join, last, length, map!, nitems, pack, pop, push, rassoc, reject!, replace, reverse, reverse!, reverse_each, rindex, shift, size, slice, slice!, sort, sort!, to_a, to_ary, to_s, uniq, uniq!, unshift.

Bignum (page 294): *Instance:* Arithmetic operations, Bit operations, <=>, [ ], size, to_f, to_i, to_s.

Binding (page 295)

Class (page 296): *Class:* inherited, new. *Instance:* new, superclass.

Continuation (page 298): *Instance:* call.

Dir (page 299): *Class:* [ ], chdir, chroot, delete, entries, foreach, getwd, glob, mkdir, new, open, pwd, rmdir, unlink. *Instance:* close, each, read, rewind, seek, tell.

Exception (page 302): *Class:* exception. *Instance:* backtrace, exception, message, set_backtrace.

FalseClass (page 305): *Instance:* &, ^, |.

File (page 305): *Class:* atime, basename, chmod, chown, ctime, delete, dirname, expand_path, ftype, join, link, lstat, mtime, new, open, readlink, rename, size, split, stat, symlink, truncate, umask, unlink, utime. *Instance:* atime, chmod, chown, ctime, flock, lstat, mtime, path, truncate.

File::Stat (page 313): *Instance:* <=>, atime, blksize, blockdev?, blocks, chardev?, ctime, dev, directory?, executable?, executable_real?, file?, ftype, gid, grpowned?, ino, mode, mtime, nlink, owned?, pipe?, rdev, readable?, readable_real?, setgid?, setuid?, size, size?, socket?, sticky?, symlink?, uid, writable?, writable_real?, zero?.

Fixnum (page 318): *Instance:* Arithmetic operations, Bit operations, <=>, [ ], id2name, size, to_f, to_i, to_s.

Float (page 319): *Instance:* Arithmetic operations, <=>, ceil, finite?, floor, infinite?, nan?, round, to_f, to_i, to_s.

Hash (page 321): *Class:* [ ], new. *Instance:* ==, [ ], [ ]=, clear, default, default=, delete, delete_if, each, each_key, each_pair, each_value, empty?, fetch, has_key?, has_value?, include?, index, indexes, indices, invert, key?, keys, length, member?, rehash, reject, reject!, replace, shift, size, sort, store, to_a, to_s, update, value?, values.

Integer (page 328): *Instance:* chr, downto, integer?, next, step, succ, times, upto.

IO (page 329): *Class:* foreach, new, pipe, popen, readlines, select. *Instance:* <<, binmode, clone, close, close_read, close_write, closed?, each, each_byte, each_line, eof, eof?, fcntl, fileno, flush, getc, gets, ioctl, isatty, lineno, lineno=, pid, pos, pos=, print, printf, putc, puts, read, readchar, readline, readlines, reopen, rewind, seek, stat, sync, sync=, sysread, syswrite, tell, to_i, to_io, tty?, ungetc, write.

MatchData (page 340): *Instance:* [ ], begin, end, length, offset, post_match, pre_match, size, string, to_a, to_s.

Method (page 342): *Instance:* [ ], arity, call, to_proc.

Module (page 343): *Class:* constants, nesting, new. *Instance:* <, <=, >, >=, <=>, ===, ancestors, class_eval, class_variables, clone, const_defined?, const_get, const_set, constants, included_modules, instance_methods, method_defined?, module_eval, name, private_class_method, private_instance_methods, protected_instance_methods, public_class_method, public_instance_methods. *Private:* alias_method, append_features, attr, attr_accessor, attr_reader, attr_writer, extend_object, include, method_added, module_function, private, protected, public, remove_const, remove_method, undef_method.

NilClass (page 353): *Instance:* &, ^, |, nil?, to_a, to_i, to_s.

Numeric (page 354): *Instance:* +@, −@, abs, coerce, divmod, eql?, integer?, modulo, nonzero?, remainder, zero?.

Object (page 356): *Instance:* ==, ===, =~, __id__, __send__, class, clone, display, dup, eql?, equal?, extend, freeze, frozen?, hash, id, inspect, instance_eval, instance_of?, instance_variables, is_a?, kind_of?, method, method_missing, methods, nil?, private_methods, protected_methods, public_methods, respond_to?, send, singleton_methods, taint, tainted?, to_a, to_s, type, untaint.

Proc (page 363): *Class:* new. *Instance:* [ ], arity, call.

Range (page 364): *Class:* new. *Instance:* ===, begin, each, end, exclude_end?, first, last, length, size.

Regexp (page 366): *Class:* compile, escape, last_match, new, quote. *Instance:* ==, ===, =~, ~, casefold?, kcode, match, source.

String (page 368): *Class:* new. *Instance:* *, +, <<, <=>, ==, ===, =~, [ ], [ ]=, ~, capitalize, capitalize!, center, chomp, chomp!, chop, chop!, concat, count, crypt, delete, delete!, downcase, downcase!, dump, each, each_byte, each_line, empty?, gsub, gsub!, hash, hex, include?, index, intern, length, ljust, next, next!, oct, replace, reverse, reverse!, rindex, rjust, scan, size, slice, slice!, split, squeeze, squeeze!, strip, strip!, sub, sub!, succ, succ!, sum, swapcase, swapcase!, to_f, to_i, to_s, to_str, tr, tr!, tr_s, tr_s!, unpack, upcase, upcase!, upto.

Struct (page 385): *Class:* new, new, members. *Instance:* ==, [ ], [ ]=, each, length, members, size, to_a, values.

Struct::Tms (page 388)

Symbol (page 388): *Instance:* id2name, inspect, to_i, to_s.

Thread (page 389): *Class:* abort_on_exception, abort_on_exception=, critical, critical=, current, exit, fork, kill, list, main, new, pass, start, stop. *Instance:* [ ], [ ]=, abort_on_exception, abort_on_exception=, alive?, exit, join, key?, kill, priority, priority=, raise, run, safe_level, status, stop?, value, wakeup.

ThreadGroup (page 396): *Class:* new. *Instance:* add, list.

Time (page 397): *Class:* at, gm, local, mktime, new, now, times, utc. *Instance:* +, −, <=>, asctime, ctime, day, gmt?, gmtime, hour, isdst, localtime, mday, min, mon, month, sec, strftime, to_a, to_f, to_i, to_s, tv_sec, tv_usec, usec, utc, utc?, wday, yday, year, zone.

TrueClass (page 404): *Instance:* &, ^, |.

Class — **Array** < Object

Arrays are ordered, integer-indexed collections of any object. Array indexing starts at 0, as in C or Java. A negative index is assumed relative to the end of the array—that is, an index of −1 indicates the last element of the array, −2 is the next to last element in the array, and so on.

Mixes in

Enumerable:
    collect, detect, each_with_index, entries, find, find_all, grep, include?, map, max, member?, min, reject, select, sort, to_a

Class methods

[ ] Array[⟨ anObject ⟩*] → *anArray*

Returns a new array populated with the given objects. Equivalent to the operator form `Array.[](...)`.

```
Array.[]( 1, ’a’, /^A/ )   →   [1, "a", /^A/]
Array[ 1, ’a’, /^A/ ]      →   [1, "a", /^A/]
[ 1, ’a’, /^A/ ]           →   [1, "a", /^A/]
```

new Array.new(*anInteger=0, anObject=nil*) → *anArray*

Returns a new array, optionally with a size and initial value (that is, *anInteger* references to the same *anObject*).

```
Array.new            →   []
Array.new(2)         →   [nil, nil]
Array.new(5, "A")    →   ["A", "A", "A", "A", "A"]
Array.new(2, Hash.new) →   [{}, {}]
```

Instance methods

& *arr* & *anOtherArray* → *anArray*

Set Intersection—Returns a new array containing elements common to the two arrays, with no duplicates.

```
[ 1, 1, 3, 5 ] & [ 1, 2, 3 ]   →   [1, 3]
```

* *arr* * *anInteger* → *anArray*
  arr * *aString* → *anOtherString*

Repetition—With a `String` argument, equivalent to *arr*.`join(aString)`. Otherwise, returns a new array built by concatenating the *anInteger* copies of *arr*.

```
[ 1, 2, 3 ] * 3   →   [1, 2, 3, 1, 2, 3, 1, 2, 3]
```

Array

+   *arr + anOtherArray → anArray*

Concatenation—Returns a new array built by concatenating the two arrays together to produce a third array.

```
[ 1, 2, 3 ] + [ 4, 5 ]  →  [1, 2, 3, 4, 5]
```

−   *arr - anOtherArray → anArray*

Set Difference—Returns a new array that is a copy of the original array, removing any items that also appear in *anOtherArray* and duplicated items.

```
[ 1, 1, 2, 2, 3, 3, 3, 4, 5 ] - [ 1, 2, 4 ]  →  [3, 5]
```

<<   *arr << anObject → arr*

Append—Pushes the given object on to the end of this array. This expression returns the array itself, so several appends may be chained together. See also **Array#push**.

```
[ 1, 2 ] << "c" << "d" << [ 3, 4 ]  →  [1, 2, "c", "d", [3, 4]]
```

<=>   *arr <=> anOtherArray → −1, 0, +1*

Comparison—Returns an integer −1, 0, or +1 if this array is less than, equal to, or greater than *anOtherArray*. Each object in each array is compared (using **<=>**). If any value isn't equal, then that inequality is the return value. If all the values found are equal, then the return is based on a comparison of the array lengths. Thus, two arrays are "equal" according to **Array#<=>** if and only if they have the same length and the value of each element is equal to the value of the corresponding element in the other array.

```
[ "a", "a", "c" ]    <=> [ "a", "b", "c" ]  →  -1
[ 1, 2, 3, 4, 5, 6 ] <=> [ 1, 2 ]           →  1
```

==   *arr == anOtherArray → true or false*

Equality—Two arrays are equal if they contain the same number of elements and if each element is equal to (according to **Object#==**) the corresponding element in the other array.

```
[ "a", "c" ]     == [ "a", "c", 7 ]  →  false
[ "a", "c", 7 ] == [ "a", "c", 7 ]  →  true
[ "a", "c", 7 ] == [ "a", "d", "f" ]  →  false
```

===   *arr === anOtherArray → true or false*

Case Equality—Equality as evaluated by **case** expressions. For arrays, this is the same as **Array#==**.

Array

[ ]

$$arr[anInteger] \rightarrow anObject \text{ or } \texttt{nil}$$
$$arr[start, length] \rightarrow aSubArray \text{ or } \texttt{nil}$$
$$arr[aRange] \rightarrow aSubArray \text{ or } \texttt{nil}$$

Element Reference—Returns the element at index *anInteger*, or returns a subarray starting at index *start* and continuing for *length* elements, or returns a subarray specified by *aRange*. Negative indices count backward from the end of the array (-1 is the last element). Returns `nil` if any indices are out of range.

```
a = [ "a", "b", "c", "d", "e" ]
a[2] +  a[0] + a[1]   →   "cab"
a[6]                  →   nil
a[1, 2]               →   ["b", "c"]
a[1..3]               →   ["b", "c", "d"]
a[4..7]               →   ["e"]
a[6..10]              →   nil
a[-3, 3]              →   ["c", "d", "e"]
```

[ ]=

$$arr[anInteger] = anObject \rightarrow anObject$$
$$arr[start, length] = aSubArray \rightarrow aSubArray$$
$$arr[aRange] = aSubArray \rightarrow aSubArray$$

Element Assignment—Sets the element at index *anInteger*, or replaces a subarray starting at index *start* and continuing for *length* elements, or replaces a subarray specified by *aRange*. If *anInteger* is greater than the current capacity of the array, the array grows automatically. A negative *anInteger* will count backward from the end of the array. Inserts elements if *length* is zero. If *subArray* is `nil`, deletes elements from *arr*. An `IndexError` is raised if a negative index points past the beginning of the array. See also `Array#push`, `Array#unshift`.

```
a = Array.new               →   []
a[4] = "4";             a   →   [nil, nil, nil, nil, "4"]
a[0, 3] = [ 'a', 'b', 'c' ]; a   →   ["a", "b", "c", nil, "4"]
a[1..2] = [ 1, 2 ];     a   →   ["a", 1, 2, nil, "4"]
a[0, 2] = "?";          a   →   ["?", 2, nil, "4"]
a[0..2] = "A";          a   →   ["A", "4"]
a[-1]   = "Z";          a   →   ["A", "Z"]
a[1..-1] = nil;         a   →   ["A"]
```

|

$$arr \mid anOtherArray \rightarrow anArray$$

Set Union—Returns a new array by joining this array with *anOtherArray*, removing duplicates.

```
[ "a", "b", "c" ] | [ "c", "d", "a" ]   →   ["a", "b", "c", "d"]
```

assoc

$$arr.assoc(anObject) \rightarrow anArray \text{ or } \texttt{nil}$$

Searches through an array whose elements are also arrays comparing *anObject* with the first element of each contained array using *anObject*`.==` . Returns the first contained array that matches (that is, the first *assoc*iated array), or `nil` if no match is found. See also `Array#rassoc`.

```
s1 = [ "colors", "red", "blue", "green" ]
s2 = [ "letters", "a", "b", "c" ]
s3 = "foo"
a  = [ s1, s2, s3 ]
a.assoc("letters")    →    ["letters", "a", "b", "c"]
a.assoc("foo")        →    nil
```

---

at   *arr*.at(*anInteger*) → *anObject* or `nil`

Returns the element at index *anInteger*. A negative index counts from the end of *arr*. Returns `nil` if the index is out of range. See also `Array#[]`. (`Array#at` is slightly faster than `Array#[]`, as it does not accept ranges and so on.)

```
a = [ "a", "b", "c", "d", "e" ]
a.at(0)    →    "a"
a.at(-1)   →    "e"
```

---

clear   *arr*.clear → *arr*

Removes all elements from *arr*.

```
a = [ "a", "b", "c", "d", "e" ]
a.clear    →    []
```

---

collect   *arr*.collect { | *obj* | *block* } → *anArray*

Returns a new array by invoking *block* once for every element, passing each element as a parameter to *block*. The result of *block* is used as the given element in the new array. See also `Array#collect!`.

```
a = [ "a", "b", "c", "d" ]
a.collect {|x| x + "!" }    →    ["a!", "b!", "c!", "d!"]
a                           →    ["a", "b", "c", "d"]
```

---

collect!   *arr*.collect! { | *obj* | *block* } → *arr*

Invokes *block* once for each element of *arr*, replacing the element with the value returned by *block*. See also `Array#collect`.

```
a = [ "a", "b", "c", "d" ]
a.collect! {|x| x + "!" }    →    ["a!", "b!", "c!", "d!"]
a                            →    ["a!", "b!", "c!", "d!"]
```

---

compact   *arr*.compact → *anArray*

Returns a new array based on the *arr* with all `nil` elements removed.

```
[ "a", nil, "b", nil, "c", nil ].compact    →    ["a", "b", "c"]
```

Array

compact!

arr.compact! → arr or <code>nil</code>

Same as **`Array#compact`**, but modifies the receiver in place. Returns **`nil`** if no changes were made.

```
[ "a", nil, "b", nil, "c" ].compact!   →   ["a", "b", "c"]
[ "a", "b", "c" ].compact!             →   nil
```

concat

arr.concat(anOtherArray) → arr

Appends the elements in *anOtherArray* to *arr*.

```
[ "a", "b" ].concat( ["c", "d"] )   →   ["a", "b", "c", "d"]
```

delete

arr.delete(anObject) → anObject or <code>nil</code>
arr.delete(anObject) { block } → anObject or <code>nil</code>

Deletes items from the self that are equal to *anObject*. If the item is not found, returns **`nil`**. If the optional code block is given, returns the result of *block* if the item is not found.

```
a = [ "a", "b", "b", "b", "c" ]
a.delete("b")                      →   "b"
a                                  →   ["a", "c"]
a.delete("z")                      →   nil
a.delete("z") { "not found" }      →   "not found"
```

delete_at

arr.delete_at(anIndex) → anObject or <code>nil</code>

Deletes the element at the specified index, returning that element, or **`nil`** if the index is out of range. See also **`Array#slice!`**.

```
a = %w( ant bat cat dog )
a.delete_at(2)    →   "cat"
a                 →   ["ant", "bat", "dog"]
a.delete_at(99)   →   nil
```

delete_if

arr.delete_if { block } → arr

Deletes every element of *arr* for which *block* evaluates to **`true`**.

```
a = [ "a", "b", "c" ]
a.delete_if {|x| x >= "b" }   →   ["a"]
```

each

arr.each {| item | block } → arr

Calls *block* once for each element in *arr*, passing that element as a parameter.

```
a = [ "a", "b", "c" ]
a.each {|x| print x, " -- " }
```

produces:

```
a -- b -- c --
```

each_index   *arr*.each_index { | *anIndex* | *block* } → *arr*

Same as `Array#each`, but passes the index of the element instead of the element itself.

```
a = [ "a", "b", "c" ]
a.each_index {|x| print x, " -- " }
```

produces:

```
0 -- 1 -- 2 --
```

empty?   *arr*.empty? → **true** or **false**

Returns **true** if *arr* array contains no elements.

```
[].empty?   →   true
```

eql?   *arr*.eql?(*anOtherArray*) → **true** or **false**

An array is equal to another array if the lengths are equal and each corresponding element is equal (according to `Object#eql?`). See also `Array#<=>`. `eql?` is used for `Hash` comparison.

```
[ "a", "b", "c" ].eql?(["a", "b", "c"])   →   true
[ "a", "b", "c" ].eql?(["a", "b"])        →   false
[ "a", "b", "c" ].eql?(["b", "c", "d"])   →   false
```

fill   *arr*.fill(*anObject*) → *arr*
                                        arr.fill(*anObject, start* ⟨ *, length* ⟩) → *arr*
                                                  arr.fill(*anObject, aRange*) → *arr*

Sets the selected elements of *arr* (which may be the entire array) to *anObject*. A *start* of `nil` is equivalent to zero. A *length* of `nil` is equivalent to *arr*.length.

```
a = [ "a", "b", "c", "d" ]
a.fill("x")        →   ["x", "x", "x", "x"]
a.fill("z", 2, 2)  →   ["x", "x", "z", "z"]
a.fill("y", 0..1)  →   ["y", "y", "z", "z"]
```

first   *arr*.first → *anObject* or **nil**

Returns the first element of the array. If the array is empty, returns **nil**.

```
a = [ "q", "r", "s", "t" ]
a.first   →   "q"
```

flatten   *arr*.flatten → *anArray*

Returns a new array that is a one-dimensional flattening of this array (recursively). That is, for every element that is an array, extract its elements into the new array.

```
s = [ 1, 2, 3 ]           →   [1, 2, 3]
t = [ 4, 5, 6, [7, 8] ]   →   [4, 5, 6, [7, 8]]
a = [ s, t, 9, 10 ]       →   [[1, 2, 3], [4, 5, 6, [7, 8]], 9, 10]
a.flatten                 →   [1, 2, 3, 4, 5, 6, 7, 8, 9, 10]
```

flatten!

arr.flatten! → arr or nil

Same as **Array#flatten**, but modifies the receiver in place. Returns **nil** if no modifications were made (i.e., *arr* contains no subarrays.)

```
a = [ 1, 2, [3, [4, 5] ] ]
a.flatten!   →   [1, 2, 3, 4, 5]
a.flatten!   →   nil
a            →   [1, 2, 3, 4, 5]
```

include?

arr.include?(*anObject*) → true or false

Returns **true** if the given object is present in *arr* (that is, if any object == *anObject*), **false** otherwise.

```
a = [ "a", "b", "c" ]
a.include?("b")   →   true
a.include?("z")   →   false
```

index

arr.index(*anObject*) → *anInteger* or nil

Returns the index of the first object in *arr* such that the object == *anObject*. Returns **nil** if no match is found.

```
a = [ "a", "b", "c" ]
a.index("b")   →   1
a.index("z")   →   nil
```

indexes

arr.indexes(*i1, i2, ... iN*) → *anArray*

Returns a new array consisting of elements at the given indices. May insert **nil** for indices out of range.

```
a = [ "a", "b", "c", "d", "e", "f", "g" ]
a.indexes(0, 2, 4)       →   ["a", "c", "e"]
a.indexes(0, 2, 4, 12)   →   ["a", "c", "e", nil]
```

indices

arr.indices(*i1, i2, ... iN*) → *anArray*

Synonym for **Array#indexes**.

join

arr.join(*aSepString=$,*) → *aString*

Returns a string created by converting each element of the array to a string, separated by *aSepString*.

```
[ "a", "b", "c" ].join        →   "abc"
[ "a", "b", "c" ].join("-")   →   "a-b-c"
```

last

arr.last → *anObject* or nil

Returns the last element of *arr*. If the array is empty, returns **nil**.

```
[ "w", "x", "y", "z" ].last   →   "z"
```

Table 22.1. Template characters for `Array#pack`

Directive	Meaning
@	Moves to absolute position
A	ASCII string (space padded, count is width)
a	ASCII string (null padded, count is width)
B	Bit string (descending bit order)
b	Bit string (ascending bit order)
C	Unsigned char
c	Char
d	Double-precision float, native format
E	Double-precision float, little-endian byte order
e	Single-precision float, little-endian byte order
f	Single-precision float, native format
G	Double-precision float, network (big-endian) byte order
g	Single-precision float, network (big-endian) byte order
H	Hex string (high nibble first)
h	Hex string (low nibble first)
I	Unsigned integer
i	Integer
L	Unsigned long
l	Long
M	Quoted printable, MIME encoding (see RFC2045)
m	Base64 encoded string
N	Long, network (big-endian) byte order
n	Short, network (big-endian) byte-order
P	Pointer to a structure (fixed-length string)
p	Pointer to a null-terminated string
S	Unsigned short
s	Short
U	UTF-8
u	UU-encoded string
V	Long, little-endian byte order
v	Short, little-endian byte order
X	Back up a byte
x	Null byte
Z	Same as "A"

length

arr.length → *anInteger*

Returns the number of elements in *arr*. May be zero.

```
[ 1, 2, 3, 4, 5 ].length   →   5
```

map!

arr.map! {| *obj* | *block* } → *arr*

Synonym for `Array#collect!`.

nitems

arr.nitems → *anInteger*

Returns the number of non-`nil` elements in *arr*. May be zero.

```
[ 1, nil, 3, nil, 5 ].nitems   →   3
```

pack

arr.pack (*aTemplateString*) → *aBinaryString*

Packs the contents of *arr* into a binary sequence according to the directives in *aTemplateString* (see Table 22.1 on the page before). Directives "A," "a," and "Z" may be followed by a count, which gives the width of the resulting field. The remaining directives also may take a count, indicating the number of array elements to convert. If the count is an asterisk ("*"), all remaining array elements will be converted. Any of the directives "sSiIlL" may be followed by an underscore ("_") to use the underlying platform's native size for the specified type; otherwise, they use a platform-independent size. Spaces are ignored in the template string. See also `String#unpack` on page 383.

```
a = [ "a", "b", "c" ]
n = [ 65, 66, 67 ]
a.pack("A3A3A3")   →   "aⵁⵁbⵁⵁcⵁⵁ"
a.pack("a3a3a3")   →   "a\000\000b\000\000c\000\000"
n.pack("ccc")      →   "ABC"
```

pop

arr.pop → *anObject* or `nil`

Removes the last element from *arr* and returns it, or `nil` if the array is empty (as with a stack).

```
a = [ "a", "m", "z" ]
a.pop   →   "z"
a       →   ["a", "m"]
```

push

arr.push(〈 *anObject* 〉+) → *arr*

Appends the given argument(s) to the end of *arr* (as with a stack).

```
a = [ "a", "b", "c" ]
a.push("d", "e", "f")   →   ["a", "b", "c", "d", "e", "f"]
```

rassoc

arr.rassoc(*key*) → *anArray* or `nil`

Searches through the array whose elements are also arrays. Compares *key* with the

second element of each contained array using ==. Returns the first contained array that
matches. See also `assoc`.

```
a = [ [ 1, "one"], [2, "two"], [3, "three"], ["ii", "two"] ]
a.rassoc("two")   →   [2, "two"]
a.rassoc("four")  →   nil
```

---

reject!   *arr*.reject! { *block* } → *arr* or `nil`

Equivalent to `Array#delete_if`, but returns `nil` if no changes were made.

---

replace   *arr*.replace(*anOtherArray*) → *arr*

Replaces the contents of *arr* with the contents of *anOtherArray*, truncating or expanding if necessary.

```
a = [ "a", "b", "c", "d", "e" ]
a.replace( [ "x", "y", "z" ] )   →   ["x", "y", "z"]
a                                →   ["x", "y", "z"]
```

---

reverse   *arr*.reverse → *anArray*

Returns a new array using *arr*'s elements in reverse order.

```
[ "a", "b", "c" ].reverse   →   ["c", "b", "a"]
[ 1 ].reverse               →   [1]
```

---

reverse!   *arr*.reverse! → *arr* or `nil`

Reverses the order of elements in *arr*, returning `nil` if *arr* is unchanged.

```
a = [ "a", "b", "c" ]
a.reverse!         →   ["c", "b", "a"]
a                  →   ["c", "b", "a"]
[ 1 ].reverse!     →   nil
```

---

reverse_each   *arr*.reverse_each { *block* }

Same as `Array#each`, but traverses *arr* in reverse order.

```
a = [ "a", "b", "c" ]
a.reverse_each {|x| print x, " " }
```

produces:

```
c b a
```

---

rindex   *arr*.rindex(*anObject*) → *anInteger* or `nil`

Returns the index of the last object in *arr* such that the object == *anObject*. Returns
`nil` if no match is found.

```
a = [ "a", "b", "b", "b", "c" ]
a.rindex("b")   →   3
a.rindex("z")   →   nil
```

shift

arr.shift → *anObject* or `nil`

Returns the first element of *arr* and removes it (shifting all other elements down by one). Returns `nil` if the array is empty.

```
args = [ "-m", "-q", "filename" ]
args.shift   →   "-m"
args         →   ["-q", "filename"]
```

size

arr.size → *anInteger*

Synonym for `Array#length`.

slice

arr.slice(*anInteger*) → *anObject*
arr.slice(*start, length*) → *aSubArray*
arr.slice(*aRange*) → *aSubArray*

Synonym for `Array#[ ]`.

```
a = [ "a", "b", "c", "d", "e" ]
a.slice(2) + a.slice(0) + a.slice(1)   →   "cab"
a.slice(6)                             →   nil
a.slice(1, 2)                          →   ["b", "c"]
a.slice(1..3)                          →   ["b", "c", "d"]
a.slice(4..7)                          →   ["e"]
a.slice(6..10)                         →   nil
a.slice(-3, 3)                         →   ["c", "d", "e"]
```

slice!

arr.slice!(*anInteger*) → *anObject* or `nil`
arr.slice!(*start, length*) → *aSubArray* or `nil`
arr.slice!(*aRange*) → *aSubArray* or `nil`

Deletes the element(s) given by an index (optionally with a length) or by a range. Returns the deleted object, subarray, or `nil` if the index is out of range. Equivalent to:

```
def slice!(*args)
  result = self[*args]
  self[*args] = nil
  result
end

a = [ "a", "b", "c" ]
a.slice!(1)     →   "b"
a               →   ["a", "c"]
a.slice!(-1)    →   "c"
a               →   ["a"]
a.slice!(100)   →   nil
a               →   ["a"]
```

---

sort

arr.sort → $anArray$

arr.sort { | a,b | $block$ } → $anArray$

Returns a new array created by sorting arr. Comparisons for the sort will be done using the <=> operator or using an optional code block. The block implements a comparison between a and b, returning −1, 0, or +1.

```
a = [ "d", "a", "e", "c", "b" ]
a.sort                 →    ["a", "b", "c", "d", "e"]
a.sort {|x,y| y <=> x }  →    ["e", "d", "c", "b", "a"]
```

---

sort!

arr.sort! → arr

arr.sort! { | a,b | $block$ } → arr

Same as **Array#sort**, but modifies the receiver in place. arr is effectively frozen while a sort is in progress.

```
a = [ "d", "a", "e", "c", "b" ]
a.sort!  →   ["a", "b", "c", "d", "e"]
a        →   ["a", "b", "c", "d", "e"]
```

---

to_a

arr.to_a → arr

Returns arr.

---

to_ary

arr.to_ary → arr

Synonym for **Array#to_a**.

---

to_s

arr.to_s → $aString$

Returns arr.join.

```
[ "a", "e", "i", "o" ].to_s   →   "aeio"
```

---

uniq

arr.uniq → $anArray$

Returns a new array by removing duplicate values in arr.

```
a = [ "a", "a", "b", "b", "c" ]
a.uniq   →   ["a", "b", "c"]
```

---

uniq!

arr.uniq! → arr or nil

Same as **Array#uniq**, but modifies the receiver in place. Returns nil if no changes are made (that is, no duplicates are found).

```
a = [ "a", "a", "b", "b", "c" ]
a.uniq!  →   ["a", "b", "c"]
b = [ "a", "b", "c" ]
b.uniq!  →   nil
```

unshift

arr.unshift(*anObject*) → *arr*

Prepends *anObject* to the front of *arr*, and shifts all other elements up one.

```
a = [ "b", "c", "d" ]
a.unshift("a")   →   ["a", "b", "c", "d"]
```

Class

Bignum < Integer

Bignum objects hold integers outside the range of Fixnum. Bignum objects are created automatically when integer calculations would otherwise overflow a Fixnum. When a calculation involving Bignum objects returns a result that will fit in a Fixnum, the result is automatically converted.

For the purposes of the bitwise operations and [ ], a Bignum is treated as if it were an infinite-length bitstring with 2's complement representation.

While Fixnum values are immediate, Bignum objects are not—assignment and parameter passing work with references to objects, not the objects themselves.

Instance methods

Arithmetic operations

Performs various arithmetic operations on *big*.

big	+	*aNumeric*	Addition
big	–	*aNumeric*	Subtraction
big	*	*aNumeric*	Multiplication
big	/	*aNumeric*	Division
big	%	*aNumeric*	Modulo
big	**	*aNumeric*	Exponentiation

Bit operations

Performs various operations on the binary representations of the Bignum.

~ *big*			Invert bits
big	|	*aNumeric*	Bitwise OR
big	&	*aNumeric*	Bitwise AND
big	^	*aNumeric*	Bitwise EXCLUSIVE OR
big	<<	*aNumeric*	Left-shift *aNumeric* bits
big	>>	*aNumeric*	Right-shift *aNumeric* bits (with sign extension)

<=>

big <=> *aNumeric* → −1, 0, +1

Comparison—Returns −1, 0, or +1 depending on whether *big* is less than, equal to, or greater than *aNumeric*. This is the basis for the tests in Comparable.

[ ]   *big*[*n*] → 0, 1

Bit Reference—Returns the *n*th bit in the (assumed) binary representation of *big*, where *big*[0] is the least significant bit.

```
a = 9**15
50.downto(0) do |n|
  print a[n]
end
```

produces:

```
0001011101101000001110000111100101001111000010111001
```

---

size   *big*.size → *anInteger*

Returns the number of bytes in the machine representation of *big*.

```
(256**10 - 1).size   →   10
(256**20 - 1).size   →   20
(256**40 - 1).size   →   40
```

---

to_f   *big*.to_f → *aFloat*

Converts *big* to a **Float**. If *big* doesn't fit in a **Float**, the result is infinity.

---

to_i   *big*.to_i → big

Returns *big*.

---

to_s   *big*.to_s → *aString*

Returns a string containing the decimal representation of *big*.

Class **Binding** < Object

Objects of class **Binding** encapsulate the execution context at some particular place in the code and retain this context for future use. The variables, methods, value of **self**, and possibly an iterator block that can be accessed in this context are all retained. Binding objects can be created using **Kernel#binding**, and are made available to the callback of **Kernel#set_trace_func**.

These binding objects can be passed as the second argument of the **Kernel#eval** method, establishing an environment for the evaluation.

```
class Demo
  def initialize(n)
    @secret = n
  end
  def getBinding
    return binding()
  end
end

k1 = Demo.new(99)
b1 = k1.getBinding
k2 = Demo.new(-3)
b2 = k2.getBinding
```

```
eval("@secret", b1)   →   99
eval("@secret", b2)   →   -3
eval("@secret")       →   nil
```

Binding objects have no class-specific methods.

Class < Module

Classes in Ruby are first-class objects—each is an instance of class `Class`.

When a new class is created (typically using `class Name ... end`), an object of type `Class` is created and assigned to a global constant (`Name` in this case). When `Name.new` is called to create a new object, the `new` method in `Class` is run by default. This can be demonstrated by overriding `new` in `Class`:

```
class Class
  alias oldNew  new
  def new(*args)
    print "Creating a new ", self.name, "\n"
    oldNew(*args)
  end
end

class Name
end

n = Name.new
```

produces:

```
Creating a new Name
```

Class methods

inherited
$aClass$.inherited($aSubClass$)

This is a singleton method (per class) invoked by Ruby when a subclass of *aClass* is created. The new subclass is passed as a parameter.

```
class Top
  def Top.inherited(sub)
    print "New subclass: ", sub, "\n"
  end
end

class Middle < Top
end

class Bottom < Middle
end
```

produces:

```
New subclass: Middle
New subclass: Bottom
```

new
Class.new($aSuperClass$=Object) → $aClass$

Creates a new anonymous (unnamed) class with the given superclass (or `Object` if no parameter is given).

Instance methods

new
$aClass$.new(⟨ $args$ ⟩*) → $anObject$

Creates a new object of *aClass*'s class, then invokes that object's `initialize` method, passing it *args*.

superclass
$aClass$.superclass → $aSuperClass$ or `nil`

Returns the superclass of *aClass*, or `nil`.

```
Class.superclass    →    Module
Object.superclass   →    nil
```

Class **Continuation** < Object

Continuation objects are generated by `Kernel#callcc`. They hold a return address and execution context, allowing a nonlocal return to the end of the `callcc` block from anywhere within a program. Continuations are somewhat analogous to a structured version of C's `setjmp/longjmp` (although they contain more state, so you might consider them closer to threads).

For instance:

```
arr = [ "Freddie", "Herbie", "Ron", "Max", "Ringo" ]
callcc{|$cc|}
puts(message = arr.shift)
$cc.call unless message =~ /Max/
```

produces:

```
Freddie
Herbie
Ron
Max
```

This (somewhat contrived) example allows the inner loop to abandon processing early:

```
callcc {|cont|
  for i in 0..4
    print "\n#{i}: "
    for j in i*5...(i+1)*5
      cont.call() if j == 17
      printf "%3d", j
    end
  end
}
print "\n"
```

produces:

```
0:   0  1  2  3  4
1:   5  6  7  8  9
2:  10 11 12 13 14
3:  15 16
```

Instance methods

call   *cont*.call(⟨ *args* ⟩*)

Invokes the continuation. The program continues from the end of the `callcc` block. If no arguments are given, the original `callcc` returns `nil`. If one argument is given, `callcc` returns it. Otherwise, an array containing *args* is returned.

```
callcc {|cont|  cont.call }        →   nil
callcc {|cont|  cont.call 1 }      →   1
callcc {|cont|  cont.call 1, 2, 3 } →  [1, 2, 3]
```

Class
Dir < Object

Objects of class `Dir` are directory streams representing directories in the underlying file system. They provide a variety of ways to list directories and their contents. See also `File`, page 305.

The directory used in these examples contains the two regular files (`config.h` and `main.rb`), the parent directory (`..`), and the directory itself (`.`).

Mixes in

Enumerable:
> collect, detect, each_with_index, entries, find, find_all, grep,
> include?, map, max, member?, min, reject, select, sort, to_a

Class methods

[ ]   Dir[*aString*] → *anArray*

Returns *anArray* of filenames found by expanding the pattern given in *aString*. Note that this pattern is not a regexp (it's closer to a shell glob) and may contain the following metacharacters:

`**`	Matches subdirectories recursively
`*`	Matches zero or more characters
`?`	Matches any single character
`[ charSet ]`	Matches any character from the given set of characters. A range of characters is written as *charFrom-charTo*. The set may be negated with an initial uparrow (`^`).
`{ opt, opt, ... }`	Matches any one of the optional strings

```
Dir["config.?"]      →    ["config.h"]
Dir["*.[a-z][a-z]"]  →    ["main.rb"]
Dir["*.[^r]*"]       →    ["config.h"]
Dir["*.{rb,h}"]      →    ["main.rb", "config.h"]
Dir["*"]             →    ["config.h", "main.rb"]
```

chdir   Dir.chdir(⟨ *aString* ⟩) → 0

Changes the current working directory of the process to the given string. When called without an argument, changes the directory to the value of the environment variable `HOME`, or `LOGDIR`. Raises a `SystemCallError` (probably `Errno::ENOENT`) if the target directory does not exist.

```
Dir.chdir("/var/spool/mail")   →    0
Dir.pwd                        →    "/var/spool/mail"
```

---

chroot   Dir.chroot(*aString*) → 0

Changes this process's idea of the file system root. Only a privileged process may make this call. Not available on all platforms. On Unix systems, see `chroot(2)` for more information.

```
Dir.chdir("/production/secure/root")
Dir.chroot("/production/secure/root")   → 0
Dir.pwd                                 → "/"
```

---

delete   Dir.delete(*aString*) → 0

Deletes the named directory. Raises a subclass of `SystemCallError` if the directory isn't empty.

---

entries   Dir.entries(*aString*) → *anArray*

Returns an array containing all of the filenames in the given directory. Will raise a `SystemCallError` if the named directory doesn't exist.

```
Dir.entries("testdir")   →   [".", "..", "config.h", "main.rb"]
```

---

foreach   Dir.foreach(*aString*) {| *filename* | *block* } → `nil`

Calls the block once for each entry in the named directory, passing the filename of each entry as a parameter to the block.

```
Dir.foreach("testdir") {|x| puts("Got " + x) }
```

produces:

```
Got .
Got ..
Got config.h
Got main.rb
```

---

getwd   Dir.getwd → *aString*

Returns the path to the current working directory of this process as a string.

```
Dir.chdir("/tmp")   →   0
Dir.getwd           →   "/tmp"
```

---

glob   Dir.glob(*aString*) → *anArray*

Synonym for `Dir.[]`.

---

mkdir   Dir.mkdir(*aString* ⟨ , *anInteger* ⟩) → 0

Makes a new directory named by *aString*, with permissions specified by the optional parameter *anInteger*. The permissions may be modified by the value of `File.umask`, and are ignored on NT. Raises a `SystemCallError` if the directory cannot be created. See also the discussion of permissions on page 305.

new   Dir.new(*aString*) → *aDir*

Returns a new directory object for the named directory.

---

open   Dir.open(*aString*) → *aDir*
Dir.open(*aString*) {| *aDir* | *block* } → `nil`

With no block, `open` is a synonym for `Dir.new`. If a block is present, it is passed *aDir* as a parameter. The directory is closed at the end of the block, and `Dir.open` returns `nil`.

---

pwd   Dir.pwd → *aString*

Synonym for `Dir.getwd`.

---

rmdir   Dir.rmdir(*aString*) → `true`

Synonym for `Dir.delete`.

---

unlink   Dir.unlink(*aString*) → `true`

Synonym for `Dir.delete`.

Instance methods

close   *dir*.close → `nil`

Closes the directory stream. Any further attempts to access *dir* will raise an `IOError`.

```
d = Dir.new("testdir")
d.close   →   nil
```

---

each   *dir*.each { *block* } → *dir*

Calls the block once for each entry in this directory, passing the filename of each entry as a parameter to the block.

```
d = Dir.new("testdir")
d.each  {|x| puts ("Got " + x) }
```

produces:

```
Got .
Got ..
Got config.h
Got main.rb
```

---

read   *dir*.read → *aString* or `nil`

Reads the next entry from *dir* and returns it as a string. Returns `nil` at the end of the stream.

```
d = Dir.new("testdir")
d.read   →   "."
d.read   →   ".."
d.read   →   "config.h"
```

---

rewind   *dir*.rewind → *dir*

Repositions *dir* to the first entry.

```
d = Dir.new("testdir")
d.read     →   "."
d.rewind   →   #<Dir:0x4018a8c4>
d.read     →   "."
```

---

seek   *dir*.seek(*anInteger*) → *dir*

Seeks to a particular location in *dir*. *anInteger* must be a value returned by `Dir#tell`.

```
d = Dir.new("testdir")
d.read       →   "."
i = d.tell
d.read       →   ".."
d.seek(i)    →   #<Dir:0x4018a6f8>
d.read       →   ".."
```

---

tell   *dir*.tell → *anInteger*

Returns the current position in *dir*. See also `Dir#seek`.

```
d = Dir.new("testdir")
d.tell   →   0
d.read   →   "."
d.tell   →   12
```

Class **Exception**   <   Object

Descendents of class `Exception` are used to communicate between `raise` methods and `rescue` statements in `begin/end` blocks. `Exception` objects carry information about the exception—its type (the exception's class name), an optional descriptive string, and optional traceback information.

The standard library defines the exceptions shown in Figure 22.1 on the facing page.

E xception

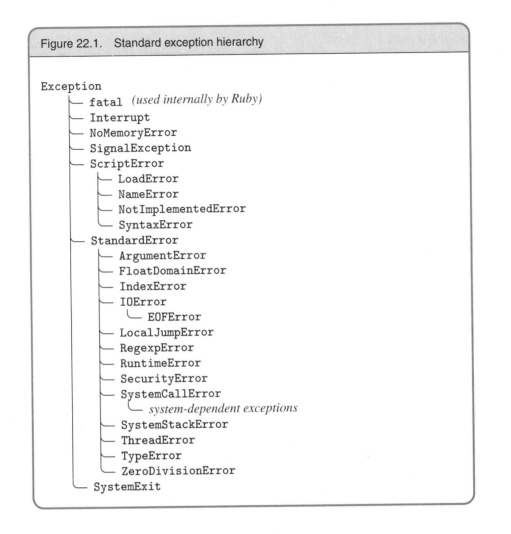

Figure 22.1.   Standard exception hierarchy

```
Exception
    └─ fatal  (used internally by Ruby)
    ── Interrupt
    ── NoMemoryError
    ── SignalException
    ── ScriptError
            ── LoadError
            ── NameError
            ── NotImplementedError
            └─ SyntaxError
    ── StandardError
            ── ArgumentError
            ── FloatDomainError
            ── IndexError
            ── IOError
                 └─ EOFError
            ── LocalJumpError
            ── RegexpError
            ── RuntimeError
            ── SecurityError
            ── SystemCallError
                 └─ system-dependent exceptions
            ── SystemStackError
            ── ThreadError
            ── TypeError
            └─ ZeroDivisionError
    └─ SystemExit
```

Class methods

exception   Exception.exception(⟨ *aString* ⟩) → *anException*

Creates and returns a new exception object, optionally setting the message to *aString*.

Exception

Instance methods

backtrace

exc.backtrace → *anArray*

Returns any backtrace associated with the exception. The backtrace is an array of strings, each containing either "filename:lineNo: in 'method'" or "filename:lineNo."

```
def a
  raise "boom"
end

def b
  a()
end

begin
  b()
rescue => detail
  print detail.backtrace.join("\n")
end
```

produces:

```
prog.rb:2:in `a'
prog.rb:6:in `b'
prog.rb:10
```

exception

exc.exception(⟨ *aString* ⟩) → *anException* or *exc*

With no argument, returns the receiver. Otherwise, creates a new exception object of the same class as the receiver, but with a different message.

message

exc.message → *aString*

Returns the message associated with this exception.

set_backtrace

exc.set_backtrace(*anArray*) → *anArray*

Sets the backtrace information associated with *exc*. The argument must be an array of String objects in the format described in Exception#backtrace.

Class **FalseClass** < Object

The global value `false` is the only instance of class `FalseClass` and represents a logically false value in boolean expressions. The class provides operators allowing `false` to participate correctly in logical expressions.

Instance methods

&
$$false \ \& \ anObject \rightarrow false$$

And—Returns `false`. *anObject* is always evaluated as it is the argument to a method call—there is no short-circuit evaluation in this case.

^
$$false \ \wedge \ anObject \rightarrow true \ \text{or} \ false$$

Exclusive Or—If *anObject* is `nil` or `false`, returns `false`; otherwise, returns `true`.

|
$$false \ | \ anObject \rightarrow true \ \text{or} \ false$$

Or—Returns `false` if *anObject* is `nil` or `false`; `true` otherwise.

Class **File** < IO

A `File` is an abstraction of any file object accessible by the program and is closely associated with class `IO`, page 329. `File` includes the methods of module `FileTest` as class methods, allowing you to write (for example) `File.exist?("foo")`.

In this section, *permission bits* are a platform-specific set of bits that indicate permissions of a file. On Unix-based systems, permissions are viewed as a set of three octets, for the owner, the group, and the rest of the world. For each of these entities, permissions may be set to read, write, or execute (or search, if a directory) the file:

Owner			Group			Other		
r	w	x	r	w	x	r	w	x
4	2	1	4	2	1	4	2	1

The permission bits `0644` (in octal) would thus be interpreted as read/write for owner, and read-only for group and other. Higher-order bits may also be used to indicate the type of file (plain, directory, pipe, socket, and so on) and various other special features.

On non-Posix operating systems, there may be only the ability to make a file read-only or not. In this case, the remaining permission bits will be synthesized to resemble typical values. For instance, on Windows NT the default permission bits are `0644`, which means read/write for owner, read-only for all others. The only change that can be made is to make the file read-only, which is reported as `0444`.

Mixes in

```
FileTest:
    blockdev?, chardev?, directory?, executable?, executable_real?,
    exist?, exists?, file?, grpowned?, owned?, pipe?, readable?,
    readable_real?, setgid?, setuid?, size, size?, socket?, sticky?,
    symlink?, writable?, writable_real?, zero?
```

Class methods

atime   File.atime(*fileName*) → *aTime*

Returns the last access time for the named file.

```
File.atime("testfile")   →   Tue Sep 19 23:31:42 CDT 2000
```

basename   File.basename(*fileName* ⟨ , *aSuffix* ⟩) → *aNewString*

Returns the last component of the filename given in *fileName*, which must be formed using forward slashes ("/ ") regardless of the separator used on the local file system. If *aSuffix* is given and present at the end of *fileName*, it is removed.

```
File.basename("/home/gumby/work/ruby.rb")          →   "ruby.rb"
File.basename("/home/gumby/work/ruby.rb", ".rb")   →   "ruby"
```

chmod   File.chmod(*aModeInt* ⟨ , *fileName* ⟩+) → *anInteger*

Changes permission bits on the named file(s) to the bit pattern represented by *aMode-Int*. Actual effects are operating system dependent (see the beginning of this section). On Unix systems, see chmod(2) for details. Returns the number of files processed.

```
File.chmod(0644, "testfile", "out")   →   2
```

chown   File.chown(*anOwnerInt, aGroupInt* ⟨ , *fileName* ⟩+) → *anInteger*

Changes the owner and group of the named file(s) to the given numeric owner and group id's. Only a process with superuser privileges may change the owner of a file. The current owner of a file may change the file's group to any group to which the owner belongs. A nil or −1 owner or group id is ignored. Returns the number of files processed.

```
File.chown(nil, 100, "testfile")
```

ctime   File.ctime(*fileName*) → *aTime*

Returns the change time for the named file (the time at which directory information about the file was changed, not the file itself).

```
File.ctime("testfile")   →   Tue Sep 19 23:32:04 CDT 2000
```

delete   File.delete(⟨ *fileName* ⟩⁺) → *aFixnum*

Deletes the named file(s). Returns the number of files processed. See also `Dir.rmdir`.

```
File.new("testrm", "w+").close   →   nil
File.delete("testrm")            →   1
```

dirname   File.dirname(*fileName*) → *fileName*

Returns all components of the filename given in *fileName* except the last one. The
filename must be formed using forward slashes ("/") regardless of the separator used
on the local file system.

```
File.dirname("/home/gumby/work/ruby.rb")   →   "/home/gumby/work"
```

expand_path   File.expand_path(*fileName* ⟨ , *aDirString* ⟩) → *fileName*

Converts a pathname to an absolute pathname. Relative paths are referenced from the
current working directory of the process unless *aDirString* is given, in which case it
will be used as the starting point. The given pathname may start with a "~", which
expands to the process owner's home directory (the environment variable `HOME` must
be set correctly). "~*user*" expands to the named user's home directory.

```
File.expand_path("~oracle/bin")        →   "/home/oracle/bin"
File.expand_path("../../bin", "/tmp/x") →   "/bin"
```

ftype   File.ftype(*fileName*) → *fileType*

Identifies the type of the named file; the return string is one of "`file`", "`directory`",
"`characterSpecial`", "`blockSpecial`", "`fifo`", "`link`", or "`socket`".

```
File.ftype("testfile")          →   "file"
File.ftype("/dev/tty")          →   "characterSpecial"
File.ftype("/tmp/.X11-unix/X0") →   "socket"
```

join   File.join(⟨ *aString* ⟩⁺) → *fileName*

Returns a new string formed by joining the strings using `File::SEPARATOR` (see
Table 22.2 on the next page).

```
File.join("usr", "mail", "gumby")   →   "usr/mail/gumby"
```

link   File.link(*anOldName*, *aNewName*) → 0

Creates a new name for an existing file using a hard link. Will not overwrite *aNew-
Name* if it already exists (raising a subclass of `SystemCallError`). Not available on
all platforms.

```
File.link("testfile", ".testfile")   →   0
IO.readlines(".testfile")[0]         →   "This is line one\n"
```

Table 22.2. Path separator constants (platform-specific)

`ALT_SEPARATOR`	Alternate path separator.
`PATH_SEPARATOR`	Character that separates filenames in a search path (such as ":" or ";").
`SEPARATOR`	Character that separates directory components in a filename (such as "\" or "/").
`Separator`	Alias for `SEPARATOR`.

lstat
File.lstat(fileName) → aStat

Same as `IO#stat`, but does not follow the last symbolic link. Instead, reports on the link itself.

```
File.symlink("testfile", "link2test")   →   0
File.stat("testfile").size              →   66
File.lstat("link2test").size            →   8
File.stat("link2test").size             →   66
```

mtime
File.mtime(fileName) → aTime

Returns the modification time for the named file.

```
File.mtime("testfile")   →   Tue Sep 19 23:11:49 CDT 2000
```

new
File.new(fileName, aModeString="r") → file
File.new(fileName ⟨ , aModeNum ⟨ , aPermNum ⟩ ⟩) → file

Opens the file named by *fileName* according to *aModeString* (default is "r") and returns a new `File` object. See Table 22.5 on page 331 for a description of *aModeString*. The file mode may optionally be specified as a `Fixnum` by *or*-ing together the flags described in Table 22.3 on the next page. Optional permission bits may be given in *aPermNum*. These mode and permission bits are platform dependent; on Unix systems, see open(2) for details.

```
f = File.new("testfile", "r")
f = File.new("newfile",  "w+")
f = File.new("newfile", 0644, File::CREAT|File::TRUNC|File::RDWR)
```

open
File.open(fileName, aModeString="r") → file
File.open(fileName ⟨ , aModeNum ⟨ , aPermNum ⟩ ⟩) → file
File.open(fileName, aModeString="r") {| file | block } → nil
File.open(fileName ⟨ , aModeNum ⟨ , aPermNum ⟩ ⟩) {| file | block } → nil

With no associated block, `open` is a synonym for `File.new`. If the optional code block is given, it will be passed *file* as an argument, and the file will automatically be closed when the block terminates. In this instance, `File.open` returns `nil`.

Table 22.3. Open-mode constants

APPEND	Open the file in append mode; all writes will occur at end of file.
CREAT	Create the file on open if it does not exist.
EXCL	When used with CREAT, open will fail if the file exists.
NOCTTY	When opening a terminal device (see IO#isatty on page 335), do not allow it to become the controlling terminal.
NONBLOCK	Open the file in nonblocking mode.
RDONLY	Open for reading only.
RDWR	Open for reading and writing.
TRUNC	Open the file and truncate it to zero length if the file exists.
WRONLY	Open for writing only.

---

readlink   File.readlink(*fileName*) → *fileName*

Returns the given symbolic link as a string. Not available on all platforms.

```
File.symlink("testfile", "link2test")   →   0
File.readlink("link2test")              →   "testfile"
```

---

rename   File.rename(*anOldName, aNewName*) → 0

Renames the given file to the new name. Raises a `SystemCallError` if the file cannot be renamed.

```
File.rename("afile", "afile.bak")   →   0
```

---

size   File.size(*fileName*) → *anInteger*

Returns the size of the file in bytes.

```
File.size("testfile")   →   66
```

---

split   File.split(*fileName*) → *anArray*

Splits the given string into a directory and a file component and returns them in a two-element array. See also `File.dirname` and `File.basename`.

```
File.split("/home/gumby/.profile")   →   ["/home/gumby", ".profile"]
```

---

stat   File.stat(*fileName*) → *aStat*

Returns a `File::Stat` object for the named file (see `File::Stat`, page 313).

```
File.stat("testfile").mtime   →   Tue Sep 19 23:11:49 CDT 2000
```

symlink   File.symlink(*anOldName, aNewName*) → 0 or `nil`

Creates a symbolic link called *aNewName* for the existing file *anOldName*. Returns `nil` on all platforms that do not support symbolic links.

```
File.symlink("testfile", "link2test")   →   0
```

truncate   File.truncate(*fileName, anInteger*) → 0

Truncates the file *fileName* to be at most *anInteger* bytes long. Not available on all platforms.

```
f = File.new("out", "w")
f.write("1234567890")     →    10
f.close                   →    nil
File.truncate("out", 5)   →    0
File.size("out")          →    5
```

umask   File.umask(⟨ *anInteger* ⟩) → *anInteger*

Returns the current umask value for this process. If the optional argument is given, set the umask to that value and return the previous value. Umask values are *subtracted* from the default permissions; so a umask of 0222 would make a file read-only for everyone. See also the discussion of permissions on page 305.

```
File.umask(0006)   →    18
File.umask         →    6
```

unlink   File.unlink(⟨ *fileName* ⟩⁺) → *anInteger*

Synonym for `File.delete`. See also `Dir.rmdir`.

utime   File.utime(*anAccessTime, aModTime* ⟨ *, fileName* ⟩⁺) → *aFixnum*

Changes the access and modification times on a number of files. The times must be instances of class **Time** or integers representing the number of seconds since epoch. Returns the number of files processed. Not available on all platforms.

```
File.utime(0, 0, "testfile")            →    1
File.mtime("testfile")                  →    Wed Dec 31 18:00:00 CST
                                             1969
File.utime(0, Time.now, "testfile")     →    1
File.mtime("testfile")                  →    Tue Sep 19 23:32:05 CDT
                                             2000
```

Instance methods

atime

file.atime → *aTime*

Returns the last access time for *file*, or epoch if *file* has not been accessed.

```
File.new("testfile").atime  →  Wed Dec 31 18:00:00 CST 1969
```

chmod

file.chmod(*aModeInt*) → 0

Changes permission bits on *file* to the bit pattern represented by *aModeInt*. Actual effects are platform dependent; on Unix systems, see chmod(2) for details. See the discussion of permissions on page 305.

```
f = File.new("out", "w");
f.chmod(0644)  →  0
```

chown

file.chown(*anOwnerInt, aGroupInt*) → 0

Changes the owner and group of *file* to the given numeric owner and group id's. Only a process with superuser privileges may change the owner of a file. The current owner of a file may change the file's group to any group to which the owner belongs. A nil or −1 owner or group id is ignored.

```
File.new("testfile").chown(502, 1000)
```

ctime

file.ctime → *aTime*

Returns the change time for *file* (that is, the time directory information about the file was changed, not the file itself).

```
File.new("testfile").ctime  →  Tue Sep 19 23:32:05 CDT 2000
```

flock

file.flock (*aLockingConstant*) → 0 or false

Locks or unlocks a file according to *aLockingConstant* (a logical *or* of the values in Table 22.4 on the next page). Returns false if File::LOCK_NB is specified and the operation would otherwise have blocked. Not available on all platforms.

```
File.new("testfile").flock(File::LOCK_UN)  →  0
```

lstat

file.lstat → *aStat*

Same as IO#stat, but does not follow the last symbolic link. Instead, reports on the link itself.

```
File.symlink("testfile", "link2test")  →  0
File.stat("testfile").size             →  66
f = File.new("link2test")
f.lstat.size                           →  8
f.stat.size                            →  66
```

Table 22.4. Lock-mode constants

LOCK_EX	Exclusive lock. Only one process may hold an exclusive lock for a given file at a time.
LOCK_NB	Don't block when locking. May be combined with other lock options using logical or.
LOCK_SH	Shared lock. Multiple processes may each hold a shared lock for a given file at the same time.
LOCK_UN	Unlock.

mtime *file*.mtime → *aTime*

Returns the modification time for *file*.

```
File.new("testfile").mtime  →  Tue Sep 19 23:32:05 CDT 2000
```

path *file*.path → *fileName*

Returns the pathname used to create *file* as a string.

```
File.new("testfile").path  →  "testfile"
```

truncate *file*.truncate(*anInteger*) → 0

Truncates *file* to at most *anInteger* bytes. The file must be opened for writing. Not available on all platforms.

```
f = File.new("out", "w")
f.syswrite("1234567890")   →   10
f.truncate(5)              →   0
f.close()                  →   nil
File.size("out")           →   5
```

Class **File::Stat** < Object

Objects of class `File::Stat` encapsulate common status information for `File` objects. The information is recorded at the moment the `File::Stat` object is created; changes made to the file after that point will not be reflected. `File::Stat` objects are returned by `IO#stat`, `File.stat`, `File#lstat`, and `File.lstat`. Many of these methods return platform-specific values, and not all values are meaningful on all systems. See also `Kernel#test` on page 429.

Mixes in

```
Comparable:
    <, <=, ==, >=, >, between?
```

Instance methods

<=>   *statfile* <=> *anOtherStat* → −1, 0, 1

Compares `File::Stat` objects by comparing their respective modification times.

```
f1 = File.new("f1", "w")
sleep 1
f2 = File.new("f2", "w")
f1.stat <=> f2.stat   →   -1
```

atime   *statfile*.atime → *aTime*

Returns the last access time for this file as an object of class `Time`.

```
File.stat("testfile").atime   →   Wed Dec 31 18:00:00 CST 1969
```

blksize   *statfile*.blksize → *anInteger*

Returns the native file system's block size. Will return 0 on platforms that don't support this information.

```
File.stat("testfile").blksize   →   4096
```

blockdev?   *statfile*.blockdev? → `true` or `false`

Returns `true` if the file is a block device, `false` if it isn't or if the operating system doesn't support this feature.

```
File.stat("testfile").blockdev?   →   false
```

blocks   *statfile*.blocks → *anInteger*

Returns the number of native file system blocks allocated for this file, or 0 if the operating system doesn't support this feature.

```
File.stat("testfile").blocks   →   2
```

---

chardev?   *statfile*.chardev? → `true` or `false`

Returns `true` if the file is a character device, `false` if it isn't or if the operating system doesn't support this feature.

```
File.stat("/dev/tty").chardev?   →   true
```

---

ctime   *statfile*.ctime → *aTime*

Returns the change time for *statfile* (that is, the time directory information about the file was changed, not the file itself).

```
File.stat("testfile").ctime   →   Tue Sep 19 23:32:05 CDT 2000
```

---

dev   *statfile*.dev → *aFixnum*

Returns an integer representing the device on which *statfile* resides.

```
File.stat("testfile").dev   →   774
```

---

directory?   *statfile*.directory? → `true` or `false`

Returns `true` if *statfile* is a directory, `false` otherwise.

```
File.stat("testfile").directory?   →   false
File.stat(".").directory?          →   true
```

---

executable?   *statfile*.executable? → `true` or `false`

Returns `true` if *statfile* is executable or if the operating system doesn't distinguish executable files from nonexecutable files. The tests are made using the effective owner of the process.

```
File.stat("testfile").executable?   →   false
```

---

executable_real?   *statfile*.executable_real? → `true` or `false`

Same as `executable?`, but tests using the real owner of the process.

---

file?   *statfile*.file? → `true` or `false`

Returns `true` if *statfile* is a regular file (not a device file, pipe, socket, etc.).

```
File.stat("testfile").file?   →   true
```

---

ftype   *statfile*.ftype → *fileType*

Identifies the type of *statfile*. The return string is one of: "`file`", "`directory`", "`characterSpecial`", "`blockSpecial`", "`fifo`", "`link`", or "`socket`".

```
File.stat("/dev/tty").ftype   →   "characterSpecial"
```

gid   *statfile*.gid → *aFixnum*

Returns the numeric group id of the owner of *statfile*.

```
File.stat("testfile").gid   →   500
```

grpowned?   *statfile*.grpowned? → **true** or **false**

Returns true if the effective group id of the process is the same as the group id of *statfile*. On Windows NT, returns **false**.

```
File.stat("testfile").grpowned?      →   true
File.stat("/etc/passwd").grpowned?   →   false
```

ino   *statfile*.ino → *aFixnum*

Returns the inode number for *statfile*.

```
File.stat("testfile").ino   →   1083669
```

mode   *statfile*.mode → *aFixnum*

Returns an integer representing the permission bits of *statfile*. The meaning of the bits is platform dependent; on Unix systems, see `stat(2)`.

```
File.chmod(0644, "testfile")   →   1
s = File.stat("testfile")
sprintf("%o", s.mode)          →   "100644"
```

mtime   *statfile*.mtime → *aTime*

Returns the modification time for *statfile*.

```
File.stat("testfile").mtime   →   Tue Sep 19 23:32:05 CDT 2000
```

nlink   *statfile*.nlink → *aFixnum*

Returns the number of hard links to *statfile*.

```
File.stat("testfile").nlink            →   1
File.link("testfile", "testfile.bak")  →   0
File.stat("testfile").nlink            →   2
```

owned?   *statfile*.owned? → **true** or **false**

Returns **true** if the effective user id of the process is the same as the owner of *statfile*.

```
File.stat("testfile").owned?      →   true
File.stat("/etc/passwd").owned?   →   false
```

pipe?   *statfile*.pipe? → **true** or **false**

Returns **true** if the operating system supports pipes and *statfile* is a pipe; **false** otherwise.

rdev
statfile.rdev → *aFixnum*

Returns an integer representing the device type on which *statfile* resides. Returns 0 if the operating system doesn't support this feature.

```
File.stat("/dev/fd0").rdev   →   512
```

readable?
statfile.readable? → `true` or `false`

Returns `true` if *statfile* is readable by the effective user id of this process.

```
File.stat("testfile").readable?   →   true
```

readable_real?
statfile.readable_real? → `true` or `false`

Returns `true` if *statfile* is readable by the real user id of this process.

```
File.stat("testfile").readable_real?   →   true
```

setgid?
statfile.setgid? → `true` or `false`

Returns `true` if *statfile* has the set-group-id permission bit set, `false` if it doesn't or if the operating system doesn't support this feature.

```
File.stat("/usr/sbin/lpc").setgid?   →   true
```

setuid?
statfile.setuid? → `true` or `false`

Returns `true` if *statfile* has the set-user-id permission bit set, `false` if it doesn't or if the operating system doesn't support this feature.

```
File.stat("/bin/su").setuid?   →   true
```

size
statfile.size → *aFixnum*

Returns the size of *statfile* in bytes.

```
File.stat("testfile").size   →   66
```

size?
statfile.size? → *aFixnum* or `nil`

Returns `nil` if *statfile* is a zero-length file; otherwise, returns the file size.

```
File.stat("testfile").size?   →   66
```

socket?
statfile.socket? → `true` or `false`

Returns `true` if *statfile* is a socket, `false` if it isn't or if the operating system doesn't support this feature.

```
File.stat("testfile").socket?   →   false
```

sticky?   *statfile*.sticky? → `true` or `false`

Returns `true` if *statfile* has its sticky bit set, `false` if it doesn't or if the operating system doesn't support this feature.

```
File.stat("testfile").sticky?   →   false
```

symlink?   *statfile*.symlink? → `true` or `false`

Returns `true` if *statfile* is a symbolic link, `false` if it isn't or if the operating system doesn't support this feature. As `File.stat` automatically follows symbolic links, `symlink?` will always be `false` for an object returned by `File.stat`.

```
File.symlink("testfile", "alink")   →   0
File.stat("alink").symlink?         →   false
File.lstat("alink").symlink?        →   true
```

uid   *statfile*.uid → *aFixnum*

Returns the numeric user id of the owner of *statfile*.

```
File.stat("testfile").uid   →   501
```

writable?   *statfile*.writable? → `true` or `false`

Returns `true` if *statfile* is writable by the effective user id of this process.

```
File.stat("testfile").writable?   →   true
```

writable_real?   *statfile*.writable_real? → `true` or `false`

Returns `true` if *statfile* is writable by the real user id of this process.

```
File.stat("testfile").writable_real?   →   true
```

zero?   *statfile*.zero? → `true` or `false`

Returns `true` if *statfile* is a zero-length file; `false` otherwise.

```
File.stat("testfile").zero?   →   false
```

Class Fixnum < Integer

A `Fixnum` holds `Integer` values that can be represented in a native machine word (minus 1 bit). If any operation on a `Fixnum` exceeds this range, the value is automatically converted to a `Bignum`.

`Fixnum` objects have immediate value. This means that when they are assigned or passed as parameters, the actual object is passed, rather than a reference to that object. Assignment does not alias `Fixnum` objects. There is effectively only one `Fixnum` object instance for any given integer value, so, for example, you cannot add a singleton method to a `Fixnum`.

Instance methods

Arithmetic operations

Performs various arithmetic operations on *fix*.

fix	+	*aNumeric*	Addition
fix	−	*aNumeric*	Subtraction
fix	*	*aNumeric*	Multiplication
fix	/	*aNumeric*	Division
fix	%	*aNumeric*	Modulo
fix	**	*aNumeric*	Exponentiation

Bit operations

Performs various operations on the binary representations of the `Fixnum`.

~ *fix*			Invert bits
fix	|	*aNumeric*	Bitwise OR
fix	&	*aNumeric*	Bitwise AND
fix	^	*aNumeric*	Bitwise EXCLUSIVE OR
fix	<<	*aNumeric*	Left-shift *aNumeric* bits
fix	>>	*aNumeric*	Right-shift *aNumeric* bits (with sign extension)

<=>   *fix* <=> *aNumeric* → −1, 0, +1

Comparison—Returns −1, 0, or +1 depending on whether *fix* is less than, equal to, or greater than *aNumeric*. This is the basis for the tests in `Comparable`.

[ ]   *fix*[*n*] → 0, 1

Bit Reference—Returns the *n*th bit in the binary representation of *fix*, where *fix*[0] is the least significant bit.

```
a = 0b11001100101010
30.downto(0) do |n| print a[n] end
```

produces:

00000000000000000011001100101010

---

id2name   *fix*.id2name → *aString* or `nil`

Returns the name of the object whose symbol id is the value of *fix*. If there is no symbol in the symbol table with this value, returns `nil`. `id2name` has nothing to do with the `Object.id` method. See also `String#intern` on page 376 and class `Symbol` on page 388.

```
symbol = :@inst_var    →   :@inst_var
id     = symbol.to_i   →   8930
id.id2name             →   "@inst_var"
```

---

size   *fix*.size → *aFixnum*

Returns the number of *bytes* in the machine representation of a `Fixnum`.

---

to_f   *fix*.to_f → *aFloat*

Converts *fix* to a `Float`.

---

to_i   *fix*.to_i → *fix*

Returns *fix*.

---

to_s   *fix*.to_s → *aString*

Returns a string containing the decimal representation of self.

Class **Float** < Numeric

`Float` objects represent real numbers using the native architecture's double-precision floating point representation.

Instance methods

Arithmetic operations

Performs various arithmetic operations on *flt*.

flt	+	*aNumeric*	Addition
flt	–	*aNumeric*	Subtraction
flt	*	*aNumeric*	Multiplication
flt	/	*aNumeric*	Division
flt	%	*aNumeric*	Modulo
flt	**	*aNumeric*	Exponentiation

<=> $\qquad$ *flt* <=> *aNumeric* → −1, 0, +1

Returns −1, 0, or +1 depending on whether *flt* is less than, equal to, or greater than *aNumeric*. This is the basis for the tests in `Comparable`.

---

ceil $\qquad$ *flt*.ceil → *anInteger*

Returns the smallest `Integer` greater than or equal to *flt*.

```
1.2.ceil      →    2
2.0.ceil      →    2
(-1.2).ceil   →    -1
(-2.0).ceil   →    -2
```

---

finite? $\qquad$ *flt*.finite? → **true** or **false**

Returns **true** if *flt* is a valid IEEE floating point number (it is not infinite, and **nan?** is **false**).

---

floor $\qquad$ *flt*.floor → *anInteger*

Returns the largest integer less than or equal to *flt*.

```
1.2.floor      →    1
2.0.floor      →    2
(-1.2).floor   →    -2
(-2.0).floor   →    -2
```

---

infinite? $\qquad$ *flt*.infinite? → **nil**, −1, +1

Returns **nil**, −1, or +1 depending on whether *flt* is finite, −∞, or +∞.

```
(0.0).infinite?        →    nil
(-1.0/0.0).infinite?   →    -1
(+1.0/0.0).infinite?   →    1
```

---

nan? $\qquad$ *flt*.nan? → **true** or **false**

Returns **true** if *flt* is an invalid IEEE floating point number.

```
a = -1.0           →    -1.0
a.nan?             →    false
a = Math.log(a)    →    NaN
a.nan?             →    true
```

---

round $\qquad$ *flt*.round → *anInteger*

Rounds *flt* to the nearest integer. Equivalent to:

```
def round
  return floor(self+0.5) if self > 0.0
  return ceil(self-0.5)  if self < 0.0
  return 0.0
end
```

```
1.5.round      →    2
(-1.5).round   →   -2
```

to_f

flt.to_f → flt

Returns *flt*.

to_i

flt.to_i → anInteger

Returns *flt* truncated to an **Integer**.

to_s

flt.to_s → aString

Returns a string containing a representation of self. As well as a fixed or exponential form of the number, the call may return "**NaN**", "**Infinity**", and "**-Infinity**".

Class # Hash < Object

A **Hash** is a collection of key-value pairs. It is similar to an **Array**, except that indexing is done via arbitrary keys of any object type, not an integer index. The order in which you traverse a hash by either key or value may seem arbitrary, and will generally not be in the insertion order.

Hashes have a *default value* that is returned when accessing keys that do not exist in the hash. By default, that value is **nil**.

Mixes in

Enumerable:
    collect, detect, each_with_index, entries, find, find_all, grep,
    include?, map, max, member?, min, reject, select, sort, to_a

Class methods

[ ]

Hash[⟨ key => value ⟩*] → aHash

Creates a new hash populated with the given objects. Equivalent to the literal **{ key, value, ... }**. Keys and values occur in pairs, so there must be an even number of arguments.

```
Hash["a", 100, "b", 200]       →   {"a"=>100, "b"=>200}
Hash["a" => 100, "b" => 200]   →   {"a"=>100, "b"=>200}
{ "a" => 100, "b" => 200 }     →   {"a"=>100, "b"=>200}
```

---

new

Hash.new(anObject=nil) → aHash

Returns a new, empty hash. If *anObject* is specified, it will be used as the *default value*.

```
h = Hash.new("Go Fish")
h["a"] = 100
h["b"] = 200
h["a"]   →   100
h["c"]   →   "Go Fish"
```

Instance methods

==

hsh == anOtherHash → `true` or `false`

Equality—Two hashes are equal if they each contain the same number of keys and if each key-value pair is equal to (according to `Object#==`) the corresponding elements in the other hash.

```
h1 = { "a" => 1, "c" => 2 }
h2 = { "a" => 1, "c" => 2, 7 => 35 }
h3 = { "a" => 1, "c" => 2, 7 => 35 }
h4 = { "a" => 1, "d" => 2, "f" => 35 }
h1 == h2   →   false
h2 == h3   →   true
h3 == h4   →   false
```

[ ]

hsh[aKeyObject] → *aValueObject*

Element Reference—Retrieves the *aValueObject* stored for *aKeyObject*. If not found, returns the *default value*.

```
h = { "a" => 100, "b" => 200 }
h["a"]   →   100
h["c"]   →   nil
```

[ ]=

hsh[aKeyObject] = aValueObject → *aValueObject*

Element Assignment—Associates the value given by *aValueObject* with the key given by *aKeyObject*. *aKeyObject* should not have its value changed while it is in use as a key (a `String` passed as a key will be duplicated and frozen).

```
h = { "a" => 100, "b" => 200 }
h["a"] = 9
h["c"] = 4
h   →   {"a"=>9, "b"=>200, "c"=>4}
```

clear

hsh.clear → *hsh*

Removes all key-value pairs from *hsh*.

```
h = { "a" => 100, "b" => 200 }   →   {"a"=>100, "b"=>200}
h.clear                          →   {}
```

default

hsh.default → *anObject*

Returns the "*default value*"—that is, the value returned for a key that does not exist in the hash. Defaults to `nil`. See also `Hash#default=`.

---

default=   *hsh*.default = *anObject* → *hsh*

Sets the "*default value*"—that is, the value returned for a key that does not exist in the hash. Defaults to `nil`.

```
h = { "a" => 100, "b" => 200 }
h.default = "Go fish"
h["a"]    →    100
h["z"]    →    "Go fish"
```

---

delete   *hsh*.delete(*aKeyObject*) → *aValueObject*

         hsh.delete(*aKeyObject*) {| *aKeyObject* | *block* } → *aValueObject*

Deletes and returns a key-value pair from *hsh* whose key is equal to *aKeyObject*. If the key is not found, returns the *default value*. If the optional code block is given and the key is not found, pass in the key and return the result of *block*.

```
h = { "a" => 100, "b" => 200 }
h.delete("a")                           →   100
h.delete("z")                           →   nil
h.delete("z") { |el| "#{el} not found" }   →   "z not found"
```

---

delete_if   *hsh*.delete_if {| *key, value* | *block* } → *hsh*

Deletes every key-value pair from *hsh* for which *block* evaluates to `true`.

```
h = { "a" => 100, "b" => 200, "c" => 300 }
h.delete_if {|key, value| key >= "b" }   →   {"a"=>100}
```

---

each   *hsh*.each {| *key, value* | *block* } → *hsh*

Calls *block* once for each key in *hsh*, passing the key and value as parameters.

```
h = { "a" => 100, "b" => 200 }
h.each {|key, value| print key, " is ", value, "\n" }
```

produces:

```
a is 100
b is 200
```

---

each_key   *hsh*.each_key {| *key* | *block* } → *hsh*

Calls *block* once for each key in *hsh*, passing the key as a parameter.

```
h = { "a" => 100, "b" => 200 }
h.each_key {|key| puts key }
```

produces:

```
a
b
```

---

each_pair   *hsh*.each_pair {| *key, value* | *block* } → *hsh*

Synonym for `Hash#each`.

each_value hsh.each_value {| value | block } → hsh

Calls *block* once for each key in *hsh*, passing the value as a parameter.

```
h = { "a" => 100, "b" => 200 }
h.each_value {|value| puts value }
```

produces:

```
100
200
```

empty? hsh.empty? → true or false

Returns `true` if *hsh* contains no key-value pairs.

```
{}.empty?   →   true
```

fetch hsh.fetch(*aKeyObject* ⟨ , *aDefObject* ⟩) → *anObject*
hsh.fetch(*aKeyObject*) {| *aKeyObject* | block } → *anObject*

Returns a value from the hash for the given key. If the key can't be found, there are several options: With no other arguments, it will raise an `IndexError` exception; if *aDefObject* is given, then that will be returned; if the optional code block is specified, then that will be run and its result returned.

```
h = { "a" => 100, "b" => 200 }
h.fetch("a")                           →    100
h.fetch("z", "go fish")                →    "go fish"
h.fetch("z") { |el| "go fish, #{el}"}  →    "go fish, z"
```

The following example shows that an exception is raised if the key is not found and a default value is not supplied.

```
h = { "a" => 100, "b" => 200 }
h.fetch("z")
```

produces:

```
prog.rb:2:in `fetch': key not found (IndexError)
from prog.rb:2
```

has_key? hsh.has_key?(*aKeyObject*) → true or false

Returns `true` if the given key is present in *hsh*.

```
h = { "a" => 100, "b" => 200 }
h.has_key?("a")   →    true
h.has_key?("z")   →    false
```

has_value? hsh.has_value?(*aValueObject*) → true or false

Returns `true` if the given value is present for some key in *hsh*.

```
h = { "a" => 100, "b" => 200 }
h.has_value?(100)   →   true
h.has_value?(999)   →   false
```

include?

hsh.include?(aKeyObject) → <code>true</code> or <code>false</code>

Synonym for `Hash#has_key?`.

index

hsh.index(aValueObject) → aKeyObject

Returns the key for a given value. If not found, returns the *default value*.

```
h = { "a" => 100, "b" => 200 }
h.index(200)   →   "b"
h.index(999)   →   nil
```

indexes

hsh.indexes(〈 key 〉⁺) → anArray

Returns a new array consisting of values for the given key(s). Will insert the *default value* for keys that are not found.

```
h = { "a" => 100, "b" => 200, "c" => 300 }
h.indexes("a", "c")        →   [100, 300]
h.indexes("a", "c", "z")   →   [100, 300, nil]
```

indices

hsh.indices(〈 key 〉⁺) → anArray

Synonym for `Hash#indexes`.

invert

hsh.invert → aHash

Returns a new hash created by using *hsh*'s values as keys, and the keys as values.

```
h = { "n" => 100, "m" => 100, "y" => 300, "d" => 200, "a" => 0 }
h.invert   →   {200=>"d", 300=>"y", 0=>"a", 100=>"n"}
```

key?

hsh.key?(aKeyObject) → <code>true</code> or <code>false</code>

Synonym for `Hash#has_key?`.

keys

hsh.keys → anArray

Returns a new array populated with the keys from this hash. See also `Hash#values`.

```
h = { "a" => 100, "b" => 200, "c" => 300, "d" => 400 }
h.keys   →   ["a", "b", "c", "d"]
```

length

hsh.length → aFixnum

Returns the number of key-value pairs in the hash.

```
h = { "d" => 100, "a" => 200, "v" => 300, "e" => 400 }
h.length        →   4
h.delete("a")   →   200
h.length        →   3
```

member?   *hsh*.member?(*aKeyObject*) → `true` or `false`

Synonym for `Hash#has_key?`.

---

rehash   *hsh*.rehash → *hsh*

Rebuilds the hash based on the current hash values for each key. If values of key objects have changed since they were inserted, this method will reindex *hsh*. If `Hash#rehash` is called while an iterator is traversing the hash, an `IndexError` will be raised in the iterator.

```
a = [ "a", "b" ]
c = [ "c", "d" ]
h = { a => 100, c => 300 }
h[a]        →    100
a[0] = "z"
h[a]        →    nil
h.rehash    →    {["c", "d"]=>300, ["z", "b"]=>100}
h[a]        →    100
```

---

reject   *hsh*.reject {| *key, value* | *block* } → *aHash*

Same as `Hash#delete_if`, but works on (and returns) a copy of the *hsh*. Equivalent to `hsh.dup.delete_if`.

---

reject!   *hsh*.reject! {| *key, value* | *block* } → *hsh* or `nil`

Equivalent to `Hash#delete_if`, but returns `nil` if no changes were made.

---

replace   *hsh*.replace(*anOtherHash*) → *hsh*

Replaces the contents of *hsh* with the contents of *anOtherHash*.

```
h = { "a" => 100, "b" => 200 }
h.replace({ "c" => 300, "d" => 400 })    →    {"c"=>300, "d"=>400}
```

---

shift   *hsh*.shift → *anArray* or `nil`

Removes a key-value pair from *hsh* and returns it as the two-item array [*key, value*], or `nil` if the hash is empty.

```
h = { 1 => "a", 2 => "b", 3 => "c" }
h.shift   →    [1, "a"]
h         →    {2=>"b", 3=>"c"}
```

---

size   *hsh*.size → *aFixnum*

Synonym for `Hash#length`.

---

sort   *hsh*.sort → *anArray*
                                              hsh.sort {| *a, b* | *block* } → *anArray*

Converts *hsh* to a nested array of [*key, value*] arrays and sorts it, using `Array#sort`.

```
h = { "a" => 20, "b" => 30, "c" => 10  }
h.sort                         →   [["a", 20], ["b", 30], ["c", 10]]
h.sort {|a,b| a[1]<=>b[1]}     →   [["c", 10], ["a", 20], ["b", 30]]
```

---

store   *hsh*.store(*aKeyObject, aValueObject*) → *aValueObject*

Synonym for Element Assignment (**Hash#[]=**).

---

to_a   *hsh*.to_a → *anArray*

Converts *hsh* to a nested array of [*key, value*] arrays.

```
h = { "c" => 300, "a" => 100, "d" => 400, "c" => 300  }
h.to_a   →   [["a", 100], ["c", 300], ["d", 400]]
```

---

to_s   *hsh*.to_s → *aString*

Converts *hsh* to a string by converting the hash to an array of [*key, value*] pairs and then converting that array to a string using **Array#join** with the default separator.

```
h = { "c" => 300, "a" => 100, "d" => 400, "c" => 300  }
h.to_s   →   "a100c300d400"
```

---

update   *hsh*.update(*anOtherHash*) → *hsh*

Adds the contents of *anOtherHash* to *hsh*, overwriting entries with duplicate keys with those from *anOtherHash*.

```
h1 = { "a" => 100, "b" => 200 }
h2 = { "b" => 254, "c" => 300 }
h1.update(h2)   →   {"a"=>100, "b"=>254, "c"=>300}
```

---

value?   *hsh*.value?(*aValueObject*) → **true** or **false**

Synonym for **Hash#has_value?**.

---

values   *hsh*.values → *anArray*

Returns a new array populated with the values from *hsh*. See also **Hash#keys**.

```
h = { "a" => 100, "b" => 200, "c" => 300 }
h.values   →   [100, 200, 300]
```

| Class | **Integer** | < | Numeric |

Subclasses: Bignum, Fixnum

Integer is the basis for the two concrete classes that hold whole numbers, **Bignum** and **Fixnum**.

Instance methods

chr

int.chr → $aString$

Returns a string containing the ASCII character represented by the receiver's value.

```
65.chr    →   "A"
?a.chr    →   "a"
230.chr   →   "\346"
```

downto

int.downto($anInteger$) {| i | $block$ } → int

Iterates *block*, passing decreasing values from *int* down to and including *anInteger*.

```
5.downto(1) { |n| print n, ".. " }
print "  Liftoff!\n"
```

produces:

```
5.. 4.. 3.. 2.. 1..    Liftoff!
```

integer?

int.integer? → **true**

Always returns **true**.

next

int.next → $anInteger$

Returns the **Integer** equal to *int* + 1.

```
1.next      →   2
(-1).next   →   0
```

step

int.step($endNum, step$) {| i | $block$ } → int

Invokes *block* with the sequence of numbers starting at *int*, incremented by *step* on each call. The loop finishes when the value to be passed to the block is greater than *endNum* (if *step* is positive) or less than *endNum* (if *step* is negative).

```
1.step(10, 2) { |i| print i, " " }
```

produces:

```
1 3 5 7 9
```

succ

int.succ → $anInteger$

Synonym for **Integer#next**.

times   *int*.times { | *i* | *block* } → *int*

Iterates block *int* times, passing in values from zero to *int* −1.

```
5.times do |i|
  print i, " "
end
print "\n"
```

produces:

```
0 1 2 3 4
```

upto   *int*.upto(*anInteger*) { | *i* | *block* } → *int*

Iterates *block*, passing in integer values from *int* up to and including *anInteger*.

```
5.upto(10) { |i| print i, " " }
```

produces:

```
5 6 7 8 9 10
```

Class **IO** < Object

Subclasses: File

Class `IO` is the basis for all input and output in Ruby. An I/O stream may be *duplexed* (that is, bidirectional), and so may use more than one native operating system stream.

Many of the examples in this section use class `File`, the only standard subclass of `IO`. The two classes are closely associated.

As used in this section, *aPortname* may take any of the following forms.

- A plain string represents a filename suitable for the underlying operating system.

- A string starting with "|" indicates a subprocess. The remainder of the string following the "|" is invoked as a process with appropriate input/output channels connected to it.

- A string equal to "|-" will create another Ruby instance as a subprocess.

Ruby will convert pathnames between different operating system conventions if possible. For instance, on a Windows system the filename "/gumby/ruby/test.rb" will be opened as "\gumby\ruby\test.rb". When specifying a Windows-style filename in a Ruby string, remember to escape the backslashes:

```
"c:\\gumby\\ruby\\test.rb"
```

Our examples here will use the Unix-style forward slashes; `File::SEPARATOR` can be used to get the platform-specific separator character.

I/O ports may be opened in any one of several different modes, which are shown in this section as *aModeString*. This mode string must be one of the values listed in Table 22.5 on the next page.

Mixes in

Enumerable:

> collect, detect, each_with_index, entries, find, find_all, grep, include?, map, max, member?, min, reject, select, sort, to_a

Class methods

foreach   IO.foreach(*aPortName, aSepString=$/*) {| *line* | *block* } → `nil`

Executes the block for every line in the named I/O port, where lines are separated by *aSepString*.

```
IO.foreach("testfile") {|x| print "GOT ", x }
```

produces:

```
GOT This is line one
GOT This is line two
GOT This is line three
GOT And so on...
```

new   IO.new(*anInteger, aModeString*) → *aFile*

Returns a new `File` object (a stream) for the given integer file descriptor and mode string. See also `IO#fileno`.

```
a = IO.new(2,"w")       # '2' is standard error
$stderr.puts "Hello"
a.puts "World"
```

produces:

```
Hello
World
```

pipe   IO.pipe → *anArray*

Creates a pair of pipe endpoints (connected to each other) and returns them as a two-element array of IO objects: [*readFile, writeFile*]. Not available on all platforms.

In the example below, the two processes close the ends of the pipe that they are not using. This is not just a cosmetic nicety. The read end of a pipe will not generate an end of file condition if there are any writers with the pipe still open. In the case of the parent process, the `rd.read` will never return if it does not first issue a `wr.close`.

Table 22.5. Mode strings

Mode	Meaning
"r"	Read-only, starts at beginning of file (default mode).
"r+"	Read-write, starts at beginning of file.
"w"	Write-only, truncates existing file to zero length or creates a new file for writing.
"w+"	Read-write, truncates existing file to zero length or creates a new file for reading and writing.
"a"	Write-only, starts at end of file if file exists, otherwise creates a new file for writing.
"a+"	Read-write, starts at end of file if file exists, otherwise creates a new file for reading and writing.
"b"	(DOS/Windows only) Binary file mode (may appear with any of the key letters listed above).

```
rd, wr = IO.pipe

if fork
  wr.close
  puts "Parent got: <#{rd.read}>"
  rd.close
  Process.wait
else
  rd.close
  puts "Sending message to parent"
  wr.write "Hi Dad"
  wr.close
end
```

produces:

```
Sending message to parent
Parent got: <Hi Dad>
```

---

popen   IO.popen(*aCmdString, aModeString*="r") → *anIO*
                        IO.popen(*aCmdString, aModeString*="r") {| *anIO* | *block* } → **nil**

Runs the specified command string as a subprocess; the subprocess's standard input and output will be connected to the returned **IO** object. If *aCmdString* starts with a "–", then a new instance of Ruby is started as the subprocess. The default mode for the new file object is "r", but *aModeString* may be set to any of the modes in Table 22.5.

If a block is given, Ruby will run the command as a child connected to Ruby with a pipe. Ruby's end of the pipe will be passed as a parameter to the block.

If a block is given with a *aCmdString* of "-", the block will be run in two separate processes: once in the parent, and once in a child. The parent process will be passed the pipe object as a parameter to the block, the child version of the block will be passed nil, and the child's standard in and standard out will be connected to the parent through the pipe. Not available on all platforms.

```
f = IO.popen("uname")
p f.readlines
puts "Parent is #{Process.pid}"
IO.popen ("date") { |f| puts f.gets }
IO.popen("-") {|f| $stderr.puts "#{Process.pid} is here, f is #{f}"}
```

produces:

```
["Linux\n"]
Parent is 14864
Tue Sep 19 23:32:09 CDT 2000
14867 is here, f is
14864 is here, f is #<IO:0x4018a66c>
```

---

readlines   IO.readlines(*aPortName, aSepString=$/*) → *anArray*

Reads the entire file specified by *aPortName* as individual lines, and returns those lines in an array. Lines are separated by *aSepString*.

```
a = IO.readlines("testfile")
a[0]   →   "This is line one\n"
```

---

select   IO.select(*readArray* ⟨ , *writeArray* ⟨ , *errorArray* ⟨ , *timeout* ⟩ ⟩ ⟩) → *anArray*

or nil

See Kernel#select on page 426.

Instance methods

<<   *ios << anObject → ios*

String Output—Writes *anObject* to *ios*. *anObject* will be converted to a string using to_s.

```
$stdout << "Hello " << "world!\n"
```

produces:

```
Hello world!
```

---

binmode   *ios.binmode → ios*

Puts *ios* into binary mode. This is useful only in MS-DOS/Windows environments. Once a stream is in binary mode, it cannot be reset to nonbinary mode.

---

clone   *ios.clone → anIO*

Creates a new I/O stream, copying all the attributes of *ios*. The file position is shared as well, so reading from the clone will alter the file position of the original, and vice-versa.

---

close   *ios*.close → `nil`

Closes *ios* and flushes any pending writes to the operating system. The stream is unavailable for any further data operations; an `IOError` is raised if such an attempt is made. I/O streams are automatically closed when they are claimed by the garbage collector.

---

close_read   *ios*.close_read → `nil`

Closes the read end of a duplex I/O stream (i.e., one that contains both a read and a write stream, such as a pipe). Will raise an `IOError` if the stream is not duplexed.

```
f = IO.popen("/bin/sh","r+")
f.close_read
f.readlines
```

produces:

```
prog.rb:3:in `readlines': not opened for reading (IOError)
from prog.rb:3
```

---

close_write   *ios*.close_write → `nil`

Closes the write end of a duplex I/O stream (i.e., one that contains both a read and a write stream, such as a pipe). Will raise an `IOError` if the stream is not duplexed.

```
f = IO.popen("/bin/sh","r+")
f.close_write
f.print "nowhere"
```

produces:

```
prog.rb:3:in `write': not opened for writing (IOError)
from prog.rb:3:in `print'
from prog.rb:3
```

---

closed?   *ios*.closed? → `true` or `false`

Returns `true` if *ios* is completely closed (for duplex streams, both reader and writer), `false` otherwise.

```
f = File.new("testfile")
f.close          →    nil
f.closed?        →    true
f = IO.popen("/bin/sh","r+")
f.close_write    →    nil
f.closed?        →    false
f.close_read     →    nil
f.closed?        →    true
```

each
$$ios.each(\ aSepString=\$/\ )\ \{\ |\ line\ |\ block\ \}\ \rightarrow ios$$

Executes the block for every line in *ios*, where lines are separated by *aSepString*. *ios* must be opened for reading or an IOerror will be raised.

```
f = File.new("testfile")
f.each {|line| puts "#{f.lineno}: #{line}" }
```

produces:

```
1: This is line one
2: This is line two
3: This is line three
4: And so on...
```

each_byte
$$ios.each\_byte\ \{\ |\ byte\ |\ block\ \}\ \rightarrow \texttt{nil}$$

Calls the given block once for each byte (0..255) in *ios*, passing the byte as an argument. The stream must be opened for reading or an IOerror will be raised.

```
f = File.new("testfile")
checksum = 0
f.each_byte {|x| checksum ^= x }   →   nil
checksum                           →   12
```

each_line
$$ios.each\_line(\ aSepString=\$/\ )\ \{\ |\ line\ |\ block\ \}\ \rightarrow ios$$

Synonym for IO#each.

eof
$$ios.eof \rightarrow \texttt{true}\ or\ \texttt{false}$$

Returns true if *ios* is at end of file. The stream must be opened for reading or an IOError will be raised.

```
f = File.new("testfile")
dummy = f.readlines
f.eof   →   true
```

eof?
$$ios.eof? \rightarrow \texttt{true}\ or\ \texttt{false}$$

Synonym for IO#eof.

fcntl
$$ios.fcntl(\ anIntegerCmd,\ anArg\ ) \rightarrow anInteger$$

Provides a mechanism for issuing low-level commands to control or query file-oriented I/O streams. Arguments and results are platform dependent. If *anArg* is a number, its value is passed directly. If it is a string, it is interpreted as a binary sequence of bytes. On Unix platforms, see fcntl(2) for details. Not implemented on all platforms.

fileno
$$ios.fileno \rightarrow aFixnum$$

Returns an integer representing the numeric file descriptor for *ios*.

```
$stdin.fileno    →   0
$stdout.fileno   →   1
```

flush   *ios*.flush → *ios*

Flushes any buffered data within *ios* to the underlying operating system (note that this is Ruby internal buffering only; the OS may buffer the data as well).

```
$stdout.print "no newline"
$stdout.flush
```

produces:

```
no newline
```

---

getc   *ios*.getc → *aFixnum* or `nil`

Gets the next 8-bit byte (0..255) from *ios*. Returns `nil` if called at end of file.

```
f = File.new("testfile")
f.getc   →   84
f.getc   →   104
```

---

gets   *ios*.gets(*aSepString*=$/) → *aString* or `nil`

Reads the next "line" from the I/O stream; lines are separated by *aSepString*. A separator of `nil` reads the entire contents, and a zero-length separator reads the input a paragraph at a time (two successive newlines in the input separate paragraphs). The stream must be opened for reading or an `IOerror` will be raised. The line read in will be returned and also assigned to `$_`. Returns `nil` if called at end of file.

```
File.new("testfile").gets   →   "This is line one\n"
$_                          →   "This is line one\n"
```

---

ioctl   *ios*.ioctl(*anIntegerCmd*, *anArg*) → *anInteger*

Provides a mechanism for issuing low-level commands to control or query I/O devices. Arguments and results are platform dependent. If *anArg* is a number, its value is passed directly. If it is a string, it is interpreted as a binary sequence of bytes. On Unix platforms, see `ioctl(2)` for details. Not implemented on all platforms.

---

isatty   *ios*.isatty → `true` or `false`

Returns `true` if *ios* is associated with a terminal device (tty), `false` otherwise.

```
File.new("testfile").isatty   →   false
File.new("/dev/tty").isatty   →   true
```

---

lineno   *ios*.lineno → *anInteger*

Returns the current line number in *ios*. The stream must be opened for reading. `lineno` counts the number of times `gets` is called, rather than the number of newlines encountered. The two values will differ if `gets` is called with a separator other than newline. See also the `$.` variable.

```
f = File.new("testfile")
f.lineno   →   0
f.gets     →   "This is line one\n"
f.lineno   →   1
f.gets     →   "This is line two\n"
f.lineno   →   2
```

---

lineno=   *ios*.lineno = *anInteger* → *anInteger*

Manually sets the current line number to the given value. **$.** is updated only on the next read.

```
f = File.new("testfile")
f.gets                         →   "This is line one\n"
$.                             →   1
f.lineno = 1000
f.lineno                       →   1000
$. # lineno of last read       →   1
f.gets                         →   "This is line two\n"
$. # lineno of last read       →   1001
```

---

pid   *ios*.pid → *aFixnum*

Returns the process ID of a child process associated with *ios*. This will be set by IO.popen.

```
pipe = IO.popen("-")
if pipe
  $stderr.puts "In parent, child pid is #{pipe.pid}"
else
  $stderr.puts "In child, pid is #{$$}"
end
```

produces:

```
In parent, child pid is 14903
In child, pid is 14903
```

---

pos   *ios*.pos → *anInteger*

Returns the current offset (in bytes) of *ios*.

```
f = File.new("testfile")
f.pos    →   0
f.gets   →   "This is line one\n"
f.pos    →   17
```

---

pos=   *ios*.pos = *anInteger* → 0

Seeks to the given position (in bytes) in *ios*.

```
f = File.new("testfile")
f.pos = 17
f.gets   →   "This is line two\n"
```

print   *ios*.print(⟨ *anObject=$_* ⟩*) → `nil`

Writes the given object(s) to *ios*. The stream must be opened for writing. If the output record separator ($\) is not `nil`, it will be appended to the output. If no arguments are given, prints `$_`. Objects that aren't strings will be converted by calling their `to_s` method. Returns `nil`.

```
$stdout.print("This is ", 100, " percent.\n")
```

produces:

```
This is 100 percent.
```

printf   *ios*.printf(*aFormatString* ⟨ , *anObject* ⟩*) → `nil`

Formats and writes to *ios*, converting parameters under control of the format string. See `Kernel#sprintf` on page 427 for details.

putc   *ios*.putc(*anObject*) → *anObject*

Writes the given character (taken from a `String` or a `Fixnum`) on *ios*.

```
$stdout.putc "A"
$stdout.putc 65
```

produces:

```
AA
```

puts   *ios*.puts(⟨ *anObject* ⟩*) → `nil`

Writes the given objects to *ios* as with `IO#print`. Writes a record separator (typically a newline) after any that do not already end with a newline sequence. If called with an array argument, writes each element on a new line. If called without arguments, outputs a single record separator.

```
$stdout.puts("this", "is", "a", "test")
```

produces:

```
this
is
a
test
```

read   *ios*.read(⟨ *anInteger* ⟩) → *aString* or `nil`

Reads at most *anInteger* bytes from the I/O stream, or to the end of file if *anInteger* is omitted. Returns `nil` if called at end of file.

```
f = File.new("testfile")
f.read(16)   →   "This is line one"
```

readchar   *ios*.readchar → *aFixnum*

Reads a character as with `IO#getc`, but raises an `EOFError` on end of file.

readline

$$ios.readline(\ aSepString=\$/\ ) \rightarrow aString$$

Reads a line as with `IO#gets`, but raises an `EOFError` on end of file.

readlines

$$ios.readlines(\ aSepString=\$/\ ) \rightarrow anArray$$

Reads all of the lines in *ios*, and returns them in *anArray*. Lines are separated by the optional *aSepString*. The stream must be opened for reading or an `IOerror` will be raised.

```
f = File.new("testfile")
f.readlines[0]   →   "This is line one\n"
```

reopen

$$ios.reopen(\ anOtherIO\ ) \rightarrow ios$$
$$ios.reopen(\ aPath, aModeStr\ ) \rightarrow ios$$

Reassociates *ios* with the I/O stream given in *anOtherIO* or to a new stream opened on *aPath*. This may dynamically change the actual class of this stream.

```
f1 = File.new("testfile")
f2 = File.new("testfile")
f2.readlines[0]   →   "This is line one\n"
f2.reopen(f1)     →   #<File:0x4018a748>
f2.readlines[0]   →   "This is line one\n"
```

rewind

$$ios.rewind \rightarrow 0$$

Positions *ios* to the beginning of input, resetting `lineno` to zero.

```
f = File.new("testfile")
f.readline   →   "This is line one\n"
f.rewind     →   0
f.lineno     →   0
f.readline   →   "This is line one\n"
```

seek

$$ios.seek(\ anInteger, whence=SEEK\_SET\ ) \rightarrow 0$$

Seeks to a given offset *anInteger* in the stream according to the value of *whence*:

`IO::SEEK_CUR`	Seeks to *anInteger* plus current position.
`IO::SEEK_END`	Seeks to *anInteger* plus end of stream (you probably want a negative value for *anInteger*).
`IO::SEEK_SET`	Seeks to the absolute location given by *anInteger*.

```
f = File.new("testfile")
f.seek(-13, IO::SEEK_END)   →   0
f.readline                  →   "And so on...\n"
```

stat

$$ios.stat \rightarrow aStat$$

Returns status information for *ios* as an object of type `File::Stat`.

```
f = File.new("testfile")
s = f.stat
"%o" % s.mode    →   "100644"
s.blksize        →   4096
s.atime          →   Tue Sep 19 23:32:10 CDT 2000
```

---

sync   *ios*.sync → `true` or `false`

Returns the current "sync mode" of *ios*. When sync mode is true, all output is immediately flushed to the underlying operating system and is not buffered by Ruby internally.

```
f = File.new("testfile")
f.sync   →   false
```

---

sync=   *ios*.sync = *aBoolean* → *aBoolean*

Sets the "sync mode" to `true` or `false`. When sync mode is true, all output is immediately flushed to the underlying operating system and is not buffered internally. Returns the new state.

```
f = File.new("testfile")
f.sync = true
```

---

sysread   *ios*.sysread(*anInteger*) → *aString*

Reads *anInteger* bytes from *ios* using a low-level read and returns them as a string. Do not mix with other methods that read from *ios* or you may get unpredictable results. Raises `SystemCallError` on error and `EOFError` at end of file.

```
f = File.new("testfile")
f.sysread(16)   →   "This is line one"
```

---

syswrite   *ios*.syswrite(*aString*) → *anInteger*

Writes the given string to *ios* using a low-level write. Returns the number of bytes written. Do not mix with other methods that write to *ios* or you may get unpredictable results. Raises `SystemCallError` on error.

```
f = File.new("out", "w")
f.syswrite("ABCDEF")   →   6
```

---

tell   *ios*.tell → *anInteger*

Synonym for IO#pos.

---

to_i   *ios*.to_i → *anInteger*

Synonym for IO#fileno.

---

to_io   *ios*.to_io → *ios*

Returns *ios*.

---

tty?   *ios*.tty? → `true` or `false`

Synonym for IO#isatty.

---

ungetc   *ios*.ungetc(*anInteger*) → `nil`

Pushes back one character onto *ios*, such that a subsequent buffered read will return it. Only one character may be pushed back before a subsequent read operation (that is, you will be able to read only the last of several characters that have been pushed back). Has no effect with unbuffered reads (such as IO#sysread).

```
f = File.new("testfile")    →    #<File:0x4018a7ac>
c = f.getc                  →    84
f.ungetc(c)                 →    nil
f.getc                      →    84
```

---

write   *ios*.write(*aString*) → *anInteger*

Writes the given string to *ios*. The stream must be opened for writing. If the argument is not a string, it will be converted to a string using `to_s`. Returns the number of bytes written.

```
count = $stdout.write( "This is a test\n" )
puts "That was #{count} bytes of data"
```

produces:

```
This is a test
That was 15 bytes of data
```

Class **MatchData** < Object

MatchData is the type of the special variable $~, and is the type of the object returned by `Regexp.match`. It encapsulates all the results of a pattern match, results normally accessed through the special variables $&, $', $`, $1, $2, and so on.

Instance methods

[ ]   *mtch*[*i*] → *anObject*
                                                                   mtch[*start, length*] → *anArray*
                                                                        mtch[*aRange*] → *anArray*

Match Reference—MatchData acts as an array, and may be accessed using the normal array indexing techniques. *mtch*[0] is equivalent to the special variable $&, and returns the entire matched string. *mtch*[1], *mtch*[2], and so on return the values of the matched backreferences (portions of the pattern between parentheses).

```
m = /(.)(.)(\d+)(\d)/.match("THX1138.")
m[0]       →    "HX1138"
m[1, 2]    →    ["H", "X"]
m[1..3]    →    ["H", "X", "113"]
m[-3, 2]   →    ["X", "113"]
```

---

begin
mtch.begin(n) → anInteger

Returns the offset of the start of the *n*th element of the match array in the string.

```
m = /(.)(.)(\d+)(\d)/.match("THX1138.")
m.begin(0)   →   1
m.begin(2)   →   2
```

---

end
mtch.end(n) → anInteger

Returns the offset of the character immediately following the end of the *n*th element of the match array in the string.

```
m = /(.)(.)(\d+)(\d)/.match("THX1138.")
m.end(0)   →   7
m.end(2)   →   3
```

---

length
mtch.length → anInteger

Returns the number of elements in the match array.

```
m = /(.)(.)(\d+)(\d)/.match("THX1138.")
m.length   →   5
m.size     →   5
```

---

offset
mtch.offset(n) → anArray

Returns a two-element array containing the beginning and ending offsets of the *n*th match.

```
m = /(.)(.)(\d+)(\d)/.match("THX1138.")
m.offset(0)   →   [1, 7]
m.offset(4)   →   [6, 7]
```

---

post_match
mtch.post_match → aString

Returns the portion of the original string after the current match. Equivalent to the special variable $'.

```
m = /(.)(.)(\d+)(\d)/.match("THX1138: The Movie")
m.post_match   →   ": The Movie"
```

---

pre_match
mtch.pre_match → aString

Returns the portion of the original string before the current match. Equivalent to the special variable $`.

```
m = /(.)(.)(\d+)(\d)/.match("THX1138.")
m.pre_match   →   "T"
```

size

mtch.size → anInteger

A synonym for `MatchData#length`.

string

mtch.string → aString

Returns a frozen copy of the string passed in to `match`.

```
m = /(.)(.)(\d+)(\d)/.match("THX1138.")
m.string   →   "THX1138."
```

to_a

mtch.to_a → anArray

Returns the array of matches.

```
m = /(.)(.)(\d+)(\d)/.match("THX1138.")
m.to_a   →   ["HX1138", "H", "X", "113", "8"]
```

to_s

mtch.to_s → aString

Returns the entire matched string.

```
m = /(.)(.)(\d+)(\d)/.match("THX1138.")
m.to_s   →   "HX1138"
```

Class **Method** < Object

Method objects are created by `Object#method`, and are associated with a particular object (not just with a class). They may be used to invoke the method within the object, and as a block associated with an iterator.

```
class Thing
  def square(n)
    n*n
  end
end
aThing  = Thing.new
aMethod = aThing.method("square")

aMethod.call(9)                   →   81
[ 1, 2, 3 ].collect(&aMethod)   →   [1, 4, 9]
```

Instance methods

[ ]

$$meth[\ \langle\ args\ \rangle^*\ ] \rightarrow anObject$$

Synonym for `Method.call`.

arity

$$meth.\text{arity} \rightarrow aFixnum$$

Returns an indication of the number of arguments accepted by a method. Returns a non-negative integer for methods that take a fixed number of arguments. For Ruby methods that take a variable number of arguments, returns $-n - 1$, where n is the number of required arguments. For methods written in C, returns -1 if the call takes a variable number of arguments.

call

$$meth.\text{call}(\ \langle\ args\ \rangle^*\ ) \rightarrow anObject$$

Invokes the *meth* with the specified arguments, returning the method's return value.

```
m = 12.method("+")
m.call(3)    →    15
m.call(20)   →    32
```

to_proc

$$meth.\text{to\_proc} \rightarrow aProc$$

Returns a `Proc` object corresponding to this method.

Class ## Module < Object

Subclasses: Class

A `Module` is a collection of methods and constants. The methods in a module may be instance methods or module methods. Instance methods appear as methods in a class when the module is included, module methods do not. Conversely, module methods may be called without creating an encapsulating object, while instance methods may not. See `Module#module_function` on page 350.

In the descriptions that follow, the parameter *aSymbol* refers to a symbol, which is either a quoted string or a `Symbol` (such as `:name`).

```
module Mod
  include Math
  CONST = 1
  def meth
    #  ...
  end
end
Mod.type              →    Module
Mod.constants         →    ["CONST", "E", "PI"]
Mod.instance_methods  →    ["meth"]
```

Class methods

constants

Module.constants → *anArray*

Returns an array of the names of all constants defined in the system. This list includes the names of all modules and classes.

```
p Module.constants.sort[1..5]
```

produces:

```
["ARGV", "ArgumentError", "Array", "Bignum", "Binding"]
```

nesting

Module.nesting → *anArray*

Returns the list of `Modules` nested at the point of call.

```
module M1
  module M2
    $a = Module.nesting
  end
end
$a              →    [M1::M2, M1]
$a[0].name      →    "M1::M2"
```

new

Module.new → *aModule*

Creates a new anonymous module.

Instance methods

<, <=, >, >=

mod `relop` *aModule* → `true` or `false`

Hierarchy Query—One module is considered *greater than* another if it is included in (or is a parent class of) the other module. The other operators are defined accordingly. If there is no relationship between the modules, returns false for all operators.

```
module Mixin
end

module Parent
  include Mixin
end

module Unrelated
end

Parent > Mixin       →    false
Parent < Mixin       →    true
Parent <= Parent     →    true
Parent < Unrelated   →    false
Parent > Unrelated   →    ·false
```

<=>
$$mod <=> aModule \rightarrow -1, 0, +1$$

Comparison—Returns -1 if *mod* includes *aModule*, 0 if *mod* is the same as *aModule*, and $+1$ if *mod* is included by *aModule* or if *mod* has no relationship with *aModule*.

===
$$mod === anObject \rightarrow \texttt{true} \text{ or } \texttt{false}$$

Case Equality—Returns **true** if *anObject* is an instance of *mod* or one of *mod*'s descendents. Of limited use for modules, but can be used in **case** statements to classify objects by class.

ancestors
$$mod.\text{ancestors} \rightarrow anArray$$

Returns a list of modules included in *mod* (including *mod* itself).

```
module Mod
  include Math
  include Comparable
end

Mod.ancestors    →    [Mod, Comparable, Math]
Math.ancestors   →    [Math]
```

class_eval
$$mod.\text{class\_eval}(aString) \rightarrow anObject$$
$$mod.\text{class\_eval} \{ block \} \rightarrow anObject$$

Synonym for `Module.module_eval`.

class_variables
$$mod.\text{class\_variables} \rightarrow anArray$$

Returns an array of the names of class variables in *mod* and the ancestors of *mod*.

```
class One
  @@var1 = 1
end
class Two < One
  @@var2 = 2
end
One.class_variables   →    ["@@var1"]
Two.class_variables   →    ["@@var2", "@@var1"]
```

clone
$$mod.\text{clone} \rightarrow aModule$$

Creates a new copy of a module.

```
m = Math.clone   →    Math
m.constants      →    ["PI", "E"]
m == Math        →    false
```

const_defined?
$$mod.\text{const\_defined?}(aSymbol) \rightarrow \texttt{true} \text{ or } \texttt{false}$$

Returns **true** if a constant with the given name is defined by *mod*.

```
Math.const_defined? "PI"   →    true
```

---

const_get   *mod*.const_get(*aSymbol*) → *anObject*

Returns the value of the named constant in *mod*.

```
Math.const_get :PI   →   3.141592654
```

---

const_set   *mod*.const_set(*aSymbol, anObject*) → *anObject*

Sets the named constant to the given object, returning that object. Creates a new constant if no constant with the given name previously existed.

```
Math.const_set("HIGH_SCHOOL_PI", 22.0/7.0)   →   3.142857143
Math::HIGH_SCHOOL_PI - Math::PI              →   0.001264489267
```

---

constants   *mod*.constants → *anArray*

Returns an array of the names of the constants accessible in *mod*. This includes the names of constants in any included modules (example at start of section).

---

included_modules   *mod*.included_modules → *anArray*

Returns the list of modules included in *mod*.

```
module Mixin
end

module Outer
  include Mixin
end

Mixin.included_modules   →   []
Outer.included_modules   →   [Mixin]
```

---

instance_methods   *mod*.instance_methods(*includeSuper*=false) → *anArray*

Returns an array containing the names of public instance methods in the receiver. For a module, these are the public methods; for a class, they are the instance (not singleton) methods. With no argument, or with an argument that is `false`, the instance methods in *mod* are returned, otherwise the methods in *mod* and *mod*'s superclasses are returned.

```
module A
  def method1()  end
end
class B
  def method2()  end
end
class C < B
  def method3()  end
end

A.instance_methods               →   ["method1"]
B.instance_methods               →   ["method2"]
C.instance_methods               →   ["method3"]
C.instance_methods(true).length  →   39
```

method_defined? `mod`.method_defined?(*aSymbol*) → `true` or `false`

Returns `true` if the named method is defined by *mod* (or its included modules and, if *mod* is a class, its ancestors).

```
module A
  def method1()  end
end
class B
  def method2()  end
end
class C < B
  include A
  def method3()  end
end

A.method_defined? :method1    →    true
C.method_defined? "method1"   →    true
C.method_defined? "method2"   →    true
C.method_defined? "method3"   →    true
C.method_defined? "method4"   →    false
```

module_eval `mod`.module_eval(*aString*) → *anObject*
`mod`.module_eval { *block* } → *anObject*

Evaluates the string or block in the context of *mod*. This can be used to add methods to a class. `module_eval` returns the result of evaluating its argument.

```
class Thing
end
a = %q{def hello() "Hello there!" end}
Thing.module_eval(a)   →    nil
Thing.new.hello()      →    "Hello there!"
```

name `mod`.name → *aString*

Returns the name of the module *mod*.

private_class_method `mod`.private_class_method(⟨ *aSymbol* ⟩⁺) → `nil`

Makes existing class methods private. Often used to hide the default constructor `new`.

```
class SimpleSingleton  # Not thread safe
  private_class_method :new
  def SimpleSingleton.create(*args, &block)
    @me = new(*args, &block) if ! @me
    @me
  end
end
```

private_instance_methods

$$mod.\text{private\_instance\_methods}(\ includeSuper=\texttt{false}\ ) \rightarrow anArray$$

Returns a list of the private instance methods defined in *mod*. If the optional parameter is not `false`, the methods of any ancestors are included.

```
module Mod
  def method1()  end
  private :method1
  def method2()  end
end
Mod.instance_methods          →    ["method2"]
Mod.private_instance_methods  →    ["method1"]
```

protected_instance_methods

$$mod.\text{protected\_instance\_methods}(\ includeSuper=\texttt{false}\ ) \rightarrow anArray$$

Returns a list of the protected instance methods defined in *mod*. If the optional parameter is not `false`, the methods of any ancestors are included.

public_class_method

$$mod.\text{public\_class\_method}(\ \langle\, aSymbol\,\rangle^{+}\ ) \rightarrow \texttt{nil}$$

Makes a list of existing class methods public.

public_instance_methods

$$mod.\text{public\_instance\_methods}(\ includeSuper=\texttt{false}\ ) \rightarrow anArray$$

Returns a list of the public instance methods defined in *mod*. If the optional parameter is not `false`, the methods of any ancestors are included.

The following methods are used mainly during the definition of classes and modules.

Private instance methods

alias_method

$$\text{alias\_method}(\ newID,\ oldID\ ) \rightarrow mod$$

Makes *newID* a new copy of the method *oldID*. This can be used to retain access to methods that are overridden.

```
module Mod
  alias_method :origExit, :exit
  def exit(code=0)
    print "Exiting with code #{code}\n"
    origExit(code)
  end
end
include Mod
exit(99)
```

produces:

```
Exiting with code 99
```

---

append_features   append_features(*aModule*) → *mod*

The constants and methods of *aModule* are added to the current module if *aModule* has not already been added to the current module or one of its ancestors. Also see `Module#include` on the following page.

---

attr   attr(*aSymbol, writable*=`false`) → `nil`

Defines a named attribute for this module, where the name is *aSymbol*.`id2name`, creating an instance variable (`@name`) and a corresponding access method to read it. If the optional *writable* argument is `true`, also creates a method called `name=` to set the attribute.

```
module Mod
  attr  :size, true
end
```

is equivalent to:

```
module Mod
  def size
    @size
  end
  def size=(val)
    @size = val
  end
end
```

---

attr_accessor   ·   attr_accessor(⟨ *aSymbol* ⟩⁺) → `nil`

Equivalent to calling "`attr` *aSymbol*, `true`" on each *aSymbol* in turn.

```
module Mod
  attr_accessor(:one, :two)
end
Mod.instance_methods.sort  →  ["one", "one=", "two", "two="]
```

---

attr_reader   attr_reader(⟨ *aSymbol* ⟩⁺) → `nil`

Creates instance variables and corresponding methods that return the value of each instance variable. Equivalent to calling "`attr` *:name*" on each name in turn.

---

attr_writer   attr_writer(⟨ *aSymbol* ⟩⁺) → `nil`

Creates an accessor method to allow assignment to the attribute *aSymbol*.`id2name`.

---

extend_object   extend_object(*anObject*) → *anObject*

Extends the specified object by adding this module's constants and methods (which are added as singleton methods). This is the callback method used by `Object#extend`.

```
module Picky
  def Picky.extend_object(o)
    if String === o
      print "Can't add Picky to a String\n"
    else
      print "Picky added to ", o.type, "\n"
      super
    end
  end
end
(s = Array.new).extend Picky  # Call Object.extend
(s = "quick brown fox").extend Picky
```

produces:

```
Picky added to Array
Can't add Picky to a String
```

---

include   include(⟨ *aModule* ⟩[+]) → *mod*

Invokes `Module.append_features` (documented on the page before) on each parameter in turn.

---

method_added   method_added(*aSymbol*)

Invoked as a callback whenever a method is added to the receiver.

```
module Chatty
  def Chatty.method_added(id)
    print "Adding ", id.id2name, "\n"
  end
  def one()   end
end
module Chatty
  def two()   end
end
```

produces:

```
Adding one
Adding two
```

---

module_function   module_function(⟨ *aSymbol* ⟩[*]) → *mod*

Creates module functions for the named methods. These functions may be called with the module as a receiver, and also become available as instance methods to classes that mix in the module. Module functions are copies of the original, and so may be changed independently. The instance-method versions are made private. If used with no arguments, subsequently defined methods become module functions.

```
module Mod
  def one
    "This is one"
  end
  module_function :one
end
class Cls
  include Mod
  def callOne
    one
  end
end
Mod.one      →   "This is one"
c = Cls.new
c.callOne    →   "This is one"
module Mod
  def one
    "This is the new one"
  end
end
Mod.one      →   "This is one"
c.callOne    →   "This is the new one"
```

private   private(⟨ *aSymbol* ⟩*) → *mod*

With no arguments, sets the default visibility for subsequently defined methods to private. With arguments, sets the named methods to have private visibility. See *Access Control* starting on page 235.

```
module Mod
  def a()  end
  def b()  end
  private
  def c()  end
  private :a
end
Mod.private_instance_methods   →   ["c", "a"]
```

protected   protected(⟨ *aSymbol* ⟩*) → *mod*

With no arguments, sets the default visibility for subsequently defined methods to protected. With arguments, sets the named methods to have protected visibility. See *Access Control* starting on page 235.

public   public(⟨ *aSymbol* ⟩*) → *mod*

With no arguments, sets the default visibility for subsequently defined methods to public. With arguments, sets the named methods to have public visibility. See *Access Control* starting on page 235.

---

remove_const   remove_const(*aSymbol*) → *anObject*

Removes the definition of the given constant, returning that constant's value. Predefined classes and singleton objects (such as *true*) cannot be removed.

---

remove_method   remove_method(*aSymbol*) → *mod*

Removes the method identified by *aSymbol* from the current class. For an example, see `Module.undef_method`.

---

undef_method   undef_method(*aSymbol*) → *mod*

Prevents the current class from responding to calls to the named method. Contrast this with `remove_method`, which deletes the method from the particular class; Ruby will still search superclasses and mixed-in modules for a possible receiver.

```ruby
class Parent
  def hello
    print "In parent\n"
  end
end
class Child < Parent
  def hello
    print "In child\n"
  end
end

c = Child.new
c.hello

class Child
  remove_method :hello   # remove from child, still in parent
end
c.hello

class Child
  undef_method :hello    # prevent any calls to 'hello'
end
c.hello
```

produces:

```
In child
In parent
prog.rb:23: undefined method `hello' for #<Child:0x4018a568> (NameError)
```

Class	**NilClass** < Object

The class of the singleton object `nil`.

Instance methods

&

nil & *anObject* → `false`

And—Returns `false`. As *anObject* is an argument to a method call, it is always evaluated; there is no short-circuit evaluation in this case.

```
nil && puts("logical and")
nil &  puts("and")
```

produces:

```
and
```

^

nil ^ *anObject* → `true` or `false`

Exclusive Or—Returns `false` if *anObject* is `nil` or `false`, `true` otherwise.

|

nil | *anObject* → `true` or `false`

Or—Returns `false` if *anObject* is `nil` or `false`, `true` otherwise.

nil?

nil.nil? → `true`

Always returns `true`.

to_a

nil.to_a → []

Always returns an empty array.

to_i

nil.to_i → 0

Always returns zero.

to_s

nil.to_s → ""

Always returns the empty string.

Class **Numeric**   <   Object

Subclasses: Float, Integer

Numeric is the fundamental base type for the concrete number classes Float, Fixnum, and Bignum.

Mixes in

Comparable:

    <, <=, ==, >=, >, between?

Instance methods

+@

$$+num \rightarrow num$$

Unary Plus—Returns the receiver's value.

–@

$$-num \rightarrow aNumeric$$

Unary Minus—Returns the receiver's value, negated.

abs

$$num.abs \rightarrow aNumeric$$

Returns the absolute value of *num*.

```
12.abs        →    12
(-34.56).abs  →    34.56
-34.56.abs    →    34.56
```

coerce

$$num.coerce(\ aNumeric\ ) \rightarrow anArray$$

If *aNumeric* is the same type as *num*, returns an array containing *aNumeric* and *num*. Otherwise, returns an array with both *aNumeric* and *num* represented as Float objects.

```
1.coerce(2.5)    →    [2.5, 1.0]
1.2.coerce(3)    →    [3.0, 1.2]
1.coerce(2)      →    [2, 1]
```

divmod

$$num.divmod(\ aNumeric\ ) \rightarrow anArray$$

Returns an array containing the quotient and modulus obtained by dividing *num* by *aNumeric*. If q, r = x.divmod(y),

$$q = floor(float(x)/float(y))$$
$$x = q \times y + r$$

The quotient is rounded toward $-\infty$. See Table 22.6 on the next page.

```
11.divmod(3)       →    [3, 2]
11.divmod(-3)      →    [-4, -1]
11.divmod(3.5)     →    [3.0, 0.5]
(-11).divmod(3.5)  →    [-4.0, 3.0]
(11.5).divmod(3.5) →    [3.0, 1.0]
```

Table 22.6. Difference between modulo and remainder. The modulo operator ("%") always has the sign of the divisor, whereas `remainder` has the sign of the dividend.

a	b	a.divmod(b)	a / b	a.modulo(b)	a.remainder(b)
13	4	3, 1	3	1	1
13	−4	−4, −3	−4	−3	1
−13	4	−4, 3	−4	3	−1
−13	−4	3, −1	3	−1	−1
11.5	4	2.0, 3.5	2.875	3.5	3.5
11.5	−4	−3.0, −0.5	−2.875	−0.5	3.5
−11.5	4	−3.0, 0.5	−2.875	0.5	−3.5
−11.5	−4	2.0, −3.5	2.875	−3.5	−3.5

---

eql?   *num*.eql?(*aNumeric*) → `true` or `false`

Returns `true` if *num* and *aNumeric* are the same type and have equal values.

```
1 == 1.0          →    true
1.eql?(1.0)       →    false
(1.0).eql?(1.0)   →    true
```

---

integer?   *num*.integer? → `true` or `false`

Returns `true` if *num* is an `Integer` (including `Fixnum` and `Bignum`).

---

modulo   *num*.modulo(*aNumeric*) → *aNumeric*

Equivalent to *num*.`divmod`(*aNumeric*) `[1]`.

---

nonzero?   *num*.nonzero? → *num* or `nil`

Returns *num* if *num* is not zero, `nil` otherwise. This behavior is useful when chaining comparisons:

```
a = %w( z Bb bB bb BB a aA Aa AA A )
b = a.sort {|a,b| (a.downcase <=> b.downcase).nonzero? || a <=> b }
b   →    ["A", "a", "AA", "Aa", "aA", "BB", "Bb", "bB", "bb", "z"]
```

---

remainder   *num*.remainder(*aNumeric*) → *aNumeric*

If *num* and *aNumeric* have different signs, returns *mod*−*aNumeric*; otherwise, returns *mod*. In both cases *mod* is the value *num*.`modulo`(*aNumeric*). The differences between `remainder` and modulo (%) are shown in Table 22.6.

---

zero?   *num*.zero? → `true` or `false`

Returns `true` if *num* has a zero value.

Class	Object

Subclasses: Array, Binding, Continuation, Data, Dir, Exception, FalseClass, File::Stat, Hash, IO, MatchingData, Method, Module, NilClass, Numeric, Proc, Range, Regexp, String, Struct, Thread, Time, TrueClass

Object is the parent class of all classes in Ruby. Its methods are therefore available to all objects unless explicitly overridden.

Object mixes in the Kernel module, making the built-in kernel functions globally accessible. Although the instance methods of Object are defined by the Kernel module, we have chosen to document them here for clarity.

In the descriptions that follow, the parameter *aSymbol* refers to a symbol, which is either a quoted string or a Symbol (such as :name).

Instance methods

==

$$obj == anObject \rightarrow \textbf{true} \text{ or } \textbf{false}$$

Equality—At the Object level, == returns **true** only if *obj* and *anObject* are the same object. Typically, this method is overridden in descendent classes to provide class-specific meaning.

===

$$obj === anObject \rightarrow \textbf{true} \text{ or } \textbf{false}$$

Case Equality—A synonym for Object#==, but typically overridden by descendents to provide meaningful semantics in case statements.

=~

$$obj =\sim anObject \rightarrow \textbf{false}$$

Pattern Match—Overridden by descendents (notably Regexp and String) to provide meaningful pattern-match semantics.

__id__

$$obj.\_\_id\_\_ \rightarrow aFixnum$$

Synonym for Object#id.

__send__

$$obj.\_\_send\_\_(aSymbol \ \langle , args \rangle^{+}) \rightarrow anObject$$

Synonym for Object#send.

class

$$obj.class \rightarrow aClass$$

Returns the class of *obj*.

clone

$$obj.clone \rightarrow anObject$$

Produces a shallow copy of *obj*—the instance variables of *obj* are copied, but not the objects they reference. Copies the frozen and tainted state of *obj*. See also the discussion under Object#dup.

```
class Klass
    attr_accessor :str
end
s1 = Klass.new        →    #<Klass:0x4018a374>
s1.str = "Hello"      →    "Hello"
s2 = s1.clone         →    #<Klass:0x4018a2d4 @str="Hello">
s2.str[1,4] = "i"     →    "i"
s1.inspect            →    "#<Klass:0x4018a374 @str=\"Hi\">"
s2.inspect            →    "#<Klass:0x4018a2d4 @str=\"Hi\">"
```

display $\qquad$ *obj*.display(*port=$>*) → nil

Prints *obj* on the given port (default $>). Equivalent to:

```
def display(port=$>)
  port.write self
end
```

dup $\qquad$ *obj*.dup → *anObject*

Produces a shallow copy of *obj*—the instance variables of *obj* are copied, but not the objects they reference. dup copies the tainted state of *obj*. See also the discussion under Object#clone. In general, clone and dup may have different semantics in descendent classes. While clone is used to duplicate an object, including its internal state, dup typically uses the class of the descendent object to create the new instance.

eql? $\qquad$ *obj*.eql?(*anObject*) → true or false

Returns true if *obj* and *anObject* have the same value. Used by Hash to test members for equality. For objects of class Object, eql? is synonymous with ==. Subclasses normally continue this tradition, but there are exceptions. Numeric types, for example, perform type conversion across ==, but not across eql?, so:

```
1 == 1.0     →    true
1.eql? 1.0   →    false
```

equal? $\qquad$ *obj*.equal?(*anObject*) → true or false

Returns true if *obj* and *anObject* have the same object ID. This method should not be overridden by subclasses.

```
a = [ 'cat', 'dog' ]
b = [ 'cat', 'dog' ]
a == b          →    true
a.id == b.id    →    false
a.eql?(b)       →    true
a.equal?(b)     →    false
```

extend $\qquad$ *obj*.extend(⟨ *aModule* ⟩⁺) → *obj*

Adds to *obj* the instance methods from each module given as a parameter.

```
module Mod
  def hello
    "Hello from Mod.\n"
  end
end

class Klass
  def hello
    "Hello from Klass.\n"
  end
end

k = Klass.new
k.hello          →    "Hello from Klass.\n"
k.extend(Mod)    →    #<Klass:0x4018a554>
k.hello          →    "Hello from Mod.\n"
```

---

freeze *obj*.freeze → *obj*

Prevents further modifications to *obj*. A `TypeError` will be raised if modification is attempted. There is no way to unfreeze a frozen object. See also `Object#frozen?`.

```
a = [ "a", "b", "c" ]
a.freeze
a << "z"
```

produces:

```
prog.rb:3:in `<<': can't modify frozen array (TypeError)
from prog.rb:3
```

---

frozen? *obj*.frozen? → `true` or `false`

Returns the freeze status of *obj*.

```
a = [ "a", "b", "c" ]
a.freeze     →    ["a", "b", "c"]
a.frozen?    →    true
```

---

hash *obj*.hash → *aFixnum*

Generates a `Fixnum` hash value for this object. This function must have the property that `a.eql?(b)` implies `a.hash == b.hash`. The hash value is used by class `Hash`. Any hash value that exceeds the capacity of a `Fixnum` will be truncated before being used.

---

id *obj*.id → *aFixnum*

Returns an integer identifier for *obj*. The same number will be returned on all calls to `id` for a given object, and no two active objects will share an id. `Object#id` is a different concept from the `:name` notation, which returns the symbol id of `name`.

---

inspect *obj*.inspect → *aString*

Returns a string containing a human-readable representation of *obj*. If not overridden, uses the `to_s` method to generate the string.

```
[ 1, 2, 3..4, 'five' ].inspect   →   "[1, 2, 3..4, \"five\"]"
Time.new.inspect                 →   "Wed Sep 20 10:35:21 CDT 2000"
```

---

instance_eval *obj*.instance_eval(*aString* ⟨ , *file* ⟨ , *line* ⟩ ⟩) → *anObject*
obj.instance_eval { *block* } → *anObject*

Evaluates a string containing Ruby source code, or the given block, within the context of the receiver (*obj*). In order to set the context, the variable `self` is set to *obj* while the code is executing, giving the code access to *obj*'s instance variables. In the version of `instance_eval` that takes a `String`, the optional second and third parameters supply a filename and starting line number that are used when reporting compilation errors.

```
class Klass
  def initialize
    @secret = 99
  end
end
k = Klass.new
k.instance_eval { @secret }   →   99
```

---

instance_of? *obj*.instance_of?(*aClass*) → `true` or `false`

Returns `true` if *obj* is an instance of the given class. See also `Object#kind_of?`.

---

instance_variables *obj*.instance_variables → *anArray*

Returns an array of instance variable names for the receiver.

---

is_a? *obj*.is_a?(*aClass*) → `true` or `false`

Synonym for `Object#kind_of?`.

---

kind_of? *obj*.kind_of?(*aClass*) → `true` or `false`

Returns `true` if *aClass* is the class of *obj*, or if *aClass* is one of the superclasses of *obj* or modules included in *obj*.

```
a = Integer.new
a.instance_of? Numeric      →   false
a.instance_of? Integer      →   true
a.instance_of? Fixnum       →   false
a.instance_of? Comparable   →   false
a.kind_of? Numeric          →   true
a.kind_of? Integer          →   true
a.kind_of? Fixnum           →   false
a.kind_of? Comparable       →   true
```

Object

method

obj.method(aSymbol) → aMethod

Looks up the named method as a receiver in *obj*, returning a `Method` object (or raising `NameError`). The `Method` object acts as a closure in *obj*'s object instance, so instance variables and the value of `self` remain available.

```ruby
class Demo
  def initialize(n)
    @iv = n
  end
  def hello()
    "Hello, @iv = #{@iv}"
  end
end

k = Demo.new(99)
m = k.method(:hello)
m.call   →   "Hello, @iv = 99"

l = Demo.new('Fred')
m = l.method("hello")
m.call   →   "Hello, @iv = Fred"
```

method_missing

obj.method_missing(aSymbol ⟨ , *args ⟩) → anObject

Invoked by Ruby when *obj* is sent a message it cannot handle. *aSymbol* is the symbol for the method called, and *args* are any arguments that were passed to it. The example below creates a class `Roman`, which responds to methods with names consisting of roman numerals, returning the corresponding integer values.

```ruby
class Roman
  def romanToInt(str)
    # ...
  end
  def method_missing(methId)
    str = methId.id2name
    romanToInt(str)
  end
end

r = Roman.new
r.iv     →   4
r.xxiii  →   23
r.mm     →   2000
```

methods

obj.methods → anArray

Returns a list of the names of methods publicly accessible in *obj*. This will include all the methods accessible in *obj*'s ancestors.

```
class Klass
  def kMethod()
  end
end
k = Klass.new
k.methods[0..9]      →    ["kMethod", "method", "kind_of?",
                          "private_methods", "methods", "frozen?",
                          "taint", "type", "eql?", "=="]
k.methods.length     →    38
```

---

nil?   *obj*.nil? → **true** or **false**

All objects except **nil** return **false**.

---

private_methods   *obj*.private_methods → *anArray*

Returns a list of private methods accessible within *obj*. This will include the private methods in *obj*'s ancestors, along with any mixed-in module functions.

---

protected_methods   *obj*.protected_methods → *anArray*

Returns the list of protected methods accessible to *obj*.

---

public_methods   *obj*.public_methods → *anArray*

Synonym for `Object#methods`.

---

respond_to?   *obj*.respond_to?(*aSymbol*, *includePriv*=**false**) → **true** or **false**

Returns **true** if *obj* responds to the given method. Private methods are included in the search only if the optional second parameter evaluates to **true**.

---

send   *obj*.send(*aSymbol* ⟨ , *args* ⟩*) → *anObject*

Invokes the method identified by *aSymbol*, passing it any arguments specified.

```
class Klass
  def hello(*args)
    "Hello " + args.join(' ')
  end
end
k = Klass.new
k.send :hello, "gentle", "readers"   →   "Hello gentle readers"
```

---

singleton_methods   *obj*.singleton_methods → *anArray*

Returns an array of the names of singleton methods for *obj*.

Object

```
class Klass
  def Klass.classMethod
  end
end
k = Klass.new
def k.sm()
end
Klass.singleton_methods   →   ["classMethod"]
k.singleton_methods       →   ["sm"]
```

taint
obj.taint → *obj*

Marks *obj* as tainted (see Chapter 20, which begins on page 257).

tainted?
obj.tainted? → `true` or `false`

Returns `true` if the object is tainted.

to_a
obj.to_a → *anArray*

Returns an array representation of *obj*. For objects of class `Object` and others that don't explicitly override the method, the return value is an array containing `self`.

```
self.to_a       →   [main]
"hello".to_a    →   ["hello"]
Time.new.to_a   →   [21, 35, 10, 20, 9, 2000, 3, 264, true, "CDT"]
```

to_s
obj.to_s → *aString*

Returns a string representing *obj*. The default `to_s` prints the object's class and an encoding of the object id. As a special case, the top-level object that is the initial execution context of Ruby programs returns "main."

type
obj.type → *aClass*

Returns the class of *obj*.

untaint
obj.untaint → *obj*

Removes the taint from *obj*.

Proc < Object

Proc objects are blocks of code that have been bound to a set of local variables. Once bound, the code may be called in different contexts and still access those variables.

```
def genTimes(factor)
  return Proc.new {|n| n*factor }
end

times3 = genTimes(3)
times5 = genTimes(5)

times3.call(12)             →   36
times5.call(5)             →   25
times3.call(times5.call(4))  →   60
```

Class methods

new   Proc.new ⟨ { block } ⟩ → aProc

Creates a new Proc object, bound to the current context. It may be called without a block only within a method with an attached block, in which case that block is converted to the Proc object.

```
def procFrom
  Proc.new
end
aProc = procFrom { "hello" }
aProc.call   →   "hello"
```

Instance methods

[ ]   prc[⟨ params ⟩*] → anObject

A synonym for Proc.call.

arity   prc.arity → anInteger

Returns the number of arguments required by the block. If the block takes no arguments, returns −1. If it takes one argument, returns −2. Otherwise, returns a positive argument count unless the last argument is prefixed with *, in which case the argument count is negated. The number of required arguments is *anInteger* for positive values, and (*anInteger*+1).abs otherwise.

```
Proc.new {||}.arity        →   -1
Proc.new {|a|}.arity       →   -2
Proc.new {|a,b|}.arity     →   2
Proc.new {|a,b,c|}.arity   →   3
Proc.new {|*a|}.arity      →   -1
Proc.new {|a,*b|}.arity    →   -2
```

call

$$prc.call(\langle params \rangle^*) \rightarrow anObject$$

Invokes the block, setting the block's parameters to the values in *params* using the same rules as used by parallel assignment. Returns the value of the last expression evaluated in the block.

```
aProc = Proc.new {|a, *b| b.collect {|i| i*a }}
aProc.call(9, 1, 2, 3)   →   [9, 18, 27]
aProc[9, 1, 2, 3]        →   [9, 18, 27]
```

Class **Range** < Object

A Range represents an interval—a set of values with a start and an end. Ranges may be constructed using the *s..e* and *s...e* literals, or with `Range.new`. Ranges constructed using .. run from the start to the end inclusively. Those created using ... exclude the end value. When used as an iterator, ranges return each value in the sequence.

```
(-1..-5).to_a     →   []
(-5..-1).to_a     →   [-5, -4, -3, -2, -1]
('a'..'e').to_a   →   ["a", "b", "c", "d", "e"]
('a'...'e').to_a  →   ["a", "b", "c", "d"]
```

Ranges can be constructed using objects of any type, as long as the objects can be compared using their <=> operator and they support the `succ` method to return the next object in sequence.

```
class Xs                  # represent a string of 'x's
  include Comparable
  attr :length
  def initialize(n)
    @length = n
  end
  def succ
    Xs.new(@length + 1)
  end
  def <=>(other)
    raise TypeError unless other.kind_of? Xs
    @length <=> other.length
  end
  def inspect
    'x' * @length
  end
end

r = Xs.new(3)..Xs.new(6)   →   xxx..xxxxxx
r.to_a                     →   [xxx, xxxx, xxxxx, xxxxxx]
r.member?(Xs.new(5))       →   true
```

Mixes in

Enumerable:
    collect, detect, each_with_index, entries, find, find_all, grep,
    include?, map, max, member?, min, reject, select, sort, to_a

Class methods

new   Range.new(*start, end, exclusive*=`false`) → *aRange*

Constructs a range using the given *start* and *end*. If the third parameter is omitted or is `false`, the range will include the end object; otherwise, it will be excluded.

Instance methods

===   *rng* === *anObject* → `true` or `false`

Returns `true` if *anObject* is an element of *rng*, `false` otherwise. Conveniently, === is the comparison operator used by `case` statements.

```
case 79
when 1..50    then    print "low\n"
when 51..75   then    print "medium\n"
when 76..100 then    print "high\n"
end
```

produces:

```
high
```

begin   *rng*.begin → *anObject*

Returns the first object of *rng*.

each   *rng*.each {| *i* | *block* } → *rng*

Iterates over the elements *rng*, passing each in turn to the block.

```
(10..15).each do |n|
   print n, ' '
end
```

produces:

```
10 11 12 13 14 15
```

end   *rng*.end → *anObject*

Returns the object that defines the end of *rng*. See also `Range#length`.

```
(1..10).end    →    10
(1...10).end   →    10
```

exclude_end?

rng.exclude_end? → `true` or `false`

Returns `true` if *rng* excludes its end value.

first

rng.first → *anObject*

Returns the first object in *rng*.

last

rng.last → *anObject*

Synonym for `Range#end`.

length

rng.length → *anInteger*

Returns the number of objects in *rng*.

```
(1..10).length   →   10
(1...10).length  →   9
```

size

rng.size → *anInteger*

Synonym for `Range#length`.

Class **Regexp** < Object

A `Regexp` holds a regular expression, used to match a pattern against strings. Regexps are created using the `/.../` and `%r...` literals, and by the `Regexp.new` constructor.

Class constants

EXTENDED	Ignore spaces and newlines in regexp.
IGNORECASE	Matches are case insensitive.
MULTILINE	Newlines treated as any other character.

Class methods

compile

Regexp.compile(*pattern* ⟨ , *options* ⟨ , *lang* ⟩ ⟩) → *aRegexp*

Synonym for `Regexp.new`.

escape

Regexp.escape(*aString*) → *aNewString*

Escapes any characters that would have special meaning in a regular expression. For any string, `Regexp.escape(`*str*`)=~`*str* will be true.

```
Regexp.escape('\\[]*?{}.')   →   \\\[\]\*\?\{\}\.
```

---

last_match $\hspace{3cm}$ Regexp.last_match → *aMatchData*

Returns the `MatchData` object generated by the last successful pattern match. Equivalent to reading the global variable `$~`. `MatchData` is described on page 340.

---

new $\hspace{3cm}$ Regexp.new(*pattern* ⟨ , *options* ⟨ , *lang* ⟩ ⟩) → *aRegexp*

Constructs a new regular expression from *pattern*, which can be either a `String` or a `Regexp` (in which case that regexp's options are not propagated). If *options* is a `Fixnum`, it should be one or more of the constants `Regexp::EXTENDED`, `Regexp::IGNORECASE`, and `Regexp::POSIXLINE`, *or*-ed together. Otherwise, if *options* is not `nil`, the regexp will be case insensitive. The *lang* parameter enables multibyte support for the regexp: 'n', 'N' = none, 'e', 'E' = EUC, 's', 'S' = SJIS, 'u', 'U' = UTF-8.

```
r1 = Regexp.new('^[a-z]+:\\s+\w+')      →   /^[a-z]+:\s+\w+/
r2 = Regexp.new(r1, true)              →   /^[a-z]+:\s+\w+/i
r3 = Regexp.new(r2, Regexp::EXTENDED)  →   /^[a-z]+:\s+\w+/x
```

---

quote $\hspace{3cm}$ Regexp.quote(*aString*) → *aNewString*

Synonym for `Regexp.escape`.

Instance methods

== $\hspace{3cm}$ *rxp* == *aRegexp* → **true** or **false**

Equality—Two regexps are equal if their patterns are identical, they have the same character set code, and their `casefold?` values are the same.

```
/abc/   == /abc/x   →   true
/abc/   == /abc/i   →   false
/abc/u == /abc/n    →   false
```

=== $\hspace{3cm}$ *rxp* === *aString* → **true** or **false**

Case Equality—Synonym for `Regexp#=~` used in case statements.

```
a = "HELLO"
case a
when /^[a-z]*$/; print "Lower case\n"
when /^[A-Z]*$/; print "Upper case\n"
else;            print "Mixed case\n"
end
```

produces:

```
Upper case
```

=~ $\hspace{3cm}$ *rxp* =~ *aString* → *anInteger* or **nil**

Match—Matches *rxp* against *aString*, returning the offset of the start of the match or `nil` if the match failed.

```
/SIT/  =~ "insensitive"  →  nil
/SIT/i =~ "insensitive"  →  5
```

~   *~ rxp → anInteger* or `nil`

Match—Matches *rxp* against the contents of `$_`. Equivalent to `rxp =~ $_`.

```
$_ = "input data"
~ /at/  →  7
```

---

casefold?   *rxp*.casefold? → `true` or `false`

Returns the value of the case-insensitive flag.

---

kcode   *rxp*.kcode → *aString*

Returns the character set code for the regexp.

---

match   *rxp*.match(*aString*) → *aMatchData* or `nil`

Returns a `MatchData` object (see page 340) describing the match, or `nil` if there was no match. This is equivalent to retrieving the value of the special variable `$~` following a normal match.

```
/(.)(.)(.)/.match("abc")[2]  →  "b"
```

---

source   *rxp*.source → *aString*

Returns the original string of the pattern.

```
/ab+c/ix.source  →  "ab+c"
```

Class **String** `<` Object

A `String` object holds and manipulates an arbitrary sequence of bytes, typically representing characters. String objects may be created using `String.new` or as literals (see page 204).

Because of aliasing issues, users of strings should be aware of the methods that modify the contents of a `String` object. Typically, methods with names ending in "!" modify their receiver, while those without a "!" return a new `String`. However, there are exceptions, such as `String#[]=`.

Mixes in

```
Comparable:
    <, <=, ==, >=, >, between?
```

Enumerable:

> collect, detect, each_with_index, entries, find, find_all, grep, include?, map, max, member?, min, reject, select, sort, to_a

Class methods

new | String.new(*aString*) → *aNewString*

Returns a new string object containing a copy of *aString*.

Instance methods

% | *str* % *arg* → *aString*

Format—Uses *str* as a format specification, and returns the result of applying it to *arg*. If the format specification contains more than one substitution, then *arg* must be an **Array** containing the values to be substituted. See **Kernel.sprintf** on page 427 for details of the format string.

```
"%05d" % 123              →    "00123"
"%-5s: %08x" % [ "ID", self.id ]   →    "ID␣␣␣:␣200cbe84"
```

* | *str* * *anInteger* → *aString*

Copy—Returns a new **String** containing *anInteger* copies of the receiver.

```
"Ho! " * 3    →    "Ho! Ho! Ho! "
```

+ | *str* + *aString* → *aNewString*

Concatenation—Returns a new **String** containing *aString* concatenated to *str*.

```
"Hello from " + self.to_s    →    "Hello from main"
```

<< | *str* << *aFixnum* → *str*
| *str* << *anObject* → *str*

Append—Concatenates the given object to *str*. If the object is a **Fixnum** between 0 and 255, it is converted to a character before concatenation.

```
a = "hello "
a << "world"    →    "hello world"
a << 33         →    "hello world!"
a               →    "hello world!"
```

<=> | *str* <=> *aString* → −1, 0, +1

Comparison—Returns −1 if *str* is less than, 0 if *str* is equal to, and +1 if *str* is greater than *aString*. If the strings are of different lengths, and the strings are equal when compared up to the shortest length, then the longer string is considered greater than the shorter one. If the variable **$=** is **false**, the comparison is based on comparing the binary values of each character in the string. If $= is not `false`, then the comparison is case insensitive.[1]

`<=>` is the basis for the methods `<`, `<=`, `>`, `>=`, and `between?`, included from module `Comparable`. The method `String#==` does not use `Comparable#==`.

```
"abcdef" <=> "abcde"     →    1
"abcdef" <=> "abcdef"    →    0
"abcdef" <=> "abcdefg"   →   -1
"abcdef" <=> "ABCDEF"    →    1
$= = true
"abcdef" <=> "ABCDEF"    →    0
```

==

$$str == anObject \rightarrow \texttt{true} \text{ or } \texttt{false}$$

Equality—If *anObject* is not a `String`, returns `false`. Otherwise, returns `true` if *str* `<=>` *anObject* returns zero.

===

$$str === anObject \rightarrow \texttt{true} \text{ or } \texttt{false}$$

Case Equality—Synonym for `String#==`.

=~

$$str =\text{\textasciitilde} anObject \rightarrow aFixnum \text{ or } \texttt{nil}$$

Match—If *anObject* is a `Regexp` or a `String`, uses it as a pattern to match against *str*. Returns the position the match starts, or `nil` if there is no match. Otherwise, invokes *anObject.*`=~`, passing *str* as an argument. The default `=~` in `Object` returns `false`.

```
"cat o' 9 tails" =~ "\\d"   →    7
"cat o' 9 tails" =~ /\d/    →    7
"cat o' 9 tails" =~ 9       →    false
```

[ ]

$$str[\ aFixnum\ ] \rightarrow aFixnum \text{ or } \texttt{nil}$$
$$str[\ aFixnum, aFixnum\ ] \rightarrow aString \text{ or } \texttt{nil}$$
$$str[\ aRange\ ] \rightarrow aString \text{ or } \texttt{nil}$$
$$str[\ aRegexp\ ] \rightarrow aString \text{ or } \texttt{nil}$$
$$str[\ aString\ ] \rightarrow aString \text{ or } \texttt{nil}$$

Element Reference—If passed a single `Fixnum`, returns the code of the character at that position. If passed two `Fixnum` objects, returns a substring starting at the offset given by the first, and a length given by the second. If given a range, a substring containing characters at offsets given by the range is returned. In all three cases, if an offset is negative, it is counted from the end of *str*. Returns `nil` if the initial offset falls outside the string, the length is negative, or the beginning of the range is greater than the end.

---

1. The locale is ignored when case-insensitive comparisons are performed, so "ö" will not match "Ö".

If a **Regexp** is supplied, the matching portion of *str* is returned. If a **String** is given, that string is returned if it occurs in *str*. In both cases, **nil** is returned if there is no match.

```
a = "hello there"
a[1]              →    101
a[1,3]            →    "ell"
a[1..3]           →    "ell"
a[-3,2]           →    "er"
a[-4..-2]         →    "her"
a[-2..-4]         →    nil
a[/th[aeiou]/]    →    "the"
a["lo"]           →    "lo"
a["bye"]          →    nil
```

[ ]=

str[*aFixnum*] = *aFixnum*
str[*aFixnum*] = *aString*
str[*aFixnum, aFixnum*] = *aString*
str[*aRange*] = *aString*
str[*aRegexp*] = *aString*
str[*aString*] = *aString*

Element Assignment—Replaces some or all of the content of *str*. The portion of the string affected is determined using the same criteria as **String#[ ]**. If the replacement string is not the same length as the text it is replacing, the string will be adjusted accordingly. The forms that take a **Fixnum** will raise an **IndexError** if the value is out of range; the **Range** form will raise a **RangeError**, and the **Regexp** and **String** forms will silently ignore the assignment.

```
a = "hello"; a[2]       = 96;      a  →   "he`lo"
a = "hello"; a[2, 4]    = "xyz";   a  →   "hexyz"
a = "hello"; a[-4, 2]   = "xyz";   a  →   "hxyzlo"
a = "hello"; a[2..4]    = "xyz";   a  →   "hexyz"
a = "hello"; a[-4..-2]  = "xyz";   a  →   "hxyzo"
a = "hello"; a[/[el]+/] = "xyz";   a  →   "hxyzo"
a = "hello"; a["l"]     = "xyz";   a  →   "hexyzlo"
a = "hello"; a["ll"]    = "xyz";   a  →   "hexyzo"
a = "hello"; a["bad"]   = "xyz";   a  →   "hello"
a = "hello"; a[2, 0]    = "xyz";   a  →   "hexyzllo"
```

~

~ *str*→ *aFixnum* or **nil**

Equivalent to `$_ =~ str`.

---

capitalize

str.capitalize → *aString*

Returns a copy of *str* with the first character converted to uppercase and the remainder to lowercase.

```
"hello".capitalize     →    "Hello"
"HELLO".capitalize     →    "Hello"
"123ABC".capitalize    →    "123abc"
```

capitalize!

str.capitalize! → *str* or `nil`

Modifies *str* by converting the first character to uppercase and the remainder to lower-case. Returns `nil` if no changes are made.

```
a = "hello"
a.capitalize!    →    "Hello"
a                →    "Hello"
a.capitalize!    →    nil
```

center

str.center(*anInteger*) → *aString*

If *anInteger* is greater than the length of *str*, returns a new `String` of length *anInteger* with *str* centered between spaces; otherwise, returns *str*.

```
"hello".center(4)     →    "hello"
"hello".center(20)    →    "␣␣␣␣␣␣␣hello␣␣␣␣␣␣␣␣"
```

chomp

str.chomp(*aString=$/*) → *aString*

Returns a new `String` with the given record separator removed from the end of *str* (if present).

```
"hello".chomp             →    "hello"
"hello\n".chomp           →    "hello"
"hello \n there".chomp    →    "hello \n there"
"hello".chomp("llo")      →    "he"
```

chomp!

str.chomp!(*aString=$/*) → *str* or `nil`

Modifies *str* in place as described for `String#chomp`, returning *str*, or `nil` if no modifications were made.

chop

str.chop → *aString*

Returns a new `String` with the last character removed. If the string ends with `\r\n`, both characters are removed. Applying `chop` to an empty string returns an empty string. `String#chomp` is often a safer alternative, as it leaves the string unchanged if it doesn't end in a record separator.

```
"string\r\n".chop    →    "string"
"string\n\r".chop    →    "string\n"
"string\n".chop      →    "string"
"string".chop        →    "strin"
"x".chop.chop        →    ""
```

chop!

str.chop! $\rightarrow$ str or `nil`

Processes str as for `String#chop`, returning str, or `nil` if str is the empty string. See also `String#chomp!`.

concat

str.concat($aFixnum$) $\rightarrow$ str
str.concat($anObject$) $\rightarrow$ str

Synonym for `String#<<`.

count

str.count($\langle\, aString\, \rangle^+$) $\rightarrow$ $aFixnum$

Each $aString$ parameter defines a set of characters to count. The intersection of these sets defines the characters to count in str. Any $aString$ that starts with a caret (^) is negated. The sequence c_1–c_2 means all characters between c_1 and c_2.

```
a = "hello world"
a.count "lo"              →    5
a.count "lo", "o"         →    2
a.count "hello", "^l"     →    4
a.count "ej-m"            →    4
```

crypt

str.crypt($aString$) $\rightarrow$ $aString$

Applies a one-way cryptographic hash to str by invoking the standard library function `crypt`. The argument is the salt string, which should be two characters long, each character drawn from `[a-zA-Z0-9./]`.

delete

str.delete($\langle\, aString\, \rangle^+$) $\rightarrow$ $aString$

Returns a copy of str with all characters in the intersection of its arguments deleted. Uses the same rules for building the set of characters as `String#count`.

```
"hello".delete "l","lo"         →    "heo"
"hello".delete "lo"             →    "he"
"hello".delete "aeiou", "^e"    →    "hell"
"hello".delete "ej-m"           →    "ho"
```

delete!

str.delete!($\langle\, aString\, \rangle^+$) $\rightarrow$ str or `nil`

Performs a `delete` operation in place, returning str, or `nil` if str was not modified.

downcase

str.downcase $\rightarrow$ $aString$

Returns a copy of str with all uppercase letters replaced with their lowercase counterparts. The operation is locale insensitive—only characters "A" to "Z" are affected.

```
"hEllO".downcase   →   "hello"
```

downcase!

str.downcase! $\rightarrow$ str or `nil`

Downcases the contents of str, returning `nil` if no changes were made.

---

dump   *str*.dump → *aString*

Produces a version of *str* with all nonprinting characters replaced by **nnn** notation and all special characters escaped.

---

each   *str*.each(*aString*=**$/**) {| *substr* | *block* } → *str*

Splits *str* using the supplied parameter as the record separator (**$/** by default), passing each substring in turn to the supplied block. If a zero-length record separator is supplied, the string is split on **n** characters, except that multiple successive newlines are appended together.

```
print "Example one\n"
"hello\nworld".each {|s| p s}
print "Example two\n"
"hello\nworld".each('l') {|s| p s}
print "Example three\n"
"hello\n\n\nworld".each('') {|s| p s}
```

produces:

```
Example one
"hello\n"
"world"
Example two
"hel"
"l"
"o\nworl"
"d"
Example three
"hello\n\n\n"
"world"
```

---

each_byte   *str*.each_byte {| *aFixnum* | *block* } → *str*

Passes each byte in *str* to the given block.

```
"hello".each_byte {|c| print c, ' ' }
```

produces:

```
104 101 108 108 111
```

---

each_line   *str*.each_line(*aString*=**$/**) {| *substr* | *block* } → *str*

Synonym for **String#each**.

---

empty?   *str*.empty? → **true** or **false**

Returns **true** if *str* has a length of zero.

```
"hello".empty?   →   false
"".empty?        →   true
```

String

gsub   *str*.gsub(*pattern, replacement*) → *aString*
                          str.gsub(*pattern*) { | *match* | *block* } → *aString*

Returns a copy of *str* with *all* occurrences of *pattern* replaced with either *replacement* or the value of the block. If a string is used as the replacement, special variables from the match (such as $& and $1) cannot be substituted into it, as substitution into the string occurs before the pattern match starts. However, the sequences \1, \2, and so on may be used to interpolate successive groups in the match. These sequences are shown in Table 22.7 on the following page.

In the block form, the current match is passed in as a parameter, and variables such as $1, $2, $`, $&, and $' will be set appropriately. The value returned by the block will be substituted for the match on each call.

The result inherits any tainting in the original string or any supplied replacement string.

```
"hello".gsub(/[aeiou]/, '*')             →    "h*ll*"
"hello".gsub(/([aeiou])/, '<\1>')        →    "h<e>ll<o>"
"hello".gsub('.') {|s| s[0].to_s + ' '}  →    "104 101 108 108 111 "
```

gsub!   *str*.gsub!(*pattern, replacement*) → *str* or nil
                          str.gsub!(*pattern*) { | *match* | *block* } → *str* or nil

Performs the substitutions of `String#gsub` in place, returning *str*, or `nil` if no substitutions were performed.

hash   *str*.hash → *aFixnum*

Generates a `Fixnum` hash value for *str*. If $= is `true`, the hash will be case insensitive.

```
$= = true
hash = { 'cat' => 'Feline', 'dog' => 'canine' }
hash['cat']                                →    "Feline"
hash['cAt']                                →    "Feline"
$= = false
hash.rehash     # re-calculate hash values →    {"dog"=>"canine",
                                                "cat"=>"Feline"}
hash['cat']                                →    "Feline"
hash['cAt']                                →    nil
```

hex   *str*.hex → *anInteger*

Treats leading characters from *str* as a string of hexadecimal digits (with an optional sign and an optional 0x) and returns the corresponding number. Zero is returned on error.

```
"0x0a".hex    →    10
"-1234".hex   →    -4660
"0".hex       →    0
"wombat".hex  →    0
```

String

Table 22.7. Backslash sequences in substitution strings

Sequence	Text That Is Substituted
\1, \2, ... \9	The value matched by the *n*th grouped subexpression
\&	The last match
\`	The part of the string before the match
\'	The part of the string after the match
\+	The highest-numbered group matched

---

include?
str.include? *aString* → `true` or `false`
str.include? *aFixnum* → `true` or `false`

Returns `true` if *str* contains the given string or character.

```
"hello".include? "lo"  →   true
"hello".include? "ol"  →   false
"hello".include? ?h    →   true
```

---

index
str.index(*aString* ⟨ , *anOffset* ⟩) → *aFixnum* or `nil`
str.index(*aFixnum* ⟨ , *anOffset* ⟩) → *aFixnum* or `nil`
str.index(*aRegexp* ⟨ , *anOffset* ⟩) → *aFixnum* or `nil`

Returns the index of the first occurrence of the given substring, character, or pattern in *str*. Returns `nil` if not found. If the second parameter is present, it specifies the position in the string to begin the search.

```
"hello".index('e')          →   1
"hello".index('lo')         →   3
"hello".index('a')          →   nil
"hello".index(101)          →   1
"hello".index(/[aeiou]/, -3) →   4
```

---

intern
str.intern → *aSymbol*

Returns the `Symbol` corresponding to *str*, creating the symbol if it did not previously exist. See `Symbol#id2name` on page 389.

```
"Koala".intern   →   :Koala
```

---

length
str.length → *anInteger*

Returns the length of *str*.

---

ljust
str.ljust(*anInteger*) → *aString*

If *anInteger* is greater than the length of *str*, returns a new `String` of length *anInteger* with *str* left justified and space padded; otherwise, returns *str*.

String

```
"hello".ljust(4)    →    "hello"
"hello".ljust(20)   →    "helloⱽⱽⱽⱽⱽⱽⱽⱽⱽⱽⱽⱽⱽⱽⱽ"
```

next
str.next → *aString*

Synonym for `String#succ`.

next!
str.next! → *str*

Synonym for `String#succ!`.

oct
str.oct → *anInteger*

Treats *str* as a string of octal digits (with an optional sign) and returns the corresponding number. Returns 0 if the conversion fails.

```
"123".oct       →    83
"-377".oct      →    -255
"bad".oct       →    0
"0377bad".oct   →    255
```

replace
str.replace(*aString*) → *str*

Replaces the contents and taintedness of *str* with the corresponding values in *aString*.

```
s = "hello"           →    "hello"
s.replace "world"     →    "world"
```

reverse
str.reverse → *aString*

Returns a new string with the characters from *str* in reverse order.

```
"stressed".reverse   →    "desserts"
```

reverse!
str.reverse! → *str*

Reverses *str* in place.

rindex
str.rindex(*aString* ⟨ , *aFixnum* ⟩) → *aFixnum* or **nil**
str.rindex(*aFixnum* ⟨ , *aFixnum* ⟩) → *aFixnum* or **nil**
str.rindex(*aRegexp* ⟨ , *aFixnum* ⟩) → *aFixnum* or **nil**

Returns the index of the last occurrence of the given substring, character, or pattern in *str*. Returns **nil** if not found. If the second parameter is present, it specifies the position in the string to end the search—characters beyond this point will not be considered.

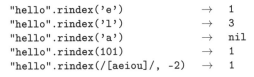

```
"hello".rindex('e')          →    1
"hello".rindex('l')          →    3
"hello".rindex('a')          →    nil
"hello".rindex(101)          →    1
"hello".rindex(/[aeiou]/, -2) →    1
```

rjust

$str.rjust(\ anInteger\ ) \rightarrow aString$

If *anInteger* is greater than the length of *str*, returns a new `String` of length *anInteger* with *str* right justified and space padded; otherwise, returns *str*.

```
"hello".rjust(4)    →   "hello"
"hello".rjust(20)   →   "⎵⎵⎵⎵⎵⎵⎵⎵⎵⎵⎵⎵⎵⎵⎵hello"
```

scan

$str.scan(\ pattern\ ) \rightarrow anArray$
$str.scan(\ pattern\ )\ \{|\ match, \ldots\ |\ block\ \}\ \rightarrow str$

Both forms iterate through *str*, matching the pattern (which may be a `Regexp` or a `String`). For each match, a result is generated and either added to the result array or passed to the block. If the pattern contains no groups, each individual result consists of the matched string, `$&`. If the pattern contains groups, each individual result is itself an array containing one entry per group.

```
a = "cruel world"
a.scan(/\w+/)        →   ["cruel", "world"]
a.scan(/.../)        →   ["cru", "el ", "wor"]
a.scan(/(...)/)      →   [["cru"], ["el "], ["wor"]]
a.scan(/(..)(..)/)   →   [["cr", "ue"], ["l ", "wo"]]
```

And the block form:

```
a.scan(/\w+/) {|w| print "<<#{w}>> " }
print "\n"
a.scan(/(.)(.)/) {|a,b| print b, a }
print "\n"
```

produces:

```
<<cruel>> <<world>>
rceu lowlr
```

size

$str.size \rightarrow anInteger$

Synonym for `String#length`.

slice

$str.slice(\ aFixnum\ ) \rightarrow aFixnum$ or `nil`
$str.slice(\ aFixnum, aFixnum\ ) \rightarrow aString$ or `nil`
$str.slice(\ aRange\ ) \rightarrow aString$ or `nil`
$str.slice(\ aRegexp\ ) \rightarrow aString$ or `nil`
$str.slice(\ aString\ ) \rightarrow aString$ or `nil`

Synonym for `String#[ ]`.

```
a = "hello there"
a.slice(1)       →   101
a.slice(1,3)     →   "ell"
a.slice(1..3)    →   "ell"
a.slice(-3,2)    →   "er"
a.slice(-4..-2)  →   "her"
```

```
a.slice(-2..-4)          →    nil
a.slice(/th[aeiou]/)     →    "the"
a.slice("lo")            →    "lo"
a.slice("bye")           →    nil
```

---

slice!

str.slice!($aFixnum$) → $aFixnum$ or nil
str.slice!($aFixnum$, $aFixnum$) → $aString$ or nil
str.slice!($aRange$) → $aString$ or nil
str.slice!($aRegexp$) → $aString$ or nil
str.slice!($aString$) → $aString$ or nil

Deletes the specified portion from *str*, and returns the portion deleted. The forms that take a `Fixnum` will raise an `IndexError` if the value is out of range; the `Range` form will raise a `RangeError`, and the `Regexp` and `String` forms will silently ignore the assignment.

```
string = "this is a string"
string.slice!(2)         →    105
string.slice!(3..6)      →    " is "
string.slice!(/s.*t/)    →    "sa st"
string.slice!("r")       →    "r"
string                   →    "thing"
```

---

split

str.split($pattern$=$\$;$, ⟨ $limit$ ⟩) → $anArray$

Divides *str* into substrings based on a delimiter, returning an array of these substrings.

If *pattern* is a `String`, then its contents are used as the delimiter when splitting *str*. If *pattern* is a single space, *str* is split on whitespace, with leading whitespace and runs of contiguous whitespace characters ignored.

If *pattern* is a `Regexp`, *str* is divided where the pattern matches. Whenever the pattern matches a zero-length string, *str* is split into individual characters.

If *pattern* is omitted, the value of `$;` is used. If `$;` is `nil` (which is the default), *str* is split on whitespace as if ' ' were specified.

If the *limit* parameter is omitted, trailing null fields are supressed. If *limit* is a positive number, at most that number of fields will be returned (if *limit* is 1, the entire string is returned as the only entry in an array). If negative, there is no limit to the number of fields returned, and trailing null fields are not supressed.

```
" now's  the time".split      →    ["now's", "the", "time"]
" now's  the time".split(' ')  →    ["now's", "the", "time"]
" now's  the time".split(/ /)  →    ["", "now's", "", "the", "time"]
"1, 2.34,56, 7".split(/,\s*/)  →    ["1", "2.34", "56", "7"]
"hello".split(//)              →    ["h", "e", "l", "l", "o"]
"hello".split(//, 3)           →    ["h", "e", "llo"]
"hi mom".split(/\s*/)          →    ["h", "i", "m", "o", "m"]
```

```
"mellow yellow".split("ello")     →   ["m", "w y", "w"]
"1,2,,3,4,,".split(',')           →   ["1", "2", "", "3", "4"]
"1,2,,3,4,,".split(',', 4)        →   ["1", "2", "", "3,4,,"]
"1,2,,3,4,,".split(',', -4)       →   ["1", "2", "", "3", "4", "", ""]
```

---

squeeze
str.squeeze(⟨ $aString$ ⟩*) → $aNewString$

Builds a set of characters from the *aString* parameter(s) using the procedure described for `String#count` on page 373. Returns a new string where runs of the same character that occur in this set are replaced by a single character. If no arguments are given, all runs of identical characters are replaced by a single character.

```
"yellow moon".squeeze             →   "yelow mon"
"  now   is  the".squeeze(" ")    →   " now is the"
"putters shoot balls".squeeze("m-z")  →   "puters shot balls"
```

---

squeeze!
str.squeeze!(⟨ $aString$ ⟩*) → str or `nil`

Squeezes *str* in place, returning either *str*, or `nil` if no changes were made.

---

strip
str.strip → $aString$

Returns a copy of *str* with leading and trailing whitespace removed.

```
"   hello   ".strip    →   "hello"
"\tgoodbye\r\n".strip  →   "goodbye"
```

---

strip!
str.strip! → str or `nil`

Removes leading and trailing whitespace from *str*. Returns `nil` if *str* was not altered.

---

sub
str.sub(*pattern*, *replacement*) → $aString$
str.sub(*pattern*) {| *match* | *block* } → $aString$

Returns a copy of *str* with the *first* occurrence of *pattern* replaced with either *replacement* or the value of the block. If the string form of the method is used, special variables such as `$&` will not be useful, as substitution into the string occurs before the pattern match starts. However, the sequences \1, \2, listed in Table 22.7 on page 376 may be used.

In the block form, the current match is passed in as a parameter, and variables such as `$1`, `$2`, `$'`, `$&`, and `$'`will be set appropriately. The value returned by the block will be substituted for the match on each call.

```
"hello".sub(/[aeiou]/, '*')           →   "h*llo"
"hello".sub(/([aeiou])/, '<\1>')      →   "h<e>llo"
"hello".sub('.') {|s| s[0].to_s + ' ' }  →   "104 ello"
```

sub!

str.sub!(*pattern*, *replacement*) → *str* or `nil`

str.sub!(*pattern*) {| *match* | *block* } → *str* or `nil`

Performs the substitutions of `String#sub` in place, returning *str*, or `nil` if no substitutions were performed.

succ

str.succ → *aString*

Returns the successor to *str*. The successor is calculated by incrementing characters starting from the rightmost alphanumeric (or the rightmost character if there are no alphanumerics) in the string. Incrementing a digit always results in another digit, and incrementing a letter results in another letter of the same case. Incrementing nonalphanumerics uses the underlying character set's collating sequence.

If the increment generates a "carry," the character to the left of it is incremented. This process repeats until there is no carry, adding an additional character if necessary.

```
"abcd".succ        →    "abce"
"THX1138".succ     →    "THX1139"
"<<koala>>".succ   →    "<<koalb>>"
"1999zzz".succ     →    "2000aaa"
"ZZZ9999".succ     →    "AAAA0000"
"***".succ         →    "**+"
```

succ!

str.succ! → *str*

Equivalent to `String#succ`, but modifies the receiver in place.

sum

str.sum(*aFixnum*=16) → *anInteger*

Returns a basic *n*-bit checksum of the characters in *str*, where *n* is the optional parameter, defaulting to 16. The result is simply the sum of the binary value of each character in *str* modulo $2^n - 1$. This is not a particularly good checksum.

swapcase

str.swapcase → *aString*

Returns a copy of *str* with uppercase alphabetic characters converted to lowercase and lowercase characters converted to uppercase.

```
"Hello".swapcase        →    "hELLO"
"cYbEr_PuNk11".swapcase →    "CyBeR_pUnK11"
```

swapcase!

str.swapcase! → *str* or *nil*

Equivalent to `String#swapcase`, but modifies the receiver in place, returning *str*, or `nil` if no changes were made.

to_f

str.to_f → *aFloat*

Returns the result of interpreting leading characters in *str* as a floating point number.

Extraneous characters past the end of a valid number are ignored. If there is not a valid number at the start of *str*, 0.0 is returned. The method never raises an exception.

```
"123.45e1".to_f       →    1234.5
"45.67 degrees".to_f  →    45.67
"thx1138".to_f        →    0.0
```

to_i

str.to_i → anInteger

Returns the result of interpreting leading characters in *str* as a decimal integer. Extraneous characters past the end of a valid number are ignored. If there is not a valid number at the start of *str*, 0 is returned. The method never raises an exception.

```
"12345".to_i           →    12345
"99 red balloons".to_i →    99
"0x0a".to_i            →    0
"hello".to_i           →    0
```

to_s

str.to_s → str

Returns the receiver.

to_str

str.to_str → str

Synonym for `String#to_s`. `to_str` is used by methods such as `String#concat` to convert their arguments to a string. Unlike `to_s`, which is supported by almost all classes, `to_str` is normally implemented only by those classes that act like strings. Of the built-in classes, only `Exception` and `String` implement `to_str`.

tr

str.tr(fromString, toString) → aString

Returns a copy of *str* with the characters in *fromString* replaced by the corresponding characters in *toString*. If *toString* is shorter than *fromString*, it is padded with its last character. Both strings may use the c_1–c_2 notation to denote ranges of characters, and *fromString* may start with a ^, which denotes all characters except those listed.

```
"hello".tr('aeiou', '*')    →    "h*ll*"
"hello".tr('^aeiou', '*')   →    "*e**o"
"hello".tr('el', 'ip')      →    "hippo"
"hello".tr('a-y', 'b-z')    →    "ifmmp"
```

tr!

str.tr!(fromString, toString) → str or nil

Translates *str* in place, using the same rules as `String#tr`. Returns *str*, or **nil** if no changes were made.

tr_s

str.tr_s(fromString, toString) → aString

Processes a copy of *str* as described under `String#tr`, then removes duplicate characters in regions that were affected by the translation.

```
"hello".tr_s('l', 'r')    →    "hero"
"hello".tr_s('el', '*')   →    "h*o"
"hello".tr_s('el', 'hx')  →    "hhxo"
```

tr_s!
str.tr_s!(fromString, toString) → str or nil

Performs `String#tr_s` processing on *str* in place, returning *str*, or **nil** if no changes were made.

unpack
str.unpack(format) → anArray

Decodes *str* (which may contain binary data) according to the format string, returning an array of each value extracted. The format string consists of a sequence of single-character directives, summarized in Table 22.8 on the following page. Each directive may be followed by a number, indicating the number of times to repeat with this directive. An asterisk ("`*`") will use up all remaining elements. The directives `sSiIlL` may each be followed by an underscore ("`_`") to use the underlying platform's native size for the specified type; otherwise, it uses a platform-independent consistent size. Spaces are ignored in the format string. See also `Array#pack` on page 290.

```
"abc \0\0abc \0\0".unpack('A6Z6')    →    ["abc", "abc "]
"abc \0\0".unpack('a3a3')            →    ["abc", " \000\000"]
"aa".unpack('b8B8')                  →    ["10000110", "01100001"]
"aaa".unpack('h2H2c')                →    ["16", "61", 97]
"\xfe\xff\xfe\xff".unpack('sS')      →    [-2, 65534]
"now=20is".unpack('M*')              →    ["now is"]
"whole".unpack('xax2aX2aX1aX2a')     →    ["h", "e", "l", "l", "o"]
```

upcase
str.upcase → aString

Returns a copy of *str* with all lowercase letters replaced with their uppercase counterparts. The operation is locale insensitive—only characters "a" to "z" are affected.

```
"hEllO".upcase   →   "HELLO"
```

upcase!
str.upcase! → str or nil

Upcases the contents of *str*, returning **nil** if no changes were made.

upto
str.upto(aString) {| s | block } → str

Iterates through successive values, starting at *str* and ending at *aString* inclusive, passing each value in turn to the block. The `String#succ` method is used to generate each value.

```
"a8".upto("b6") {|s| print s, ' ' }
for s in "a8".."b6"
  print s, ' '
end
```

produces:

```
a8 a9 b0 b1 b2 b3 b4 b5 b6
a8 a9 b0 b1 b2 b3 b4 b5 b6
```

Table 22.8. Directives for `String#unpack`

Format	Function	Returns
A	String with trailing nulls and spaces removed.	String
a	String.	String
B	Extract bits from each character (msb first).	String
b	Extract bits from each character (lsb first).	String
C	Extract a character as an unsigned integer.	Fixnum
c	Extract a character as an integer.	Fixnum
d	Treat *sizeof(double)* characters as a native double.	Float
E	Treat *sizeof(double)* characters as a double in little-endian byte order.	Float
e	Treat *sizeof(float)* characters as a float in little-endian byte order.	Float
f	Treat *sizeof(float)* characters as a native float.	Float
G	Treat *sizeof(double)* characters as a double in network byte order.	Float
g	Treat *sizeof(float)* characters as a float in network byte order.	Float
H	Extract hex nibbles from each character (most significant first).	String
h	Extract hex nibbles from each character (least significant first).	String
I	Treat *sizeof(int)*[1] successive characters as an unsigned native integer.	Integer
i	Treat *sizeof(int)*[1] successive characters as a signed native integer.	Integer
L	Treat four[1] successive characters as an unsigned native long integer.	Integer
l	Treat four[1] successive characters as a signed native long integer.	Integer
M	Extract a quoted-printable string.	String
m	Extract a base64 encoded string.	String
N	Treat four characters as an unsigned long in network byte order.	Fixnum
n	Treat two characters as an unsigned short in network byte order.	Fixnum
P	Treat *sizeof(char *)* characters as a pointer, and return *len* characters from the referenced location.	String
p	Treat *sizeof(char *)* characters as a pointer to a null-terminated string.	String
S	Treat two[1] successive characters as an unsigned short in native byte order.	Fixnum
s	Treat two[1] successive characters as a signed short in native byte order.	Fixnum
U	Extract UTF-8 characters as unsigned integers.	Integer
u	Extract a UU-encoded string.	String
V	Treat four characters as an unsigned long in little-endian byte order.	Fixnum
v	Treat two characters as an unsigned short in little-endian byte order.	Fixnum
X	Skip backward one character.	—
x	Skip forward one character.	—
Z	String with trailing nulls removed.	String
@	Skip to the offset given by the length argument.	—

[1] May be modified by appending "_" to the directive.

Struct < Object

Class

Subclasses: Struct::Tms

A **Struct** is a convenient way to bundle a number of attributes together, using accessor methods, without having to write an explicit class.

The **Struct** class is a generator of specific classes, each one of which is defined to hold a set of variables and their accessors. In these examples, we'll call the generated class "*Customer*," and we'll show an example instance of that class as "*joe*."

In the descriptions that follow, the parameter *aSymbol* refers to a symbol, which is either a quoted string or a **Symbol** (such as **:name**).

Mixes in

Enumerable:
    collect, detect, each_with_index, entries, find, find_all, grep,
    include?, map, max, member?, min, reject, select, sort, to_a

Class methods

new   Struct.new($\langle$ *aString* $\rangle$ $\langle$, *aSym* $\rangle^+$) $\rightarrow$ *Customer*

Creates a new class, named by *aString*, containing accessor methods for the given symbols. If the name *aString* is omitted, an anonymous structure class will be created. Otherwise, the name of this struct will appear as a constant in class **Struct**, so it must be unique for all **Struct**s in the system and should start with a capital letter.

Struct.new returns a new **Class** object, which can then be used to create specific instances of the new structure. The remaining methods listed below (class and instance) are defined for this generated class. See the description that follows for an example.

new   *Customer*.new($\langle$ *anObject* $\rangle^+$) $\rightarrow$ *joe*

Creates a new instance. The number of actual parameters must be less than or equal to the number of attributes defined for this class; unset parameters default to **nil**. Passing too many parameters will raise an **ArgumentError**.

```
Customer = Struct.new( "Customer", :name, :address, :zip )
joe = Customer.new( "Joe Smith", "123 Maple, Anytown NC", 12345 )
joe.name    →   "Joe Smith"
joe.zip     →   12345
```

members   *Customer*.members $\rightarrow$ *anArray*

Returns an array of strings representing the names of the instance variables.

```
Customer = Struct.new( "Customer", :name, :address, :zip )
Customer.members   →   ["name", "address", "zip"]
```

Instance methods

==

$$joe == anOtherStruct \rightarrow \text{true or false}$$

Equality—Returns **true** if *anOtherStruct* is equal to this one: they must be of the same class as generated by `Struct.new`, and the values of all instance variables must be equal (according to `Object#==`).

```
Customer = Struct.new( "Customer", :name, :address, :zip )
joe   = Customer.new( "Joe Smith", "123 Maple, Anytown NC", 12345 )
joejr = Customer.new( "Joe Smith", "123 Maple, Anytown NC", 12345 )
jane  = Customer.new( "Jane Doe", "456 Elm, Anytown NC", 12345 )
joe == joejr   →   true
joe == jane    →   false
```

[ ]

$$joe[\ aSymbol \ ] \rightarrow anObject$$
$$joe[\ anInteger \ ] \rightarrow anObject$$

Attribute Reference—Returns the value of the instance variable named by *aSymbol*, or indexed $(0..length-1)$ by *anInteger*. Will raise `NameError` if the named variable does not exist, or `IndexError` if the index is out of range.

```
Customer = Struct.new( "Customer", :name, :address, :zip )
joe = Customer.new( "Joe Smith", "123 Maple, Anytown NC", 12345 )

joe["name"]   →   "Joe Smith"
joe[:name]    →   "Joe Smith"
joe[0]        →   "Joe Smith"
```

[ ]=

$$joe[\ aSymbol \ ] = anObject \rightarrow anObject$$
$$joe[\ anInteger \ ] = anObject \rightarrow anObject$$

Attribute Assignment—Assigns to the instance variable named by *aSymbol* or *anInteger* the value *anObject* and returns it. Will raise a `NameError` if the named variable does not exist, or an `IndexError` if the index is out of range.

```
Customer = Struct.new( "Customer", :name, :address, :zip )
joe = Customer.new( "Joe Smith", "123 Maple, Anytown NC", 12345 )

joe["name"] = "Luke"
joe[:zip]   = "90210"

joe.name   →   "Luke"
joe.zip    →   "90210"
```

each

$$joe.\text{each} \ \{ \ | anObject | \ block \ \} \ \rightarrow joe$$

Calls *block* once for each instance variable, passing the value as a parameter.

```
Customer = Struct.new( "Customer", :name, :address, :zip )
joe = Customer.new( "Joe Smith", "123 Maple, Anytown NC", 12345 )
joe.each {|x| puts(x) }
```

Struct

produces:

```
Joe Smith
123 Maple, Anytown NC
12345
```

length
joe.length → *anInteger*

Returns the number of instance variables.

```
Customer = Struct.new( "Customer", :name, :address, :zip )
joe = Customer.new( "Joe Smith", "123 Maple, Anytown NC", 12345 )
joe.length   →   3
```

members
joe.members → *anArray*

Returns an array of strings representing the names of the instance variables.

```
Customer = Struct.new( "Customer", :name, :address, :zip )
joe = Customer.new( "Joe Smith", "123 Maple, Anytown NC", 12345 )
joe.members   →   ["name", "address", "zip"]
```

size
joe.size → *anInteger*

Synonym for `Struct#length`.

to_a
joe.to_a → *anArray*

Returns the values for this instance as an array.

```
Customer = Struct.new( "Customer", :name, :address, :zip )
joe = Customer.new( "Joe Smith", "123 Maple, Anytown NC", 12345 )
joe.to_a[1]   →   "123 Maple, Anytown NC"
```

values
joe.values → *anArray*

Synonym for `to_a`.

Struct

Class Struct::Tms < Struct

This structure is returned by `Time.times`. It holds information on process times on those platforms that support it. Not all values are valid on all platforms.

This structure contains the following instance variables and the corresponding accessors:

`utime`	Amount of User CPU time, in seconds
`stime`	Amount of System CPU time, in seconds
`cutime`	Completed child processes' User CPU time, in seconds (always 0 on Windows NT)
`cstime`	Completed child processes' System CPU time, in seconds (always 0 on Windows NT)

See also `Struct` on page 385 and `Time.times` on page 398.

```
t = Time.times
[ t.utime, t.stime]        →    [0.02, 0.0]
[ t.cutime, t.cstime ]     →    [0.0, 0.0]
```

Class Symbol < Object

A `Symbol` object represents a Ruby name and is generated automatically using the `:name` literal syntax. The same `Symbol` object will be created for a given name string for the duration of a program's execution, regardless of the context or meaning of that name. Thus if `Fred` is a constant in one context, a method in another, and a class in a third, the `Symbol` `:Fred` will be the same object in all three contexts.

```
module One
  class Fred
  end
  $f1 = :Fred
end
module Two
  Fred = 1
  $f2 = :Fred
end
def Fred()
end
$f3 = :Fred
$f1.id   →   2286862
$f2.id   →   2286862
$f3.id   →   2286862
```

Symbol

Instance methods

id2name
sym.id2name → *aString*

Returns the name corresponding to *sym*.

```
:fred.id2name   →   "fred"
```

inspect
sym.inspect → *aString*

Returns the representation of *sym* as a symbol literal.

```
:fred.inspect   →   ":fred"
```

to_i
sym.to_i → *aFixnum*

Returns an integer that is unique for each symbol within a particular execution of a program.

to_s
sym.to_s → *aString*

Synonym for `Symbol#id2name`.

Class **Thread** < Object

`Thread` encapsulates the behavior of a thread of execution, including the main thread of the Ruby script. See the tutorial in Chapter 11, beginning on page 113.

In the descriptions that follow, the parameter *aSymbol* refers to a symbol, which is either a quoted string or a `Symbol` (such as `:name`).

Class methods

abort_on_exception
Thread.abort_on_exception → `true` or `false`

Returns the status of the global "abort on exception" condition. The default is `false`. When set to `true`, will cause all threads to abort (the process will `exit(0)`) if an exception is raised in any thread. See also `Thread.abort_on_exception=`.

abort_on_exception=
Thread.abort_on_exception= *aBoolean*→ `true` or `false`

When set to `true`, all threads will abort if an exception is raised. Returns the new state.

```
Thread.abort_on_exception = true
t1 = Thread.new do
  puts "In second thread"
  raise "Raise exception"
end
t1.join
print "not reached\n"
```

produces:

```
In second thread
prog.rb:4: Raise exception (RuntimeError)
from prog.rb:2:in `initialize'
from prog.rb:2:in `new'
from prog.rb:2
```

---

critical   Thread.critical → `true` or `false`

Returns the status of the global "thread critical" condition.

---

critical=   Thread.critical= *aBoolean* → `true` or `false`

Sets the status of the global "thread critical" condition and returns it. When set to `true`, prohibits scheduling of any existing thread. Does not block new threads from being created and run. Certain thread operations (such as stopping or killing a thread, sleeping in the current thread, and raising an exception) may cause a thread to be scheduled even when in a critical section.

```
count=0
Thread.new { while true; sleep(1); print "a "; count+=1; end }
while count < 3 do end # no-op wait
Thread.critical = true
puts "no more a's will come out."
```

produces:

```
a a a no more a's will come out.
```

---

current   Thread.current → *aThread*

Returns the currently executing thread.

```
Thread.current    →    #<Thread:0x401935c8 run>
```

---

exit   Thread.exit

Terminates the currently running thread and schedules another thread to be run. If this thread is already marked to be killed, `exit` returns the **Thread**. If this is the main thread, or the last thread, exit the process.

---

fork   Thread.fork { *block* } → *aThread*

Synonym for `Thread.new`.

---

kill   Thread.kill(*aThread*)

Causes the given thread to exit (see `Thread.exit`).

```
count = 0
a = Thread.new { while true do  count += 1 end }
sleep(1)            →    1
Thread.kill(a)      →    nil
count               →    892796
a.alive?            →    false
```

---

list   Thread.list → *anArray*

Returns an array of **Thread** objects for all threads that are either runnable or stopped.

```
Thread.new { sleep(200) }
Thread.new { 1000000.times {|i| i*i } }
Thread.new { Thread.stop }
l = Thread.list
l    →   [#<Thread:0x401757d0 sleep>, #<Thread:0x4018a824 run>,
          #<Thread:0x4018a860 sleep>, #<Thread:0x401935c8 run>]
```

---

main   Thread.main → *aThread*

Returns the main thread for the process.

```
Thread.main   →   #<Thread:0x401935c8 run>
```

---

new   Thread.new(⟨ *arg* ⟩*) {| *args* | *block* } → *aThread*

Creates a new thread to execute the instructions given in *block*, and begins running it. Any arguments passed to **Thread.new** are passed into the block.

```
x = Thread.new { sleep .1; print "x"; print "y"; print "z" }
a = Thread.new { print "a"; print "b"; sleep .2; print "c" }
x.join # Let the threads finish before
a.join # main thread exits...
```

produces:

```
abxyzc
```

---

pass   Thread.pass

Invokes the thread scheduler to pass execution to another thread.

```
a = Thread.new { print "a"; Thread.pass;
                 print "b"; Thread.pass;
                 print "c" }
b = Thread.new { print "x"; Thread.pass;
                 print "y"; Thread.pass;
                 print "z" }
a.join
b.join
```

produces:

```
axbycz
```

---

start   Thread.start(⟨ *args* ⟩*) {| *args* | *block* } → *aThread*

Basically the same as `Thread.new`. However, if class `Thread` is subclassed, then calling `start` in that subclass will not invoke the subclass's `initialize` method.

---

stop   Thread.stop

Stops execution of the current thread, putting it into a "sleep" state, and schedules execution of another thread. Resets the "critical" condition to `false`.

```
a = Thread.new { print "a"; Thread.stop; print "c" }
Thread.pass
print "b"
a.run
a.join
```

produces:

```
abc
```

Instance methods

[ ]   *thr*[*aSymbol*] → *anObject* or `nil`

Attribute Reference—Returns the value of a thread-local variable, using either a symbol or a string name. If the specified variable does not exist, returns `nil`.

```
a = Thread.new { Thread.current["name"] = "A"; Thread.stop }
b = Thread.new { Thread.current[:name]  = "B"; Thread.stop }
c = Thread.new { Thread.current["name"] = "C"; Thread.stop }
Thread.list.each {|x| print x.inspect, x[:name], "\n" }
```

produces:

```
#<Thread:0x4018a540 sleep>C
#<Thread:0x4018a590 sleep>B
#<Thread:0x4018a5f4 sleep>A
#<Thread:0x401935c8 run>nil
```

[ ]=   *thr*[*aSymbol*] = *anObject* → *anObject*

Attribute Assignment—Sets or creates the value of a thread-local variable, using either a symbol or a string. See also `Thread#[]`.

---

abort_on_exception   *thr*.abort_on_exception → `true` or `false`

Returns the status of the "abort on exception" condition for *thr*. The default is `false`. See also `Thread.abort_on_exception=`.

---

abort_on_exception=   *thr*.abort_on_exception= `true` or `false` → `true` or `false`

When set to `true`, causes all threads (including the main program) to abort if an exception is raised in *thr*. The process will effectively `exit(0)`.

---

alive?   *thr*.alive? → `true` or `false`

Returns `true` if *thr* is running or sleeping.

```
Thread.current.alive?   →   true
```

---

exit   *thr*.exit → *thr* or `nil`

Terminates *thr* and schedules another thread to be run. If this thread is already marked
to be killed, `exit` returns the `Thread`. If this is the main thread, or the last thread, exits
the process.

---

join   *thr*.join → *thr*

The calling thread will suspend execution and run *thr*. Does not return until *thr* exits.
Any threads not joined will be killed when the main program exits.

```
a = Thread.new { print "a"; sleep(10); print "b"; print "c" }
x = Thread.new { print "x"; Thread.pass; print "y"; print "z" }
x.join # Let x thread finish, a will be killed on exit.
```

produces:

```
axyz
```

---

key?   *thr*.key?(*aSymbol*) → `true` or `false`

Returns `true` if the given string (or symbol) exists as a thread-local variable.

```
me = Thread.current
me[:oliver] = "a"
me.key?(:oliver)   →   true
me.key?(:stanley)  →   false
```

---

kill   *thr*.kill

Synonym for `Thread#exit`.

---

priority   *thr*.priority → *anInteger*

Returns the priority of *thr*. Default is zero; higher-priority threads will run before lower-
priority threads.

```
Thread.current.priority   →   0
```

---

priority=   *thr*.priority= *anInteger* → *thr*

Sets the priority of *thr* to *anInteger*. Higher-priority threads will run before lower-
priority threads.

```
count1 = count2 = 0
a = Thread.new do
      loop { count1 += 1 }
    end
```

Thread

```
a.priority = -1
b = Thread.new do
      loop { count2 += 1 }
    end
b.priority = -2
sleep 1    →    1
Thread.critical = 1
count1    →    620815
count2    →    6183
```

raise

thr.raise(anException)

Raises an exception (see `Kernel.raise` on page 424 for details) from *thr*. The caller does not have to be *thr*.

```
Thread.abort_on_exception = true
a = Thread.new { sleep(200) }
a.raise("Gotcha")
```

produces:

```
prog.rb:3: Gotcha (RuntimeError)
from prog.rb:2:in `initialize'
from prog.rb:2:in `new'
from prog.rb:2
```

run

thr.run → thr

Wakes up *thr*, making it eligible for scheduling. If not in a critical section, then invokes the scheduler.

```
a = Thread.new { puts "a"; Thread.stop; puts "c" }
Thread.pass
puts "Got here"
a.run
a.join
```

produces:

```
a
Got here
c
```

safe_level

thr.safe_level → anInteger

Returns the safe level in effect for *thr*.

```
Thread.current.safe_level    →    0
```

status

thr.status → aString, false or nil

Returns the status of *thr*: "sleep" if *thr* is sleeping or waiting on I/O, "run" if *thr* is executing, false if *thr* terminated normally, and nil if *thr* terminated with an exception.

```
a = Thread.new { raise("die now") }
b = Thread.new { Thread.stop }
c = Thread.new { Thread.exit }
a.status                →    nil
b.status                →    "sleep"
c.status                →    false
Thread.current.status   →    "run"
```

---

stop?   *thr*.stop? → true or false

Returns **true** if *thr* is dead or sleeping.

```
a = Thread.new { Thread.stop }
b = Thread.current
a.stop?   →   true
b.stop?   →   false
```

---

value   *thr*.value → *anObject*

Waits for *thr* to complete (via **Thread#join**) and returns its value.

```
a = Thread.new { 2+2 }
a.value   →   4
```

---

wakeup   *thr*.wakeup → *thr*

Marks *thr* as eligible for scheduling (it may still remain blocked on I/O, however). Does not invoke the scheduler (see **Thread#run**).

```
c = Thread.new { Thread.stop; puts "hey!" }
c.wakeup
```

produces:

```
hey!
```

Thread

Class **ThreadGroup** < Object

ThreadGroup provides a means of keeping track of a number of threads as a group. A **Thread** can belong to only one **ThreadGroup** at a time; adding a thread to a new group will remove it from any previous group.

Newly created threads belong to the same group as the thread from which they were created.

ThreadGroup constants

Default   Default thread group.

Class methods

new   ThreadGroup.new → *thgrp*

Returns a newly created **ThreadGroup**. The group is initially empty.

Instance methods

add   *thgrp*.add(*aThread*) → *thgrp*

Adds the given thread to this group, removing it from any other group to which it may have previously belonged.

```
puts "Initial group is #{ThreadGroup::Default.list}"
tg = ThreadGroup.new
t1 = Thread.new { sleep 10 }
t2 = Thread.new { sleep 10 }
puts "t1 is #{t1}"
puts "t2 is #{t2}"
tg.add( t1 )
puts "Initial group now #{ThreadGroup::Default.list}"
puts "tg group now #{tg.list}"
```

produces:

```
Initial group is #<Thread:0x401935c8>
t1 is #<Thread:0x4018a554>
t2 is #<Thread:0x4018a518>
Initial group now #<Thread:0x4018a518>#<Thread:0x401935c8>
tg group now #<Thread:0x4018a554>
```

list   *thgrp*.list → *anArray*

Returns an array of all existing **Thread** objects that belong to this group.

```
ThreadGroup::Default.list   →   [#<Thread:0x401935c8 run>]
```

`Time` is an abstraction of dates and times. Time is stored internally as the number of seconds and microseconds since the *epoch*, January 1, 1970 00:00 UTC. Also see the library modules `Date` and `ParseDate`, documented beginning on pages 443 and 457, respectively.

The `Time` class treats GMT (Greenwich Mean Time) and UTC (Coordinated Universal Time)[2] as equivalent. GMT is the older way of referring to these baseline times but persists in the names of calls on Posix systems.

All times are stored with some number of microseconds. Be aware of this fact when comparing times with each other—times that are apparently equal when displayed may be different when compared.

Mixes in

```
Comparable:
    <, <=, ==, >=, >, between?
```

Class methods

at

$$\text{Time.at(} aTime \text{)} \rightarrow aTime$$
$$\text{Time.at(} seconds \ \langle , microseconds \rangle \text{)} \rightarrow aTime$$

Creates a new time object with the value given by *aTime*, or the given number of *seconds* (and optional *microseconds*) from epoch.

```
Time.at(0)          →   Wed Dec 31 18:00:00 CST 1969
Time.at(946702800)  →   Fri Dec 31 23:00:00 CST 1999
```

gm

$$\text{Time.gm(} year \ \langle , month, day, hour, min, sec, usec \rangle \text{)} \rightarrow aTime$$
$$\text{Time.gm(} sec, min, hour, day, month, year, wday, yday, isdst, tz \text{)} \rightarrow aTime$$

Creates a time based on given values, interpreted as UTC (GMT). The year must be specified. Other values default to the minimum value for that field (and may be `nil` or omitted). Months may be specified by numbers from 1 to 12, or by the three-letter English month names. Hours are specified on a 24-hour clock (0..23). Raises an `ArgumentError` if any values are out of range. Will also accept ten arguments in the order output by `Time#to_a`.

```
Time.gm(2000,"jan",1,20,15,1)   →   Sat Jan 01 20:15:01 UTC 2000
```

---

2. Yes, UTC really does stand for Coordinated Universal Time. There was a committee involved.

local

> Time.local(*year* 〈 *, month, day, hour, min, sec, usec* 〉) → *aTime*
> Time.local(*sec, min, hour, day, month, year, wday, yday, isdst, tz*) → *aTime*

Same as `Time.gm`, but interprets the values in the local time zone.

```
Time.local(2000,"jan",1,20,15,1)   →   Sat Jan 01 20:15:01 CST 2000
```

mktime

> Time.mktime(*year, month, day, hour, min, sec, usec*) → *aTime*

Synonym for `Time.local`.

new

> Time.new → *aTime*

Returns a `Time` object initialized to the current system time. **Note:** The object created will be created using the resolution available on your system clock, and so may include fractional seconds.

```
a = Time.new        →   Wed Sep 20 10:35:29 CDT 2000
b = Time.new        →   Wed Sep 20 10:35:29 CDT 2000
a == b              →   false
"%.6f" % a.to_f     →   "969464129.197427"
"%.6f" % b.to_f     →   "969464129.197973"
```

now

> Time.now → *aTime*

Synonym for `Time.new`.

times

> Time.times → *aStructTms*

Returns a `Tms` structure (see `Struct::Tms` on page 388) that contains user and system CPU times for this process.

```
t = Time.times
[ t.utime, t.stime ]   →   [0.01, 0.0]
```

utc

> Time.utc(*year* 〈 *, month, day, hour, min, sec, usec* 〉) → *aTime*
> Time.utc(*sec, min, hour, day, month, year, wday, yday, isdst, tz*) → *aTime*

Synonym for `Time.gm`.

```
Time.utc(2000,"jan",1,20,15,1)   →   Sat Jan 01 20:15:01 UTC 2000
```

Instance methods

+

> *time* + *aNumeric* → *aTime*

Addition—Adds some number of seconds (possibly fractional) to *time* and returns that value as a new time.

```
t = Time.now        →   Wed Sep 20 10:35:29 CDT 2000
t + (60 * 60 * 24)  →   Thu Sep 21 10:35:29 CDT 2000
```

> *time - aTime → aFloat*
> *time - aNumeric → aTime*

Difference—Returns a new time that represents the difference between two times, or subtracts the given number of seconds in *aNumeric* from *time*.

```
t = Time.now      →   Wed Sep 20 10:35:29 CDT 2000
t2 = t + 2592000  →   Fri Oct 20 10:35:29 CDT 2000
t2 - t            →   2592000.0
t2 - 2592000      →   Wed Sep 20 10:35:29 CDT 2000
```

<=>
> *time <=> anOtherTime → −1, 0, +1*
> *time <=> aNumeric → −1, 0, +1*

Comparison—Compares *time* with *anOtherTime* or with *aNumeric*, which is the number of seconds (possibly fractional) since epoch.

```
t = Time.now      →   Wed Sep 20 10:35:29 CDT 2000
t2 = t + 2592000  →   Fri Oct 20 10:35:29 CDT 2000
t <=> t2          →   -1
t2 <=> t          →   1
t <=> t           →   0
```

---

asctime
> *time*.asctime → *aString*

Returns a canonical string representation of *time*.

```
Time.now.asctime   →   "Wed Sep 20 10:35:29 2000"
```

---

ctime
> *time*.ctime → *aString*

Synonym for `Time#asctime`.

---

day
> *time*.day → *aFixnum*

Returns the day of the month (1..*n*) for *time*.

```
t = Time.now   →   Wed Sep 20 10:35:29 CDT 2000
t.day          →   20
```

---

gmt?
> *time*.gmt? → **true** or **false**

Returns **true** if *time* represents a time in UTC (GMT).

```
t = Time.now                     →   Wed Sep 20 10:35:29 CDT 2000
t.gmt?                           →   false
t = Time.gm(2000,"jan",1,20,15,1) →   Sat Jan 01 20:15:01 UTC 2000
t.gmt?                           →   true
```

---

gmtime
> *time*.gmtime → *time*

Converts *time* to UTC (GMT), modifying the receiver.

ime

```
t = Time.now      →    Wed Sep 20 10:35:29 CDT 2000
t.gmt?            →    false
t.gmtime          →    Wed Sep 20 15:35:29 UTC 2000
t.gmt?            →    true
```

hour

time.hour → aFixnum

Returns the hour of the day (0..23) for *time*.

```
t = Time.now      →    Wed Sep 20 10:35:29 CDT 2000
t.hour            →    10
```

isdst

time.isdst → true or false

Returns **true** if *time* occurs during Daylight Saving Time in its time zone.

```
t  = Time.local(2000, 7, 1)   →    Sat Jul 01 00:00:00 CDT 2000
t.isdst                       →    true
t2 = Time.local(2000, 1, 1)   →    Sat Jan 01 00:00:00 CST 2000
t2.isdst                      →    false
```

localtime

time.localtime → time

Converts *time* to local time (using the local time zone in effect for this process) modifying the receiver.

```
t = Time.gm(2000, "jan", 1, 20, 15, 1)
t.gmt?            →    true
t.localtime       →    Sat Jan 01 14:15:01 CST 2000
t.gmt?            →    false
```

mday

time.mday → aFixnum

Synonym for Time#day.

min

time.min → aFixnum

Returns the minute of the hour (0..59) for *time*.

```
t = Time.now      →    Wed Sep 20 10:35:29 CDT 2000
t.min             →    35
```

mon

time.mon → aFixnum

Returns the month of the year (1..12) for *time*.

```
t = Time.now      →    Wed Sep 20 10:35:29 CDT 2000
t.mon             →    9
```

month

time.month → aFixnum

Synonym for Time#mon.

sec   *time*.sec → *aFixnum*

Returns the second of the minute $(0..60)^3$ for *time*.

```
t = Time.now   →   Wed Sep 20 10:35:29 CDT 2000
t.sec          →   29
```

strftime   *time*.strftime(*aString*) → *aString*

Formats *time* according to the directives in the given format string. See Table 22.9 on the next page for the available values. Any text not listed as a directive will be passed through to the output string.

```
t = Time.now
t.strftime("Printed on %m/%d/%Y")   →   "Printed on 09/20/2000"
t.strftime("at %I:%M%p")            →   "at 10:35AM"
```

to_a   *time*.to_a → *anArray*

Returns a ten-element *anArray* of values for *time*: [sec, min, hour, day, month, year, wday, yday, isdst, zone]. See the individual methods for an explanation of the valid ranges of each value. The ten elements can be passed directly to Time.utc or Time.local to create a new Time.

```
now = Time.now   →   Wed Sep 20 10:35:29 CDT 2000
t = now.to_a     →   [29, 35, 10, 20, 9, 2000, 3, 264, true, "CDT"]
```

to_f   *time*.to_f → *aFloat*

Returns the value of *time* as a floating point number of seconds since epoch.

```
t = Time.now
"%10.5f" % t.to_f   →   "969464129.71943"
t.to_i              →   969464129
```

to_i   *time*.to_i → *anInteger*

Returns the value of *time* as an integer number of seconds since epoch.

```
t = Time.now
"%10.5f" % t.to_f   →   "969464129.74653"
t.to_i              →   969464129
```

to_s   *time*.to_s → *aString*

Returns a string representing *time*. Equivalent to calling Time#strftime with a format string of "%a %b %d %H:%M:%S %Z %Y".

```
Time.now.to_s   →   "Wed Sep 20 10:35:29 CDT 2000"
```

---

3. Yes, seconds really can range from zero to 60. This allows the system to inject leap seconds every now and then to correct for the fact that years are not really a convenient number of hours long.

Table 22.9. `Time#strftime` directives

Format	Meaning
%a	The abbreviated weekday name ("Sun")
%A	The full weekday name ("Sunday")
%b	The abbreviated month name ("Jan")
%B	The full month name ("January")
%c	The preferred local date and time representation
%d	Day of the month (01..31)
%H	Hour of the day, 24-hour clock (00..23)
%I	Hour of the day, 12-hour clock (01..12)
%j	Day of the year (001..366)
%m	Month of the year (01..12)
%M	Minute of the hour (00..59)
%p	Meridian indicator ("AM" or "PM")
%S	Second of the minute (00..60)
%U	Week number of the current year, starting with the first Sunday as the first day of the first week (00..53)
%W	Week number of the current year, starting with the first Monday as the first day of the first week (00..53)
%w	Day of the week (Sunday is 0, 0..6)
%x	Preferred representation for the date alone, no time
%X	Preferred representation for the time alone, no date
%y	Year without a century (00..99)
%Y	Year with century
%Z	Time zone name
%%	Literal "%" character

Time

---

tv_sec   *time*.tv_sec → *anInteger*

Synonym for `Time#to_i`.

---

tv_usec   *time*.tv_usec → *anInteger*

Synonym for `Time#usec`.

---

usec   *time*.usec → *anInteger*

Returns just the number of microseconds for *time*.

```
t = Time.now          →    Wed Sep 20 10:35:29 CDT 2000
"%10.6f" % t.to_f     →    "969464129.802889"
t.usec                →    802889
```

---

utc   *time*.utc → *time*

Synonym for `Time#gmtime`.

```
t = Time.now   →   Wed Sep 20 10:35:29 CDT 2000
t.utc?         →   false
t.utc          →   Wed Sep 20 15:35:29 UTC 2000
t.utc?         →   true
```

---

utc?   *time*.utc? → `true` or `false`

Returns `true` if *time* represents a time in UTC (GMT).

```
t = Time.now                    →   Wed Sep 20 10:35:29 CDT 2000
t.utc?                          →   false
t = Time.gm(2000,"jan",1,20,15,1)   →   Sat Jan 01 20:15:01 UTC 2000
t.utc?                          →   true
```

---

wday   *time*.wday → *aFixnum*

Returns an integer representing the day of the week, 0..6, with Sunday == 0.

```
t = Time.now   →   Wed Sep 20 10:35:29 CDT 2000
t.wday         →   3
```

---

yday   *time*.yday → *aFixnum*

Returns an integer representing the day of the year, 1..366.

```
t = Time.now   →   Wed Sep 20 10:35:29 CDT 2000
t.yday         →   264
```

---

year   *time*.year → *aFixnum*

Returns the year for *time* (including the century).

```
t = Time.now   →   Wed Sep 20 10:35:29 CDT 2000
t.year         →   2000
```

---

zone   *time*.zone → *aString*

Returns the name of the time zone used for *time*.

```
t = Time.gm(2000, "jan", 1, 20, 15, 1)
t.zone   →   "GMT"
t = Time.local(2000, "jan", 1, 20, 15, 1)
t.zone   →   "CST"
```

Class **TrueClass** < Object

The global value **true** is the only instance of class **TrueClass** and represents a logically true value in boolean expressions. The class provides operators allowing **true** to be used in logical expressions.

Instance methods

&

$$\text{\textbf{true} \& } anObject \rightarrow anObject$$

And—Returns **false** if *anObject* is **nil** or **false**, **true** otherwise.

^

$$\text{\textbf{true} ^ } anObject \rightarrow !anObject$$

Exclusive Or—Returns **true** if *anObject* is **nil** or **false**, **false** otherwise.

|

$$\text{\textbf{true} | } anObject \rightarrow \text{\textbf{true}}$$

Or—Returns **true**. As *anObject* is an argument to a method call, it is always evaluated; there is no short-circuit evaluation in this case.

```
true |  puts("or")
true || puts("logical or")
```

produces:

```
or
```

## Chapter 23

Built-in Modules

This chapter lists the modules built in to the Ruby system.

Alphabetical Listing

Comparable (page 406): *Instance:* Comparisons, between?.

Enumerable (page 407): *Instance:* collect, detect, each_with_index, entries, find, find_all, grep, include?, map, max, member?, min, reject, select, sort, to_a.

Errno (page 410)

FileTest (page 411)

GC (page 414): *Class:* disable, enable, start. *Instance:* garbage_collect.

Kernel (page 415): *Class:* Array, Float, Integer, String, ` (backquote), abort, at_exit, autoload, binding, block_given?, callcc, caller, catch, chomp, chomp!, chop, chop!, eval, exec, exit, exit!, fail, fork, format, gets, global_variables, gsub, gsub!, iterator?, lambda, load, local_variables, loop, open, p, print, printf, proc, putc, puts, raise, rand, readline, readlines, require, scan, select, set_trace_func, singleton_method_added, sleep, split, sprintf, srand, sub, sub!, syscall, system, test, throw, trace_var, trap, untrace_var.

Marshal (page 432): *Class:* dump, load, restore.

Math (page 433): *Class:* atan2, cos, exp, frexp, ldexp, log, log10, sin, sqrt, tan.

ObjectSpace (page 434): *Class:* _id2ref, define_finalizer, each_object, garbage_collect, undefine_finalizer.

Process (page 435): *Class:* egid, egid=, euid, euid=, exit!, fork, getpgid, getpgrp, getpriority, gid, gid=, kill, pid, ppid, setpgid, setpgrp, setpriority, setsid, uid, uid=, wait, wait2, waitpid, waitpid2.

Module	
Comparable	

Relies on: <=>

The `Comparable` mixin is used by classes whose objects may be ordered. The class must define the <=> operator, which compares the receiver against another object, returning −1, 0, or +1 depending on whether the receiver is less than, equal to, or greater than the other object. `Comparable` uses <=> to implement the conventional comparison operators (<, <=, ==, >=, and >) and the method `between?`.

```
class SizeMatters
  include Comparable
  attr :str
  def <=>(anOther)
    str.size <=> anOther.str.size
  end
  def initialize(str)
    @str = str
  end
  def inspect
    @str
  end
end

s1 = SizeMatters.new("Z")
s2 = SizeMatters.new("YY")
s3 = SizeMatters.new("XXX")
s4 = SizeMatters.new("WWWW")
s5 = SizeMatters.new("VVVVV")

s1 < s2                      →    true
s4.between?(s1, s3)          →    false
s4.between?(s3, s5)          →    true
[ s3, s2, s5, s4, s1 ].sort  →    [Z, YY, XXX, WWWW, VVVVV]
```

Instance methods

Comparisons

$anObject < otherObject$ → **true** or **false**
$anObject <= otherObject$ → **true** or **false**
$anObject == otherObject$ → **true** or **false**
$anObject >= otherObject$ → **true** or **false**
$anObject > otherObject$ → **true** or **false**

Compares two objects based on the receiver's <=> method.

between?

$anObject$.between?(min, max) → **true** or **false**

Returns **false** if *anObject* <=> *min* is less than zero or if *anObject* <=> *max* is greater than zero, **true** otherwise.

```
3.between?(1, 5)              →   true
6.between?(1, 5)              →   false
'cat'.between?('ant', 'dog')  →   true
'gnu'.between?('ant', 'dog')  →   false
```

Module **Enumerable**

Relies on: each, <=>

The `Enumerable` mixin provides collection classes with several traversal and searching methods, and with the ability to sort. The class must provide a method `each`, which yields successive members of the collection. If `Enumerable#max`, `#min`, or `#sort` is used, the objects in the collection must also implement a meaningful <=> operator, as these methods rely on an ordering between members of the collection.

Instance methods

collect   *enumObj*.collect { | *obj* | *block* } → *anArray*

Returns a new array with the results of running *block* once for every element in *enumObj*.

```
(1..4).collect {|i| i*i }  →  [1, 4, 9, 16]
(1..4).collect { "cat" }   →  ["cat", "cat", "cat", "cat"]
```

detect   *enumObj*.detect { | *obj* | *block* } → *anObject* or `nil`

Passes each entry in *enumObj* to *block*. Returns the first for which *block* is not `false`. Returns `nil` if no object matches.

```
(1..10).detect  {|i| i % 5 == 0 and i % 7 == 0 }  →  nil
(1..100).detect {|i| i % 5 == 0 and i % 7 == 0 }  →  35
```

each_with_index   *enumObj*.each_with_index { | *obj, i* | *block* } → `nil`

Calls *block* with two arguments, the item and its index, for each item in *enumObj*.

```
hash = Hash.new
%w(cat dog wombat).each_with_index {|item, index|
  hash[item] = index
}
hash   →   {"dog"=>1, "wombat"=>2, "cat"=>0}
```

entries   *enumObj*.entries → *anArray*

Synonym for `Enumerable#to_a`.

find   *enumObj*.find { | *obj* | *block* } → *anObject* or `nil`

Synonym for `Enumerable#detect`.

---

find_all   *enumObj*.find_all { | *obj* | *block* } → *anArray*

Returns an array containing all elements of *enumObj* for which *block* is not `false` (see also `Enumerable#reject`).

```
(1..10).find_all {|i|  i % 3 == 0 }   →   [3, 6, 9]
```

---

grep   *enumObj*.grep(*pattern*) → *anArray*
                              enumObj.grep(*pattern*) { | *obj* | *block* } → *anArray*

Returns an array of every element in *enumObj* for which `Pattern === element`. If the optional *block* is supplied, each matching element is passed to it, and the block's result is stored in the output array.

```
(1..100).grep 38..44   →   [38, 39, 40, 41, 42, 43, 44]
c = IO.constants
c.grep(/SEEK/)         →   ["SEEK_END", "SEEK_CUR", "SEEK_SET"]
res = c.grep(/SEEK/) {|v| IO.const_get(v) }
res                    →   [2, 1, 0]
```

---

include?   *enumObj*.include?(*anObject*) → `true` or `false`

Returns `true` if any member of *enumObj* equals *anObject*. Equality is tested using ==.

```
IO.constants.include? "SEEK_SET"         →   true
IO.constants.include? "SEEK_NO_FURTHER"  →   false
```

---

map   *enumObj*.map { | *obj* | *block* } → *anArray*

Synonym for `Enumerable#collect`.

---

max   *enumObj*.max → *anObject*
                                    enumObj.max { | *a,b* | *block* } → *anObject*

Returns the object in *enumObj* with the maximum value. The first form assumes all objects implement `Comparable`; the second uses the block to return *a* <=> *b*.

```
a = %w(albatross dog horse)
a.max                                 →   "horse"
a.max {|a,b| a.length <=> b.length }  →   "albatross"
```

---

member?   *enumObj*.member?(*anObject*) → `true` or `false`

Synonym for `Enumerable#include?`.

---

min   *enumObj*.min → *anObject*
                                    enumObj.min { | *a,b* | *block* } → *anObject*

Returns the object in *enumObj* with the minimum value. The first form assumes all objects implement `Comparable`; the second uses the block to return *a* <=> *b*.

```
a = %w(albatross dog horse)
a.min                                →    "albatross"
a.min {|a,b| a.length <=> b.length } →    "dog"
```

---

reject   *enumObj*.reject { | *obj* | *block* } → *anArray*

Returns an array for all elements of *enumObj* for which *block* is `false` (see also **Enumerable#find_all**).

```
(1..10).reject {|i|  i % 3 == 0 }   →   [1, 2, 4, 5, 7, 8, 10]
```

---

select   *enumObj*.select { | *obj* | *block* } → *anArray*

Synonym for `Enumerable#find_all`.

---

sort   *enumObj*.sort → *anArray*
                                       enumObj.sort { | *a, b* | *block* } → *anArray*

Returns an array containing the items in *enumObj* sorted, either according to their own <=> method, or by using the results of the supplied block. The block should return −1, 0, or +1 depending on the comparison between *a* and *b*.

```
%w(rhea kea flea).sort      →   ["flea", "kea", "rhea"]
(1..10).sort {|a,b| b <=> a} →   [10, 9, 8, 7, 6, 5, 4, 3, 2, 1]
```

The following code sorts some files on modification time.

```
files = Dir["*"]
sorted = files.sort {|a,b| File.new(a).mtime <=> File.new(b).mtime}
sorted   →   ["mon", "tues", "wed", "thurs"]
```

This sort is inefficient: it generates two new `File` objects during every comparison. A slightly better technique is to use the `Kernel#test` method to generate the modification times directly.

```
files = Dir["*"]
sorted = files.sort { |a,b|
  test(?M, a) <=> test(?M, b)
}
sorted   →   ["mon", "tues", "wed", "thurs"]
```

This still generates many unnecessary `Time` objects. A more efficient technique is to cache the sort keys (modification times in this case) before the sort. Perl users often call this approach a Schwartzian Transform, after Randal Schwartz. We construct a temporary array, where each element is an array containing our sort key along with the filename. We sort this array, and then extract the filename from the result.

```
sorted = Dir["*"].collect { |f|
   [test(?M, f), f]
}.sort.collect { |f| f[1] }
sorted   →   ["mon", "tues", "wed", "thurs"]
```

to_a $\qquad$ *enumObj*.to_a → *anArray*

Returns an array containing the items in *enumObj*.

```
(1..7).to_a                        →    [1, 2, 3, 4, 5, 6, 7]
{ 'a'=>1, 'b'=>2, 'c'=>3 }.to_a    →    [["a", 1], ["b", 2], ["c", 3]]
```

Module Errno

Ruby exception objects are subclasses of `Exception`. However, operating systems typically report errors using plain integers. Module `Errno` is created dynamically to map these operating system errors to Ruby classes, with each error number generating its own subclass of `SystemCallError`. As the subclass is created in module `Errno`, its name will start `Errno::`.

```
Exception
    StandardError
        SystemCallError
            Errno::xxx
```

The names of the `Errno::` classes depend on the environment in which Ruby runs. On a typical Unix or Windows platform, there are `Errno` classes such as `Errno::EACCES`, `Errno::EAGAIN`, `Errno::EINTR`, and so on.

The integer operating system error number corresponding to a particular error is available as the class constant `Errno::`*error*`::Errno`.

```
Errno::EACCES::Errno    →    13
Errno::EAGAIN::Errno    →    11
Errno::EINTR::Errno     →    4
```

The full list of operating system errors on your particular platform are available as the constants of `Errno`.

```
Errno.constants    →    E2BIG, EACCES, EADDRINUSE, EADDRNOTAVAIL,
                        EADV, EAFNOSUPPORT, EAGAIN, ...
```

Module FileTest

`FileTest` implements file test operations similar to those used in `File::Stat`.

---

blockdev?   FileTest.blockdev?(*aString*) → true or false

Returns `true` if the named file is a block device, `false` if it isn't or if the operating system doesn't support this feature.

```
FileTest.blockdev?( "testfile" )   →   false
```

---

chardev?   FileTest.chardev?(*aString*) → true or false

Returns `true` if the named file is a character device, `false` if it isn't or if the operating system doesn't support this feature.

```
FileTest.chardev?( "/dev/tty" )   →   true
```

---

directory?   FileTest.directory?(*aString*) → true or false

Returns `true` if this named file is a directory, `false` otherwise.

```
FileTest.directory?( "." )   →   true
```

---

executable?   FileTest.executable?(*aString*) → true or false

Returns `true` if the named file is executable. The tests are made using the effective owner of the process.

```
FileTest.executable?( "testfile" )   →   false
```

---

executable_real?   FileTest.executable_real?(*aString*) → true or false

Same as `FileTest#executable?`, but tests using the real owner of the process.

---

exist?   FileTest.exist? (*aString*) → true or false

Returns `true` if the named file exists.

```
FileTest.exist?( "testfile" )   →   true
```

---

exists?   FileTest.exists? (*aString*) → true or false

Synonym for `FileTest.exist?`.

---

file?   FileTest.file?(*aString*) → true or false

Returns `true` if the named file is a regular file (not a device file, pipe, socket, etc.).

```
FileTest.file?( "testfile" )   →   true
```

grpowned?

FileTest.grpowned?(*aString*) → `true` or `false`

Returns `true` if the effective group id of the process is the same as the group id of the named file. On Windows NT, returns `false`.

```
FileTest.grpowned?( "/etc/passwd" )   →   false
```

owned?

FileTest.owned?(*aString*) → `true` or `false`

Returns `true` if the effective user id of the process is the same as the owner of the named file.

```
FileTest.owned?( "/etc/passwd" )   →   false
```

pipe?

FileTest.pipe?(*aString*) → `true` or `false`

Returns `true` if the operating system supports pipes and the named file is a pipe, `false` otherwise.

```
FileTest.pipe?( "testfile" )   →   false
```

readable?

FileTest.readable?(*aString*) → `true` or `false`

Returns `true` if the named file is readable by the effective user id of this process.

```
FileTest.readable?( "testfile" )   →   true
```

readable_real?

FileTest.readable_real?(*aString*) → `true` or `false`

Returns `true` if the named file is readable by the real user id of this process.

```
FileTest.readable_real?( "testfile" )   →   true
```

setgid?

FileTest.setgid?(*aString*) → `true` or `false`

Returns `true` if the named file's set-group-id permission bit is set, and `false` if it isn't or if the operating system doesn't support this feature.

```
FileTest.setgid?( "/usr/sbin/lpc" )   →   true
```

setuid?

FileTest.setuid?(*aString*) → `true` or `false`

Returns `true` if the named file's set-user-id permission bit is set, and `false` if it isn't or if the operating system doesn't support this feature.

```
FileTest.setuid?( "/bin/su" )   →   true
```

size

FileTest.size(*aString*) → *anInteger*

Returns the size of the named file in bytes.

```
FileTest.size( "testfile" )   →   66
```

size?   FileTest.size?(*aString*) → *aFixnum* or `nil`

Returns `nil` if the named file is of zero length; otherwise, returns a nonzero *aFixnum*.

```
FileTest.size?( "testfile" )   →   66
FileTest.size?( "/dev/zero" )  →   nil
```

---

socket?   FileTest.socket?(*aString*) → `true` or `false`

Returns `true` if the named file is a socket, `false` if it isn't or if the operating system doesn't support this feature.

---

sticky?   FileTest.sticky?(*aString*) → `true` or `false`

Returns `true` if the named file has its sticky bit set, `false` if it doesn't or if the operating system doesn't support this feature.

---

symlink?   FileTest.symlink?(*aString*) → `true` or `false`

Returns `true` if the named file is a symbolic link, `false` if it isn't or if the operating system doesn't support this feature.

---

writable?   FileTest.writable?(*aString*) → `true` or `false`

Returns `true` if the named file is writable by the effective user id of this process.

---

writable_real?   FileTest.writable_real?(*aString*) → `true` or `false`

Returns `true` if the named file is writable by the real user id of this process.

---

zero?   FileTest.zero?(*aString*) → `true` or `false`

Returns `true` if the named file is of zero length, `false` otherwise.

| Module | GC |

The GC module provides an interface to Ruby's mark and sweep garbage collection mechanism. Some of the underlying methods are also available via the ObjectSpace module, described beginning on page 434.

Module methods

disable
GC.disable → true or false

Disables garbage collection, returning true if garbage collection was already disabled.

```
GC.disable   →   false
GC.disable   →   true
```

enable
GC.enable → true or false

Enables garbage collection, returning true if garbage collection was disabled.

```
GC.disable   →   false
GC.enable    →   true
GC.enable    →   false
```

start
GC.start → nil

Initiates garbage collection, unless manually disabled.

```
GC.start   →   nil
```

Instance methods

garbage_collect
garbage_collect → nil

Equivalent to GC.start.

```
include GC
garbage_collect   →   nil
```

Module Kernel

The Kernel module is included by class Object, so its methods are available in every Ruby object. The Kernel instance methods are documented in class Object beginning on page 356. This section documents the module methods. These methods are called without a receiver and thus can be called in functional form.

Module methods

Array <div align="right">Array(*arg*) → *anArray*</div>

Returns *arg*.to_a.

```
Array(1..5)   →   [1, 2, 3, 4, 5]
```

Float <div align="right">Float(*arg*) → *aFloat*</div>

Returns *arg* converted to a float. Numeric types are converted directly, nil is converted to 0.0, and the rest are converted using *arg*.to_f.

```
Float(1)         →    1.0
Float(nil)       →    0.0
Float("123.456") →    123.456
```

Integer <div align="right">Integer(*arg*) → *anInteger*</div>

Converts *arg* to a Fixnum or Bignum. Numeric types are converted directly (with floating point numbers being truncated). If *arg* is a String, leading radix indicators (0, 0b, and 0x) are honored. This behavior is different from that of String#to_i.

```
Integer(123.999)  →    123
Integer("0x1a")   →    26
Integer(Time.new) →    969464130
```

String <div align="right">String(*arg*) → *aString*</div>

Converts *arg* to a String by calling its to_s method.

```
String(self)      →    "main"
String(self.type) →    "Object"
String(123456)    →    "123456"
```

**` (backquote)** <div align="right">`cmd` → *aString*</div>

Returns the standard output of running *cmd* in a subshell. The built-in syntax %x{...} described on page 75 uses this method.

```
`date`                →    "Wed Sep 20 10:35:30 CDT 2000\n"
`ls testdir`.split[1] →    "main.rb"
```

abort

abort

Terminate execution immediately, effectively by calling `Kernel.exit(1)`.

at_exit

at_exit { block } → aProc

Converts *block* to a `Proc` object (and therefore binds it at the point of call) and registers it for execution when the program exits. If multiple handlers are registered, they are executed in reverse order of registration.

```
def do_at_exit(str1)
  at_exit { print str1 }
end
at_exit { puts "cruel world" }
do_at_exit("goodbye ")
exit
```

produces:

```
goodbye cruel world
```

autoload

autoload(aModule, aFile) → <tt>nil</tt>

Registers *aFile* to be loaded (using `Kernel.require`) the first time that *aModule* (which may be a `String` or a symbol) is accessed.

```
autoload :MyModule, "/usr/local/lib/modules/my_module.rb"
```

binding

binding → aBinding

Returns a `Binding` object, describing the variable and method bindings at the point of call. This object can be used when calling `eval` to execute the evaluated command in this environment. Also see the description of `Binding` beginning on page 295.

```
def getBinding(param)
  return binding
end
b = getBinding("hello")
eval "param", b   →   "hello"
```

block_given?

block_given? → <tt>true</tt> or <tt>false</tt>

Returns `true` if `yield` would execute a block in the current context.

```
def try
  if block_given?
    yield
  else
    "no block"
  end
end
try                →   "no block"
try { "hello" }    →   "hello"
try do "hello" end →   "hello"
```

callcc

callcc { | *cont* | *block* } → *anObject*

Generates a `Continuation` object, which it passes to the associated block. Performing a *cont*.`call` will cause the `callcc` to return (as will falling through the end of the block). The value returned by the `callcc` is the value of the block, or the value passed to *cont*.`call`. See `Continuation` on page 298 for more details. Also see `Kernel.throw` for an alternative mechanism for unwinding a call stack.

caller

caller(⟨ *anInteger* ⟩) → *anArray*

Returns the current execution stack—an array containing strings in the form "*file:line*" or "*file:line: in 'method'*". The optional *anInteger* parameter determines the number of initial stack entries to omit from the result.

```
def a(skip)
  caller(skip)
end
def b(skip)
  a(skip)
end
def c(skip)
  b(skip)
end
c(0)  →  ["prog:2:in `a'", "prog:5:in `b'", "prog:8:in `c'",
          "prog:10"]
c(1)  →  ["prog:5:in `b'", "prog:8:in `c'", "prog:11"]
c(2)  →  ["prog:8:in `c'", "prog:12"]
c(3)  →  ["prog:13"]
```

catch

catch(*symbol*) { *block* } → anObject

`catch` executes its block. If a `throw` is executed, Ruby searches up its stack for a `catch` block with a tag corresponding to the `throw`'s *symbol*. If found, that block is terminated, and `catch` returns the value given to `throw`. If `throw` is not called, the block terminates normally, and the value of `catch` is the value of the last expression evaluated. `catch` expressions may be nested, and the `throw` call need not be in lexical scope.

```
def routine(n)
  puts n
  throw :done if n <= 0
  routine(n-1)
end

catch(:done) { routine(3) }
```

produces:

```
3
2
1
0
```

K ernel

chomp

chomp(⟨ *aString* ⟩) → $_ or *aString*

Equivalent to `$_ = $_.chomp(aString)`. See `String#chomp` on page 372.

```
$_ = "now\n"
chomp          →    "now"
$_             →    "now"
chomp "ow"     →    "n"
$_             →    "n"
chomp "xxx"    →    "n"
$_             →    "n"
```

chomp!

chomp!(⟨ *aString* ⟩) → $_ or `nil`

Equivalent to `$_.chomp!(aString)`. See `String#chomp!`

```
$_ = "now\n"
chomp!         →    "now"
$_             →    "now"
chomp! "x"     →    nil
$_             →    "now"
```

chop

chop → *aString*

Equivalent to `($_.dup).chop!`, except `nil` is never returned. See `String#chop!` on page 372.

```
a   =  "now\r\n"
$_ = a
chop     →    "now"
$_       →    "now"
chop     →    "no"
chop     →    "n"
chop     →    ""
chop     →    ""
a        →    "now\r\n"
```

chop!

chop! → $_ or `nil`

Equivalent to `$_.chop!`.

```
a   =  "now\r\n"
$_ = a
chop!    →    "now"
chop!    →    "no"
chop!    →    "n"
chop!    →    ""
chop!    →    nil
$_       →    ""
a        →    ""
```

eval eval(*aString* ⟨ *, aBinding* ⟨ *, file* ⟨ *, line* ⟩ ⟩ ⟩) → *anObject*

Evaluates the Ruby expression(s) in *aString*. If *aBinding* is given, the evaluation is performed in its context. The binding may be a `Binding` object or a `Proc` object. If the optional *file* and *line* parameters are present, they will be used when reporting syntax errors.

```
def getBinding(str)
  return binding
end
str = "hello"
eval "str + ' Fred'"                   →    "hello Fred"
eval "str + ' Fred'", getBinding("bye")   →    "bye Fred"
```

exec exec(*command* ⟨ *, args* ⟩)

Replaces the current process by running the given external command. If **exec** is given a single argument, that argument is taken as a line that is subject to shell expansion before being executed. If multiple arguments are given, the second and subsequent arguments are passed as parameters to *command* with no shell expansion. If the first argument is a two-element array, the first element is the command to be executed, and the second argument is used as the `argv[0]` value, which may show up in process listings. In MSDOS environments, the command is executed in a subshell; otherwise, one of the `exec(2)` system calls is used, so the running command may inherit some of the environment of the original program (including open file descriptors).

```
exec "echo *"      # echoes list of files in current directory
# never get here

exec "echo", "*"   # echoes an asterisk
# never get here
```

exit exit(*anInteger*=0)

Initiates the termination of the Ruby script by raising the `SystemExit` exception. This exception may be caught. The optional parameter is used to return a status code to the invoking environment.

```
begin
  exit
  puts "never get here"
rescue SystemExit
  puts "rescued a SystemExit exception"
end
puts "after begin block"
```

produces:

```
rescued a SystemExit exception
after begin block
```

Kernel

Just prior to termination, Ruby executes any `at_exit` functions and runs any object finalizers (see `ObjectSpace` beginning on page 434).

```
at_exit { puts "at_exit function" }
ObjectSpace.define_finalizer(self,  proc { puts "in finalizer" })
exit
```

produces:

```
at_exit function
in finalizer
```

---

exit!   exit!(*anInteger*=-1)

Similar to `Kernel.exit`, but exception handling, `at_exit` functions, and finalizers are bypassed.

---

fail   fail

fail(*aString*)

fail(*anException* ⟨ , *aString* ⟨ , *anArray* ⟩ ⟩)

Synonym for `Kernel.raise`.

---

fork   fork ⟨ { *block* } ⟩ → *aFixnum* or `nil`

Creates a subshell. If a block is specified, that block is run in the subshell, and the subshell terminates with a status of zero. Otherwise, the `fork` call returns twice, once in the parent, returning the process id of the child, and once in the child, returning `nil`. The child process can exit using `Kernel.exit!` to avoid running any `at_exit` functions. The parent process should use `Process.wait` to collect the termination statuses of its children; otherwise, the operating system may accumulate zombie processes.

```
fork do
  3.times {|i| puts "Child: #{i}" }
end
3.times {|i| puts "Parent: #{i}" }
Process.wait
```

produces:

```
Parent: 0
Child: 0
Child: 1
Parent: 1
Child: 2
Parent: 2
```

---

format   format(*aString* ⟨ , *anObject* ⟩*) → *aString*

Synonym for `Kernel.sprintf`.

---

gets   gets(*aString*=$/) → *aString* or `nil`

Returns (and assigns to `$_`) the next line from the list of files in `ARGV` (or `$*`), or from standard input if no files are present on the command line. Returns `nil` at end of file. The optional argument specifies the record separator. The separator is included with the contents of each record. A separator of `nil` reads the entire contents, and a zero-length separator reads the input one paragraph at a time, where paragraphs are divided by two consecutive newlines. If multiple filenames are present in `ARGV`, `gets(nil)` will read the contents one file at a time.

```
ARGV << "testfile"
print while gets
```

produces:

```
This is line one
This is line two
This is line three
And so on...
```

---

global_variables　　　　　　　　　　　　　　　　　　　　global_variables → *anArray*

Returns an array of the names of global variables.

```
global_variables.grep /std/   →   ["$stderr", "$stdout", "$stdin"]
```

---

gsub　　　　　　　　　　　　　　　　　　　gsub(*pattern, replacement*) → *aString*
　　　　　　　　　　　　　　　　　　　　　　gsub(*pattern*) { *block* } → *aString*

Equivalent to `$_.gsub...`, except that `$_` receives the modified result.

```
$_ = "quick brown fox"
gsub /[aeiou]/, '*'   →   "q**ck br*wn f*x"
$_                    →   "q**ck br*wn f*x"
```

---

gsub!　　　　　　　　　　　　　　　gsub!(*pattern, replacement*) → *aString* or `nil`
　　　　　　　　　　　　　　　　　　　　gsub!(*pattern*) { *block* } → *aString* or `nil`

Equivalent to `Kernel.gsub`, except `nil` is returned if `$_` is not modified.

```
$_ = "quick brown fox"
gsub! /cat/, '*'   →   nil
$_                 →   "quick brown fox"
```

---

iterator?　　　　　　　　　　　　　　　　　　　　　　　iterator? → `true` or `false`

Synonym for `Kernel.block_given?`. The `iterator?` method will be removed in Ruby 1.8.

---

lambda　　　　　　　　　　　　　　　　　　　　　　　　lambda { *block* } → *aProc*

Synonym for `Kernel.proc`.

---

load　　　　　　　　　　　　　　　　　　load(*aFileName, wrap=*`false`) → `true`

Loads and executes the Ruby program in the file *aFileName*. If the filename does not

resolve to an absolute path, the file is searched for in the library directories listed in
$:. If the optional *wrap* parameter is **true**, the loaded script will be executed under
an anonymous module, protecting the calling program's global namespace. Any local
variables in the loaded file will not be propagated to the loading environment.

---

local_variables   local_variables → *anArray*

Returns the names of the current local variables.

```
fred = 1
for i in 1..10
   # ...
end
local_variables   →   ["fred", "i"]
```

---

loop   loop { *block* }

Repeatedly executes the block.

```
loop {
  print "Input: "
  break if !gets or $_ =~ /^[qQ]/
  # ...
}
```

---

open   open(*aString* ⟨ , *aMode* ⟨ , *perm* ⟩ ⟩) → *anIO* or **nil**
                                    open(*aString* ⟨ , *aMode* ⟨ , *perm* ⟩ ⟩) {| *anIO* | *block* } → **nil**

Creates an **IO** object connected to the given stream, file, or subprocess.

If *aString* does not start with a pipe character ("|"), treat it as the name of a file to open
using the specified mode defaulting to "**r**" (see the table of valid modes on page 331).
If a file is being created, its initial permissions may be set using the integer third parameter.

If a block is specified, it will be invoked with the **File** object as a parameter, and the
file will be automatically closed when the block terminates. The call always returns
nil in this case.

If *aString* starts with a pipe character, a subprocess is created, connected to the caller
by a pair of pipes. The returned **IO** object may be used to write to the standard input
and read from the standard output of this subprocess. If the command following the "|"
is a single minus sign, Ruby forks, and this subprocess is connected to the parent. In
the subprocess, the **open** call returns **nil**. If the command is not "-", the subprocess
runs the command. If a block is associated with an **open("|-")** call, that block will be
run twice—once in the parent and once in the child. The block parameter will be an **IO**
object in the parent and **nil** in the child. The parent's **IO** object will be connected to
the child's **$stdin** and **$stdout**. The subprocess will be terminated at the end of the
block.

```
open("testfile") do |f|
  print f.gets
end
```

produces:

```
This is line one
```

Open a subprocess and read its output:

```
cmd = open("|date")
print cmd.gets
cmd.close
```

produces:

```
Wed Sep 20 10:35:30 CDT 2000
```

Open a subprocess running the same Ruby program:

```
f = open("|-", "w+")
if f == nil
  puts "in Child"
  exit
else
  puts "Got: #{f.gets}"
end
```

produces:

```
Got: in Child
```

Open a subprocess using a block to receive the I/O object:

```
open("|-") do |f|
  if f == nil
    puts "in Child"
  else
    puts "Got: #{f.gets}"
  end
end
```

produces:

```
Got: in Child
```

---

p $\qquad\qquad$ p($\langle \textit{anObject} \rangle^+$) $\rightarrow$ nil

---

For each object, directly writes *anObject*.inspect followed by the current output record separator to the program's standard output. p bypasses the Ruby I/O libraries.

```
p self
```

produces:

```
main
```

print

print(⟨ *anObject* ⟩*) → nil

Prints each object in turn to $defout. If the output field separator ($,) is not nil, its contents will appear between each field. If the output record separator ($\) is not nil, it will be appended to the output. If no arguments are given, prints $_. Objects that aren't strings will be converted by calling their to_s method.

```
print "cat", [1,2,3], 99, "\n"
$, = ", "
$\ = "\n"
print "cat", [1,2,3], 99
```

produces:

```
cat12399
cat, 1, 2, 3, 99
```

printf

printf(*anIO, aString* ⟨ , *anObject* ⟩*) → nil
printf(*aString* ⟨ , *anObject* ⟩*) → nil

Equivalent to:

> *anIO*.write sprintf(*aString, anObject* ...)

or

> $defout.write sprintf(*aString, anObject* ...)

proc

proc { *block* } → *aProc*

Creates a new procedure object from the given block. Equivalent to Proc.new.

```
aProc = proc { "hello" }
aProc.call   →   "hello"
```

putc

putc(*anInteger*) → *anInteger*

Equivalent to $defout.putc(*anInteger*).

puts

puts(⟨ *args* ⟩*) → nil

Equivalent to $defout.puts(*args*).

raise

raise
raise(*aString*)
raise(*anException* ⟨ , *aString* ⟨ , *anArray* ⟩ ⟩)

With no arguments, raises the exception in $! or raises a RuntimeError if $! is nil. With a single String argument, raises a RuntimeError with the string as a message. Otherwise, the first parameter should be the name of an Exception class (or an object that returns an Exception when sent exception). The optional second parameter sets the message associated with the exception, and the third parameter is an array of callback information. Exceptions are caught by the `rescue` clause of `begin...end` blocks.

```
raise "Failed to create socket"
raise ArgumentError, "No parameters", caller
```

---

rand   rand(*max=0*) → *aNumber*

Converts *max* to an integer using $max_1 = max.\texttt{to\_i.abs}$. If the result is zero, returns a pseudorandom floating point number greater than or equal to 0.0 and less than 1.0. Otherwise, returns a pseudorandom integer greater than or equal to zero and less than max_1. `Kernel.srand` may be used to ensure repeatable sequences of random numbers between different runs of the program.

```
srand 1234                →  0
[ rand, rand ]            →  [0.7408769294, 0.2145348572]
[ rand(10), rand(1000) ]  →  [3, 323]
srand 1234                →  1234
[ rand, rand ]            →  [0.7408769294, 0.2145348572]
```

---

readline   readline(⟨ *aString=$/* ⟩) → *aString*

Equivalent to `Kernel.gets`, except `readline` raises `EOFError` at end of file.

---

readlines   readlines(⟨ *aString=$/* ⟩) → *anArray*

Returns an array containing the lines returned by calling `Kernel.gets(aString)` until the end of file.

---

require   require(*aString*) → `true` or `false`

Ruby tries to load the library named *aString*, returning `true` if successful. If the filename does not resolve to an absolute path, it will be searched for in the directories listed in `$:`. If the file has the extension ".rb", it is loaded as a source file; if the extension is ".so", ".o", or ".dll",[1] Ruby loads the shared library as a Ruby extension. Otherwise, Ruby tries adding ".rb", ".so", and so on to the name. The name of the loaded feature is added to the array in `$"`. A feature will not be loaded if it already appears in `$"`. `require` returns `true` if the feature was successfully loaded.

```
require "my-library.rb"
require "db-driver"
```

---

scan   scan(*pattern*) → *anArray*
                                       scan(*pattern*) { *block* } → $_

Equivalent to calling `$_.scan`. See `String#scan` on page 378.

---

1. Or whatever the default shared library extension is on the current platform.

select select(*readArray* ⟨ , *writeArray* ⟨ , *errorArray* ⟨ , *timeout* ⟩ ⟩ ⟩) → *anArray* or `nil`

> Performs a low-level `select` call, which waits for data to become available from input/output devices. The first three parameters are arrays of IO objects or `nil`. The last is a timeout in seconds, which should be an `Integer` or a `Float`. The call waits for data to become available for any of the IO objects in *readArray*, for buffers to have cleared sufficiently to enable writing to any of the devices in *writeArray*, or for an error to occur on the devices in *errorArray*. If one or more of these conditions are met, the call returns a three-element array containing arrays of the IO objects that were ready. Otherwise, if there is no change in status for *timeout* seconds, the call returns `nil`. If all parameters are `nil`, the current thread sleeps forever.

```
select( [$stdin], nil, nil, 1.5 )   →   [[#<IO:0x4018f144>], [], []]
```

set_trace_func set_trace_func(*aProc*) → *aProc*
set_trace_func(nil) → `nil`

> Establishes *aProc* as the handler for tracing, or disables tracing if the parameter is `nil`. *aProc* takes up to six parameters: an event name, a filename, a line number, an object id, a binding, and the name of a class. *aProc* is invoked whenever an event occurs. Events are: `c-call` (call a C-language routine), `c-return` (return from a C-language routine), `call` (call a Ruby method), `class` (start a class or module definition), `end` (finish a class or module definition), `line` (execute code on a new line), `raise` (raise an exception), and `return` (return from a Ruby method). Tracing is disabled within the context of *aProc*.

See the example starting on page 271 for more information.

singleton_method_added singleton_method_added(*aFixnum*) → `nil`

> Invoked with a symbol id whenever a singleton method is added to a module or a class. The default implementation in `Kernel` ignores this, but subclasses may override the method to provide specialized functionality.

```
class Test
  def Test.singleton_method_added(id)
    puts "Added #{id.id2name} to Test"
  end
  def a() end
  def Test.b() end
end
def Test.c() end
```

produces:

```
Added singleton_method_added to Test
Added b to Test
Added c to Test
```

sleep   sleep(⟨ *aNumeric* ⟩) → *aFixnum*

Suspends the current thread for *aNumber* seconds (which may be a `Float` with fractional seconds). Returns the actual number of seconds slept (rounded), which may be less than that asked for if the thread was interrupted by a `SIGALRM`, or if another thread calls `Thread#run`. An argument of zero causes `sleep` to sleep forever.

```
Time.new     →    Wed Sep 20 10:35:31 CDT 2000
sleep 1.2    →    1
Time.new     →    Wed Sep 20 10:35:32 CDT 2000
sleep 1.9    →    2
Time.new     →    Wed Sep 20 10:35:34 CDT 2000
```

split   split(⟨ *pattern* ⟨ , *limit* ⟩ ⟩) → *anArray*

Equivalent to `$_.split(pattern, limit)`. See `String#split` on page 379.

sprintf   sprintf(*aFormatString* ⟨ , *arguments* ⟩*) → *aString*

Returns the string resulting from applying *aFormatString* to any additional arguments. Within the format string, any characters other than format sequences are copied to the result. A format sequence consists of a percent sign, followed by optional flags, width, and precision indicators, then terminated with a field type character. The field type controls how the corresponding `sprintf` argument is to be interpreted, while the flags modify that interpretation. The flag characters are shown in Table 23.1 on the following page, and the field type characters are listed in Table 23.2.

The field width is an optional integer, followed optionally by a period and a precision. The width specifies the minimum number of characters that will be written to the result for this field. For numeric fields, the precision controls the number of decimal places displayed. For string fields, the precision determines the maximum number of characters to be copied from the string. (Thus, the format sequence `%10.10s` will always contribute exactly ten characters to the result.)

```
sprintf("%d %04x", 123, 123)             →    "123␣007b"
sprintf("%08b '%4s'", 123, 123)          →    "01111011␣'␣123'"
sprintf("%*2$s %d", "hello", 10)         →    "␣␣␣␣␣hello␣10"
sprintf("%*2$s %d", "hello", -10)        →    "hello␣␣␣␣␣␣-10"
sprintf("%+g:% g:%-g", 1.23, 1.23, 1.23) →    "+1.23:␣1.23:1.23"
```

srand   srand(⟨ *aNumber* ⟩) → *oldSeed*

Seeds the pseudorandom number generator to the value of *aNumber*`.to_i.abs`. If *aNumber* is omitted or zero, seeds the generator using a combination of the time, the process id, and a sequence number. (This is also the behavior if `Kernel.rand` is called without previously calling `srand`, but without the sequence.) By setting the seed to a known value, scripts can be made deterministic during testing. The previous seed value is returned. Also see `Kernel.rand` on page 425.

Table 23.1. `sprintf` flag characters

Flag	Applies to	Meaning
␣ (space)	bdeEfgGioxXu	Leave a space at the start of positive numbers.
#	beEfgGoxX	Use an alternative format. For the conversions 'o', 'x', 'X', and 'b', prefix the result with "0", "0x", "0X", and "0b", respectively. For 'e', 'E', 'f', 'g', and 'G', force a decimal point to be added, even if no digits follow. For 'g' and 'G', do not remove trailing zeros.
+	bdeEfgGioxXu	Add a leading plus sign to positive numbers.
-	all	Left-justify the result of this conversion.
0 (zero)	all	Pad with zeros, not spaces.
*	all	Use the next argument as the field width. If negative, left-justify the result. If the asterisk is followed by a number and a dollar sign, use the indicated argument as the width.

Table 23.2. `sprintf` field types

Field	Conversion
b	Convert argument as a binary number.
c	Argument is the numeric code for a single character.
d	Convert argument as a decimal number.
E	Equivalent to 'e', but uses an uppercase E to indicate the exponent.
e	Convert floating point argument into exponential notation with one digit before the decimal point. The precision determines the number of fractional digits (defaulting to six).
f	Convert floating point argument as [␣-]`ddd.ddd`, where the precision determines the number of digits after the decimal point.
G	Equivalent to 'g', but use an uppercase 'E' in exponent form.
g	Convert a floating point number using exponential form if the exponent is less than −4 or greater than or equal to the precision, or in `d.dddd` form otherwise.
i	Identical to 'd'.
o	Convert argument as an octal number.
s	Argument is a string to be substituted. If the format sequence contains a precision, at most that many characters will be copied.
u	Treat argument as an unsigned decimal number.
X	Convert argument as a hexadecimal number using uppercase letters.
x	Convert argument as a hexadecimal number.

---

sub
$$\text{sub}(\textit{ pattern, replacement }) \rightarrow \$\_$$
$$\text{sub}(\textit{ pattern }) \ \{ \textit{ block } \} \rightarrow \$\_$$

Equivalent to `$_.sub(args)`, except that `$_` will be updated if substitution occurs.

---

sub!
$$\text{sub!}(\textit{ pattern, replacement }) \rightarrow \$\_ \text{ or } \texttt{nil}$$
$$\text{sub!}(\textit{ pattern }) \ \{ \textit{ block } \} \rightarrow \$\_ \text{ or } \texttt{nil}$$

Equivalent to `$_.sub!(args)`.

---

syscall
$$\text{syscall}(\textit{ aFixnum } \langle \text{ , } \textit{args} \rangle^*) \rightarrow \textit{anInteger}$$

Calls the operating system function identified by *aFixnum*, passing in the arguments, which must be either `String` objects, or `Integer` objects that ultimately fit within a native `long`. Up to nine parameters may be passed (14 on the Atari-ST). The function identified by *Fixnum* is system dependent. On some Unix systems, the numbers may be obtained from a header file called `syscall.h`.

```
syscall 4, 1, "hello\n", 6   # '4' is write(2) on our box
```

produces:

```
hello
```

---

system
$$\text{system}(\textit{ aCmd } \langle \text{ , } \textit{args} \rangle^*) \rightarrow \texttt{true} \text{ or } \texttt{false}$$

Executes *aCmd* in a subshell, returning `true` if the command was found and ran successfully, `false` otherwise. A detailed error code is available in `$?`. The arguments are processed in the same way as for `Kernel.exec` on page 419.

```
system("echo *")
system("echo", "*")
```

produces:

```
config.h main.rb
*
```

---

test
$$\text{test}(\textit{aCmd, file1 } \langle \text{ , } \textit{file2} \rangle) \rightarrow \textit{anObject}$$

Uses the integer *aCmd* to perform various tests on *file1* (Table 23.3 on the next page) or on *file1* and *file2* (Table 23.4).

---

throw
$$\text{throw}(\textit{ aSymbol } \langle \text{ , } \textit{anObject} \rangle)$$

Transfers control to the end of the active `catch` block waiting for *aSymbol*. Raises `NameError` if there is no `catch` block for the symbol. The optional second parameter supplies a return value for the `catch` block, which otherwise defaults to `nil`. For examples, see `Kernel.catch` on page 417.

Table 23.3. File tests with a single argument

Integer	Description	Returns
?A	Last access time for *file1*	Time
?b	True if *file1* is a block device	true or false
?c	True if *file1* is a character device	true or false
?C	Last change time for *file1*	Time
?d	True if *file1* exists and is a directory	true or false
?e	True if *file1* exists	true or false
?f	True if *file1* exists and is a regular file	true or false
?g	True if *file1* has the `setgid` bit set (false under NT)	true or false
?G	True if *file1* exists and has a group ownership equal to the caller's group	true or false
?k	True if *file1* exists and has the sticky bit set	true or false
?l	True if *file1* exists and is a symbolic link	true or false
?M	Last modification time for *file1*	Time
?o	True if *file1* exists and is owned by the caller's effective uid	true or false
?O	True if *file1* exists and is owned by the caller's real uid	true or false
?p	True if *file1* exists and is a fifo	true or false
?r	True if file is readable by the effective uid/gid of the caller	true or false
?R	True if file is readable by the real uid/gid of the caller	true or false
?s	If *file1* has nonzero size, return the size, otherwise return `nil`	Integer or `nil`
?S	True if *file1* exists and is a socket	true or false
?u	True if *file1* has the setuid bit set	true or false
?w	True if *file1* exists and is writable by the effective uid/gid	true or false
?W	True if *file1* exists and is writable by the real uid/gid	true or false
?x	True if *file1* exists and is executable by the effective uid/gid	true or false
?X	True if *file1* exists and is executable by the real uid/gid	true or false
?z	True if *file1* exists and has a zero length	true or false

Table 23.4. File tests with two arguments

Integer	Description
?-	True if *file1* is a hard link to *file2*
?=	True if the modification times of *file1* and *file2* are equal
?<	True if the modification time of *file1* is prior to that of *file2*
?>	True if the modification time of *file1* is after that of *file2*

trace_var

trace_var(*aSymbol*, *aCmd*) → `nil`
trace_var(*aSymbol*) { | *val* | *block* } → `nil`

Controls tracing of assignments to global variables. The parameter *aSymbol* identifies the variable (as either a string name or a symbol identifier). *cmd* (which may be a string or a `Proc` object) or block is executed whenever the variable is assigned. The block or `Proc` object receives the variable's new value as a parameter. Also see `Kernel.untrace_var`.

```
trace_var :$_, proc {|v| puts "$_ is now '#{v}'" }
$_ = "hello"
$_ = ' there'
```

produces:

```
$_ is now 'hello'
$_ is now ' there'
```

trap

trap(*signal*, *cmd*) → *anObject*
trap(*signal*) { *block* } → *anObject*

Specifies the handling of signals. The first parameter is a signal name (a string such as "SIGALRM", "SIGUSR1", and so on) or a signal number. The characters "SIG" may be omitted from the signal name. The command or block specifies code to be run when the signal is raised. If the command is the string "IGNORE" or "SIG_IGN", the signal will be ignored. If the command is "DEFAULT" or "SIG_DFL", the operating system's default handler will be invoked. If the command is "EXIT", the script will be terminated by the signal. Otherwise, the given command or block will be run.

The special signal name "EXIT" or signal number zero will be invoked just prior to program termination.

`trap` returns the previous handler for the given signal.

```
trap 0, proc { puts "Terminating: #{$$}" }
trap("CLD") { puts "Child died" }
fork && Process.wait
```

produces:

```
Terminating: 21546
Child died
Terminating: 21545
```

untrace_var

untrace_var(*aSymbol* ⟨ , *aCmd* ⟩) → *anArray* or `nil`

Removes tracing for the specified command on the given global variable and returns `nil`. If no command is specified, removes all tracing for that variable and returns an array containing the commands actually removed.

Module Marshal

The marshaling library converts collections of Ruby objects into a byte stream, allowing them to be stored outside the currently active script. This data may subsequently be read and the original objects reconstituted. Marshaling is described starting on page 272.

Some objects cannot be dumped: if the objects to be dumped include bindings, procedure objects, instances of class IO, or singleton objects, a **TypeError** will be raised.

If your class has special serialization needs (for example, if you want to serialize in some specific format), or if it contains objects that would otherwise not be serializable, you can implement your own serialization strategy by defining two methods, **_dump** and **_load**:

Method Type	Signature	Returns
Instance	_dump(aDepth)	Returns a **String**
Class	_load(aString)	Returns a reconstituted **Object**

The instance method **_dump** should return a **String** object containing all the information necessary to reconstitute objects of this class and all referenced objects up to a maximum depth of *aDepth* (a value of −1 should disable depth checking). The class method **_load** should take a **String** and return an object of this class.

Module methods

dump

$$dump(\ anObject\ \langle\ ,\ anIO\ \rangle\ ,\ limit=100\ ) \rightarrow anIO$$

Serializes *anObject* and all descendent objects. If *anIO* is specified, the serialized data will be written to it, otherwise the data will be returned as a **String**. If *limit* is specified, the traversal of subobjects will be limited to that depth. If *limit* is negative, no checking of depth will be performed.

```
class Klass
  def initialize(str)
    @str = str
  end
  def sayHello
    @str
  end
end

o = Klass.new("hello\n")
data = Marshal.dump(o)
obj = Marshal.load(data)
obj.sayHello   →   "hello\n"
```

load ⟶ $load(\,from\ \langle\,,aProc\,\rangle\,) \to anObject$

Returns the result of converting the serialized data in *from* into a Ruby object (possibly with associated subordinate objects). *from* may be either an instance of IO or an object that responds to `to_str`. If *proc* is specified, it will be passed each object as it is deserialized.

restore ⟶ $restore(\,from\ \langle\,,aProc\,\rangle\,) \to anObject$

A synonym for `Marshal.load`.

Module ## Math

The `Math` module contains module functions for basic trigonometric and transcendental functions.

Module constants

E   Value of *e* (base of natural logarithms)
PI   Value of π

Module methods

atan2 ⟶ $Math.atan2(\,y,\,x\,) \to aFloat$

Computes the arc tangent given *y* and *x*. Returns $-\pi..\pi$.

cos ⟶ $Math.cos(\,aNumeric\,) \to aFloat$

Computes the cosine of *aNumeric* (expressed in radians). Returns $-1..1$.

exp ⟶ $Math.exp(\,aNumeric\,) \to aFloat$

Returns *e* raised to the power of *aNumeric*.

frexp ⟶ $Math.frexp(\,aNumeric\,) \to anArray$

Returns a two-element array ([*aFloat, aFixnum*]) containing the normalized fraction and exponent of *aNumeric*.

ldexp ⟶ $Math.ldexp(\,aFloat,\,anInteger\,) \to aFloat$

Returns the value of $aFloat \times 2^{anInteger}$.

log ⟶ $Math.log(\,aNumeric\,) \to aFloat$

Returns the natural logarithm of *aNumeric*.

log10	Math.log10(*aNumeric*) → *aFloat*

Returns the base 10 logarithm of *aNumeric*.

sin	Math.sin(*aNumeric*) → *aFloat*

Computes the sine of *aNumeric* (expressed in radians). Returns −1..1.

sqrt	Math.sqrt(*aNumeric*) → *aFloat*

Returns the non-negative square root of *aNumeric*. Raises `ArgError` if *aNumeric* is less than zero.

tan	Math.tan(*aNumeric*) → *aFloat*

Returns the tangent of *aNumeric* (expressed in radians).

Module ObjectSpace

The `ObjectSpace` module contains a number of routines that interact with the garbage collection facility and allow you to traverse all living objects with an iterator.

`ObjectSpace` also provides support for object finalizers, procs that will be called when a specific object is about to be destroyed by garbage collection.

```
include ObjectSpace

a = "A"
b = "B"
c = "C"

define_finalizer(a, proc {|id| puts "Finalizer one on #{id}" })
define_finalizer(a, proc {|id| puts "Finalizer two on #{id}" })
define_finalizer(b, proc {|id| puts "Finalizer three on #{id}" })
```

produces:

```
Finalizer three on 537678616
Finalizer one on 537678626
Finalizer two on 537678626
```

Module methods

_id2ref	ObjectSpace._id2ref(*anId*) → *anObject*

Converts an object id to a reference to the object. May not be called on an object id passed as a parameter to a finalizer.

```
s = "I am a string"              →    "I am a string"
r = ObjectSpace._id2ref(s.id)    →    "I am a string"
r == s                           →    true
```

define_finalizer   ObjectSpace.define_finalizer(*anObject*, *aProc*=proc())

Adds *aProc* as a finalizer, to be called when *anObject* is about to be destroyed.

---

each_object   ObjectSpace.each_object(⟨ *aClassOrMod* ⟩) {| *anObj* | *block* } → *aFixnum*

Calls the block once for each living, nonimmediate object in this Ruby process. If *aClassOrMod* is specified, calls the block for only those classes or modules that match (or are a subclass of) *aClassOrMod*. Returns the number of objects found.

```
a = 102.7
b = 95
ObjectSpace.each_object(Numeric) {|x| p x }
print "Total count: ", ObjectSpace.each_object {} ,"\n"
```

produces:

```
102.7
2.718281828
3.141592654
Total count: 376
```

---

garbage_collect   ObjectSpace.garbage_collect → nil

Initiates garbage collection (see module GC on page 414).

---

undefine_finalizer   ObjectSpace.undefine_finalizer(*anObject*)

Removes all finalizers for *anObject*.

Module **Process**

The Process module is a collection of methods used to manipulate processes.

Module constants

PRIO_PGRP	Process Group priority.
PRIO_PROCESS	Process priority.
PRIO_USER	User priority.
WNOHANG	Do not block if no child has exited. Not available on all platforms.
WUNTRACED	Return stopped children as well. Not available on all platforms.

Module methods

egid Process.egid → *aFixnum*

Returns the effective group id for this process.

```
Process.egid   →   500
```

egid= Process.egid= *aFixnum* → *aFixnum*

Sets the effective group id for this process.

euid Process.euid → *aFixnum*

Returns the effective user id for this process.

```
Process.euid   →   501
```

euid= Process.euid= *aFixnum*

Sets the effective user id for this process. Not available on all platforms.

exit! Process.exit!(*aFixnum*=−1)

Exits the process immediately. No exit handlers are run. *aFixnum* is returned to the underlying system as the exit status.

```
Process.exit!(0)
```

fork Process.fork ⟨ { *block* } ⟩ → *aFixnum* or `nil`

See `Kernel.fork` on page 420.

getpgid Process.getpgid(*anInteger*) → *anInteger*

Returns the process group id for the given process id. Not available on all platforms.

```
Process.getpgid(Process.ppid())   →   13542
```

getpgrp Process.getpgrp → *anInteger*

Returns the process group id for this process. Not available on all platforms.

```
Process.getpgid(0)    →   13542
Process.getpgrp       →   13542
```

getpriority Process.getpriority(*aKind, anInteger*) → *aFixnum*

Gets the scheduling priority for specified process, process group, or user. *aKind* indicates the kind of entity to find: one of `Process::PRIO_PGRP`, `Process::PRIO_USER`, or `Process::PRIO_PROCESS`. *anInteger* is an id indicating the particular process, process group, or user (an id of 0 means *current*). Lower priorities are more favorable for scheduling. Not available on all platforms.

```
Process.getpriority(Process::PRIO_USER, 0)      →   19
Process.getpriority(Process::PRIO_PROCESS, 0)   →   19
```

---

gid   Process.gid → *aFixnum*

Returns the group id for this process.

```
Process.gid   →   500
```

---

gid=   Process.gid= *aFixnum* → *aFixnum*

· Sets the group id for this process.

---

kill   Process.kill(*aSignal*, ⟨ *aPid* ⟩$^{+}$) → *aFixnum*

Sends the given signal to the specified process id(s), or to the current process if *aPid* is zero. *aSignal* may be an integer signal number or a POSIX signal name (either with or without a `SIG` prefix). If *aSignal* is negative (or starts with a "-" sign), kills process groups instead of processes. Not all signals are available on all platforms.

```
trap("SIGHUP") { close_then_exit }
Process.kill("SIGHUP", 0)
```

---

pid   Process.pid → *aFixnum*

Returns the process id of this process. Not available on all platforms.

```
Process.pid   →   15652
```

---

ppid   Process.ppid → *aFixnum*

Returns the process id of the parent of this process. Always returns 0 on NT. Not available on all platforms.

```
print "I am ", Process.pid, "\n"
Process.fork { print "Dad is ", Process.ppid, "\n" }
```

produces:

```
I am 15654
Dad is 15654
```

---

setpgid   Process.setpgid(*aPid*, *anInteger*) → 0

Sets the process group id of *aPid* (0 indicates this process) to *anInteger*. Not available on all platforms.

---

setpgrp   Process.setpgrp → 0

Equivalent to `setpgid(0,0)`. Not available on all platforms.

---

setpriority   Process.setpriority(*kind*, *anInteger*, *anIntPriority*) → 0

See `Process#getpriority`.

```
Process.setpriority(Process::PRIO_USER, 0, 19)      →   0
Process.setpriority(Process::PRIO_PROCESS, 0, 19)   →   0
Process.getpriority(Process::PRIO_USER, 0)          →   19
Process.getpriority(Process::PRIO_PROCESS, 0)       →   19
```

---

setsid   *Process.setsid → aFixnum*

Establishes this process as a new session and process group leader, with no controlling tty. Returns the session id. Not available on all platforms.

```
Process.setsid   →   15659
```

---

uid   *Process.uid → aFixnum*

Returns the user id of this process.

```
Process.uid   →   501
```

---

uid=   *Process.uid= anInteger → aNumeric*

Sets the (integer) user id for this process. Not available on all platforms.

---

wait   *Process.wait → aFixnum*

Waits for any child process to exit and returns the process id of that child. Raises a **SystemError** if there are no child processes. Not available on all platforms.

```
Process.fork { exit 1; }   →   15664
Process.wait               →   15664
```

---

wait2   *Process.wait2 → anArray*

Waits for any child process to exit and returns an array containing the process id and the exit status of that child. Raises a **SystemError** if there are no child processes.

```
Process.fork { exit 1 }   →   15667
Process.wait2             →   [15667, 256]
```

---

waitpid   *Process.waitpid(aPid, anInteger=0) → aPid*

Waits for the given child process to exit. *anInteger* may be a logical or of the flag value **Process::WNOHANG** (do not block if no child available) or **Process::WUNTRACED** (return stopped children that haven't been reported). Not all flags are available on all platforms, but a flag value of zero will work on all platforms.

```
include Process
pid = fork { sleep 3 }             →   15670
Time.now                           →   Tue Sep 19 23:32:29 CDT 2000
waitpid(pid, Process::WNOHANG)     →   nil
Time.now                           →   Tue Sep 19 23:32:29 CDT 2000
waitpid(pid, 0)                    →   15670
Time.now                           →   Tue Sep 19 23:32:32 CDT 2000
```

---

waitpid2 Process.waitpid2(*aPid, anInteger*=0) → *anArray*

Waits for the given child process to exit, returning that child's process id and exit status. *anInteger* may be a logical or of the flag value `Process::WNOHANG` (do not block if no child available) or `Process::WUNTRACED` (return stopped children that haven't been reported). Not all flags are available on all platforms, but a flag value of zero will work on all platforms.

## Chapter 24

Standard Library

Ruby comes "out of the box" with a large and useful library of modules and classes. This chapter contains a sampling of the more useful of these.

Interestingly, and unlike some of the code in later chapters, all of these libraries are written in Ruby. You'll find the source in the `lib` subdirectory of the standard Ruby distribution.

Class **Complex** < Numeric · · · · · · · · · · · · · · · · · **require** **"complex"**

```
require "complex"

v1 = Complex(2,3)      →     Complex(2, 3)
v2 = 2.im              →     Complex(0, 2)
v1 + v2                →     Complex(2, 5)
v1 * v2                →     Complex(-6, 4)
v2**2                  →     Complex(-4, 0)
Math.sin(v1)           →     Complex(9.154499147, -4.16890696)
v1 < v2                →     false
v2**2 == -4            →     true
```

Class constants

Complex::I $0 + 1_i$

Class methods

new   Complex.new(a, b) $\rightarrow$ *aComplex*

Returns $a + b_i$.

In addition to the `Complex.new` constructor, the `Complex` library defines the method `Numeric.im`, such that *aNumeric*`.im` returns $0 + aNumeric_i$. Complex numbers are also constructed using the global method `Complex`, which takes one or two arguments. The value it returns depends on the type of its arguments:

a	b	Result
Number	Number	$a + b_i$
Complex	0	a
Complex	Complex	`Complex(` a`.real - ` b`.image, ` a`.image + ` b`.real )`
Number	Complex	`Complex(` a` - ` b`.image, ` b`.real )`

Instance methods

Arithmetic operations

Performs various arithmetic operations on *cmplx*.

cmplx	+	*aNumeric* → *aComplex*	Addition
cmplx	-	*aNumeric* → *aComplex*	Subtraction
cmplx	*	*aNumeric* → *aComplex*	Multiplication
cmplx	/	*aNumeric* → *aComplex*	Division
cmplx	%	*aNumeric* → *aComplex*	Remainder
cmplx	**	*aNumeric* → *aComplex*	Exponentiation (real and complex power)

<=>
$$cmplx <=> other \rightarrow -1, 0, +1$$

Returns *cmplx*.abs <=> *other*.abs.

==
$$cmplx == anObject \rightarrow \text{true or false}$$

If *anObject* is a complex number, returns **true** if its real and imaginary parts match *cmplx*. If *anObject* is a simple number, returns **true** if *cmplx*.**real** equals *anObject* and *cmplx*.**image** is zero. Otherwise, attempts to coerce *anObject* to a complex number and compares the result.

abs
$$cmplx.abs \rightarrow aFloat$$

Absolute value.

abs2
$$cmplx.abs2 \rightarrow aFloat$$

Square of absolute value.

arg
$$cmplx.arg \rightarrow aFloat$$

Argument (angle from (1,0)).

conjugate
$$cmplx.conjugate \rightarrow aComplex$$

Complex conjugate.

image $\hspace{6cm}$ *cmplx*.image → *aNumeric*

The imaginary part of *cmplx*.

polar $\hspace{6cm}$ *cmplx*.polar → *anArray*

Returns the two-element array: [*c*.abs, *c*.arg].

real $\hspace{6cm}$ *cmplx*.real → *aNumeric*

The real part of *cmplx*.

to_f $\hspace{6cm}$ *cmplx*.to_f → *aComplex*

Returns `Complex(real.to_f, image.to_f)`.

to_i $\hspace{6cm}$ *cmplx*.to_i → *aComplex*

Returns `Complex(real.to_i, image.to_i)`.

to_r $\hspace{6cm}$ *cmplx*.to_r → *aComplex*

Returns `Complex(real.to_r, image.to_r)`, converting both parts of the complex
to a rational number.

to_s $\hspace{6cm}$ *cmplx*.to_s → *aString*

String representation of *cmplx*.

In addition, the `Math` functions `sqrt`, `exp`, `cos`, `sin`, `tan`, `log`, `log10`, and `atan2` are
extended to support a `Complex` argument.

Class **Date** < Object	require **"date"**

```
require 'date'

d = Date.new(2000, 3, 31)            →   #<Date: 2451635,2299161>
[d.year, d.yday, d.wday]             →   [2000, 91, 5]
[d.month, d.mday]                    →   [3, 31]
[d.cwyear, d.cweek, d.cwday]         →   [2000, 13, 5]
[d.jd, d.mjd]                        →   [2451635, 51634.5]
(d << 1).to_s                        →   "2000-02-29"
d.succ.to_s                          →   "2000-04-01"
(d + 100).to_s                       →   "2000-07-09"
d.leap?                              →   true
Date.new(2000, 3, -10).to_s          →   "2000-03-22"
d1 = Date.neww(2000, 13, 7)          →   #<Date: 2451637,2299161>
d1.to_s                              →   "2000-04-02"
[d1.cwday, d1.wday]                  →   [7, 0]
```

The `date` library implements class `Date`, which provides a comprehensive set of facilities for storing, manipulating, and converting dates. To document its options, we need to take a brief historical detour to establish some vocabulary.

Internally a date is stored as a Julian day number, the number of days since midday, January 1st, 4713 BCE.[1] The rules for converting a Julian day number to a calendar date are complicated because the Romans estimated the length of a year incorrectly. In the Julian calendar (often called Old Style, or O.S.), every year divisible by 4 is a leap year. The `Date` class has options to convert dates using this as an assumption.

By the sixteenth century, the inaccuracies in this measurement had become apparent. An edict from Pope Gregory XIII in 1582 created the New Style (N.S.) or Gregorian calendar, where years divisible by 100 were no longer leap years unless they were also divisible by 400. This system was adopted by most Catholic countries immediately, but religious differences held up a wider adoption. England (and several other countries) switched in 1752, with some countries following later. The `Date` class allows you to determine whether to implement the cutover in 1582 (the `Date::ITALY` option), 1752 (`Date::ENGLAND`), or another date of your choosing.

The `Date` class also provides conversions to Modified Julian Day (MJD) numbers. MJD values count from midnight, November 17, 1858. Because these values count from midnight, not midday, there is a half-day added to the conversion factor.

The descriptions that follow use the abbreviations listed in Table 24.1 on the facing page.

Class `Date` exports the constant arrays `Date::MONTHNAMES` and `Date::DAYNAMES`, which can be indexed by *mon* and *wday* values to return the corresponding English names.

The `Date` class also provides low-level date-conversion methods:

- `civil_to_jd`
- `commercial_to_jd`
- `ordinal_to_jd`
- `jd_to_mjd`
- `jd_to_civil`
- `jd_to_commercial`
- `jd_to_ordinal`
- `mjd_to_jd`

These methods perform limited error checking of their parameters, and are not documented here. The somewhat confusingly named `exist..?` routines perform conversions from different formats into a Julian day number with error checking. These routines also automatically normalize their parameters.

---

1. In the code, you may find references to the year −4712. As astronomical dates include a year zero, 4713 BCE is the same year as −4712.

Table 24.1. Abbreviations used describing dates

Field	Meaning
cwday	An ISO 8601 calendar weekday. 1 is Monday, 7 is Sunday.
cweek	An ISO 8601 calendar week. Week 1 is the week containing the first Thursday (or equivalently the week that contains January 4th).
cwyear	An ISO 8601 calendar-week-based year. May be different from *year*, as it rolls forward only on a Monday.
jd	The Julian day number—the number of days since January 1st, 4713 BCE.
mday	The day of the month (1..31).
mjd	A modified Julian day number.
mon	The month of the year (1..12).
sg	The start of the Gregorian correction: `Date::ITALY` (the default) for 1582, `Date::ENGLAND` for 1752, or `JULIAN`, meaning no correction. You may also provide an arbitrary Julian day number for this parameter, in which case the correction will start from this date.
wday	The day of the week (0 is Sunday).
week	The week number into a year (1..53).
yday	The day into the year (1..366).
year	A year (1966, 2001, and the like).

Mixes in

`Comparable:`
   `<, <=, ==, >=, >, between?`

Class methods

exist2?   Date.exist2?(*year*, *yday*, *sg*=`Date::ITALY`) → *jd*

Converts a *year* and *yday* into a Julian day number, returning `nil` on error.

exist?   Date.exist?(*year*, *mon*, *mday*, *sg*=`Date::ITALY`) → *jd*

Converts a *year*, *mon*, and *mday* into a Julian day number, or `nil` if the parameters are invalid.

existw?   Date.existw?(*cyear*, *cweek*, *cwday*, *sg*=`Date::ITALY`) → *jd*

Converts a *cyear*, *cweek*, and *cwday* into a Julian day number.

gregorian_leap?   Date.gregorian_leap?(*year*) → `true` or `false`

If *year* does not end with "00", returns `true` if *year* is divisible by 4, otherwise returns `true` if *year* is divisible by 400.

julian_leap?   Date.julian_leap?(*year*) → `true` or `false`

Returns `true` if *year* is divisible by 4.

---

leap?   Date.leap?(*year*) → `true` or `false`

Synonym for `Date.gregorian_leap?`.

---

new   Date.new(*year*=−4712, *mon*=1, *mday*=1, *sg*=`Date::ITALY`) → *aNewDate*

Returns a `Date` for the given *year*, *mon*, and *mday*. If *mon* is negative, it counts back from the end of the year. If *mday* is negative, it counts back from the end of the month.

---

new1   Date.new1(*jd*, *sg*=`Date::ITALY`) → *aNewDate*

Creates a `Date` corresponding to the given Julian day number.

---

new2   Date.new2(*year*=−4712, *yday*=1, *sg*=`Date::ITALY`) → *aNewDate*

Returns a `Date` for the given *year* and *yday*. If *yday* is negative, it counts back from the end of the year.

---

new3   Date.new3(*year*=−4712, *mon*=1, *mday*=1, *sg*=`Date::ITALY`) → *aNewDate*

Synonym for `Date.new`.

---

neww   Date.neww(*cyear*=1582, *cweek*=41, *cwday*=5, *sg*=`Date::ITALY`) → *aNewDate*

Returns a `Date` for the given *cyear*, *cweek*, and *cwday*. If *cweek* is negative, it counts back from the end of the year. If *cwday* is negative, it counts back from the end of the week.

---

today   Date.today(*sg*=`Date::ITALY`) → *aNewDate*

Returns a `Date` for today.

Instance methods

Accessors   *aDate*.year → *year*
                                                            aDate.yday → *yday*
                                                            aDate.mjd → *mjd*
                                                            aDate.mon → *mon*
                                                            aDate.month → *mon*
                                                            aDate.mday → *mday*
                                                            aDate.day → *mday*
                                                       aDate.cwyear → *cwyear*
                                                            aDate.cweek → *cweek*
                                                            aDate.cwday → *cwday*
                                                            aDate.wday → *wday*

Returns the given component of *aDate* as a number.

+   *aDate + anInteger → aNewDate*

Returns a new **Date** *anInteger* days from *aDate*.

−   *aDate − anInteger → aNewDate*
           aDate − anOtherDate → anInteger

The first form returns a new **Date** *anInteger* days before *aDate*. The second form returns the number of days between *aDate* and *anOtherDate*.

<<   *aDate << anInteger → aNewDate*

Returns a new **Date** formed by subtracting *anInteger* months to *aDate*, adjusting the *mday* value back to the last day of the month if it otherwise exceeds it.

<=>   *aDate <=> anOther → −1, 0, +1*

anOther must be a **Numeric**, in which case it is treated as a Julian day number, or a **Date**. Returns −1, 0, +1 if *aDate* is less than, equal to, or greater than *anOther*. See module **Comparable** on page 406.

===   *aDate === anOther →* **true** or **false**

anOther must be a **Numeric**, in which case it is treated as a Julian day number, or a **Date**. Returns **true** if the Julian day number of *anOther* is the same as *aDate*.

>>   *aDate >> anInteger → aNewDate*

Returns a new **Date** formed by adding *anInteger* months to *aDate*, adjusting the *mday* value back to the last day of the month if it otherwise exceeds it.

---

downto   *aDate*.downto(*aDateMin*) {| *date* | *block* } → *aDate*

Invokes block with dates from *aDate* down to *aDateMin*.

---

england   *aDate*.england → *aDate*

Equivalent to *aDate*.**newsg(Date::ENGLAND)**.

---

gregorian   *aDate*.gregorian → *aDate*

Equivalent to *aDate*.**newsg(Date::GREGORIAN)**.

---

italy   *aDate*.italy → *aDate*

Equivalent to *aDate*.**newsg(Date::ITALY)**.

---

jd   *aDate*.jd → *jd*

Returns the Julian day number for *aDate*.

julian *aDate*.julian → *aDate*

Equivalent to *aDate*.`newsg(Date::JULIAN)`.

leap? *aDate*.leap? → `true` or `false`

Returns `true` if *aDate* falls within a leap year.

mjd *aDate*.mjd → *mjd*

Returns the Julian day number of *aDate* converted to a modified Julian day number.

newsg *aDate*.newsg(*sg*=`Date::ITALY`) → *aNewDate*

Returns a new `Date`.

next *aDate*.next → *aNewDate*

Synonym for *aDate*.succ.

ns? *aDate*.ns? → `true` or `false`

Returns `true` if *aDate* falls in the period of New Style dates.

os? *aDate*.os? → `true` or `false`

Returns `true` if *aDate* falls in the period of Old Style dates.

sg *aDate*.sg → *anInteger*

Returns the Julian day number of the start of New Style dates for *aDate*.

step *aDate*.step(*aDateLimit, step*) {| *date* | *block* } → *aDate*

Invokes block with dates starting at *aDate*, incrementing by *step* days, ending at the first date greater than *aDateLimit* (less than for a negative step).

succ *aDate*.succ → *aNewDate*

Returns the date of *aDate* plus one day.

to_s *aDate*.to_s → *aString*

Returns `self` as "year-mon-mday."

upto *aDate*.upto(*aDateMax*) {| *date* | *block* } → *aDate*

Invokes block with dates from *aDate* to *aDateMax*.

English

```
require "English"

$OUTPUT_FIELD_SEPARATOR = ' -- '
"waterbuffalo" =~ /buff/
print $LOADED_FEATURES, $POSTMATCH, $PID, "\n"
print $", $', $$, "\n"
```

produces:

```
English.rb -- alo -- 15692 --
English.rb -- alo -- 15692 --
```

Include the English library file in a Ruby script, and you can reference the global variables such as $_ using less cryptic names, listed in the following table.

$*	$ARGV	$"	$LOADED_FEATURES
$?	$CHILD_STATUS	$&	$MATCH
$<	$DEFAULT_INPUT	$.	$NR
$>	$DEFAULT_OUTPUT	$,	$OFS
$!	$ERROR_INFO	$\	$ORS
$@	$ERROR_POSITION	$\	$OUPUT_RECORD_SEPARATOR
$;	$FIELD_SEPARATOR	$,	$OUTPUT_FIELD_SEPARATOR
$;	$FS	$$	$PID
$=	$IGNORECASE	$'	$POSTMATCH
$.	$INPUT_LINE_NUMBER	$`	$PREMATCH
$/	$INPUT_RECORD_SEPARATOR	$$	$PROCESS_ID
$~	$LAST_MATCH_INFO	$0	$PROGRAM_NAME
$+	$LAST_PAREN_MATCH	$/	$RS
$_	$LAST_READ_LINE		

| Module | **Find** | require | "find" |

```
require "find"
Find.find("/etc/passwd", "/var/spool/lp1", ".") do |f|
  Find.prune if f == "."
  puts f
end
```

produces:

```
/etc/passwd
/var/spool/lp1
/var/spool/lp1/status
/var/spool/lp1/lock
/var/spool/lp1/.seq
```

The `Find` module supports the top-down traversal of a set of file paths.

Module methods

find   Find.find(⟨ *aName* ⟩*) {| *aFileName* | *block* }

Calls the associated block with the name of every file and directory listed as arguments, then recursively on their subdirectories, and so on.

---

prune   Find.prune

Skips the current file or directory, restarting the loop with the next entry. If the current file is a directory, that directory will not be recursively entered. Meaningful only within the block associated with `Find.find`.

| Class | **File** < IO | require | "ftools" |

```
require 'ftools'

File.copy 'testfile', 'testfile1'     →     true
File.compare 'testfile', 'testfile1'  →     true
```

The `FTools` library adds several methods to the built-in `File` class. These methods are particularly useful to programs that move and copy files, such as installers.

Class methods

cmp   File.cmp(*name1*, *name2*, *verbose*=`false`) → `true` or `false`

Synonym for `File.compare`.

---

compare   File.compare(*name1*, *name2*, *verbose*=`false`) → `true` or `false`

Returns `true` only if the contents of files *name1* and *name2* are identical.

---

copy   File.copy(*fromName*, *toName*, *verbose*=`false`) → `true` or `false`

Equivalent to calling `File.syscopy`, but logs the attempt to `$stderr` if *verbose* is not `false`.

---

cp   File.cp(*fromName*, *toName*, *verbose*=`false`) → `true` or `false`

Synonym for `File.copy`.

---

install   File.install(*fromName*, *toName*, *aMode*=`nil`, *verbose*=`false`)

Copies file *fromName* to file *toName* using `File.syscopy`, unless *toName* already exists and has the same content as *fromName*. Sets the mode of the resulting file to *aMode* unless *aMode* is `nil`.

---

makedirs   File.makedirs(⟨ *dirName* ⟩* ⟨ , *aBoolean* ⟩)

Creates the given directories, logging each attempt to `$stderr` if the last parameter is `true`. Creates any missing parent directories as required.

---

mkpath   File.mkpath(⟨ *dirName* ⟩* ⟨ , *aBoolean* ⟩)

Synonym for `File.makedirs`.

---

move   File.move(*fromName*, *toName*, *verbose*=`false`) → `true` or `false`

Effectively renames *fromName* to *toName*, logging to `$stderr` if *verbose* is not `false`.

---

mv   File.mv(*fromName*, *toName*, *verbose*=`false`) → `true` or `false`

Synonym for `File.move`.

---

rm_f   File.rm_f(⟨ *fileName* ⟩* ⟨ , *aBoolean* ⟩) → *anInteger*

Synonym for `File.safe_unlink` (the name refers to the Unix `rm -f` command).

---

safe_unlink   File.safe_unlink(⟨ *fileName* ⟩* ⟨ , *aBoolean* ⟩) → *anInteger* or `nil`

Unlinks (deletes) the given files, logging to `$stderr` if the last parameter is `true`. The method attempts to make all files writable before unlinking them, so no errors will occur deleting read-only files. Returns the number of files deleted, or `nil` on error.

---

syscopy   File.syscopy(*fromName*, *toName*) → `true` or `false`

Efficiently copies the file named *fromName* to *toName*. If *toName* names a directory, the destination will be a file in that directory with the same basename as *fromName*. After the copy, the file mode of *toName* will be the same as that of *fromName*. Returns `true` on success.

Class	GetoptLong < Object	require "getoptlong"

```
# Call using "ruby example.rb --size 10k -v -q a.txt b.doc"

require 'getoptlong'

# specify the options we accept and initialize
# the option parser

opts = GetoptLong.new(
  [ "--size",    "-s",            GetoptLong::REQUIRED_ARGUMENT ],
  [ "--verbose", "-v",            GetoptLong::NO_ARGUMENT ],
  [ "--query",   "-q",            GetoptLong::NO_ARGUMENT ],
  [ "--check",   "--valid", "-c", GetoptLong::NO_ARGUMENT ]
)

# process the parsed options

opts.each do |opt, arg|
  puts "Option: #{opt}, arg #{arg.inspect}"
end

puts "Remaining args: #{ARGV.join(', ')}"
```

produces:

```
Option: --size, arg "10k"
Option: --verbose, arg ""
Option: --query, arg ""
Remaining args: a.txt, b.doc
```

Class `GetoptLong` supports GNU-style command-line option parsing. Options may be a minus sign ('-') followed by a single character, or two minus signs ('--') followed by a name (a long option). Long options may be abbreviated to their shortest unambiguous lengths.

A single internal option may have multiple external representations. For example, the option to control verbose output could be any of `-v`, `--verbose`, or `--details`. Some options may also take an associated value.

Each internal option is passed to `GetoptLong` as an array, containing strings representing the option's external forms and a flag. The flag (`NO_ARGUMENT`, `REQUIRE_ARGUMENT`, or `OPTIONAL_ARGUMENT`) specifies how `GetoptLong` is to associate an argument with the option.

If the environment variable `POSIXLY_CORRECT` is set, all options must precede nonoptions on the command line. Otherwise, the default behavior of `GetoptLong` is to reorganize the command line to put the options at the front. This behavior may be changed by setting `GetoptLong#ordering=` to one of the constants `PERMUTE`, `REQUIRE_ORDER`, or `RETURN_IN_ORDER`. `POSIXLY_CORRECT` may not be overridden.

Class constants

Per-option constants	
NO_ARGUMENT	Flags an option that takes no argument.
OPTIONAL_ARGUMENT	A nonoption following this option will be used as this option's argument.
REQUIRED_ARGUMENT	This option must be followed by an argument.

Overall constants	
PERMUTE	Options and their arguments will be shuffled to the front of the command line.
REQUIRE_ORDER	Options and their arguments must appear at the start of the command line. The first nonoption terminates option processing.
RETURN_IN_ORDER	Return options in the order in which they occur on the command line.

Class methods

new   GetoptLong.new(⟨ *options* ⟩*) → *getopt*

Returns a new option parser. Any *options* are passed to *getopt*.set_options.

Instance methods

each   *getopt*.each {| *anOption, anArgument* | *block* }

Loops calling GetoptLong#get, passing the returned option and argument to the associated block. The loop ends when get returns nil for *anOption*.

error?   *getopt*.error? → *anException*

Returns an Exception object documenting any error that has occurred, or nil if there has not been an error.

error_message   *getopt*.error_message → *aString*

Returns the text of the last error message.

get   *getopt*.get → [*anOption, anArgument*]

Returns the next option, along with any associated argument. If there is no argument, nil is returned for *anArgument*. If there are no remaining unprocessed options, or if there is an error in option processing and quiet has been set, nil is returned for *anOption*. Otherwise, if there is an error, a message is written to $stderr and an exception (a subclass of StandardError) is raised.

The option string returned is the first option that was given in the corresponding array passed to `set_options`.

---

get_option   *getopt*.get_option → [*anOption, anArgument*]

Synonym for `GetoptLong#get`.

---

ordering   *getopt*.ordering → *aFixnum*

Returns the current ordering.

---

ordering=   *getopt*.ordering = *aFixnum*

Sets the ordering to one of **PERMUTE, REQUIRE_ORDER**, or **RETURN_IN_ORDER**. Quietly ignored if the environment variable **POSIXLY_CORRECT** is set. Ordering may not be changed once option processing has been started.

---

quiet   *getopt*.quiet → **true** or **false**

Returns the current value of the `quiet` attribute.

---

quiet=   *getopt*.quiet = **true** or **false**

Sets the current value of the `quiet` attribute. If **false**, any errors encountered are reported to **$stderr**.

---

quiet?   *getopt*.quiet? → **true** or **false**

Synonym for `GetoptLong#quiet`.

---

set_options   *getopt*.set_options(⟨ *anOptArray* ⟩*) → *getopt*

Each parameter is an array specifying a single internal option. The array contains one or more strings specifying the external form(s) of the option, and one of the flags **NO_ARGUMENT, OPTIONAL_ARGUMENT**, or **REQUIRED_ARGUMENT**. See the sample code on page 452 for examples of use.

---

terminate   *getopt*.terminate → *getopt*

Terminates option processing. Any remaining arguments are written back to **ARGV**. This may be called from within a `GetoptLong#each` or on its own. For example, calling the following program using "`ruby example.rb -size 10k -v -term -q a.txt b.doc`" will leave the -q and filenames in **ARGV**.

```
require 'getoptlong'

opts = GetoptLong.new(
  [ "--size",    "-s",    GetoptLong::REQUIRED_ARGUMENT ],
  [ "--verbose", "-v",    GetoptLong::NO_ARGUMENT ],
  [ "--term",    "-t",    GetoptLong::NO_ARGUMENT ],
  [ "--query",   "-q",    GetoptLong::NO_ARGUMENT ],
```

```
[ "--check",    "--valid", "-c", GetoptLong::NO_ARGUMENT ]
)

opts.each do |opt, arg|
  puts "Option: #{opt}, arg #{arg.inspect}"
  opts.terminate if (opt == '--term')
end

puts "Remaining args: #{ARGV.join(', ')}"
```

produces:

```
Option: --size, arg "10k"
Option: --verbose, arg ""
Option: --term, arg ""
Remaining args: -q, a.txt, b.doc
```

---

terminated?   *getopt*.terminated? → `true` or `false`

Returns `true` if option processing has been terminated.

| Module **mkmf** | require **"mkmf"** |

The `mkmf` library is used by Ruby extension modules to help create `Makefiles`. When writing an extension, you create a program named "`extconf.rb`", which may be as simple as:

```
require 'mkmf'
create_makefile("Test")
```

When run, this script will produce a `Makefile` suited to the target platform. `mkmf` contains several methods you can use to find libraries and include files and to set compiler flags.

For more information on creating extension modules, see Chapter 17, which begins on page 171.

Module constants

PLATFORM	A constant string that describes the platform on which Ruby is running, such as "mswin32" or "i686-linux."
$CFLAGS	Global variable for compiler flags.
$LDFLAGS	Global variable for linker flags.

Instance methods

create_makefile   create_makefile(*target*)

Creates a `Makefile` for an extension named *target*. If this method is not called, no `Makefile` is created.

dir_config   dir_config(*name*)

Looks for directory configuration options for *name* given as arguments to this program or to the original build of Ruby. These arguments may be one of:

```
--with-name-dir=directory
--with-name-include=directory
--with-name-lib=directory
```

The given directories will be added to the appropriate search paths (include or link) in the `Makefile`.

find_library   find_library(*name, function,* ⟨ *path* ⟩⁺) → `true` or `false`

Same as `have_library`, but will also search in the given directory paths.

have_func   have_func(*function*) → `true` or `false`

If the named function exists in the standard compile environment, adds the directive -D HAVE_*FUNCTION* to the compile command in the `Makefile` and returns `true`.

have_header   have_header(*header*) → `true` or `false`

If the given header file can be found in the standard search path, adds the directive -D HAVE_*HEADER* to the compile command in the `Makefile` and returns `true`.

have_library   have_library(*library, function*) → `true` or `false`

If the given function exists in the named library, which must exist in the standard search path or in a directory added with `dir_config`, adds the library to the link command in the `Makefile` and returns `true`.

ParseDate

The `ParseDate` module defines a single method, `ParseDate.parsedate`, which converts a date and/or time string into its constituents. It uses heuristics that handle a wide variety of date and time formats, including a subset of ISO 8601, Unix `ctime`, and most common written variants. The following table shows some examples.

String	Guess?	yy	mm	dd	hh	min	sec	zone	wd
1999-09-05 23:55:21+0900	F	1999	9	5	23	55	21	+0900	–
1983-12-25	F	1983	12	25	–	–	–	–	–
1965-11-10 T13:45	F	1965	11	10	13	45	–	–	–
10/9/75 1:30pm	F	75	10	9	13	30	–	–	–
10/9/75 1:30pm	T	1975	10	9	13	30	–	–	–
Mon Feb 28 17:15:49 CST 2000	F	2000	2	28	17	15	49	CST	1
Tue, 02-Mar-99 11:20:32 GMT	F	99	3	2	11	20	32	GMT	2
Tue, 02-Mar-99 11:20:32 GMT	T	1999	3	2	11	20	32	GMT	2
12-January-1990, 04:00 WET	F	1990	1	12	4	0	–	WET	–
4/3/99	F	99	4	3	–	–	–	–	–
4/3/99	T	1999	4	3	–	–	–	–	–
10th February, 1976	F	1976	2	10	–	–	–	–	–
March 1st, 84	T	1984	3	1	–	–	–	–	–
Friday	F	–	–	–	–	–	–	–	5

Module methods

parsedate   ParseDate.parsedate(*aString*, *guessYear*=`false`)
→ [*year*, *mon*, *mday*, *hour*, *min*, *sec*, *zone*, *wday*]

Parses a string containing a date and/or a time, returning an array of `Fixnum` objects containing the various components. `nil` is returned for fields that cannot be parsed from *aString*. If the result contains a year that is less than 100 and *guessYear* is true, `parsedate` will return a year value equal to *year* plus 2000 if *year* is less than 69, *year* plus 1900 otherwise.

The `profile` library prints to `$stderr` a summary of the number of calls to, and the time spent in, each method in a Ruby program. The output is sorted by the total time spent in each method. Profiling can be enabled from the command line using the `-rprofile` option, or from within a source program by requiring the `profile` module.

```ruby
require 'profile'
def ackerman(m, n)
  if m == 0 then  n+1
  elsif n == 0 and m > 0 then ackerman(m-1, 1)
  else ackerman(m-1, ackerman(m, n-1))
  end
end
ackerman(3,3)
```

produces:

% time	cumulative seconds	self seconds	calls	self ms/call	total ms/call	name
73.53	2.75	2.75	2432	1.13	47.19	Object#ackerman
12.03	3.20	0.45	3676	0.12	0.12	Fixnum#==
7.49	3.48	0.28	1188	0.24	0.24	Fixnum#+
6.95	3.74	0.26	2431	0.11	0.11	Fixnum#-
0.00	3.74	0.00	57	0.00	0.00	Fixnum#>
0.00	3.74	0.00	1	0.00	0.00	Module#method_added
0.00	3.74	0.00	1	0.00	3740.00	#toplevel

The `PStore` class provides transactional, file-based persistent storage of Ruby objects. The following example stores two hierarchies in a PStore. The first, identified by the key "**names**", is an array of Strings. The second, identified by "**tree**", is a simple binary tree.

```ruby
require "pstore"

class T
  def initialize(val, left=nil, right=nil)
    @val, @left, @right = val, left, right
  end
  def to_a
    [ @val, @left.to_a, @right.to_a ]
  end
end

store = PStore.new("/tmp/store")
store.transaction do
  store['names'] = [ 'Douglas', 'Barenberg', 'Meyer' ]
```

```
    store['tree']  = T.new('top',
                        T.new('A', T.new('B')),
                        T.new('C', T.new('D', nil, T.new('E'))))
end

# now read it back in

store.transaction do
    puts "Roots: #{store.roots.join(', ')}"
    puts store['names'].join(', ')
    puts store['tree'].to_a.inspect
end
```

produces:

```
Roots: names, tree
Douglas, Barenberg, Meyer
["top", ["A", ["B", [], []], []], ["C", ["D", [], ["E", [], []]], []]]
```

Each PStore can store several object hierarchies. Each hierarchy has a root, identified by a key (often a string). At the start of a PStore transaction, these hierarchies are read from a disk file and made available to the Ruby program. At the end of the transaction, the hierarchies are written back to the file. Any changes made to objects in these hierarchies are therefore saved on disk, to be read at the start of the next transaction that uses that file.

In normal use, a PStore object is created and then is used one or more times to control a transaction. Within the body of the transaction, any object hierarchies that had previously been saved are made available, and any changes to object hierarchies, and any new hierarchies, are written back to the file at the end.

Class methods

new   PStore.new(*aFilename*) → *aPStore*

Returns a new PStore object associated with the given file. If the file exists, its contents must have been previously written by PStore.

Instance methods

[ ]   *pStore*[*anObject*] → *anOtherObject*

Root Access—Returns the root of an object hierarchy identified by *anObject*. An exception is raised if *anObject* does not identify a root.

[ ]=   *pStore*[*anObject*] = *anOtherObject* → *anOtherObject*

Root Creation—Sets *anOtherObject* as the base of the object hierarchy to be identified using *anObject*.

---

abort *pStore*.abort

Terminates this transaction, losing any changes made to the object hierarchies.

---

commit *pStore*.commit

Terminates the current transaction, saving the object hierarchies into the store's file.

---

path *pStore*.path → *aString*

Returns the name of the file associated with this store.

---

root? *pStore*.root?(*anObject*) → `true` or `false`

Returns `true` if *anObject* is the key of a root in this store.

---

roots *pStore*.roots → *anArray*

Returns an array containing the keys of the root objects available in this store.

---

transaction *pStore*.transaction {| pStore | *block* } → *anObject*

If the file associated with *pStore* exists, reads in the object hierarchies from it. It then executes the associated block, passing in *pStore*. The block may use this parameter to access the roots of the hierarchies and hence access the persistent objects. If the block calls `PStore#abort`, or if it raises an exception, no data is saved back to the associated file. Otherwise, if it invokes `PStore#commit`, or if it terminates normally, the object hierarchies are written back to the file. The value returned is the value returned by the block.

Class **Tempfile** < [IO]   **require** `"tempfile"`

```
require "tempfile"

tf = Tempfile.new("afile")
tf.path                    →    "/tmp/afile15742.0"
tf.puts("Cosi Fan Tutte")  →    nil
tf.close                   →    nil
tf.open                    →    #<File:0x4016d094>
tf.gets                    →    "Cosi Fan Tutte\n"
tf.close(true)             →    #<File:0x4016d094>
```

Class `Tempfile` creates managed temporary files. Although they behave the same as any other `IO` objects, temporary files are automatically deleted when the Ruby program terminates. Once a `Tempfile` object has been created, the underlying file may be opened and closed a number of times in succession.

Tempfile does not directly inherit from IO. Instead, it delegates calls to a **File** object. From the programmer's perspective, apart from the unusual **new, open,** and **close** semantics, a **Tempfile** object behaves as if it were an IO object.

Class methods

new   Tempfile.new(*basename, tmpdir*=<see below>) → *aTempfile*

Constructs a temporary file in the given directory. The file name is built by concatenating *basename*, the current process id and (as an extension) a unique sequence number. If the *tmpdir* parameter is not supplied, it defaults to the value of one of the environment variables TMPDIR, TMP, or TEMP, or to the directory /tmp.

The file is then opened using mode "w+", which allows reading and writing and deletes any existing content (see Table 22.5 on page 331).

open   Tempfile.open(*basename, tmpdir*) → *aTempfile*

Synonym for **Tempfile.new**.

Instance methods

close   *aTempfile*.close(*final*=**false**)

Closes *aTempfile*. If *final* is **true**, deletes the underlying real file. If *final* is **false**, *aTempfile* may be subsequently reopened. In all cases, the underlying file is deleted when the program terminates.

open   *aTempfile*.open

Reopens *aTempfile* using mode "r+", which allows reading and writing but does not delete existing content.

path   *aTempfile*.path → *aString*

Returns the full path of the underlying file.

Tempfile

Class **Mutex** < Object   **require** **"thread"**

```
require 'thread'
sema4 = Mutex.new

a = Thread.new {
  sema4.synchronize {
    # access shared resource
  }
}

b = Thread.new {
  sema4.synchronize {
    # access shared resource
  }
}
```

`Mutex` implements a simple semaphore that can be used to coordinate access to shared data from multiple concurrent threads.

Instance methods

lock   *aMutex*.lock → *aMutex*

Attempts to grab the lock and waits if it isn't available.

---

locked?   *aMutex*.locked? → `true` or `false`

Returns `true` if this lock is currently held by some thread.

---

synchronize   *aMutex*.synchronize { *block* } → *aMutex*

Obtains a lock (using `Mutex#lock`), runs the block, and releases the lock when the block completes.

---

try_lock   *aMutex*.try_lock → `true` or `false`

Attempts to obtain the lock and returns immediately. Returns `true` if the lock was granted.

---

unlock   *aMutex*.unlock → *aMutex* or `nil`

Releases the lock. Returns `nil` if *aMutex* wasn't locked.

ConditionVariable < Object

```
require 'thread'
mutex = Mutex.new
resource = ConditionVariable.new

a = Thread.new {
  mutex.synchronize {
    # Thread 'a' now needs the resource
    resource.wait(mutex)
    # 'a' can now have the resource
  }
}

b = Thread.new {
  mutex.synchronize {
    # Thread 'b' has finished using the resource
    resource.signal
  }
}
```

ConditionVariable objects augment class Mutex. Using condition variables, it is possible to suspend while in the middle of a critical section until a resource becomes available (see the discussion on page 119).

Instance methods

broadcast
aCond.broadcast

Wakes up all threads waiting for this lock.

signal
aCond.signal

Wakes up the first thread in line waiting for this lock.

wait
aCond.wait(*aMutex*) → *aMutex*

Releases the lock held in *aMutex* and waits; reacquires the lock on wakeup.

timeout

```
require "timeout"

for snooze in 1..2
  puts "About to sleep for #{snooze}"
  timeout(1.5) do
    sleep(snooze)
  end
  puts "That was refreshing"
end
```

produces:

```
About to sleep for 1
That was refreshing
About to sleep for 2
/tc/usr/lib/ruby/1.6/timeout.rb:37: execution expired (TimeoutError)
from prog.rb:5:in `timeout'
from prog.rb:5
from prog.rb:3:in `each'
from prog.rb:3
```

The `timeout` method takes a single parameter, representing a timeout period in seconds, and a block. The block is executed, and a timer is run concurrently. If the block terminates before the timeout, `timeout` returns `true`. Otherwise, a `TimeoutError` exception is raised.

WeakRef < Delegator

```
require "weakref"

ref = "fol de rol"
puts "Initial object is #{ref}"
ref = WeakRef.new(ref)
puts "Weak reference is #{ref}"
ObjectSpace.garbage_collect
puts "But then it is #{ref}"
```

produces:

```
Initial object is fol de rol
Weak reference is fol de rol
prog.rb:8: Illegal Reference - probably recycled (WeakRef::RefError)
```

In Ruby, objects are not eligible for garbage collection if there are still references to them. Normally, this is a Good Thing—it would be disconcerting to have an object simply evaporate while you were using it. However, sometimes you may need more flexibility. For example, you might want to implement an in-memory cache of commonly used file contents. As you read more files, the cache grows. At some point, you may run low on memory. The garbage collector will be invoked, but the objects in the cache are all referenced by the cache data structures, and so will not be deleted.

A weak reference behaves exactly as any normal object reference with one important exception—the referenced object may be garbage collected, even while references to it exist. In the cache example, if the cached files were accessed using weak references, once memory runs low they will be garbage collected, freeing memory for the rest of the application.

Weak references introduce a slight complexity. As the object referenced can be deleted by garbage collection at any time, code that accesses these objects must take care to ensure that the references are valid. Two techniques can be used. First, the code can reference the objects normally. Any attempt to reference an object that has been garbage collected will raise a `WeakRef::RefError` exception.

An alternative approach is to use the `WeakRef#weakref_alive?` method to check that a reference is valid before using it. Garbage collection must be disabled during the test and subsequent reference to the object. In a single-threaded program, you could use something like:

```
ref = WeakRef.new(someObject)
#
# .. some time later
#
gcWasDisabled = GC.disable
if ref.weakref_alive?
  # do stuff with 'ref'
end
GC.enable unless gcWasDisabled
```

Class methods

new   WeakRef.new(*anObject*) → *ref*

Creates and returns a weak reference to *anObject*. All future references to *anObject* should be made using *ref*.

Instance methods

weakref_alive?   *ref*.weakref_alive? → `true` or `false`

Returns `false` if the object referenced by *ref* has been garbage collected.

## Chapter 25

Object-Oriented Design Libraries

One of the interesting things about Ruby is the way it blurs the distinction between design and implementation. Ideas that have to be expressed at the design level in other languages can be implemented directly in Ruby.

To help in this process, Ruby has support for some design-level strategies.

- **The Visitor pattern** (Design Patterns, [GHJV95]) is a way of traversing a collection without having to know the internal organization of that collection.

- **Delegation** is a way of composing classes more flexibly and dynamically than can be done using standard inheritance.

- **The Singleton pattern** is a way of ensuring that only one instantiation of a particular class exists at a time.

- **The Observer pattern** implements a protocol allowing one object to notify a set of interested objects when certain changes have occurred.

Normally, all four of these strategies require explicit code each time they're implemented. With Ruby, they can be abstracted into a library and reused freely and transparently.

Before we get into the proper library descriptions, let's get the simplest strategy out of the way.

The Visitor Pattern

It's the method `each`.

Library		require
delegate		**"delegate"**

Object delegation is a way of *composing* objects—extending an object with the capabilities of another—at runtime. This promotes writing flexible, decoupled code, as there are no compile-time dependencies between the users of the overall class and the delegates.

The Ruby `Delegator` class implements a simple but powerful delegation scheme, where requests are automatically forwarded from a master class to delegates or their ancestors, and where the delegate can be changed at runtime with a single method call.

The `delegate.rb` library provides two mechanisms for allowing an object to forward messages to a delegate.

1. For simple cases where the class of the delegate is fixed, arrange for the master class to be a subclass of `DelegateClass`, passing the name of the class to be delegated as a parameter (Example 1). Then, in your class's `initialize` method, you'd call the superclass, passing in the object to be delegated. For example, to declare a class `Fred` that also supports all the methods in `Flintstone`, you'd write

```
class Fred < DelegateClass(Flintstone)
  def initialize
    # ...
    super(Flintstone.new(...))
  end
  # ...
end
```

This is subtly different from using subclassing. With subclassing, there is only one object, which has the methods and the defined class, its parent, and their ancestors. With delegation there are two objects, linked so that calls to one may be delegated to the other.

2. For cases where the delegate needs to be dynamic, make the master class a subclass of `SimpleDelegator` (Example 2). You can also add delegation capabilities to an existing object using `SimpleDelegator` (Example 3). In these cases, you can call the `__setobj__` method in `SimpleDelegator` to change the object being delegated at runtime.

Example 1. Use the `DelegateClass` method and subclass the result when you need a class with its own behavior that also delegates to an object of another class. In this example, we assume that the `@sizeInInches` array is large, so we want only one copy of it. We then define a class that accesses it, converting the values to feet.

```
require 'delegate'

sizeInInches = [ 10, 15, 22, 120 ]
```

```
class Feet < DelegateClass(Array)
  def initialize(arr)
    super(arr)
  end
  def [](*n)
    val = super(*n)
    case val.type
    when Numeric; val/12.0
    else;         val.collect {|i| i/12.0}
    end
  end
end

sizeInFeet = Feet.new(sizeInInches)
sizeInInches[0..3]  →  [10, 15, 22, 120]
sizeInFeet[0..3]    →  [0.8333333333, 1.25, 1.833333333, 10.0]
```

Example 2. Use subclass `SimpleDelegator` when you want an object that both has its own behavior *and* delegates to different objects during its lifetime. This is an example of the State pattern[GHJV95]. Objects of class `TicketOffice` sell tickets if a seller is available, or tell you to come back tomorrow if there is no seller.

```
require 'delegate'

class TicketSeller
  def sellTicket()
    return 'Here is a ticket'
  end
end

class NoTicketSeller
  def sellTicket()
    "Sorry-come back tomorrow"
  end
end

class TicketOffice < SimpleDelegator
  def initialize
    @seller = TicketSeller.new
    @noseller = NoTicketSeller.new
    super(@seller)
  end
  def allowSales(allow = true)
    __setobj__(allow ? @seller : @noseller)
    allow
  end
end

to = TicketOffice.new
to.sellTicket        →  "Here is a ticket"
to.allowSales(false) →  false
to.sellTicket        →  "Sorry-come back tomorrow"
to.allowSales(true)  →  true
to.sellTicket        →  "Here is a ticket"
```

Example 3. Create `SimpleDelegator` objects when you want a single object to delegate all its methods to two or more other objects.

```
# Example 3 - delegate from existing object
seller   = TicketSeller.new
noseller = NoTicketSeller.new
to = SimpleDelegator.new(seller)
to.sellTicket   →   "Here's a ticket"
to.sellTicket   →   "Here's a ticket"
to.__setobj__(noseller)
to.sellTicket   →   "Sorry-come back tomorrow"
to.__setobj__(seller)
to.sellTicket   →   "Here's a ticket"
```

Library observer   require **"observer"**

The Observer pattern[GHJV95], also known as Publish/Subscribe, provides a simple mechanism for one object to inform a set of interested third-party objects when its state changes.

In the Ruby implementation, the notifying class mixes in the `Observable` module, which provides the methods for managing the associated observer objects.

add_observer(*obj*)	Add *obj* as an observer on this object. *obj* will now receive notifications.
delete_observer(*obj*)	Delete *obj* as an observer on this object. It will no longer receive notifications.
delete_observers	Delete all observers associated with this object.
count_observers	Return the count of observers associated with this object.
changed(*newState*=`true`)	Set the changed state of this object. Notifications will be sent only if the changed state is `true`.
changed?	Query the changed state of this object.
notify_observers(**args*)	If this object's changed state is true, invoke the `update` method in each currently associated observer in turn, passing it the given arguments. The changed state is then set to `false`.

The observers must implement the `update` method to receive notifications.

```
require "observer"

  class Ticker # Periodically fetch a stock price
    include Observable

    def initialize(symbol)
      @symbol = symbol
    end
```

```
    def run
      lastPrice = nil
      loop do
        price = Price.fetch(@symbol)
        print "Current price: #{price}\n"
        if price != lastPrice
          changed                 # notify observers
          lastPrice = price
          notify_observers(Time.now, price)
        end
      end
    end
  end

  class Warner
    def initialize(ticker, limit)
      @limit = limit
      ticker.add_observer(self)   # all warners are observers
    end
  end

  class WarnLow < Warner
    def update(time, price)       # callback for observer
      if price < @limit
        print "--- #{time.to_s}: Price below #@limit: #{price}\n"
      end
    end
  end

  class WarnHigh < Warner
    def update(time, price)       # callback for observer
      if price > @limit
        print "+++ #{time.to_s}: Price above #@limit: #{price}\n"
      end
    end
  end

ticker = Ticker.new("MSFT")
WarnLow.new(ticker, 80)
WarnHigh.new(ticker, 120)
ticker.run
```

produces:

```
Current price: 83
Current price: 75
--- Tue Sep 19 23:32:40 CDT 2000: Price below 80: 75
Current price: 90
Current price: 134
+++ Tue Sep 19 23:32:40 CDT 2000: Price above 120: 134
Current price: 134
Current price: 112
Current price: 79
--- Tue Sep 19 23:32:40 CDT 2000: Price below 80: 79
```

Library **singleton**	require **"singleton"**

The Singleton design pattern[GHJV95] ensures that only one instance of a particular class may be created.

The **singleton** library makes this simple to implement. Mix the **Singleton** module into each class that is to be a singleton, and that class's **new** method will be made private. In its place, users of the class call the method **instance**, which returns a singleton instance of that class.

In this example, the two instances of **MyClass** are the same object.

```
require 'singleton'

class MyClass
  include Singleton
end

a = MyClass.instance   →   #<MyClass:0x40189aa0>
b = MyClass.instance   →   #<MyClass:0x40189aa0>
```

## Chapter 26

Network and Web Libraries

Ruby provides two levels of access to network services. At a low level, you can access the basic socket support in the underlying operating system, which allows you to implement clients and servers for both connection-oriented and connectionless protocols. These are documented in the next section.

Ruby also has libraries that provide higher-level access to specific application-level network protocols, such as FTP, HTTP, and so on. These are documented starting on page 486.

Finally, the CGI libraries, documented beginning on page 501, provide server-side developers with a convenient interface for developing Web applications.

Socket-Level Access

Sockets are the endpoints of a bidirectional communications channel. Sockets may communicate within a process, between processes on the same machine, or between processes on different continents. Sockets may be implemented over a number of different channel types: Unix domain sockets, TCP, UDP, and so on. The socket library provides specific classes for handling the common transports as well as a generic interface for handling the rest. All functionality in the socket library is accessible through a single extension library. Access it using

```
require 'socket'
```

Sockets have their own vocabulary:

domain The family of protocols that will be used as the transport mechanism. These values are constants such as PF_INET, PF_UNIX, PF_X25, and so on.

type The type of communications between the two endpoints, typically SOCK_STREAM for connection-oriented protocols and SOCK_DGRAM for connectionless protocols.

protocol Typically zero, this may be used to identify a variant of a protocol within a domain and type.

hostName The identifier of a network interface:

- a string, which can be a host name, a dotted-quad address, or an IPV6 address in colon (and possibly dot) notation,

- the string "<broadcast>", which specifies an `INADDR_BROADCAST` address,

- a zero-length string, which specifies `INADDR_ANY`, or

- an `Integer`, interpreted as a binary address in host byte order.

port (sometimes called **service**) Each server listens for clients calling on one or more ports. A port may be a `Fixnum` port number, a string containing a port number, or the name of a service.

Sockets are children of class `IO`. Once a socket has been successfully opened, the conventional I/O methods may be used. However, greater efficiency is sometimes obtained by using socket-specific methods. As with other I/O classes, socket I/O blocks by default. The hierarchy of the socket classes is shown in Figure 26.1 on the facing page.

For more information on the use of sockets, see your operating system documentation. You'll also find a comprehensive treatment in W. Richard Stevens, *Unix Network Programming, Volumes 1 and 2* [Ste98a, Ste98b].

Class	**BasicSocket** < IO	**require** "socket"

`BasicSocket` is an abstract base class for all other socket classes.

This class and its subclasses often manipulate addresses using something called a `struct sockaddr`, which is effectively an opaque binary string.[1]

Class methods

do_not_reverse_lookup   BasicSocket.do_not_reverse_lookup → `true` or `false`

Returns the value of the global reverse lookup flag. If set to `true`, queries on remote addresses will return the numeric address but not the host name.

---

do_not_reverse_lookup=   BasicSocket.do_not_reverse_lookup = `true` or `false`

Sets the global reverse lookup flag.

---

1.   In reality, it maps onto the underlying C-language `struct sockaddr` set of structures, documented in the man pages and in the books by Stevens.

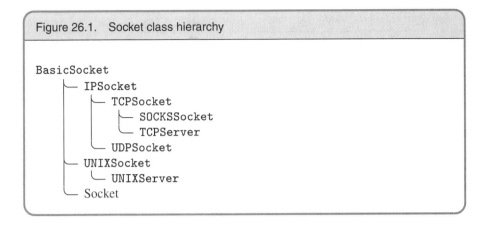

Figure 26.1. Socket class hierarchy

```
BasicSocket
    ├── IPSocket
    │      ├── TCPSocket
    │      │      ├── SOCKSSocket
    │      │      └── TCPServer
    │      └── UDPSocket
    ├── UNIXSocket
    │      └── UNIXServer
    └── Socket
```

---

lookup_order   BasicSocket.lookup_order → *aFixnum*

Returns the global address lookup order, one of:

Order	Families Searched
LOOKUP_UNSP	AF_UNSPEC
LOOKUP_INET	AF_INET, AF_INET6, AF_UNSPEC
LOOKUP_INET6	AF_INET6, AF_INET, AF_UNSPEC

---

lookup_order=   BasicSocket.lookup_order = *aFixnum*

Sets the global address lookup order.

Instance methods

close_read   *sock*.close_read → `nil`

Closes the readable connection on this socket.

---

close_write   *sock*.close_write → `nil`

Closes the writable connection on this socket.

---

getpeername   *sock*.getpeername → *aString*

Returns the `struct sockaddr` structure associated with the other end of this socket connection.

---

getsockname   *sock*.getsockname → *aString*

Returns the `struct sockaddr` structure associated with *sock*.

---

getsockopt   *sock*.getsockopt(*level, optname*) → *aString*

Returns the value of the specified option.

---

recv   *sock*.recv(*len*, ⟨ , *flags* ⟩) → *aString*

Receives up to *len* bytes from *sock*.

---

send   *sock*.send(*aString*, *flags*, ⟨ , *to* ⟩) → *aFixnum*

Sends *aString* over *sock*. If specified, *to* is a **struct sockaddr** specifying the recipient address. *flags* are the sum or one or more of the **MSG_** options (listed on page 482). Returns the number of characters sent.

---

setsockopt   *sock*.setsockopt(*level*, *optname*, *optval*) → 0

Sets a socket option. *level* is one of the socket-level options (listed on page 482). *optname* and *optval* are protocol specific—see your system documentation for details.

---

shutdown   *sock*.shutdown(*how=2*) → 0

Shuts down the receive (*how* == 0), or send (*how* == 1), or both (*how* == 2), parts of this socket.

<table>
<tr><td>Class</td><td>IPSocket < BasicSocket</td><td>require</td><td>"socket"</td></tr>
</table>

Class **IPSocket** is a base class for sockets using IP as their transport. **TCPSocket** and **UDPSocket** are based on this class.

Class methods

getaddress   IPSocket.getaddress(*hostName*) → *aString*

Returns the dotted-quad IP address of *hostName*.

```
a = IPSocket.getaddress('www.ruby-lang.org')
a   →   "210.251.121.211"
```

Instance methods

addr   *sock*.addr → *anArray*

Returns the domain, port, name, and IP address of *sock* as a four-element array. The name will be returned as an address if the **do_not_reverse_lookup** flag is **true**.

```
u = UDPSocket.new
u.bind('localhost', 8765)
u.addr   →   ["AF_INET", 8765, "localhost", "127.0.0.1"]
BasicSocket.do_not_reverse_lookup = true
u.addr   →   ["AF_INET", 8765, "127.0.0.1", "127.0.0.1"]
```

---

peeraddr   *sock*.peeraddr → *anArray*

Returns the domain, port, name, and IP address of the peer.

```
t = TCPSocket.new('localhost', 'ftp')
t.gets    →    "220 zip.local.thomases.com FTP server (Version
                6.2/OpenBSD/Linux-0.11) read..."
t.close   →    nil
```

Class methods

gethostbyname   TCPSocket.gethostbyname(*hostName*) → *anArray*

Looks up *hostName* and returns its canonical name, an array containing any aliases, the address type (**AF_INET**), and the dotted-quad IP address.

```
a = TCPSocket.gethostbyname('ns.pragprog.com')
a    →    ["pragprog.com", [], 2, "63.68.129.131"]
```

new   TCPSocket.new(*hostName, port*) → *sock*

Opens a TCP connection to *hostName* on the *port*.

open   TCPSocket.open(*hostName, port*) → *sock*

Synonym for **TCPSocket.new**.

Instance methods

recvfrom   *sock*.recvfrom(*len* ⟨ *, flags* ⟩) → *anArray*

Receives up to *len* bytes on the connection. *flags* is zero or more of the **MSG_** options (listed on page 482). Returns a two-element array. The first element is the received data, the second is an array containing information about the peer.

```
t = TCPSocket.new('localhost', 'ftp')
data = t.recvfrom(30)
data    →    ["220 zip.local.thomases.com FTP", ["AF_INET", 21,
              "localhost", "127.0.0.1"]]
```

Socket

| Class | **SOCKSSocket** < TCPSocket | require | **"socket"** |

Class SOCKSSocket supports connections based on the SOCKS protocol.

Class methods

new   SOCKSSocket.new(*hostName, port*) → *sock*

Opens a SOCKS connection to *port* on *hostName*.

open   SOCKSSocket.open(*hostName, port*) → *sock*

Synonym for SOCKSSocket.new.

Instance methods

close   *sock*.close → nil

Closes this SOCKS connection.

| Class | **TCPServer** < TCPSocket | require | **"socket"** |

A TCPServer accepts incoming TCP connections. Here is a Web server that listens on a given port and returns the time.

```
require 'socket'
port = (ARGV[0] || 80).to_i
server = TCPServer.new('localhost', port)
while (session = server.accept)
  puts "Request: #{session.gets}"
  session.print "HTTP/1.1 200/OK\r\nContent-type: text/html\r\n\r\n"
  session.print "<html><body><h1>#{Time.now}</h1></body></html>\r\n"
  session.close
end
```

Class methods

new   TCPServer.new(⟨ *hostName,* ⟩ *port*) → *sock*

Creates a new socket on the given interface (identified by *hostName* and port). If *host-Name* is omitted, the server will listen on all interfaces on the current host (equivalent to an address of 0.0.0.0).

open   TCPServer.open(⟨ *hostName,* ⟩ *port*) → *sock*

Synonym for TCPServer.new.

Instance methods

accept   *sock*.accept → *aTCPSocket*

Waits for a connection on *sock*, and returns a new `TCPSocket` connected to the caller.
See the example on the facing page.

Class **UDPSocket** < IPSocket   **require** **"socket"**

UDP sockets send and receive datagrams. In order to receive data, a socket must be
bound to a particular port. You have two choices when sending data: you can connect
to a remote UDP socket and thereafter send datagrams to that port, or you can specify
a host and port for use with every packet you send. This example is a UDP server that
prints the message it receives. It is called by both connectionless and connection-based
clients.

```
require 'socket'

$port = 4321

sThread = Thread.start do      # run server in a thread
  server = UDPSocket.open
  server.bind(nil, $port)
  2.times { p server.recvfrom(64) }
end

# Ad-hoc client
UDPSocket.open.send("ad hoc", 0, 'localhost', $port)

# Connection based client
sock = UDPSocket.open
sock.connect('localhost', $port)
sock.send("connection-based", 0)
sThread.join
```

produces:
```
["ad hoc", ["AF_INET", 1580, "localhost", "127.0.0.1"]]
["connection-based", ["AF_INET", 1581, "localhost", "127.0.0.1"]]
```

Class methods

new   UDPSocket.new(*family* = `AF_INET`) → *sock*

Creates an endpoint for UDP communications, optionally specifying the address family.

---

open   UDPSocket.open(*family* = `AF_INET`) → *sock*

Synonym for `UDPSocket.new`.

Instance methods

bind

$sock.\text{bind}(\ hostName, port\ ) \rightarrow 0$

Associates the local end of the UDP connection with a given *hostName* and *port*. Must be used by servers to establish an accessible endpoint.

connect

$sock.\text{connect}(\ hostName, port\ ) \rightarrow 0$

Creates a connection to the given *hostName* and *port*. Subsequent `UDPSocket#send` requests that don't override the recipient will use this connection. Multiple `connect` requests may be issued on *sock*: the most recent will be used by `send`.

recvfrom

$sock.\text{recvfrom}(\ len\ \langle\ , flags\ \rangle\ ) \rightarrow anArray$

Receives up to *len* bytes from *sock*. *flags* is zero or more of the `MSG_` options (listed on page 482). The result is a two-element array containing the received data and information on the sender. See the example on the preceding page.

send

$sock.\text{send}(\ aString, flags\ ) \rightarrow aFixnum$
$sock.\text{send}(\ aString, flags, hostName, port\ ) \rightarrow aFixnum$

The two-parameter form sends *aString* on an existing connection. The four-parameter form sends *aString* to *port* on *hostName*.

Class **UNIXSocket**   <   BasicSocket   **require**   **"socket"**

Class `UNIXSocket` supports interprocess communications using the Unix domain protocol. Although the underlying protocol supports both datagram and stream connections, the Ruby library provides only a stream-based connection.

```
require 'socket'

$path = "/tmp/sample"

sThread = Thread.start do        # run server in a thread
  sock = UNIXServer.open($path)
  s1 = sock.accept
  p s1.recvfrom(124)
end

client = UNIXSocket.open($path)
client.send("hello", 0)
client.close

sThread.join
```

produces:

```
["hello", ["AF_UNIX", ""]]
```

Class methods

new   UNIXSocket.new(*path*) → *sock*

Opens a new domain socket on *path*, which must be a pathname.

open   UNIXSocket.open(*path*) → *sock*

Synonym for `UNIXSocket.new`.

Instance methods

addr   *sock*.addr → *anArray*

Returns the address family and path of this socket.

path   *sock*.path → *aString*

Returns the path of this domain socket.

peeraddr   *sock*.peeraddr → *anArray*

Returns the address family and path of the server end of the connection.

recvfrom   *sock*.recvfrom(*len* ⟨ , *flags* ⟩) → *anArray*

Receives up to *len* bytes from *sock*. *flags* is zero or more of the `MSG_` options (listed on the next page). The first element of the returned array is the received data, and the second contains (minimal) information on the sender.

Class **UNIXServer** < UNIXSocket   **require** **"socket"**

Class `UNIXServer` provides a simple Unix domain socket server. See `UNIXSocket` for example code.

Class methods

new   UNIXServer.new(*path*) → *sock*

Creates a server on the given *path*. The corresponding file must not exist at the time of the call.

open   UNIXServer.open(*path*) → *sock*

Synonym for `UNIXServer.new`.

Instance methods

accept   *sock*.accept → *aUnixSocket*

Waits for a connection on the server socket and returns a new socket object for that connection. See the example for `UNIXSocket` on page 480.

| Class | **Socket** < BasicSocket | require "socket" |

Class `Socket` provides access to the underlying operating system socket implementation. It can be used to provide more operating system-specific functionality than the protocol-specific socket classes, but at the expense of greater complexity. In particular, the class handles addresses using `struct sockaddr` structures packed into Ruby strings, which can be a joy to manipulate.

Class constants

Class `Socket` defines constants for use throughout the socket library. Individual constants are available only on architectures that support the related facility.

Types:
> SOCK_DGRAM, SOCK_PACKET, SOCK_RAW, SOCK_RDM, SOCK_SEQPACKET, SOCK_STREAM.

Protocol families:
> PF_APPLETALK, PF_AX25, PF_INET6, PF_INET, PF_IPX, PF_UNIX, PF_UNSPEC.

Address families:
> AF_APPLETALK, AF_AX25, AF_INET6, AF_INET, AF_IPX, AF_UNIX, AF_UNSPEC.

Lookup-order options:
> LOOKUP_INET6, LOOKUP_INET, LOOKUP_UNSPEC.

Send/receive options:
> MSG_DONTROUTE, MSG_OOB, MSG_PEEK.

Socket-level options:
> SOL_ATALK, SOL_AX25, SOL_IPX, SOL_IP, SOL_SOCKET, SOL_TCP, SOL_UDP.

Socket options:
> SO_BROADCAST, SO_DEBUG, SO_DONTROUTE, SO_ERROR, SO_KEEPALIVE, SO_LINGER, SO_NO_CHECK, SO_OOBINLINE, SO_PRIORITY, SO_RCVBUF, SO_REUSEADDR, SO_SNDBUF, SO_TYPE.

QOS options:
> SOPRI_BACKGROUND, SOPRI_INTERACTIVE, SOPRI_NORMAL.

Multicast options:

IP_ADD_MEMBERSHIP, IP_DEFAULT_MULTICAST_LOOP, IP_DEFAULT_MULTICAST_TTL,
IP_MAX_MEMBERSHIPS, IP_MULTICAST_IF, IP_MULTICAST_LOOP,
IP_MULTICAST_TTL.

TCP options:

TCP_MAXSEG, TCP_NODELAY.

getaddrinfo error codes:

EAI_ADDRFAMILY, EAI_AGAIN, EAI_BADFLAGS, EAI_BADHINTS, EAI_FAIL,
EAI_FAMILY, EAI_MAX, EAI_MEMORY, EAI_NODATA, EAI_NONAME, EAI_PROTOCOL,
EAI_SERVICE, EAI_SOCKTYPE, EAI_SYSTEM.

ai_flags values:

AI_ALL, AI_CANONNAME, AI_MASK, AI_NUMERICHOST, AI_PASSIVE,
AI_V4MAPPED_CFG.

Class methods

---

for_fd   Socket.for_fd(*anFD*) → *sock*

Wraps an already open file descriptor into a socket object.

---

getaddrinfo   Socket.getaddrinfo(*hostName, port,*
⟨ *family* ⟨ *, socktype* ⟨ *, protocol* ⟨ *, flags* ⟩ ⟩ ⟩ ⟩) → *anArray*

Returns an array of arrays describing the given host and port (optionally qualified as shown). Each subarray contains the address family, port number, host name, host IP address, protocol family, socket type, and protocol.

```
for line in Socket.getaddrinfo('www.microsoft.com', 'http')
  puts line.join(", ")
end
```

produces:

```
AF_INET, 80, microsoft.net, 207.46.130.149, 2, 1, 6
AF_INET, 80, microsoft.net, 207.46.131.137, 2, 1, 6
AF_INET, 80, microsoft.com, 207.46.230.218, 2, 1, 6
AF_INET, 80, microsoft.com, 207.46.230.219, 2, 1, 6
AF_INET, 80, microsoft.net, 207.46.130.14, 2, 1, 6
```

---

gethostbyaddr   Socket.gethostbyaddr(*addr, type*=**AF_INET**) → *anArray*

Returns the host name, address family, and **sockaddr** component for the given address.

```
a = Socket.gethostbyname("63.68.129.130")
res = Socket.gethostbyaddr(a[3], a[2])
res.join(', ')   →   "somewhere.in.pragprog.com, , 2, ?D\201\202"
```

---

gethostbyname   Socket.gethostbyname(*hostName*) → *anArray*

Returns a four-element array containing the canonical host name, a subarray of host aliases, the address family, and the address portion of the **sockaddr** structure.

```
a = Socket.gethostbyname("63.68.129.130")
a.join(', ')   →   "somewhere.in.pragprog.com, , 2, ?D\201\202"
```

---

gethostname   *sock*.gethostname → *aString*

Returns the name of the current host.

---

getnameinfo   Socket.getnameinfo(*addr* ⟨ , *flags* ⟩) → *anArray*

Looks up the given address, which may be either a string containing a sockaddr or a three- or four-element array. If *sockaddr* is an array, it should contain the string address family, the port (or nil), and the host name or IP address. If a fourth element is present and not **nil**, it will be used as the host name. Returns a canonical hostname (or address) and port number as an array.

```
a = Socket.getnameinfo(["AF_INET", '23', 'www.ruby-lang.org'])
a   →   ["hydrogen.ruby-lang.org", "telnet"]
```

---

getservbyname   Socket.getservbyname(*service, proto*=**tcp**) → *aFixnum*

Returns the port corresponding to the given service and protocol.

```
Socket.getservbyname("telnet")   →   23
```

---

new   Socket.new(*domain, type, protocol*) → *sock*

Creates a socket using the given parameters.

---

open   Socket.open(*domain, type, protocol*) → *sock*

Synonym for **Socket.new**.

---

pair   Socket.pair(*domain, type, protocol*) → *anArray*

Returns a pair of connected, anonymous sockets of the given domain, type, and protocol.

---

socketpair   Socket.socketpair(*domain, type, protocol*) → *anArray*

Synonym for **Socket.pair**.

Instance methods

accept

sock.accept → *anArray*

Accepts an incoming connection returning an array containing a new **Socket** object and a string holding the **struct sockaddr** information about the caller.

bind

sock.bind(*sockaddr*) → 0

Binds to the given **struct sockaddr**, contained in a string.

connect

sock.connect(*sockaddr*) → 0

Connects to the given **struct sockaddr**, contained in a string.

listen

sock.listen(*aFixnum*) → 0

Listens for connections, using the specified *aFixnum* as the backlog.

recvfrom

sock.recvfrom(*len* ⟨ , *flags* ⟩) → *anArray*

Receives up to *len* bytes from *sock*. *flags* is zero or more of the **MSG_** options. The first element of the result is the data received. The second element contains protocol-specific information on the sender.

Higher-Level Access

Ruby provides a set of classes to facilitate writing clients for:

- File Transfer Protocol (FTP)
- HyperText Transfer Protocol (HTTP)
- Post Office Protocol (POP)
- Simple Mail Transfer Protocol (SMTP)
- Telnet

HTTP, POP, and SMTP are layered on top of a helper class, `lib/net/protocol`. Although we don't document the `Protocol` class here, you should probably study it if you are considering writing your own network client.

Class **Net::FTP** < Object   **require** `"net/ftp"`

```
require 'net/ftp'

ftp = Net::FTP.new('ftp.netlab.co.jp')
ftp.login
files = ftp.chdir('pub/lang/ruby/contrib')
files = ftp.list('n*')
ftp.getbinaryfile('nif.rb-0.91.gz', 'nif.gz', 1024)
ftp.close
```

The `net/ftp` library implements a File Transfer Protocol (FTP) client.

Class constants

FTP_PORT   Default port for FTP connections (21).

Class methods

new   FTP.new(*host*=`nil`, *user*=`nil`, *passwd*=`nil`, *acct*=`nil`) → *ftp*

Creates and returns a new `FTP` object. If the host parameter is not `nil`, a connection is made to that host. Additionally, if the *user* parameter is not `nil`, the given user name, password, and (optionally) account are used to log in. See the description of `FTP#login` on page 488.

---

open   FTP.open(*host*, *user*=`nil`, *passwd*=`nil`, *acct*=`nil`) → *ftp*

A synonym for `FTP.new`, but with a mandatory *host* parameter.

Instance methods

Server commands

> *ftp*.acct(*account*)
> *ftp*.chdir(*dir*)
> *ftp*.delete(*remoteFile*)
> *ftp*.mdtm(*remoteFile*) → *aString*
> *ftp*.mkdir(*dir*)
> *ftp*.nlst(*dir*=`nil`) → *anArray*
> *ftp*.rename(*fromname, toname*)
> *ftp*.rmdir(*dir*)
> *ftp*.pwd → *aString*
> *ftp*.size(*remoteFile*) → *anInteger*
> *ftp*.status → *aString*
> *ftp*.system → *aString*

Issues the corresponding server command and returns the result.

close

> *ftp*.close

Closes the current connection.

closed?

> *ftp*.closed? → `true` or `false`

Returns `true` if the current connection is closed.

connect

> *ftp*.connect(*host, port*=FTP_PORT)

Establishes an FTP connection to *host*, optionally overriding the default port. If the environment variable `SOCKS_SERVER` is set, sets up the connection through a SOCKS proxy. Raises an exception (typically `Errno::ECONNREFUSED`) if the connection cannot be established.

debug_mode

> *ftp*.debug_mode → `true` or `false`

Returns the current debug mode.

debug_mode=

> *ftp*.debug_mode = `true` or `false`

If the debug mode is `true`, all traffic to and from the server is written to `$stdout`.

dir

> *ftp*.dir(⟨ pattern ⟩*) → *anArray*
> *ftp*.dir(⟨ pattern ⟩*) {| *line* | *block* }

Synonym for `FTP#list`.

getbinaryfile *ftp*.getbinaryfile(*remotefile, localfile, blocksize, callback=`nil`*)
ftp.getbinaryfile(*remotefile, localfile, blocksize*) {| *data* | *block* }

Retrieves *remotefile* in binary mode, storing the result in *localfile*. If *callback* or an associated block is supplied, calls it, passing in the retrieved data in *blocksize* chunks.

---

gettextfile *ftp*.gettextfile(*remotefile, localfile, callback=`nil`*)
ftp.gettextfile(*remotefile, localfile*) {| *data* | *block* }

Retrieves *remotefile* in ASCII (text) mode, storing the result in *localfile*. If *callback* or an associated block is supplied, calls it, passing in the retrieved data one line at a time.

---

lastresp *ftp*.lastresp → *aString*

Returns the host's last response.

---

list *ftp*.list(⟨ pattern ⟩*) → *anArray*
ftp.list(⟨ pattern ⟩*) {| *line* | *block* }

Fetches a directory listing of files matching the given pattern(s). If a block is associated with the call, invokes it with each line of the result. Otherwise, returns the result as an array of strings.

---

login *ftp*.login(*user*="anonymous", *passwd*=`nil`, *acct*=nil) → aString

Logs into the remote host. *ftp* must have been previously connected. If *user* is the string "anonymous" and the password is `nil`, a password of *user*@*host* is synthesized. If the *acct* parameter is not `nil`, an FTP `ACCT` command is sent following the successful login. Raises an exception on error (typically `Net::FTPPermError`).

---

ls *ftp*.ls(⟨ pattern ⟩*) → *anArray*
ftp.ls(⟨ pattern ⟩*) {| *line* | *block* }

Synonym for `FTP#list`.

---

mtime *ftp*.mtime(*remoteFile, local*=`false`) → *aTime*

Returns the last-modified time of *remoteFile*, interpreting the server's response as a GMT time if *local* is `false`, or as a local time otherwise.

---

passive *ftp*.passive → `true` or `false`

Returns the state of the `passive` flag.

---

passive= *ftp*.passive = `true` or `false`

Puts the connection into passive mode if `true`.

putbinaryfile

ftp.putbinaryfile(*localfile, remotefile, blocksize, callback*=**nil**)
ftp.putbinaryfile(*localfile, remotefile, blocksize*) {| *data* | *block* }

Transfers *localfile* to the server in binary mode, storing the result in *remotefile*. If *callback* or an associated block is supplied, calls it, passing in the transmitted data in *blocksize* chunks.

puttextfile

ftp.puttextfile(*localfile, remotefile, callback*=**nil**)
ftp.puttextfile(*localfile, remotefile, blocksize*) {| *data* | *block* }

Transfers *localfile* to the server in ASCII (text) mode, storing the result in *remotefile*. If *callback* or an associated block is supplied, calls it, passing in the transmitted data one line at a time.

resume

ftp.resume → **true** or **false**

Returns the status of the *resume* flag (see FTP#**resume**=). Default is **false**.

resume=

ftp.resume=*aBoolean*

Sets the status of the *resume* flag. When *resume* is **true**, partially received files will resume where they left off, instead of starting from the beginning again. This is done by sending a REST command (RESTart incomplete transfer) to the server.

retrbinary

ftp.retrbinary(*cmd, blocksize*) {| *data* | *block* }

Puts the connection into binary (image) mode, issues the given command, and fetches the data returned, passing it to the associated block in chunks of *blocksize* characters. Note that *cmd* is a server command (such as "RETR myfile").

retrlines

ftp.retrlines(cmd) {| *line* | *block* }

Puts the connection into ASCII (text) mode, issues the given command, and passes the resulting data, one line at a time, to the associated block. If no block is given, prints the lines. Note that *cmd* is a server command (such as "RETR myfile").

return_code

ftp.return_code → *aFixnum*

Returns the return code from the last operation.

storbinary

ftp.storbinary(*cmd, fileName, blocksize, callback*=**nil**)
ftp.storbinary(*cmd, fileName, blocksize*) {| *data* | *block* }

Puts the connection into binary (image) mode, issues the given server-side command (such as "STOR myfile"), and sends the contents of the file named *fileName* to the server. If the optional block is given, or if the *callBack* parameter is a **Proc**, also passes it the data, in chunks of *blocksize* characters.

storlines

ftp.storlines(*cmd, fileName, callback*=**nil**)
ftp.storlines(*cmd, fileName*) {| *data* | *block* }

Puts the connection into ASCII (text) mode, issues the given server-side command (such as "STOR myfile"), and sends the contents of the file named *fileName* to the server, one line at a time. If the optional block is given, or if the *callBack* parameter is a **Proc**, also passes it the lines.

welcome

ftp.welcome → *aString*

Returns the host's welcome message.

Class **Net::HTTP** < Net::Protocol   **require** **"net/http"**

```
require 'net/http'

h = Net::HTTP.new('www.pragmaticprogrammer.com', 80)
resp, data = h.get('/index.html', nil )
puts "Code = #{resp.code}"
puts "Message = #{resp.message}"
resp.each {|key, val| printf "%-14s = %-40.40s\n", key, val }
p data[0..55]
```

produces:

```
Code = 200
Message = OK
content-type   = text/html
last-modified  = Thu, 24 Aug 2000 14:10:37 GMT
date           = Thu, 14 Sep 2000 17:15:39 GMT
connection     = close
accept-ranges  = bytes
etag           = "804d98-23c5-39a52cdd"
content-length = 9157
server         = Rapidsite/Apa-1.3.4 FrontPage/4.0.4.3
"<!DOCTYPE HTML PUBLIC \"-//W3C//DTD HTML 4.0 Transitional"
```

The **net/http** library provides a simple client to fetch headers and Web page contents using the HTTP protocol.

The **get**, **post**, and **head** requests raise exceptions on any error, including some HTTP status responses that would normally be considered recoverable. There are two ways of handling these.

1. Each method has a corresponding version **get2**, **post2**, or **head2** that does not raise an exception. These versions are documented in the source.

2. Recoverable errors raise a **Net::ProtoRetriableError** exception. This exception contains a **data** attribute containing the response returned by the server.

(margin) Net/http

The code below illustrates the handling of an HTTP status 301, a redirect. It uses Tomoyuki Kosimizu's URI package, available in the RAA.

```
h = Net::HTTP.new(ARGV[0] || 'www.ruby-lang.org', 80)
url = ARGV[1] || '/'

begin
  resp, data = h.get(url, nil) { |a| }
rescue Net::ProtoRetriableError => detail
  head = detail.data

  if head.code == "301"
    uri = URI.create(head['location'])

    host = uri['host']
    url  = uri['path']
    port = uri['port']

    h.finish
    h = Net::HTTP.new(host, port)

    retry
  end
end
```

Class methods

new   Net::HTTP.new(*host*=**nil**, *port*=80) → *http*

Creates and returns a new **HTTP** object. No connection is made until **HTTP#start** is called.

port   Net::HTTP.port → *aFixnum*

Returns the default HTTP port (80).

start   Net::HTTP.start(*host*=**nil**, *port*=80)
                              Net::HTTP.start(*host*=**nil**, *port*=80) {| http | *block* }

Equivalent to `Net::HTTP.new(host, port).start`.

Instance methods

get   *http*.get(*path*, *headers*=**nil**, *dest*="") → *anArray*
                              http.get(*path*, *headers*=**nil**) {| *result* | *block* } → *anArray*

Retrieves headers and content from the specified *path* on the host specified when *http* was created. If specified, the *headers* parameter is a **Hash** containing additional header names and values to be sent with the request. The method returns a two-element array. The first element is an **HTTPResponse** object (documented in the next section). The second element is the page's content. The page's content is also passed to the < < method of the *dest* parameter, or to the block if specified. This result is built network block by network block, not line by line. An exception is raised if an error is encountered. Multiple **get** calls may be made on *http*. Unless **Protocol#finish** is explicitly called, the connection will use the HTTP/1.1 keep-alive protocol, and will not close between requests.

head
$$http.head(path, headers=\texttt{nil}) \rightarrow aHash$$

Retrieves headers from the specified *path* on the host specified when *http* was created. If specified, the *headers* parameter is a hash containing additional header names and values to be sent with the request. The method returns a hash of received headers. An exception is raised if an error is encountered. Multiple **head** calls may be made on *http*.

post
$$http.post(path, data, headers=\texttt{nil}, dest="") \rightarrow anArray$$
$$http.post(path, data, headers=\texttt{nil}) \{ | result | block \} \rightarrow anArray$$

Sends *data* to *path* using an HTTP POST request. *headers* is a hash containing additional headers. Assigns the result to *data* or to the block, as for **Net::HTTP#get**. Returns a two-element array containing an HTTPResponse object and the reply body.

start
$$http.start$$
$$http.start \{ | http | block \}$$

Establishes a connection to the host associated with *http*. (**start** is actually a method in **Net::Protocol**, but its use is required in HTTP objects.) In the block form, closes the session at the end of the block.

Class ▐ **Net::HTTPResponse**   **require** **"net/http"**

Represents an HTTP response to a GET or POST request.

Instance methods

[ ]
$$resp[aKey] \rightarrow aString$$

Returns the header corresponding to the case-insensitive key. For example, a key of "Content-type" might return "text/html".

[ ]=
$$resp[aKey] = aString$$

Sets the header corresponding to the case-insensitive key.

code
$$resp.code \rightarrow aString$$

Returns the result code from the request (for example, "404").

each
$$resp.each \{ | key, val | block \}$$

Iterates over all the header key-value pairs.

key?	*resp*.key?(*aKey*) → `true` or `false`

Returns `true` only if a header with the given key exists.

message	*resp*.message → *aString*

Returns the result message from the request (for example, "Not found").

Class **Net::POP** < Net::Protocol   **require** **"net/pop"**

```
require 'net/pop'
pop = Net::POP3.new('server.ruby-stuff.com')
pop.start('user', 'secret')
msg = pop.mails[0]

# Print the 'From:' header line
puts msg.header.split("\r\n").grep(/^From: /)

# Put message to $stdout (by calling <<)
puts "\nFull message:\n"
msg.all($stdout)
```

produces:

```
From: Dave Thomas <dave@pragmaticprogrammer.com>

Full message:
Return-Path: <dave@pragmaticprogrammer.com>
Received: (from dave@pragmaticprogrammer.com)
by pragmaticprogrammer.com (8.8.7/8.8.7) id XAA10537;
Sun, 21 May 2000 23:45:58 -0500
Date: Sun, 21 May 2000 23:45:58 -0500
From: Dave Thomas <dave@pragmaticprogrammer.com>
Message-Id: <200005220445.XAA10537@pragmaticprogrammer.com>
To: user@ruby-stuff.com
Subject: New Ruby Version
Status:   O

Just to let you know there's a new Ruby version out.
```

The net/pop library provides a simple client to fetch and delete mail on a Post Office Protocol (POP) server.

The class Net::POP3 is used to access a POP server, returning a list of Net::POPMail objects, one per message stored on the server. These POPMail objects are then used to fetch and/or delete individual messages. The library also provides an alternative to the POP3 class that performs APOP authentication.

net/pop

Class methods

new
$$HTTP.new(\textit{host}=localhost, \textit{port}=100) \rightarrow \textit{pop}$$

Creates and returns a new POP3 object. No connection is made until POP3#start is called.

Instance methods

each
$$\textit{pop}.each \; \{ \; | \; \textit{popmail} \; | \; \textit{block} \; \}$$

Calls the associated block once for each e-mail stored on the server, passing in the corresponding POPMail object.

mails
$$\textit{pop}.mails \rightarrow \textit{anArray}$$

Returns an array of POPMail objects, where each object corresponds to an e-mail message stored on the server.

start
$$\textit{pop}.start(\; \textit{user}, \textit{password} \;)$$
$$\textit{pop}.start(\; \textit{user}, \textit{password} \;) \; \{ \; | \; \textit{pop} \; | \; \textit{block} \; \}$$

Establishes a connection to the pop server, using the supplied username and password. Fetches a list of mail held on the server, which may be accessed using the POP3#mails and POP3#each methods.

Class **Net::APOP** < Net::POP3   **require** **"net/pop"**

Instance methods

start
$$\textit{apop}.start(\; \textit{user}, \textit{password} \;)$$

Establishes a connection to the APOP server.

| Class | **Net::POPMail** < Object | require **"net/pop"** |

Instance methods

all

mail.all → *aString*
mail.all(*dest*)
mail.all { | *aString* | *block* }

Fetches the corresponding e-mail from the server. With no argument or associated block, returns the e-mail as a string. With an argument but no block, appends the e-mail to *dest* by invoking *dest*< < for each line in the e-mail. With an associated block, invokes the block once for each line in the e-mail.

delete

mail.delete

Deletes the e-mail from the server.

delete!

mail.delete!

Synonym for POPMail#delete.

header

mail.header → *aString*

Returns the header lines for the corresponding e-mail message.

size

mail.size → *aFixnum*

Returns the size in bytes of the corresponding e-mail.

top

mail.top(*lines*) → *aString*

Returns the header lines, plus *lines* message lines for the corresponding e-mail message.

uidl

mail.uidl → *aString*

Returns the server-specific unique identifier for the corresponding e-mail.

Class			require	
Net::SMTP	<	Net::Protocol		**"net/smtp"**

```
require 'net/smtp'

# --- Send using class methods
msg = [ "Subject: Test\n", "\n", "Now is the time\n" ]
Net::SMTP.start do |smtp|
  smtp.sendmail( msg, 'dave@localhost', ['dave'] )
end

# --- Send using SMTP object and an adaptor
smtp = Net::SMTP.new
smtp.start('pragprog.com')
smtp.ready('dave@localhost', 'dave') do |a|
  a.write "Subject: Test1\r\n"
  a.write "\r\n"
  a.write "And so is this"
end
```

The **net/smtp** library provides a simple client to send electronic mail using the Simple Mail Transfer Protocol (SMTP).

Class methods

new
$$\text{Net::SMTP.new}(\textit{server}=\text{'localhost'}, \textit{port}=25) \rightarrow \textit{smtp}$$

Returns a new **SMTP** object connected to the given server and port.

---

start
$$\text{Net::SMTP.start}(\textit{server}=\text{'localhost'}, \textit{port}=25, \textit{domain}=\text{ENV['HOSTNAME']},$$
$$\textit{acct}=\text{nil}, \textit{passwd}=\text{nil}, \textit{authtype}=\text{:cram\_md5}) \rightarrow \textit{smtp}$$
$$\text{Net::SMTP.start}(\textit{server}=\text{'localhost'}, \textit{port}=25, \textit{domain}=\text{ENV['HOSTNAME']},$$
$$\textit{acct}=\text{nil}, \textit{passwd}=\text{nil}, \textit{authtype}=\text{:cram\_md5}) \{ | \textit{smtp} | \textit{block} \}$$

Equivalent to `Net::SMTP.new(server, port).start(...)`. For an explanation of the remainder of the parameters, see the instance method `Net::SMTP#start`. Creates a new **SMTP** object. The *domain* parameter will be used in the initial HELO or EHLO transaction with the SMTP server. In the block form, the *smtp* object is passed into the block. When the block terminates, the session is closed.

Instance methods

ready
$$\textit{smtp}.\text{ready}(\textit{from}, \textit{to}) \{ | \textit{anAdaptor} | \textit{block} \}$$

Equivalent to `sendmail(from, to) { ... }`. Sends header and body lines to the sendmail server. The *from* parameter is used as the sender's name in the MAIL FROM: command, and the *to* is either a string or an array of strings containing the recipients for the RCPT TO: command. The block is passed an adaptor object. Lines are sent to the server by calling the adaptor's **write** method. The terminating '.' and QUIT are sent automatically.

---

sendmail   *smtp*.sendmail(*src, from, to*)

Sends header and body lines to the sendmail server. The *from* parameter is used as the sender's name in the `MAIL FROM:` command, and *to* is either a string or an array of strings containing the recipients for the `RCPT TO:` command. Lines to be sent are fetched by invoking *src*.`each`. The terminating '.' and `QUIT` are sent automatically.

---

start   *smtp*.start(*domain*=ENV['HOSTNAME'], *acct*=`nil`, *passwd*=`nil`,
                                   authtype=:cram_md5) → `true` or `false`
                                   smtp.start(*domain*=ENV['HOSTNAME'], *acct*=`nil`, *passwd*=`nil`,
                                   authtype=:cram_md5) {| *smtp* | *block* } → `true` or `false`

Starts an SMTP session by connecting to the given domain (host). If *acct* and *passwd* are given, authentication will be attempted using the given authentication type (`:plain` or `:cram_md5`). If a block is supplied, it will be invoked with *smtp* as a parameter. The connection will be closed when the block terminates.

Class **Net::Telnet** < [Socket]   **require** `"net/telnet"`

Connect to a `localhost`, run the "date" command, and disconnect.

```
require 'net/telnet'

tn = Net::Telnet.new({})
tn.login "guest", "secret"
tn.cmd "date"   →   "date\r\nWed Sep 20 10:35:35 CDT 2000\n\r> "
```

Monitor output as it occurs. We associate a block with each of the library calls; this block is called whenever data becomes available from the host.

```
require 'net/telnet'

tn = Net::Telnet.new({})       { |str| print str }
tn.login("guest", "secret")    { |str| print str }
tn.cmd("date")   { |str| print str }
```

produces:

```
Trying localhost...
Connected to localhost.
Welcome to SuSE Linux 6.2 (i386) - Kernel 2.2.10-smp (pts/10).
login: guest
Password:
Last login: Wed Sep 20 10:35:34 from localhost

> date
Wed Sep 20 10:35:36 CDT 2000

>
```

Net/telnet

Get the time from an NTP server.

```
require 'net/telnet'
tn = Net::Telnet.new('Host'         => 'tick.gatech.edu',
                     'Port'         => 'time',
                     'Timeout'      => 60,
                     'Telnetmode'   => false)
atomicTime = tn.recv(4).unpack('N')[0]
puts "Atomic time: " + Time.at(atomicTime - 2208988800).to_s
puts "Local time:  " + Time.now.to_s
```

produces:

```
Atomic time: Wed Sep 20 10:35:34 CDT 2000
Local time:  Wed Sep 20 10:35:37 CDT 2000
```

The `net/telnet` library provides a complete implementation of a telnet client and includes features that make it a convenient mechanism for interacting with non-telnet services.

Although the class description that follows indicates that `Net::Telnet` is a subclass of class `Socket`, this is a lie. In reality, the class delegates to `Socket`. The net effect is the same: the methods of `Socket` and its parent, class `IO`, are available through `Net::Telnet` objects.

The methods `new`, `cmd`, `login`, and `waitfor` take an optional block. If present, the block is passed output from the server as it is received by the routine. This can be used to provide realtime output, rather than waiting for (for example) a login to complete before displaying the server's response.

Class methods

new

Net::Telnet.new(*options*) → *tn*

Net::Telnet.new(*options*) {| *str* | *block* } → *tn*

Connects to a server. *options* is a **Hash** with zero or more of the following:

Option	Default	Meaning
Binmode	false	If true, no end-of-line processing will be performed.
Host	localhost	Name or address of server's host.
Port	23	Name or number of service to call.
Prompt	/[$%#>]/	Pattern that matches the host's prompt.
Telnetmode	true	If false, ignore the majority of telnet embedded escape sequences. Used when talking with a non-telnet server.
Timeout	10	Time in seconds to wait for a server response (both during connection and during regular data transmission).
Waittime	0	Time to wait for prompt to appear in received data stream.

Instance methods

---

binmode $\qquad\qquad\qquad\qquad\qquad\qquad\qquad\qquad$ *tn*.binmode → `true` or `false`

Returns the current value of the `Binmode` flag.

---

binmode= $\qquad\qquad\qquad\qquad\qquad\qquad\qquad$ *tn*.binmode = `true` or `false`

Sets the `Binmode` flag, returning the new value.

---

cmd $\qquad\qquad\qquad\qquad\qquad\qquad\qquad\qquad$ *tn*.cmd(*options*) → *aString*

$\qquad\qquad\qquad\qquad$ *tn*.cmd(*options*) { | *str* | *block* } → *aString*

Sends a string to the server and waits (using a timeout) for a string that matches a pattern to be returned by the server. If the parameter is not a `Hash`, it is sent as a string to the server, and the pattern to match and the timeout are the `Prompt` and `Timeout` options given when *tn* was created. If *options* is a `Hash`, then *options['String']* is sent to the server. *options['Match']* may be used to override the class `Prompt` parameter, and *options['Timeout']* the timeout. The method returns the complete server response.

---

login $\qquad\qquad\qquad\qquad\qquad$ *tn*.login(*options, password*=nil) → *aString*

$\qquad\qquad$ *tn*.login(*options, password*=nil) { | *str* | *block* } → *aString*

If *options* is a `Hash`, a username is taken from *options['Name']* and a password from *options['Password']*; otherwise, *options* is assumed to be the username, and *password* the password. The method waits for the server to send the string matching the pattern `/login[:␣]*\z/` and sends the username. If a password is given, it then waits for the server to send `/Password[:␣]*\z/` and sends the password. The method returns the full server response.

---

print $\qquad\qquad\qquad\qquad\qquad\qquad\qquad\qquad\qquad$ *tn*.print(*aString*)

Sends *aString* to the server, honoring `Telnetmode`, `Binarymode`, and any additional modes negotiated with the server.

---

telnetmode $\qquad\qquad\qquad\qquad\qquad\qquad\qquad$ *tn*.telnetmode → `true` or `false`

Returns the current value of the `Telnetmode` flag.

---

telnetmode= $\qquad\qquad\qquad\qquad\qquad\qquad$ *tn*.telnetmode= `true` or `false`

Sets the `Telnetmode` flag, returning the new value.

---

waitfor $\qquad\qquad\qquad\qquad\qquad\qquad\qquad$ *tn*.waitfor(*options*) → *aString*

$\qquad\qquad\qquad$ *tn*.waitfor(*options*) { | *str* | *block* } → *aString*

Waits for the server to respond with a string that matches a string or pattern. If *options* is not a `Hash`, it is compared against the cumulative server output as that output is received using *options.===*. It is likely that you will want to use a regular expression in this case.

If *options* is a **Hash**, then *options['Match']*, *options['Prompt']*, or *options['String']* provides the match. In the latter case, the string will be converted to a regular expression before being used. *options* may also include the keys "Timeout" and "Waittime" to override the class options of the same names.

---

write   *tn*.write(*aString*)

Writes *aString* to the server with no translation.

CGI Development

Class	CGI < Object	require "cgi"

```ruby
require "cgi"
cgi = CGI.new("html3")  # add HTML generation methods
cgi.out {
  CGI.pretty (
    cgi.html {
      cgi.head { cgi.title{"TITLE"} } +
      cgi.body {
        cgi.form {
          cgi.textarea("get_text") +
          cgi.br +
          cgi.submit
        } +
        cgi.h1 { "This is big!" } +
        cgi.center { "Jazz Greats of the 20" +
          cgi.small {"th"} + " century" + cgi.hr
        } + cgi.p + cgi.table ('BORDER' => '5') {
          cgi.tr { cgi.td {"Artist"} + cgi.td {"Album"} } +
          cgi.tr { cgi.td {"Davis, Miles"} +
          cgi.td {"Kind of Blue"} }
        }
      }
    }
  ) # CGI.pretty is a method call, not a block
}
```

(The output of this script is shown in Figure 26.2 on page 503.)

The CGI class provides support for programs used as a Web server CGI (Common Gateway Interface) script. It contains several methods for accessing fields in a CGI form, manipulating "cookies" and the environment, and outputting formatted HTML.

Since environment variables contain a lot of useful information for a CGI script, CGI makes accessing them very easy—environment variables are accessible as attributes of CGI objects. For instance, cgi.auth_type returns the value of ENV["AUTH_TYPE"]. To create the method name, the environment variable name is translated to all lowercase, and the "HTTP_" prefix is stripped off. Thus, HTTP_USER_AGENT would be available as the method user_agent.

Cookies are represented using a separate object of class CGI::Cookie, containing the following accessors:

Accessor	Description
name	Name of this cookie
value	Array of values
path	Path (optional)
domain	Domain (optional)
expires	Time of expiry, defaults to `Time.now` (optional)
secure	`true` for a secure cookie

You create a cookie object using `CGI::Cookie.new`, which takes as arguments the accessors listed above, or `CGI::Cookie.parse`, which takes an encoded string and returns a cookie object.

Class methods

escape
$\hfill$ CGI.escape(*aString*) → *aNewString*

Returns a URL-encoded string made from the given argument, where unsafe characters (not alphanumeric, "_", "-", or ".") are encoded using "%xx" escapes.

escapeElement
$\hfill$ CGI.escapeElement(*aString* ⟨ , *elements* ⟩*) → *aNewString*

Returns a string made from the given argument with certain HTML-special characters escaped. The HTML elements given in *elements* will be escaped; other HTML elements will not be affected.

```
print CGI::escapeElement('<BR><A HREF="url"></A><P>', "A", "IMG")
```

produces:

```
<BR>&lt;A HREF=&quot;url&quot;&gt;&lt;/A&gt;<P>
```

escapeHTML
$\hfill$ CGI.escapeHTML(*aString*) → *aNewString*

Returns a string made from the given argument with HTML-special characters (such as "&","\"","<",">") quoted using "&", """, "<", ">", and so on.

new
$\hfill$ CGI.new(⟨ *aString* ⟩*) → *aCgi*

Returns a new `CGI` object. If HTML output is required, the desired standards level must be given in *aString* (otherwise, no output routines will be created). The level may be one of:

String	Standards Level	String	Standards Level
"html3"	HTML 3.2	"html4"	HTML 4.0 Strict
"html4Tr"	HTML 4.0 Transitional	"html4Fr"	HTML 4.0 Frameset

Figure 26.2. Output of sample CGI code

```
Content-Type: text/html
Content-Length: 773

<!DOCTYPE HTML PUBLIC "-//W3C//DTD HTML 3.2 Final//EN">
<HTML>
  <HEAD>
    <TITLE>
      TITLE
    </TITLE>
  </HEAD>
  <BODY>
    <FORM METHOD="post" ENCTYPE="application/x-www-form-urlencoded">
      <TEXTAREA COLS="70" NAME="get_text" ROWS="10">
      </TEXTAREA>
      <BR>
      <INPUT TYPE="submit">
    </FORM>
    <H1>
      This is big!
    </H1>
    <CENTER>
      Jazz Greats of the 20
      <SMALL>
        th
      </SMALL>
       century
      <HR>
    </CENTER>
    <P>
    <TABLE BORDER="5">
      <TR>
        <TD>
          Artist
        </TD>
        <TD>
          Album
        </TD>
      </TR>
      <TR>
        <TD>
          Davis, Miles
        </TD>
        <TD>
          Kind of Blue
        </TD>
      </TR>
    </TABLE>
  </BODY>
</HTML>
```

---

parse CGI.parse(*aString*) → *aHash*

Parses a query string and returns a hash of its *key-value* pairs.

---

pretty CGI.pretty(*anHTMLString, aLeaderString=" ") → *aCgi*

Formats the given *anHTMLString* in a nice, readable format, optionally prefixing each line with *aLeaderString*.

---

rfc1123_date CGI.rfc1123_date(*aTime*) → *aString*

Returns a string representing the given time according to RFC 1123 (for instance, `Mon, 1 Jan 2001 00:00:00 GMT`).

---

unescape CGI.unescape(*aString*) → *aNewString*

Returns a string containing "unsafe" characters made from the given URL-encoded argument, where unsafe characters were encoded using "%" escapes.

---

unescapeElement CGI.unescapeElement(*aString* ⟨ , *elements* ⟩*) → *aNewString*

Returns a string with the selected escaped HTML elements expanded to the actual characters.

---

unescapeHTML CGI.unescapeHTML(*aString*) → *aNewString*

Returns a string made from the given argument with HTML-special quoted characters expanded to the actual characters.

Instance methods

[ ] *aCgi*[⟨ *aString* ⟩+] → *anArray*

Returns the values of the given field names from the CGI form in an `Array`. See the note on multipart forms on page 507.

---

cookies *aCgi*.cookies → *aHash*

Returns a new `Hash` object containing *key-value* pairs of cookie keys and values.

---

has_key? *aCgi*.has_key(*aString*) → `true` or `false`

Returns `true` if the form contains a field named *aString*.

---

header *aCgi*.header(*aContentType*="text/html") → *aString*
aCgi.header(*aHash*) → *aString*

Returns a string containing the given headers (in the `MOD_RUBY` environment, the resulting header is sent immediately instead). If a hash is given as an argument, then the *key-value* pairs will be used to generate headers.

---

keys   *aCgi*.keys → *anArray*

Returns an array of all existing field names for the form.

---

out   *aCgi*.out(*aContentType*="text/html") { *block* } → `nil`

                                          aCgi.out(*aHash*) { *block* } → `nil`

Generates HTML output using the results of the block as the content. Headers are generated as with `CGI#header`. See the example at the start of this section.

---

params   *aCgi*.params → *aHash*

Returns a new `Hash` object containing *key-value* pairs of field names and values from the form.

HTML Output Methods

In addition, `CGI` supports the following HTML output methods. Each of these methods is named after the corresponding HTML feature (or close to it). Those tags that require content (such as `blockquote`) take an optional block; the block should return a `String` that will be used as the content for the feature. These methods may take arguments as indicated, or as a hash with the given names as keys.

`a(` *url* `)`
`a( HREF ⇒ )`

`base(` *url* `)`
`base( HREF ⇒ )`

`blockquote(` *cite=""* `) {` *aString* `}`
`blockquote( CITE ⇒ ) {` *aString* `}`

`caption(` *align=nil* `) {` *aString* `}`
`caption( ALIGN ⇒ ) {` *aString* `}`

`checkbox(` *name=*`nil`*, value=*`nil`*, checked=*`nil` `)`
`checkbox( NAME ⇒, VALUE ⇒, CHECKED ⇒ )`

`checkbox_group(` *name=*`nil`*,* ⟨ *items* ⟩[+] `)`
`checkbox_group( NAME ⇒, VALUES ⇒ )`
    Items may be individual `String` names, or any of: an array of [*name, checked*], an array of [*value, name*], or an array of [*value, name, checked*]. The value for the hash key VALUES should be an array of these items.

`file_field(` *name=""*, *size=*20, *maxlength=*`nil` `)`
`file_field( NAME ⇒, SIZE ⇒, MAXLENGTH ⇒ )`

`form(` *method=*"post", *action=*`nil`, *enctype=*"application/x-www-form-urlencoded" `) {` *aStr* `}`
`form( METHOD ⇒, ACTION ⇒, ENCTYPE ⇒ ) {` *aStr* `}`

`hidden(` *name=""*, *value=*`nil` `)`
`hidden( NAME ⇒, VALUE ⇒ )`

Cgi

```
html( ) { aString }
html( PRETTY ⇒, DOCTYPE ⇒ ) { aString }

img_button( src="", name=nil, alt=nil )
img_button( SRC ⇒, NAME ⇒, ALT ⇒ )

img( src="", alt="", width=nil, height=nil )
img( SRC ⇒, ALT ⇒, WIDTH ⇒, HEIGHT ⇒ )

multipart_form( action=nil, enctype="multipart/form-data" ) { aString }
multipart_form( METHOD ⇒, ACTION ⇒, ENCTYPE ⇒ ) { aString }

password_field( name="", value=nil, size=40, maxlength=nil )
password_field( NAME ⇒, VALUE ⇒, SIZE ⇒, MAXLENGTH ⇒ )

popup_menu( name="", items )
popup_menu( NAME ⇒, SIZE ⇒, MULTIPLE ⇒, VALUES ⇒ (array of items) )
```
>   Items may be individual **String** names, or any of: an array of [*name*, *selected*], an array
>   of [*value*, *name*], or an array of [*value*, *name*, *selected*]. The value for the hash key
>   VALUES should be an array of these items.

```
radio_button( name="", value=nil, checked=nil )
radio_button( NAME ⇒, VALUE ⇒, CHECKED ⇒ )

radio_group( name="", items )
radio_group( NAME ⇒, VALUES ⇒ (array of items) )
```
>   Items may be individual **String** names, or any of: an array of [*name*, *selected*], an array
>   of [*value*, *name*], or an array of [*value*, *name*, *selected*]. The value for the hash key
>   VALUES should be an array of these items.

```
reset( value=nil, name=nil )
reset( VALUE ⇒, NAME ⇒ )

scrolling_list( alias for popup_menu )

submit( value=nil, name=nil )
submit( VALUE ⇒, NAME ⇒ )

text_field( name="", value=nil, size=40, maxlength=nil )
text_field( NAME ⇒, VALUE ⇒, SIZE ⇒, MAXLENGTH )

textarea( name="", cols=70, rows=10 )
textarea( NAME ⇒, COLS ⇒, ROWS ⇒ )
```

In addition, all HTML tags are supported as methods, including `title`, `head`, `body`, `br`, `pre`, and so on. The block given to the method must return a `String`, which will be used as the content for that tag type. Not all tags require content: <P>, for example, does not. The available tags vary according to the supported HTML level—Table 26.1 on the facing page lists the complete set. For these methods, you can pass in a hash with attributes for the given tag. For instance, you might pass in 'BORDER'=>'5' to the `table` method to set the border width of the table.

Table 26.1. HTML tags available as methods

HTML 3

a address applet area b base basefont big blockquote body br caption center cite code dd dfn dir div dl dt em font form h1 h2 h3 h4 h5 h6 head hr html i img input isindex kbd li link listing map menu meta ol option p param plaintext pre samp script select small strike strong style sub sup table td textarea th title tr tt u ul var xmp

HTML 4

a abbr acronym address area b base bdo big blockquote body br button caption cite code col colgroup dd del dfn div dl dt em fieldset form h1 h2 h3 h4 h5 h6 head hr html i img input ins kbd label legend li link map meta noscript object ol optgroup option p param pre q samp script select small span strong style sub sup table tbody td textarea tfoot th thead title tr tt ul var

HTML 4 Transitional

a abbr acronym address applet area b base basefont bdo big blockquote body br button caption center cite code col colgroup dd del dfn dir div dl dt em fieldset font form h1 h2 h3 h4 h5 h6 head hr html i iframe img input ins isindex kbd label legend li link map menu meta noframes noscript object ol optgroup option p param pre q s samp script select small span strike strong style sub sup table tbody td textarea tfoot th thead title tr tt u ul var

HTML 4 Frameset *Same as HTML4TR, plus:*

frame frameset

Multipart Form Values

When dealing with a multipart form, the array returned by `CGI#[]` is composed of objects of class `Tempfile`, with the following dynamically added methods:

Method	Description
read	Body
local_path	Path to local file containing the content
original_filename	Original filename of the content
content_type	Content type

Class **CGI::Session** < Object **require** "cgi/session"

A `CGI::Session` maintains a persistent state for web users in a CGI environment. Sessions may be memory-resident or may be stored on disk. See the discussion on page 148 for details.

Class methods

new   CGI::Session.new(*aCgi*, ⟨ *aHash* ⟩*) → *aSession*

Returns a new session object for the `CGI` query. Options that may be given in *aHash* include:

Option	Description
session_key	Name of CGI key for session identification.
session_id	Value of session id.
new_session	If **true**, create a new session id for this session.
database_manager	Class to use to save sessions; may be `CGI::Session::File-Store` or `CGI::Session::MemoryStore` (or user defined if you're brave). Default is `FileStore`.
tmpdir	For `FileStore`, directory for session files.
prefix	For `FileStore`, prefix of session filenames.

Instance methods

[ ]   *aSession*[*aKey*] → *aValue*

Returns the value for the given key.

[ ]=   *aSession*[*aKey*] = *aValue* → *aValue*

Sets the value for the given key.

delete   *aSession*.delete

Calls the **delete** method of the underlying database manager. For `FileStore`, deletes the physical file containing the session. For `MemoryStore`, removes the session from memory.

update   *aSession*.update

Calls the **update** method of the underlying database manager. For `FileStore`, writes the session data out to disk. Has no effect with `MemoryStore`.

## Chapter 27

Microsoft Windows Support

The three libraries documented in this chapter turn Ruby into a powerful and convenient Windows scripting language. Now you have the power to control your applications, but in a controlled, object-oriented environment.

| Class | **WIN32OLE** < Object | require | "win32ole" |

```
require 'win32ole'
ie = WIN32OLE.new('InternetExplorer.Application')
ie.visible = true
ie.gohome
```

WIN32OLE provides a client interface to Windows 32 OLE Automation servers. See the tutorial description on page 166 for more information.

Class constants

WIN32OLE::VERSION   *Current version number*

Class methods

connect   WIN32OLE.connect(*aString*) → *ole*

Returns a new OLE automation client connected to an existing instance of the named automation server.

---

const_load   WIN32OLE.const_load(*ole*, ⟨ *aClass=WIN32OLE* ⟩) → nil

Defines the constants from the specified automation server as class constants in *aClass*.

---

new   WIN32OLE.new(*aString*) → *ole*

Returns a new OLE automation client connected to a new instance of the automation server named by *aString*.

Instance methods

[ ]	*ole*[*aString*] → *anObject*

Returns the named property from the OLE automation object.

[ ]=	*ole*[*aString*] = *aValue* → nil

Sets the named property in the OLE automation object.

each	*ole*.each {	*anObj*	*block* } → nil

Iterates over each item of this OLE server that supports the **IEnumVARIANT** interface.

invoke	*ole*.invoke (*aCmdString*, ⟨ *args* ⟩*) → *anObject*

Invokes the command given in *aCmdString* with the given *args*. *args* may be a **Hash** of named parameters and values. You don't need to call **invoke** explicitly; this class uses **method_missing** to forward calls through **invoke**, so you can simply use the OLE methods as methods of this class.

Class   **WIN32OLE_EVENT**   <   Object   **require**   **"win32ole"**

This (slightly modified) example from the Win32OLE 0.1.1 distribution shows the use of an event sink.

```
require 'win32ole'

$urls = []

def navigate(url)
  $urls << url
end

def stop_msg_loop
  puts "IE has exited..."
  throw :done
end

def default_handler(event, *args)
  case event
  when "BeforeNavigate"
    puts "Now Navigating to #{args[0]}..."
  end
end

ie = WIN32OLE.new('InternetExplorer.Application')
ie.visible = TRUE
ie.gohome
ev = WIN32OLE_EVENT.new(ie, 'DWebBrowserEvents')
```

Win32ole

```
      ev.on_event {|*args| default_handler(*args)}
      ev.on_event("NavigateComplete") {|url| navigate(url)}
      ev.on_event("Quit") {|*args| stop_msg_loop}

      catch(:done) {
        loop {
          WIN32OLE_EVENT.message_loop
        }
      }

      puts "You Navigated to the following URLs: "
      $urls.each_with_index do |url, i|
        puts "(#{i+1}) #{url}"
      end
```

WIN32OLE_EVENT is used in conjunction with the WIN32OLE class to add callbacks for Windows 32 events.

Class methods

message_loop   WIN32OLE_EVENT.message_loop → nil

Executes the Windows event loop, translating and dispatching events.

new   WIN32OLE_EVENT.new (*anOle, aName*) → *oleEvent*

Returns a new WIN32OLE_EVENT (an event sink) for the given WIN32OLE object and named event source. If *aName* is nil, it will attempt to use the default source and will raise a RuntimeError if it cannot find one.

Instance methods

on_event   *oleEvent*.on_event (⟨ *anEvent* ⟩) {| *args* | *block* } → nil

Defines a callback for the named *anEvent*. If *anEvent* is nil, then this callback is associated with all events. The block will be given any arguments appropriate for this event.

Win32API < Object   "Win32API"

This example is from the Ruby distribution, in `ext/Win32API`:

```
require 'Win32API'

getCursorPos = Win32API.new("user32", "GetCursorPos", ['P'], 'V')

lpPoint = " " * 8 # store two LONGs
getCursorPos.Call(lpPoint)
x, y = lpPoint.unpack("LL") # get the actual values

print "x: ", x, "\n"
print "y: ", y, "\n"

ods = Win32API.new("kernel32", "OutputDebugString", ['P'], 'V')
ods.Call("Hello, World\n")

GetDesktopWindow = Win32API.new("user32", "GetDesktopWindow", [], 'L')
GetActiveWindow = Win32API.new("user32", "GetActiveWindow", [], 'L')
SendMessage = Win32API.new("user32", "SendMessage", ['L'] * 4, 'L')
SendMessage.Call(GetDesktopWindow.Call, 274, 0xf140, 0)
```

The `Win32API` module allows access to any arbitrary Windows 32 function. Many of these functions take or return a `Pointer` datatype—a region of memory corresponding to a C string or structure type.

In Ruby, these pointers are represented using class `String`, which contains a sequence of 8-bit bytes. It is up to you to pack and unpack the bits in the `String`. See the reference section for unpack on page 383 and pack on page 290 for details.

Class methods

new	Win32API.new(*dllname, procname, importArray, export*) → *wapi*

Returns a new object representing a Windows 32 API function. *dllname* is the name of the DLL containing the function, such as "user32" or "kernel32." *procname* is the name of the desired function. *importArray* is an array of strings representing the types of arguments to the function. *export* is a string representing the return type of the function. Strings "n" and "l" represent numbers, "i" represent integers, "p" represents pointers to data stored in a string, and "v" represents a void type (used for export parameters only). These strings are case-insensitive.

Instance methods

call   *wapi*.call(⟨ *args* ⟩*) → *anObject*

Calls this API function with the given arguments, which must match the signature specified to **new**.

Call   *wapi*.Call(⟨ *args* ⟩*) → *anObject*

Synonym for `Win32API#call`.

Part V

Appendices

Embedded Documentation

So you've written a masterpiece, a class in a class of its own, and you'd like to share it with the world. But, being a responsible developer, you feel the need to document your creation. What do you do? The simplest solution is to use Ruby's built-in documentation format, RD, and `rdtool`, a Ruby utility suite that converts this documentation into a variety of output formats.

`rdtool` scans a file for `=begin` and `=end` pairs, and extracts the text between them all. This text is assumed to be documentation in RD format. The text is then processed according to a simple set of rules:

- Lines of text flush to the left margin are converted to paragraphs.

- Lines starting with one to four equals signs are headings. "=" is a first-level heading, "==" a second-level heading, and so on. "+" and "++" can be used to signal fifth- and sixth-level headings if you really want to go that deep.

  ```
  = Top Level Heading
  == Second Level Heading
  ...
  ```

- Lines in which the first nonspace is an asterisk indicate the beginnings of bullet lists. Continuation lines for each bullet item should line up with the text on the first line. Lists may be nested.

  ```
  This is normal text
  * start of a
    multiline bullet item
  * and another
    * nested item
    * second nested
  * third item at top level
  ```

- Lines where the first nonspace characters are digits between parentheses indicate numbered lists. The actual digits used are ignored. Again, lists may be nested.

Figure A.1.   rd source file

```
=begin
= Synopsis
   require "tempfile"
   tf = Tempfile.new("afile")
   tf.path
   tf.puts("Cosi Fan Tutte")
   tf.close
   tf.open
   tf.gets
   tf.close(true)
= Description
Class (({Tempfile})) creates managed temporary files. Although they
behave like any other (({IO})) object, temporary files are automatically
deleted when the Ruby program terminates. Once a (({Tempfile})) object
has been created, the underlying file may be opened and closed a number
of times in succession.
(({Tempfile})) does not directly inherit from (({IO})). Instead, it
delegates calls to a (({File})) object. From the programmer's
perspective, apart from the unusual ((<(({new}))|Tempfile.new>)),
((<(({open}))|Tempfile#open>)), and ((<(({close}))|Tempfile#close>))
semantics, a (({Tempfile})) object behaves as if it were an (({IO}))
object.
= Class Methods
--- Tempfile.new( basename, tmpdir=see below )
    Constructs a temporary file in the given directory. The filename
    is built by concatenating ((|basename|)), the current process id,
    and (as an extension) a unique sequence number. If the ((|tmpdir|))
    parameter is not supplied, it defaults to the value of one of the
    environment variables (({TMPDIR})), (({TMP})), or (({TEMP})), or to
    the directory (({/tmp})).  The file is then opened using mode
    ``w+'', which allows reading and writing and deletes any
    existing content.
--- Tempfile.open( basename, tmpdir )
     Synonym for ((<Tempfile.new>)).
= Instance Methods
--- Tempfile#open
    Reopens ((|aTempfile|)) using mode ``r+'', which allows reading and
    writing but does not delete existing content.
--- Tempfile#close( final=false )
    Closes ((|aTempfile|)). If ((|final|)) is true, deletes the
    underlying real file. If ((|final|)) is false, ((|aTempfile|)) may
    be subsequently reopened. In all cases, the underlying file is
    deleted when the program terminates.
--- Tempfile#path
    Returns the full path of the underlying file.
= History
    $Id: tempfile.rd,v 1.3 2000/08/26 02:38:05 andy Exp $
=end
```

Figure A.2.   Output from source in Figure A.1

Synopsis

```
require "tempfile"

tf = Tempfile.new("afile")
tf.path
tf.puts("Cosi Fan Tutte")
tf.close
tf.open
tf.gets
tf.close(true)
```

Description

Class `Tempfile` creates managed temporary files. Although they behave like any other `IO` object, temporary files are automatically deleted when the Ruby program terminates. Once a `Tempfile` object has been created, the underlying file may be opened and closed a number of times in succession.

`Tempfile` does not directly inherit from `IO`. Instead, it delegates calls to a `File` object. From the programmer's perspective, apart from the unusual `new`, `open`, and `close` semantics, a `Tempfile` object behaves as if it were an `IO` object.

Class Methods

`Tempfile.new( basename, tmpdir=see below )`
>   Constructs a temporary file in the given directory. The filename is built by concatenating *basename*, the current process id, and (as an extension) a unique sequence number. If the *tmpdir* parameter is not supplied, it defaults to the value of one of the environment variables TMPDIR, TMP, or TEMP, or to the directory /tmp. The file is then opened using mode "w+", which allows reading and writing and deletes any existing content.

`Tempfile.open( basename, tmpdir )`
>   Synonym for Tempfile.new.

Instance Methods

`Tempfile#open`
>   Reopens *aTempfile* using mode "r+", which allows reading and writing but does not delete existing content.

`Tempfile#close( final=false )`
>   Closes *aTempfile*. If *final* is true, deletes the underlying real file. If *final* is false, *aTempfile* may be subsequently reopened. In all cases, the underlying file is deleted when the program terminates.

`Tempfile#path`
>   Returns the full path of the underlying file.

History

```
$Id: tempfile.rd,v 1.3 2000/08/26 02:38:05 andy Exp $
```

```
(1) A numbered item
    * subitem in a bulleted list
    * subitem
(2) Second numbered item
(9) This will actually be labeled '3.'
```

- Lines starting with a colon indicate labeled lists. The text on the colon line is the label. The immediately following text (which may not be indented less than the label) is the descriptive text. Again, each type of list may be nested.

```
: red
  when the light is red, you
  must stop
: amber
  the amber light means that things are about to change. Either:
  * step on the gas, or
  * slam on the brakes
: green
  green means GO
```

- Lines starting with three minus signs are a special kind of labeled list, when the labels are method names and signatures. The source in Figure A.1 on page 518 shows a handful of these in action.

Indented text that isn't part of a list is set verbatim (such as the stuff under "Synopsis" in Figures A.1 and A.2).

Inline Formatting

Within blocks of text and headings, you can use special *inline sequences* to control text formatting. All sequences are nested within a set of double parentheses.

Sequence	Example	Intended Use
((*emphasis*))	*emphasis*	Emphasis (normally italic)
(({code stuff}))	`code stuff`	Code
((|variable|))	*variable*	Variable name
((%type me%))	`type me`	Keyboard input
((:index term:))	index term	Target of a cross reference
((<reference>))	*reference*	Hyperlink reference
((-footnote-))	text.[4]	Footnote text. A reference is placed inline, and the text of the footnote appears at the bottom of the page.
(('verb'))	verb	Verbatim text

Cross References

The content of headings, the labels of labeled lists, the names of methods, and the contents of `((:index terms:))` are automatically made into potential cross reference targets. You make links to these targets from elsewhere in the document by citing their contents in the `((<...>))` construct.

```
= Synopsis
...
See ((<Return Codes>)) for details.
..
== Instance Methods

--- Tempfile.open( filename )
    Opens the file...

== Return Codes
..
The method ((<Tempfile.open>)) raises an (({IOException}))...
```

If a reference starts with "URL:", `rdtool` attempts to format it as an external hyperlink.

The reference `((<display part|label>))` generates a link to `label` but places the text "display part" in the output document. This is used in the description section of the example in Figure A.1 on page 518 to generate references to the method names:

```
perspective, apart from the unusual ((<(({new}))|Tempfile.new>)),
...
```

This construct displays the word "new" in code font but uses it as a hyperlink to the method `Tempfile.new`.

Method Names

`rdtool` makes certain assumptions about the format of method names. Class or module methods should appear as `Class.method`, instance methods as `Class#method`, and class or module constants as `Class::Const`.

```
--- Tempfile::IOWRITE
    Open the file write-only.
    ...
--- Tempfile.new( filename )
    Constructs a temporary file in the given directory. The file
    ...
--- Tempfile#open
    Reopens ((|aTempfile|)) using mode ``r+'', which allows reading
    ..
```

Including Other Files

The contents of *filename* will be inserted wherever the document contains

```
<<< filename
```

If the file is specified with an `.rd` or `.rb` extension, it will be interpreted as RD documentation.

If the filename has no extension, `rdtool` will look for a file with an extension that matches the type of output being produced (`.html` for HTML files, `.man` for man files, and so on) and interpolate that file's contents in the `output` stream. Thus, a line such as:

```
<<< header
```

could be used to add an output-dependent header to a document.

Using rdtool

RD documentation can be included directly in a Ruby source program or written into a separate file (which by convention will have the extension `.rd`). These files are processed using the `rd2` command to produce appropriately formatted output.

```
rd2 [ options ] inputfile [ >outputfile ]
```

Some common options include:

-rformat	Select an output format. `-rrd/rd2html-lib.rb` produces HTML output (the default). `-rrd/rd2man-lib.rb` produces Unix man page output.
-oname	Set the base part of the output filename.
`-help`	List the full set of options.

Mandatory Disclaimer

As we are writing this, RD and `rdtool` are undergoing continuous development. It is likely that some of the details we give here will be out of date (or just plain wrong) by the time you read this.

Included with the `rdtool` distribution is the file **README.rd**. We suggest you do so, as it will give you the current scoop on producing Ruby documentation.

Interactive Ruby Shell

Back on page 126 we introduced irb, a Ruby module that lets you enter Ruby programs interactively and see the results immediately. This appendix goes into more detail on using and customizing irb.

Command Line

`irb` is run from the command line.

> irb [*irb-options*] [*ruby_script*] [*options*]

The command-line options for irb are listed in Table B.1 on the following page. Typically, you'll run irb with no options, but if you want to run a script and watch the blow-by-blow description as it runs, you can provide the name of the Ruby script and any options for that script.

Initialization File

irb uses an initialization file in which you can set commonly used options or execute any required Ruby statements. When irb is run, it will try to load an initialization file from one of the following sources in order: `~/.irbrc`, `.irbrc`, `irb.rc`, `_irbrc`, and `$irbrc`.

Within the initialization file you may run any arbitrary Ruby code. You can also set any of the configuration values that correspond to command-line arguments as shown in Table B.2 on the next page.

As an interesting twist on configuring irb, you can set `IRB.conf[:IRB_RC]` to a `Proc` object. This proc will be invoked whenever the irb context is changed, and will receive that new context as a parameter. You can use this facility to change the configuration dynamically based on the context.

Table B.1. irb command-line options

Option	Description
-f	Suppress reading ~/.irbrc.
-m	Math mode (fraction and matrix support is available).
-d	Set $DEBUG to true (same as "ruby -d").
-r load-module	Same as "ruby -r".
--inspect	Use "inspect" for output (the default, unless in math mode).
--noinspect	Do not use inspect for output.
--readline	Use Readline extension module.
--noreadline	Do not use Readline extension module.
--prompt *prompt-mode*	Switch prompt mode. Predefined prompt modes are "default", "simple", "xmp", and "inf-ruby".
--prompt-mode *prompt-mode*	Same as --prompt.
--inf-ruby-mode	Sets up irb to run in inf-ruby-mode under Emacs. Changes the prompt and suppresses --readline.
--simple-prompt	Simple prompt mode.
--noprompt	Do not display a prompt.
--tracer	Display trace for execution of commands.
--back-trace-limit *n*	Display backtrace information using the top n and last n entries. The default value is 16.
--irb_debug *n*	Set internal debug level to n (only for irb development).
-v, --version	Print the version of irb.

Table B.2. irb configuration values

IRB.conf[:IRB_NAME] = "irb"	IRB.conf[:MATH_MODE] = false
IRB.conf[:USE_TRACER] = false	IRB.conf[:USE_LOADER] = false
IRB.conf[:IGNORE_SIGINT] = true	IRB.conf[:IGNORE_EOF] = false
IRB.conf[:INSPECT_MODE] = nil	IRB.conf[:IRB_RC] = nil
IRB.conf[:BACK_TRACE_LIMIT] = 16	IRB.conf[:USE_LOADER] = false
IRB.conf[:USE_READLINE] = nil	IRB.conf[:USE_TRACER] = false
IRB.conf[:IGNORE_SIGINT] = true	IRB.conf[:IGNORE_EOF] = false
IRB.conf[:PROMPT_MODE] = :DEFAULT	IRB.conf[:PROMPT] = { ... }
IRB.conf[:DEBUG_LEVEL] = 0	IRB.conf[:VERBOSE] = true

Commands

At the irb prompt, you can enter any valid Ruby expression and see the results. You can also use any of the following commands to control the irb session.

`exit, quit, irb_exit`
> Quits this irb session or subsession. If you've used `cb` to change bindings (see below), exits from this binding mode.

`conf, irb_context`
> Displays current configuration. Modifying the configuration is achieved by invoking methods of `conf`.

`conf.back_trace_limit` n
> Sets display lines of backtrace as top n and tail n. The default value is 16.

`conf.debug_level =` N
> Sets debug level of irb.

`conf.ignore_eof = true/false`
> Specifies the behavior of an end of file received on input. If true, it will be ignored; otherwise, it will quit irb.

`conf.ignore_sigint= true/false`
> Specifies the behavior of ^C (control-c). If false, ^C will quit irb. If true, ^C during input will cancel input and return to the top level; during execution, ^C will abort the current operation.

`conf.inf_ruby_mode = true/false`
> If `true`, changes the prompt and disables readline support, allowing irb to work with `inf-ruby-mode`.[1] The default value is false.

`conf.inspect_mode = true/false/nil`
> Specifies inspect mode according to the following values:
>
> | | |
> |---|---|
> | `true` | Display inspect (default). |
> | `false` | Display to_s. |
> | `nil` | Inspect mode in non-math mode, non-inspect mode in math mode. |

`conf.irb_level`
> Displays the current binding level (see `cb`).

`conf.math_mode`
> Displays whether or not Ruby is in math mode.

---

1.   `inf-ruby-mode` allows Emacs users to interact with Ruby while editing programs. See the file `inf_ruby.el` in the `misc` directory of the distribution for more details.

`conf.use_loader = true/false`
> Specifies whether or not irb's own file reader method is used with **load/require**.

`conf.prompt_c`
> The prompt for a continuing statement (for example, immediately after an "if").

`conf.prompt_i`
> The standard, top-level prompt.

`conf.prompt_s`
> The prompt for a continuing string.

`conf.rc = true/false`
> Specifies whether or not to use the initialization file `~/.irbrc`.

`conf.use_prompt = true/false`
> Specifies whether or not to display prompts.

`conf.use_readline = true/false/nil`
> Specifies whether or not to use Readline according to the following values:

true	Use Readline.
false	Do not use Readline.
nil	Use Readline except for **inf-ruby-mode** (default).

`conf.verbose=true/false`
> Specifies whether or not verbose messages are displayed.

`cb, irb_change_binding ⟨ obj ⟩`
> Creates and enters a new binding that has its own scope for local variables. If *obj* is given, it will be used as self in the new binding.

`irb ⟨ obj ⟩`
> Starts an irb subsession. If *obj* is given, it will be used as self.

`jobs, irb_jobs`
> Lists irb subsessions.

`fg n, irb_fg n`
> Switches into the specified irb subsession. *n* may be any of the following values:
>
> irb subsession number
> thread id
> irb object
> self (the *obj* that launched a particular subsession)

`kill n, irb_kill n`
> Kills an irb subsession. *n* may be any of the values as described for **irb_fg**.

Configuring the Prompt

You have a lot of flexibility in configuring the prompts that irb uses. Sets of prompts are stored in the prompt hash:

```
IRB.conf[:PROMPT]
```

For example, to establish a new prompt mode called "MY_PROMPT", you might enter the following (either directly at an irb prompt or in the .irbrc file):

```
IRB.conf[:PROMPT][:MY_PROMPT] = { # name of prompt mode
  :PROMPT_I => "...",             # normal prompt
  :PROMPT_S => "...",             # prompt for continuing strings
  :PROMPT_C => "...",             # prompt for continuing statement
  :RETURN => "    ==>%s\n"        # format to return value
}
```

Then, invoke irb with the prompt mode above by

```
% irb --prompt my-prompt
```

Or set the following configuration value:

```
IRB.conf[:PROMPT_MODE] = :MY_PROMPT
```

The constants PROMPT_I, PROMPT_S, and PROMPT_C specify the format for each of the prompt strings. Within the prompt format, the following flags are available and will expand to the given text:

Flag	Description
%N	Current command.
%m	to_s of the main object (self).
%M	inspect of the main object (self).
%l	Delimiter type. In strings that are continued across a line break, %l will display the type of delimiter used to begin the string, so you'll know how to end it. The delimiter will be one of ", ', /,], or '.
%ni	Indent level. The optional number n is used as a width specification to printf, as printf("%nd").
%nn	Current line number (n used as with the indent level).
%%	A literal percent sign.

For instance, the default prompt mode is defined as follows:

```
IRB.conf[:PROMPT_MODE][:DEFAULT] = {
    :PROMPT_I => "%N(%m):%03n:%i> ",
    :PROMPT_S => "%N(%m):%03n:%i%l ",
    :PROMPT_C => "%N(%m):%03n:%i* ",
    :RETURN => "%s\n"
}
```

Restrictions

Because of the way irb works, there is a minor incompatibility between it and the standard Ruby interpreter. The problem lies in the determination of local variables.

Normally, Ruby looks for an assignment statement to determine if something is a variable—if a name hasn't been assigned to, then Ruby assumes that name is a method call.

```
eval "a = 0"
a
```

produces:

```
prog.rb:2: undefined local variable or method `a'
for #<Object:0x40197d08> (NameError)
```

In this case, the assignment is there, but it's within a string, so Ruby doesn't take it into account.

irb, on the other hand, executes statements as they are entered.

```
irb(main):001:0> eval "a = 0"
0
irb(main):002:0> a
0
```

In irb, the assignment was executed before the second line was encountered, so "a" is correctly identified as a local variable.

If you need to match the Ruby behavior more closely, you can place these statements within a **begin/end** pair.

```
irb(main):001:0> begin
irb(main):002:1*    eval "a = 0"
irb(main):003:1>    a
irb(main):004:1> end
NameError: undefined local variable or method `a'
(irb):3:in `irb_binding'
```

rtags, xmp, and the Frame Class

The base version of irb is installed along with Ruby itself. But there is an extended version of irb in the archives containing a few extra goodies that need mentioning.

rtags

rtags is a command used to create a **TAGS** file for use with either the emacs or vi editor.

```
rtags [ -vi ] [ files ]...
```

By default, rtags makes a **TAGS** file suitable for emacs (see etags.el). The `-vi` option makes a TAGS file for use with vi.

rtags needs to be installed in the same manner as irb (that is, you need to install irb in the library path and make a link from `irb/rtags.rb` to `bin/rtags`).

xmp

irb's xmp is an "example printer"—that is, a pretty-printer that shows the value of each expression as it is run (much like the script we wrote to format the examples in this book). There is also another stand-alone xmp in the archives.

xmp can be used as follows:

```
require "irb/xmp"

xmp <<END
artist = "Doc Severinsen"
artist
END
```

produces:

```
artist = "Doc Severinsen"
    ==>"Doc Severinsen"
artist
    ==>"Doc Severinsen"
```

Or, it can be used as an object instance. Used in this fashion, the object maintains context between invocations:

```
require "irb/xmp"

x = XMP.new
x.puts <<END
artist = "Louis Prima"
END

x.puts <<END
artist
END
```

produces:

```
artist = "Louis Prima"
    ==>"Louis Prima"
artist
    ==>"Louis Prima"
```

You can explicitly provide a binding with either form; otherwise, xmp uses the caller's environment.

```
xmp code_string, abinding
XMP.new(abinding)
```

Note that xmp does not work with multithreading.

The Frame Class

The IRB::Frame class represents the interpreter's stack and allows easy access to the Binding environment in effect at different stack levels.

IRB::Frame.top($n = 0$)	Returns a Binding for the nth context from the top. The 0th context is topmost, most recent frame.
IRB::Frame.bottom($n = 0$)	Returns a Binding for the nth context from the bottom. The 0th context is the bottommost, initial frame.
IRB::Frame.sender	Returns the object (the sender) that invoked the current method.

You can use this facility, for instance, to examine local variables from the method that called the current method:

```
require 'irb/frame'

def outie
  b = IRB::Frame.top(1)
  eval "p my_local", b
end

def innie
  my_local = 102.7
  outie
end

innie
```

produces:

```
102.7
```

Note that this doesn't work with multithreaded programs.

Support

One of the major features of Open Source projects is the technical support. Articles in the mass media often criticize open source efforts for not having the same tech support that a commercial product has. And boy is that a good thing! Instead of dialing up some overworked and understaffed help desk and being treated to Music On Hold for an hour or so *without* ever getting the answer you need, we have a better solution: the Ruby community. The author of Ruby, the authors of this book, and many other Ruby users are willing and able to lend you a hand, should you need it.

The syntax of Ruby remains fairly stable, but as with all evolving software, new features are added every now and again. As a result, both printed books and the online documentation can fall behind. All software has bugs, and Ruby is no exception. There aren't many, but they do crop up. See the bug reporting section on page 533 for details.

If you experience a problem with Ruby, feel free to ask in the mailing lists or on the newsgroup (more on those in just a minute). Generally you'll get timely answers from Matz himself, the author of the language, from other gurus, and from those who've solved problems similar to your own.

There might be similar questions in the mailing lists or on the newsgroup, and it is good "netiquette" to read through recent postings before asking. If you can't find the answer you need, ask, and a correct answer will usually show up with remarkable speed and precision.

Web Sites

The official Ruby Home Page is `http://www.ruby-lang.org`.

You can also find Ruby information at `http://www.rubycentral.com`. In particular, you'll find complete online references to Ruby's built-in classes and modules at `www.rubycentral.com/ref/`, and to the Ruby FAQ at `www.rubycentral.com/faq/`.

While you're surfing, drop in on `http://www.pragmaticprogrammer.com` and see what we're up to.

Download Sites

The latest version of Ruby can be downloaded from: `http://www.ruby-lang.org/en/download.html`.

Mirror sites are:

- `ftp://ftp.TokyoNet.AD.JP/pub/misc/ruby`
- `ftp://ftp.iij.ad.jp/pub/lang/ruby`
- `ftp://blade.nagaokaut.ac.jp/pub/lang/ruby`
- `ftp://ftp.krnet.ne.jp/pub/ruby`
- `ftp://mirror.nucba.ac.jp/mirror/ruby`
- `http://mirror.nucba.ac.jp/mirror/ruby`

Precompiled Windows binaries (using cygwin) are in the `pc/` subdirectory.

Usenet Newsgroup

Ruby has its own newsgroup, `comp.lang.ruby`. Traffic on this group is archived and mirrored to the `ruby-talk` mailing list.

Mailing Lists

There are five mailing lists now talking about Ruby. The first is in English, the last four in Japanese:

`ruby-talk@netlab.co.jp`	English language discussion of Ruby (mirrored to `comp.lang.ruby`).
`ruby-list@netlab.co.jp`	Japanese language discussion of Ruby.
`ruby-dev@netlab.co.jp`	List for Ruby developers.
`ruby-ext@netlab.co.jp`	List for people writing extensions for or with Ruby.
`ruby-math@netlab.co.jp`	Ruby in mathematics.

See `http://www.ruby-lang.org/en/ml.html` for details on joining a mailing list.

The mailing lists are archived, and can be searched using `http://blade.nagaokaut.ac.jp/ruby/ruby-talk/index.shtml`.

Bug Reporting

If you think you've spotted a bug in Ruby, you may want to browse the bug database at `http://www.ruby-lang.org/cgi-bin/ruby-bugs`. You may also want to check to see if a new version of Ruby is available—perhaps the bug you've found has already been fixed.

You can submit a bug report either by using the Web page mentioned above or by sending an e-mail to `ruby-bugs@ruby-lang.org`.

When reporting a suspected bug, it would be a good idea to include the output of "`ruby -v`" along with any problematic source code. People will also need to know the operating system you're running. If you compiled your own version of Ruby, it might be a good idea to attach your `rbconfig.rb` file as well.

If you have a problem using irb, be aware of its limitations (see the reference section beginning on page 523). See what happens using just Ruby itself.

Bibliography

[Fri97]   Jeffrey E. F. Friedl. *Mastering Regular Expressions: Powerful Techniques for Perl and Other Tools.* O'Reilly & Associates, Inc., Sebastopol, CA, 1997.

[GHJV95]   Erich Gamma, Richard Helm, Ralph Johnson, and John Vlissides. *Design Patterns: Elements of Reusable Object-Oriented Software.* Addison-Wesley, Reading, MA, 1995.

[HT00]   Andrew Hunt and David Thomas. *The Pragmatic Programmer: From Journeyman to Master.* Addison-Wesley, Reading, MA, 2000.

[Lid98]   Stephen Lidie. *Perl/Tk Pocket Reference.* O'Reilly & Associates, Inc., Sebastopol, CA, 1998.

[Mey97]   Bertrand Meyer. *Object-Oriented Software Construction.* Prentice Hall, Englewood Cliffs, NJ, second edition, 1997.

[Ste98a]   W. Richard Stevens. *Unix Network Programming, Volume 1: Networking APIs: Sockets and Xti.* Prentice Hall, Englewood Cliffs, NJ, second edition, 1998.

[Ste98b]   W. Richard Stevens. *Unix Network Programming, Volume 2: Interprocess Communications.* Prentice Hall, Englewood Cliffs, NJ, second edition, 1998.

[Wal99]   Nancy Walsh. *Learning Perl/Tk: Graphical User Interfaces with Perl.* O'Reilly & Associates, Inc., Sebastopol, CA, 1999.

Index

Every built-in and library method described in this book is indexed at least twice, once under the method's name and again under the name of the class or module that contains it. These entries have the method and class/module names in **typewriter** font, and have the word method, class, or module appended. If you want to know what methods class `String` contains, you can look up "`String` class" in the index. If instead you want to know which classes and modules support a method called `index`, look under "`index` method." A bold page number for these method listings shows the reference section entry.

When a class or method name corresponds with a broader concept (such as String), we've indexed the class separately from the concept.

Symbols are sorted using ASCII collation. The table on the right might help those who haven't yet memorized the positions of the punctuation characters.

Practical Tools from the Pragmatic Programmers

"If I'm putting together a project, it's the authors of this book that I want.... And failing that I'd settle for people who've read their book."
—Ward Cunningham

Straight from the programming trenches, **The Pragmatic Programmer** cuts through the increasing specialization and technicalities of modern software development to examine the core process—taking a requirement and producing working, maintainable code that delights its users. It covers topics ranging from personal responsibility and career development to architectural techniques for keeping your code flexible and easy to adapt and reuse. Written as a series of self-contained sections and filled with entertaining anecdotes, thoughtful examples, and interesting analogies, **The Pragmatic Programmer** illustrates the best practices and major pitfalls of many different aspects of software development.

"Use Ruby and you'll write better code, be more productive, and enjoy programming more."
—From the *Programming Ruby* preface

Programming Ruby: the Pragmatic Programmer's Guide is a complete Ruby resource. You'll find a tutorial and overview of the language; a detailed description of Ruby's structure, syntax, and operation; a guide to building applications with Ruby; and a comprehensive reference that documents more than eight hundred methods, forty built-in classes, and many useful library modules that come with the language. Numerous fully functional examples appear throughout the book. You will come away with an appreciation for Ruby's power, flexibility, and clarity.

⋏⋏ Addison-Wesley